DEC 14 1999

THE SOCIAL

HISTORY

OF THE

THIRD REICH

By the same author:

The Nazi Question

THE SOCIAL
HISTORY
OF THE
THIRD REICH
1933–1945

Translated from the French by Janet Lloyd

PIERRE AYÇOBERRY

THE NEW PRESS   NEW YORK

Library of Congress Cataloging-in-Publication Data

Ayçoberry, Pierre.
   [Société allemande sous le IIIe Reich.   English]
   The social history of the Third Reich : 1933-1945 / Pierre
Ayçoberry ; translated from the French by Janet Lloyd.
      p.   cm.
   Includes bibliographical references and index.
   ISBN 1-56584-549-8
     1. National socialism—Germany.   2. National characteristics,
German.   3. Germany—Politics and government—1933-1945.
4. Germany—Social conditions—1933-1945.   5. Political culture—
Germany.   I. Title.
DD256.5.A87313   2000
943.086—dc21   99-14059
                                                           CIP

Published in the United States by The New Press, New York
Distributed by W. W. Norton & Company, Inc., New York

The New Press was established in 1990 as a not-for-profit alternative to the large, commercial publishing houses currently dominating the book publishing industry. The New Press operates in the public interest rather than for private gain, and is committed to publishing, in innovative ways, works of educational, cultural, and community value that are often deemed insufficiently profitable.

www.thenewpress.com

Printed in the United States of America

95 96 97 98 9 8 7 6 5 4 3 2 1

The New Press is grateful for support of this publication from the French Ministry of Culture.

Contents

THE SOCIAL

HISTORY

OF THE

THIRD REICH

Introduction

THE DIFFICULTIES FACED
BY A HISTORY OF A SOCIETY
UNDER A TOTALITARIAN REGIME

Half a century after its collapse, is it possible to study the Third Reich with detachment? Some scholars in Germany are beginning to claim that it is, as if the reunification of their country has marked a new year zero. Let us be done with the rhetoric of prosecution and defense, they write: surely the years between 1933 and 1945 are no longer of interest to anyone but scholars and reclusive analysts, years which fascinate in the same measure as more ancient periods do.

If I question that ostensible "objectivization," it is not through any visceral anti-Germanism. However, that does not make the task any easier. For no field of study can be more confusing and taxing for a historian. The sources for the period are all polluted, and every word must be treated with suspicion. At every stage ethical debates arise, casting doubt upon the classical rules of methodology. Even history "starting at the bottom," the great innovation of recent years, may be suspected of "political incorrectness." So even a simple account of what is known, such as the present study, must be accompanied by an introductory description of the difficulties encountered in this research, many of which seem insoluble, and the methods chosen to resolve them.

The corrupt language used by Hitler and thousands of his imitators has long been exposed by Viktor Klemperer, who traced its influence even in the words of the most innocent of contemporary writers. But historians are somewhat at a loss when trying to cope with that strange amalgam of borrowings from romantic literature, religious texts, and the human sciences: the archaisms and vulgarities "of Novalis and Barnum" and the whole vocabulary of *Kitsch*.[1] [*] One handy way to indicate to the reader that certain terms should be taken with a considerable pinch of salt would be to put these words and phrases in quotation marks. The most fastidious writers might go so far as do likewise with terms used by the opposite camp, such as "Nazi," an acronym that has always been pejorative. But at that rate historical discourse would become virtually unreadable.[2] In opposition to such exaggerated scruples, common sense suggests that words now accepted as current vocabulary (such as führer, Third Reich, Gestapo, SS, SA . . .) should not be translated or even underlined, and that simple equivalents should be proposed for overblown titles and bombastic expressions. Even then, all too many words remain loaded with sinister connotations, words that need to be stigmatized by some external sign each time they appear.

Even the term "Germans" has been the object of many distortions. As well as designating those inhabitants and citizens of the German state living within its original frontiers, it came to cover others who, with varying degrees of willingness, joined it such as Austrians, Sudetens and, during the war, all the "ethnic Germans" transported across Europe to settle in and reinforce the marches of the fatherland—men and women whose membership as German people was defined by the SS anthropologists in purely pseudoscientific terms. Some of these "Germans" were not even German speakers. In contrast, many others such as political exiles were stripped of their nationality or, as in the case of the Jews, their citizenship. There is no reason why a historian anxious to delimit his subject need follow the variations dictated by imperialism, a spirit of vengeance, or racist doctrine. But to avoid extending his field of vision beyond all reasonable measure, he must content himself with allusions to Austrians, Sudetens, and "ethnic Germans." And clearly, he should exclude neither the exiles—even if their dispersion throughout the world may force him to oversimplify—nor the Jews.

The interpretation of documents is even more delicate. It's

not that the deciphering of criminal correspondence presents great problems: all specialists agree that "special treatment" meant "to be killed." But in less tragic domains, the fastidiousness of critics bent on precision may produce confusing or even contradictory results. On the one hand, the authorities received hundreds of reports from prefects, magistrates, and the *SD* (Sicherheistdienst, the SS information service). The mandate of the SS, which was served by countless informers, was never to conceal the slightest signs of discontent: so presumably one can place one's trust in the descriptions given by this veritable "early-warning" system.[3] Yet it is possible that either as a result of professional pressures or in order to demonstrate the unpopularity of their rivals—the party mandarins—these policemen ascribed undue importance to what were in truth simply manifestations of disgruntlement with the regime. In any event, because of what was considered their exaggerated pessimism,[4] their activities were certainly curtailed in 1944 following a decision from on high. The police reports thus need to be compared alongside the "reports from Germany" that clandestine militants of the Social Democratic Party and the *Neu Beginnen* group sent to their friends in exile—reports based on identical mandates of total objectivity. The picture that emerges constitutes as it were a negative of the *SD* photograph, showing a working class that is altogether passive if not positively won over by the regime! The symmetry goes even further, for the leading socialist organs, outraged by a pessimism that undermined their hopes, likewise decided to put an end to this correspondence.[5] How is one to decide which picture to accept? The question is certainly of some importance, for on it depends whether or not the taboo of the immunity of the working class, no less, should be broken. The present state of research on this matter will be described below, but for the moment we should at least note that under this repressive state all written discourse, that of conformists and opponents alike, was affected by a bias: the police saw potential rebels on every side, while those who resisted the regime detected cowards or accomplices everywhere.

The perversity of the system not only contaminates its legacy to posterity, namely the documents, but also forces whoever wishes to understand it to disobey a fundamental rule of the historian discipline. Historians cannot help remembering Marc Bloch's warning: "One cannot condemn or absolve without taking sides on a set of values that no longer stems from any positive science;"[6] but at the same time, they cannot forget the virtually contemporary (1939) observation of Karl Barth: "To explain evil is to efface the scandal, and in a sense to accept it as natural, as inevitable . . ."[7] The one bids us to explain without judging; the other to judge without explaining. Historians must struggle to resolve the moral dilemma for themselves.

Fortunately the path to follow is well signposted. The same Karl Barth, meditating in 1945 on the notions of collective culpability and responsibility, wrote the following words which may seem to retract his earlier condemnation and to encourage historical research: "It is not primarily a matter of the crimes that took place, but rather . . . of the path that led—and was bound to lead—to those crimes (Ouradour, etc.)."[8] But it is above all from the eighties onward that German and Anglo-Saxon historiography, fertile in methodological reflection, has provided us with guidelines. It has in particular set us on our guard against the form of moralistic judgmentalism that borrows its categories from a Manichaean psychology, assuming the appearance of objective distancing but in truth only in order to excuse the poverty of its analyses. Thus Karl Ferdinand Werner, when examining the behavior of his former university teachers, issued the following warning: "The convictions that we shall discover [them to have held] themselves result from a historical process, not simply from their evident cleverness, blindness, foolishness, or malice."[9] The historians of the Resistance for their part have become historians of many kinds of resistance, that is to say a whole spread of attitudes ranging between the two extremes of submission and rebellion. Martin Broszat has suggested summarizing these using the term *Resistenz*, which might be translated as "passivity," "immunity," or better still "a refractory attitude," while Ian Kershaw has suggested the English term "dissent" or "nonconformism."[10] This kind of classification has in its turn been criticized, in particular by the Canadian Michael Kater who regarded it as merely an artificial etiquette that was supposed to define subjective experiences but in truth made use of criteria that were anachronisitic and moralistic; . . . yet he then went on to adopt it himself when he divided the doctors who were party members into fanatics and careerists on the one hand and, on the other those whose allegiance was coerced.[11] In the meantime M. Broszat had extended this somewhat Byzantine debate and, in an article that soon became famous, suggested a whole program for "the historization of National Socialism." It involved avoiding anachronisms, not assuming that the end of the story was already known by the actors of its early days, nuancing the various types of support for the regime, and tracking back to before 1933 in order to illuminate the genesis of various patterns of behaviour.[12]

But that was not the end of the controversy. If one ruled out any kind of indictment even in the form of an indirect inventory of attitudes, was there not a risk of slipping into indulgence? Broszat himself was not suspected of promoting a whitewashing strategy, but others, encouraged by the conservative "swing" of public opinion in the late eighties, did seem to be tending in that direction however much they claimed the best of intentions. So the discussion started up again. What I have in mind here is *not* the all too well-known 1986 "quarrel of the historians" which was a spectacular and sterile kind of confrontation, but rather the slightly later dialogue between M. Broszat and Saul Friedländer which for its part truly was scholarly albeit sometimes somewhat strained.[13] Simplifying slightly, it is fair to say that the two adversaries each in turn explored two fields, that of "history starting at the bottom" and that of the relations between history and memory. Broszat, the great initiator in the former field, reckoned that purely political and ideological history "starting at the top" had certainly made a great contribution but had ended up with a "Manichaean construction" in which all one could make out were "goodies" and "baddies." He thought it was now time to focus attention upon ordinary, more or less passive citizens and believed that this comprehensive approach, far from whitewashing them, would on the contrary reveal the full extent to which the criminal dimension of the regime infiltrated daily life. Friedländer in contrast reckoned that focusing on ordinary, everyday life in this way risked marginalizing the essential element, namely the violence and the crimes. Subsequently, when confronted with the memories of victims, in particular those of Jewish survivors, Broszat began by recognizing that the latter might "feel that they had been deprived of their own memories if scholarly research, with its typical academic arrogance, claimed a monopoly over the business of discovery and conceptualization." But he nevertheless drew a contrast between the historians' scholarly perception of the past and the victims' myth (in the most noble sense of the word) of it. Whereas the latter reconstructed history moving backward from Auschwitz, the historians were bound to reject such teleology. At this point Friedländer more or less vehemently reintroduced the exigencies of morality: no, the historians could not claim to be more emancipated from their personal pasts than the survivors; and yes, Auschwitz did have to remain the focus of their reflections. This debate thus unfolded at a far higher level than the usual ritual accusations of left-wing moralism opposed by hypocritical absolutionism that usually punctuate German university life. The lessons to be drawn from it are clear. The first stems from the line taken by Broszat: all the testimonies produced after 1945, both those recording great pain and those laying claim to clean consciences, ought to be treated quite differently or even reserved for separate studies; and the reason for this is that memory is quite a different matter from the history of the facts on which memory feeds.[14] The other lesson is more difficult to follow for it endeavors to respect the warnings from both sides. While avoiding the over-facile nature of an indictment, we must guard against the complicity that every author spontaneously feels with his subject. The endeavor to seek comprehension from a distance assuredly involves taking a chance, but dozens of works of social history at any rate prove that it is tenable and that, as Norbert Elias has observed apropos the Eichmann trial, "an attempt to explain is not necessarily an attempt to excuse."[15]

Despite its objective appearance social history is thus, as much as if not more than rival disciplines, exposed to the triple temptation of moralism, cold aloofness, and empathy. It also needs to avoid certain methodological traps by which it in particular is beset.

When it describes the behavior of a group on the basis of the behavior of a handful of people assumed to be representative, there is a danger of it forgetting its specific task of studying collective societies. This happens above all in the cases of small minorities whose basic composition remains unclear: for example resistance groups, which the historian may tend to reduce to their leaders and martyrs; the university community, where an age-old respect leads to its consideration as a gallery of personalities, not a caste; or writers and artists who, having set themselves up as so many symbols, continue to be analyzed as such by their interpreters. . . . Strictly speaking, proper names ought to be eliminated. Although a few will appear in the present work, it is not on the grounds that they are representative but because their parallel biographies make it possible to include them together as a particular type: for instance an eminent philosopher, an eminent doctor, and an eminent composer whose involvement with National Socialism between 1933 and 1938 evolved following the same cycle of illusion, collusion, disillusion, and disgrace.

Next the historian is faced with the daunting problem of stratification. What frameworks of reference should be used? Social circles, orders (*Stände*), classes, professions, grass roots communities? The first in that list is too vague. The second was, in the official literature of the period, no more than a rhetorical illusion designed to win over conservatives. Yet, among those conservatives, particularly in professions with pretensions toward autonomy which encompassed the various elites, the notion of the *Stände* remained rooted in the consciousness of individuals and at the very least served them as a defensive argument. Their history thus suggests that in their case at any rate this category is still usable. Third in the list, classes, is too polyvalent: even if one ignores the oversimplifications of the Third International and its heirs, the classes described by the Marxists and the Weberians can hardly be made to overlap with classes as conceived by Anglo-Saxon authors. One must therefore be resigned to adopting a double view. Of the classes described by the Marxists, let us ignore the "petite bourgeoisie," which is no more than a label designed to cover certain divergent interests, attitudes, and sentiments and is furthermore a deeply disparaging label. The "working class" did exist in 1933 or at least thought of itself as such; whether it subsequently became dislocated as a result of intimidation or flattery remains to be seen. This is even more true of the "ruling class," the economic, bureaucratic, and military elites whose internal rivalries and rivalry with the new party elite has been impressively studied by Franz Neumann.[16] As for the threefold division into upper-middle, lower-middle, and lower classes, it has dominated Anglo-Saxon studies of electoral sociology and politics to such an extent that it is now impossible to ignore.

The professions for their part are easier to pick out, which no doubt accounts for the proliferation of monographs studying the journalists, officers, engineers, artisans, and so on in the Third Reich; that is to say the reciprocal relations between those professions and politics. For the years leading up to 1933 it is important to determine how much the various professions contributed to the battalions of electors and members of the party. The trouble is that each profession comprised its own aristocracy and its own masses, even its own plebs. Furthermore, an exclusive use of this professional grid rests upon a number of assumptions. Thomas Childers, a relatively explicit author and a specialist on elections held in the twenties and thirties, thus declared that the professions are fundamental to determining social status and hence to a large extent voting patterns. In support of this assertion he points to the targeting of various economic sectors by the Nazi party's propaganda departments.[17] However, another American specialist has questioned "the validity of the logic of the *cui bono*" and wonders whether the representation of interests really does determine a political movement.[18] In other words, was it for exclusively economic reasons that a business proprietor, official, or artisan voted for the party, joined it, or became a militant supporter of it? It is dangerously tempting to fill the space separating a profession and the political domain by a circular argument, explaining the overrepresentation of a particular category amid the Nazi electors by its particular affinity with Nazism, and then explaining that this affinity is due to the image the party projected when targeting that category. . . .

Besides, once past the threshold represented by 1933, that kind of professional sociography applied to the supporters of the authorities and those in power does not really account for the nature of that power; it only explains "the conditions that rendered the autonomy of the political party possible."[19] Was it not precisely in order to safeguard its own liberty against the appetites of the professions that the party's political leaders set up a no more than pseudocorporative structure and tried (with uneven success) to channel the professional lobbies into a wide range of "attached organizations"? Research accordingly needs to focus on the reverse relationship, namely the nazification of the professional bodies. And from their concrete activities rather than from the overall behavior of each social class, facts have been rediscovered that are both compromising and embarrassing to their collective honor (and to that of their successors, as can be seen from the hesitancy with which many present-day federations and trade unions confront their image in the historians' mirror). It is not the denunciation of some leading figure's ereors that provokes the greatest scandal (for the relevant corporation finds it easy enough to dissociate itself from those), but the revelation of evidence of the "continuum that stretched from 'normality' all the way to barbarity,"[20] from satisfaction in work well done and in one's own projected career, legitimate in itself, to first tolerance of and then cooperation in crime.

But that kind of study still did not reach down to life as it was concretely lived. What was needed was the microscope of "the history of daily life" in order to get down to the level of small communities: individual town quarters, workshops, parishes, and so on. This new discipline made its appearance in the eighties, not by chance but as a result of the rise of new generations. During this decade the age groups active in the Reich reached retirement and began to answer questions put to them by their grandchildren, who were less inhibited by respect and taboos than their parents had been. With the help of tape recorders oral history took off. Then came the exploration of local archives. For the first time (setting aside a handful of precursors) historians took an interest in "the ways in which individuals and groups had been touched by the effects of the system and how those effects, either as brakes or propellers, influenced the processes unfolding in society and in the State." The university researchers who collaborated with amateurs in these "history workshops" found themselves faced with a twofold task as historians: first they had to pick out "aspects of macrosociological structures such as a nation, or a class . . . that only became visible when refracted from below in the primary units of a particular sociocultural circle"; secondly, they had to discover in preceding decades the origins of "life experiences" that subsequently led to greater or lesser degrees of acceptance or rejection of the regime.[21]

Distinguished university professors, even left-wing ones, claimed that pretentious terms such as "system" or "structures" made up for elements of weakness in their thought. In response,

M. Broszat on one hand and proponents of the new historical method on the other set out their theory in a series of programmatic texts. What had to be done was test out the validity of general theories (such as fascism, etc.) at the level of microsocieties: find out how overarching political and social structures affected the grassroots level through day to day events; study the pressures exerted by the Nazi apparatus upon modest and apparently apolitical people; and investigate how fascism pervaded colloquial discourse as the latter digested propaganda and transformed it into an ongoing disposition toward, for instance, a permanent competitiveness (at which point Pierre Bourdieu would be cited).[22] This was a very political program and one which on that very account rebuffed criticisms of the partisans of "grand history." But at the same time it aroused the suspicions of right-minded people alarmed at the possibility of a parallel being drawn between the Nazi slogan of "performance" and praise that continued to be showered upon productivity! It was certainly an ambitious program for the researchers, but one that succeeded in registering attitudes relating in particular to life at work and the private lives of working people in a manner at last unencumbered by moral judgments.

The translation policy of French publishers — tardy and parsimonious, but frequently perspicacious in its choices — has made it possible for French readers to be correctly informed about the important debates taking place in German and Anglo-Saxon seats of learning. But the same has not applied to the immense literature of monographs: studies of different regions, towns, businesses, professions, resistance groups, and lobbies more or less close to the source of power.[23] Despite their seemingly narrow horizons, the best of those monographs now make it possible to answer the following question: how did people live, survive, or disappear under the Third Reich? It is a question every bit as fundamental as the one that first captured the public imagination: namely, *why* did it happen? Without dismissing the various theoretical positions that separate the authors of those works, it is perfectly possible to fasten upon the points on which they converge.[24] The plan and content of the present summary of "the state of our knowledge to date" require no particular commentary except on two points: periodization, and how the works selected were chosen.

Should the Third Reich be presented as a single block or as an evolving process? As twelve real years, not the prophesied thousands? With hindsight, this would appear to be history in the short term insofar as the seeds of the decomposition and recomposition of social units, which constitute its principal subject, were already detectable in the preceding decade and were to continue to exist beyond 1945, which is taken to be the year zero. But from another point of view the surgical interventions of the political authorities persistently accelerated those developments, and that fact suggests that we should adopt a more subtle division of time. Accordingly, rejecting the alternative between a static picture and a description of an evolution in several stages, the present work will distinguish only between the years of peace and the years of war or, more precisely, between 1933–38, the transitional period of 1938–39 (for it was then, not in September 1939, that the regime entered what Pierre Milza calls the stiffening phase),[25] and finally 1939–45. The caesura represented by 30 June 1934 (see Chronology), which is virtually obligatory in political history, does not seem fundamental in the present context. Nor does the separation of the war years into two periods, the "lightning war" and "total war," since recent studies prove that as early as 1940–41 civil society was turned upside down by the demands of modern warfare combined with the regime's totalitarian objectives.

The method used for selecting documentation also needs to be explained. An initial, relatively easy trawl revealed the major works, those works reviewed the most, and the most sustained debates that have served as landmarks for the methodology of "history starting at the bottom."[26] However, research work is constantly moving forward (however disconcerting this is for those with a preference for certainties). When a theory long since "accepted" by the community of historians eventually proves to be out-of-date—in some cases even in the eyes of its author—it has to be pushed aside to make room for more recent ones. As we shall see, examples are readily provided by electoral sociology and histories of the German working class. Next, in plumbing specialized studies to illustrate some general thesis, be aware that the choices made were inevitably arbitrary and, furthermore, affected by a lacuna in local history, namely an underrepresentation of the eastern provinces, because the archives of East Germany and Poland were virtually inaccessible. The upheavals of recent years have opened these up to research workers on all sides, but it is too early to assess all these new explorations.

Another consequence of the "turning-point" of 1989-90 is the proliferation of comparisons drawn between the National Socialist regime and the "socialism actually existing" in East Germany. The best of these, those that take into account the differences in context, duration, and ideologies, have made interesting contributions to the theory of totalitarianism, which until now has remained extremely abstract. But they presuppose a historical culture equally developed in the two domains, and since that is an illusion it is hard to see how they can be pertinent. The present work will therefore not be taking those studies into account. Nor will it be mentioning the ultra right-wing groups that have arisen since 1945 in various European countries. Over and above any ideological resemblances, any comparison between an apparatus holding power and movements still at the stage of aspiring to it would be vitiated from the outset. It is certainly tempting to draw civic lessons from history, but we do need to be circumspect.

NOTES

1. Klemperer V., passim, for example p. 84, 192, 272, 323-24. See also the commentaries of linguists: Sauer W. W., and Vodoz I.

*In the endnotes, the complete reference is given for only a few books and articles that are marginal to the subject and for that reason do not appear in the bibliography. In all other cases endnote references are abbreviated as follows:

—for collections of articles and documents: the *number* in the bibliography, pages, and dates,

—for books and articles: the author's name, the key word in the title (where the same author is cited for several publications), pages.

2. Backes U., Jesse E., Zitelmann R., *37*, p. 54 n. 46.
3. Herbert U., *Fremdarbeiter*, p. 71.
4. Boberach H., "Einleitung."
5. Voges M., p. 332–41; Stöver B. passim.
6. Bloch M., *Apologie pour l'histoire, ou Métier d'historien*, Paris, 1949, pp. 69–70.
7. Cited by Calef M., "La Shoah, mémoire collective de l'Occident," *Traces 3* (1982).
8. Cited by Vollnhals C., "Kirche," *44*, pp. 135–36.
9. Werner K. F., "Machtstaat," p. 328.
10. Cf. the collection edited by Schmädeke J. and Steinbach P., *Widerstand* (46), passim; Broszat M., "Resistenz;" and Kershaw I., *L'Opinion allemande*, in particular p. 34.
11. Kater M., Doctors, pp. 74–75, 86–87, 297 n. 2.
12. Broszat M., "Historisation."
13. Friedländer S., "Réflexions;" Broszat M., and Friedländer S., "De l'historisation . . ."
14. See the similar warnings of two specialists of retrospective interviews: Niethammer L., "Einleitung," p. 23; id., "Heimat und Front," p. 164; and Herbert U., "Die guten und die schlechten Zeiten. Uberlegungen zur diachronischen Analyse lebensgeschichtlicher Interviews," p. 68, in Niethammer L. (Hg.), *"Die Jahre weiss man nivht, wo man die heute hinsetzen soll."Faschismuserfahrungen im Ruhrgebiet. Lebensgesschichte und Sozialstruktur im Rurhrgebiet 1930 bis 1960*, Bd. 1, Berlin and Bonn, 1983.
15. Elias N., p. 396.
16. Neumann F., *Béhémoth*, part 3: "La nouvelle société."
17. Childers T., p. 10.
18. Baldwin P., passim. Note that the major synthesis by Kater M., *The Nazi Party*, in general avoids this kind of determinism.
19. Ibid.
20. Kershaw I., *Nazisme*, p. 307.
21. Peukert D. and Reulecke J., "Einleitung"; Broszat M., "Alltagsgeschichte."
22. Lüdtke A., "Alltagsgeschichte"; Gerstenberger H.
23. Rousso H., in his preface to the recent French translation of the book by Frei N, *L'État hitlérien et la Société allemande, 1933–1945*, assesses the contributions and lacunas of the French edition.
24. The synthesis by Frei N. cited above is a brilliant achievement, but the constraints of the German collection in which it first appeared inevitably limited the range of the sections on social history.
25. Milza P., Les Fascismes, Paris, 1985, in particular p. 379.
26. For example: Kershaw I., *Nazisme*, chap. 7 and 8.

Part One

THE INVASION
OF POLITICS
1933–1939

1—Violence

Why tackle the violence right at the outset? That is no mere rhetorical question. Certain works including some of the most classic approach this question only after they have described the more ordinary—political, economic, and cultural—aspects of the regime. They certainly do not do so in order to minimize the importance of the apparatus and its methods of repression, but rather so as to present them as crowning the system, as the characteristic mark of its radical nature, and then to move on in a natural transition, to the history of the victims, those who were persecuted and those who resisted, in such a way that the last touches to the picture are of a kind to salvage the honor of the German people.[1] Others proceed the other way round, and the present work will follow their example.[2] To begin by describing the violence is surely to reproduce the perception of contemporaries more faithfully, and it also constitutes a rejection of the excuses that conservatives present *a posteriori* in the name of what appears to be scrupulous historicism: "Between 1933 and 1935, it was not possible for anyone to foresee, even distantly, what would one day become the crimes of the National Socialists."[3]

What appears to justify these selective memory lacunas of posterity, these attempts to convey a picture of normality, is the undeniable fact that from June 1934 on the brutalities did more or less disappear from the public scene, giving way to methods and an apparatus that were less glaringly obvious but every bit as effective. A study of the two types of author (Täter), one after the other, will also reveal the strategic continuity of the authorities that lay behind the rivalry between the SA and the SS.

BRUTE VIOLENCE: THE SA

To anyone who happened to be in Berlin on 30 January 1933, the torchlit procession of the SA that evening must have revealed the true nature of those newly come to power. The fact that propaganda later exaggerated the number of those who took part in the procession is of secondary importance. The essential point is that the minute Hitler was appointed chancellor by a legal procedure, he immediately so to speak invited his warriors to make free with the streets and proved to what could still be called public opinion that his 1924 prophecy had been realized: "We shall make Marxism understand that National Socialism is the future master of the streets and that it will one day be master of the State."[4] What is more, these troops in uniform (but not visibly armed so as not to offend the military) had from the start been called "assault sections" (*Sturmabteilungen*, *SA*), in flagrant contradiction to their official vocation of providing protection at party meetings.

Organizations of this kind always justify their aggression by glorifying their martyrs. In the course of 1933 alone and in Berlin alone, the SA claimed to have suffered eighty-four deaths and close to ten thousand wounded. (Communist losses seem to have been even heavier: seventy-five deaths in six months; Socialist losses were considerably lighter). But whatever the polemics over which side was responsible for each skirmish, it is manifestly clear that the initiative came from the Nazi camp, whose regional chief (*gauleiter*), Joseph Goebbels had since 1926 been masterminding the reconquest of the "red fortresses." The battle was all the more relentless given that the recruitment of basic troops on both sides took place within more or less the same proletarian circles. In 1931, 50 percent of the membership of the SA in the capital were workers (most of them skilled rather than unskilled, in contrast to the shock troops of the Communists). In other large towns that percentage was in some cases lower (30 percenet in Nuremberg), in some even higher (57 percent in one national sample which admittedly included agricultural workers). But everywhere the SA attracted an overwhelming majority of under-thirty-year-olds as well as a smaller but definite majority of unemployed. These men were generally young, poor, out of work, and unmarried, with no political past. Contrary to a self-perpetuating legend later maintained by a number of historians, defectors from Communism accounted for no more than a small minority, in Berlin at any rate. In any event, well before the capture of power at the top the SA claimed to be the masters of the capital and, as that claimed success led to real success, it had swelled from eight hundred men in the entire city in 1928 to 1,300 in the Neukölln quarter alone three years later. The men were organized into thirteen detachments, each centered on a particular inn.[5]

SA activity had also spread to more rural regions. In Silesia as in East Prussia, one-third of the members were peasants, one quarter artisans, and one fifth-employees: the often misused expression "a middle-class revolt" truly is appropriate here. What was happening was that traditionally restless bands of young men both rural and urban were being organized by older leaders, many of them veterans from vigilante groups, from higher social strata. The army meanwhile was keen to help these auxiliaries despite their lack of discipline, as they might eventually be used to defend the frontier provinces. In this way eastern Germany also came to be put to the fire and sword (the crimes of Potempa in Silesia provide the most famous of many examples), and here too the hundred or so dead "martyrs" and the thousands of wounded (in the year 1932 alone) presaged further bouts of vengeance. Yet had Hitler not won the chancellorship, the hour of retreat for these eastern militiamen might well have been at hand: toward the end of 1932 the police appeared to be regaining control of the situation, and in the November elections the fall in the number of Nazi votes may well have been attributable at least in part to the excesses of the SA.[6]

By allowing free rein to these young, radicalized members of the proletariat, had the Nazi party not fallen into the trap of the sorcerer's apprentice? The essential reason for their joining the SA was "a sense of impotence that could only be dispelled by a demonstrative use of force" (D. Peukert).[7] The autobiographies that some of them produce as early as 1934 for an American sociologist reveal that they were fascinated by the personality of the Great Leader and even more so by the atmosphere of virile and resentful solidarity that reigned in the SA inns—but not at all by either the program or the apparatus of the Party.[8] In their eyes the latter was composed entirely of "civilians," timid bourgeois. Many of them refused to join it, claiming that the subscription charge was too heavy. The party meanwhile officially manifested its gratitude by setting up collective kitchens for them or distributing funds to help their wounded. But many of its regional organizers were unenthusiastic about the SA members and left them on their own to manage financially by dint of fund-raising, borrowing, or racketeering. This explains the revolts that broke out, such as the one led by Walther Stennes in 1931 which afforded a ray of hope to the SA's adversaries. The Communists even interpreted the revolts as expressions of class warfare, pitting the proletarian base against its bourgeois leaders within an extreme right-wing context. But they were to be disappointed: the prestige of the führer proved enough to calm things down temporarily. All the same, the marches of January 1933 masked a persistent underlying grudge.

It was thus not without justification that the now official propaganda fabricated the somewhat revolutionary expression "seizure of power" (*Machtergreifung*) to describe the events of 30 January 1933. Thanks to the SA the streets were already conquered or partially so; and SA members quite naturally imagined that other centers of power such as the administrative departments, businesses, and even barracks would fall in the same way.

The first months of "Germany's renewal" witnessed a huge flood of new members: the total SA force increased from five hundred thousand or six hundred thousand to close to three million men. Within this mass it is possible to pick out "veterans" now in the minority, for recruitment had always been characterized by strong rotation; new members, consisting of volunteers, opportunists, and men newly unemployed (the economic situation having, if anything, worsened that winter) who quite simply wished to manifest a show of zeal while avoiding joining the party; and finally, half a million "active" steel-helmeted members, that is to say adolescents and young men between the ages of eighteen and thirty-five conscripted by the authorities. The social composition of the SA groups was, however, little changed: a national poll of about four thousand individuals, in the years 1933–34 indicated as before that 51 percent were skilled workers and 17 percent unskilled (including agricultural workers). As for the officers, these came from higher social strata: employees and minor officials filled the positions of higher uncommissioned officers; in the officer corps the proportion of former secondary school pupils increased regularly the higher the hierarchical rank. But here it was not so much a matter of social origin as of military experience: over half the SA officers had served in war with a similar rank and many had subsequently transferred to vigilante groups. All in all the sociological spectrum in the SA was somewhat different from that of the party, but it could still not be considered truly homogeneous.[9]

In the context of a basis of relatively uncultivated men and a hierarchy that was more cultivated but emphasized activism, there could be no question of imposing any doctrinal education. The principal intellectual fare consisted of a collection of "SA novels": cheap little books, an idea of the Communist Party. Literary critics of our own day who condescended to analyze the contents of this tatty literature discovered a mixture that reflected both brutality and sentiments that were conventionally acceptable. The brutality was that of public life: to win the reader's sympathy, countless brawls were described in the familiar style of German "westerns" such as the works of Karl May, found on all family bookshelves. Socialists were depicted as fuddy-duddy old bourgeois and Communists as an amalgam of criminals and valiant fighters, with the latter inevitably ending up converted to the good cause, switching over "from one red flag to the other." Meanwhile the private life of the SA hero was bathed in an idyllic light: when he returned home he celebrated

Christmas with his excellent wife and children in a nice little house surrounded by a nice little garden. It was perhaps this modest collection of stories, a compound of *kitsch* and terror, that created the alloy that was to characterize the whole Nazi culture, even the daily lives of its murderers.[10]

For what purpose could the SA now be used? In the first place, for state terrorism. For a few months, from 22 February to 2 August 1933 to be precise, Hermann Goering as minister of the interior in East Prussia engaged several thousand SA members as "auxiliary policemen." It was a pseudoregularization that revealed the strategy of the authorities: namely to give free rein to instincts of violence, to protect the perpetrators from any intervention on the part of the last remaining defenders of the law; then to bring them to heel once their principal opponents had been destroyed. While the anti-Communist struggle fell mainly to the regular police, the SA specialized in attacking first Socialist militants, then, in May, trade unionists. There were many old scores to be settled between the mandarins of the moderate Left, formerly pillars of the Republic and longstanding masters of the Prussian police, and their street-brawling opponents. And settled they were: by arrests, torture in places known as "wild concentration camps," and assassinations. The lists of adversaries to be struck down included Catholic militants here, Poles there, depending on the region. The case of the Jews demonstrates the extent to which the SA was manipulated by political authorities: it was purely on Goering's initiative that on 10 March they began to harass Jewish people and destroy or confiscate their possessions, thereby providing Goebbels with the pretext for the boycott of 1 April, officially presented as being "born out of popular anger."

Hardly a single major town was spared these waves of criminality. Consider the bloody week in Köpenick, one of the "Red" suburbs of Berlin, which between 21 and 26 June produced at least twenty deaths as well as hundreds of wounded, provoking an indignant petition from the local doctors; or the "wild camp" set up in a factory in Wuppertal by an SA colonel with a very checkered past (twenty wounds and fourteen sentences), the sinister echoes of which spread all the way to Berlin: all judicial inquiries were blocked even after the discovery of corpses, and the legal authorities' way of dealing with the culprit was simply to convict him of fraud. It was not until news broke of another such camp in the neighborhood of Stettin that Goering was moved to urge the Prussian minister of justice to set up a commission of procurators specializing in "delicate affairs." In this particular case—virtually the only one—the commission managed to condemn the culprits. Around the same date, shortly after Hitler proclaimed "the end of the revolution," the Bavarian judiciary also endeavored to bring to justice the SA leaders who—to the great indignation of the archbishop of Munich, who had denounced them for using methods "worthy of the Tcheka"—were guilty of brutalities against Catholic militants. However, in order to achieve any results at all, it had to promise those guilty that if they presented themselves in court, they would be treated leniently.[11]

Meanwhile, this kind of leniency shown to the "bully-boys" did nothing to improve the lot of their out-of-work comrades. However, a number of special projects were designed for party "veterans," many of whom thus managed to find reemployment, mostly as minor civil servants. A number of mass appointments to municipal and state offices helped complete this well-targeted reemployment policy. But as we have seen, the posts of auxiliary policemen did not last long, for they were abolished that very autumn. The army was clearly disinclined to integrate into its own ranks men so badly disciplined, and its distrust of them increased from month to month. Conversely, the major construction sites of the Labor Service and the motor roads, which were keen to employ the jobless, attracted few jobseekers. The private sector represented an alternative, but economic recovery was slow in coming and SA applicants were frequently turned away because they were underqualified. Here, too, local leaders initiated many moves that shocked the supporters of order: in one place an SA section would descend upon a business to force it to take on workers; in another, SA members taken on only recently would start absenting themselves "for reasons of SA service." The business proprietors protested and on at least two occasions, in the autumn of 1933 and in June 1934, received in response communiqués from the SA high command. This correspondence lay at the origin of what was claimed to be SA socialism: It consisted of a series of individual complaints rather than a doctrine of collective emancipation, complaints encouraged by SA leader Ernst Röhm's appeals for "a second revolution." The SA's ritualistic enumeration of enemies to be struck down more frequently included—alongside Reds, Jews, and Blacks (Catholics)—the "capitalists," among whom the communiqué of June 1934 cited Goering, Reichs Bank president Horace Greeley Hjalmar Schacht, and steel industrialist Fritz Thyssen. In the cacophony of discontent that spring the voice of the SA dominated the din.[12]

This is not the place to recount the events of 30 June 1934.[13] For us, particularly interesting are the reasons for the collapse of the imposing-seeming edifice of the SA and its subsequent slump into insignificance. All the evidence (which is however mostly of a retrospective nature) suggests that the reason the basic troops did not react to the annihilation of their leaders was not solely because the operation was so sudden and they were faced with the combined strength of so many adversaries: the army, the SS, the business bosses, and the party. It was because the coherence of the organization had foundered amid so many local splinter groups, because lack of discipline had been set up as a virtue, and because mere slogans had taken the place of ideology.

The task of reorganizing and reactivating this bewildered mass now fell to new leaders headed by the pallid SA chief of staff Viktor Lutze. After the bloody purge a series of internal trials took place followed by exclusions and, for many, loss of rank. Those principally targeted were cadres and veterans, that is to say the very backbone of the movement. In all close to two thousand disciplinary procedures took place during the remaining prewar years. Care was taken not to mention political divergences. But all infractions of traditional morality such as alcoholism, homosexuality, adultery, corruption, and even physical brutality in the SA were skilfully exploited, thereby satisfying public opinion. It was a far cry from the days when Hitler, defending his henchmen, had exclaimed, "After all, the SA is not an institution for well-brought-up young girls!"

The problem of finding occupations for the unemployed masses remained, for although their numbers continued to shrink there still were over one million in 1938. The SA jobless were regarded askance by employers and the streets were full of them, so tens of thousands had to be prodded in the direction of institutions that went by the sad name of "emergency labor camps." Where the rest were concerned, justification had to be found for the SA rallies and, by the same token, for the very existence of the SA apparatus with all its permanent staff. The military preparation of the young and the ongoing training of reservists under the wary supervision of professional officers was a dispiriting business. Eventually even ceremonial duties palled, except perhaps those connected with the major Nuremberg parades, which were followed by drinking bouts; but for many units these displays were now quite out of the question as they lacked the means to equip themselves with suitable uniforms. Nevertheless, alongside the lukewarm in the SA, whose motive for joining or remaining was to avoid the heavier duties that would fall upon them if they became party members, some were still nostalgic for the heady days of the past. These could be relied upon to fabricate a number of "spontaneous manifestations of popular anger" against the Jews, once as a prelude to the adoption of the Nuremberg Laws in 1935 and again during the pogrom of November 1938. But by those two dates the SA could no longer claim the debatable honor of holding a monopoly on violence.[14]

SYSTEMATIC TERROR: THE SS

In contrast to the overt aggressiveness of the "assault sections," the "protection squads" (*Schutzstaffel*, *SS*) seemed by virtue of their very name to be intended for defensive tasks. Unlike the three-million-strong SA, in 1933 the SS numbered a mere two hundred thousand or so, of whom only a few were located in barracks, and even these relied on the regular army for their military training and means of transport.[15] But while Röhm was dreaming of a total SA subversion of the state, SS chief Heinrich Himmler had already made sure that a number of vital centers were taken over by special SS detachments, making the most of the juridical fiction of a statute of private law. To understand the development of what was to become an empire within an empire, we must examine first its various branches, then the mode of recruitment and the philosophy that soldered them together.

As early as the end of 1934 at least seven categories of SS could be distinguished, three operating on a part-time basis, four working full-time. The first three categories consisted of the "Honorary SS," figures of importance rewarded by the right occasionally to don the black uniform; the SS cavalry regiment, a smart equestrian club; and on the periphery a "circle of bene-factors" made up of thousands of generous patrons. The four units with permanent personnel were called "the Deployable SS," "the Death's Heads," "the Security Service," and "the General SS." It is worth noting immediately that in the latter four sections the rotation of cadres, if not of the rank and file, was strongly developed right from the start.

The history of the "Deployable SS" describes the creation of a new army, initially a protégé of the regular army and later its rival.[16] Following the destruction of SA power, achieved by the two groups working together, the Ministry of War showed its gratitude by arming and paying for three regiments of these "po-litical soldiers" for whose moral and doctrinal training the SS high command made itself responsible. It was not long before the army became alarmed: the schools for SS cadres planned to produce five hundred officers each year. No doubt most of them would be sent to serve elsewhere than among the "Deployable SS" troops. But quite apart from the fact that in times of war they would constitute a strong body of politicized reservists, their rotation between barracks, police stations, and concentration camps — which in 1937 was still openly approved by Himmler — was bound to shock the General Staff Office. That distrust was further strengthened by the 1938 decree that confirmed the hybrid status of these regiments: they constituted "a permanent armed troop at the exclusive disposal of the Führer," and would come under the command of the army only in the event of general mobilization. The following year, when the top military leaders had been brought into line, they ended up constituting a division of twenty thousand men, equipped with artillery. It was at this point that the "Deployable SS" received their definitive name, "the Armed SS" (*Waffen-SS*).

In 1936 the supervisors of concentration camps changed their anodyne name of "Guard Units" to the seemingly more grandiose "Death's Head Formation." Their intention was probably in part to proclaim themselves the heirs to an old Prussian elite unit, the "Hussars of Death," whose macabre emblem they had taken over, but also to broadcast their absolute authority over those held in the camps. Like so many other initiatives of the regime, their creation was the result of circumstance: by the end of the winter of 1933 the "wild" SA camps, which were not located in sufficiently remote places, were shocking their surrounding neighborhoods and their anarchic proliferation was worrying the professional police, whose loyalty it was preferable to preserve. Bavaria in particular had prisons full to overflowing. Himmler, as prefect of the Munich police, now set up the first official camp in a surburban factory in Dachau. He lost no time in setting his SS to guard it, but they in their turn proved uncontrollable and he was obliged to find a director who was at once unburdened by scruples and a good organizer. Colonel Eicke presented the necessary *curriculum vitae*, having seen active wartime service and worked in police stations and prisons, in heavy industry and terrorism, in exile, and even in a psychiatric hospital. To him may be attributed the invention of a new technique of imprisonment: bureaucratic terror. From now on the detainees would be their own administrators in day-to-day life (Eicke had noted the efficiency of gangster bosses in prisons during the Republic), and the SS would do no more than command, supervise, and punish: if this involved killing, it would be sanctioned by the rules. In this way a small garrison would suffice to control thousands of prisoners and the official proclamation of punishments would salve the consciences of those who had to execute them. Even the local neighborhood could be informed by press announcements of "incidents," that is to say the executions or so-called "suicides" that occurred inside the camp.

Once appointed inspector-general, Eicke was able to extend the "Dachau model" to other regular camps. Nevertheless their geographic distribution remained uncertain until 1936, when economic imperatives (the mobilization of labor for great urban development projects) and policing needs dictated the solution of building giant camps. After Dachau a series of camps were opened in Sachsenhausen near Berlin, Buchenwald near Weimar, Flossenbürg near the Czech frontier, Mauthausen, once Austria was annexed, and finally Ravensbrück in Mecklenburg, for women. On the eve of the war, about twenty-five thousand prisoners were in the hands of 14,000 "Death's Head" SS: the system was thus still potentially extendable, as had been shown at the time of the waves of arrests of Jews in 1938.[17]

At its foundation the Security Service (*SD*) consisted of one single employee, ex-naval officer Reinhard Heydrich. By 1933 it was staffed by 120 individuals with headquarters in Munich, close to the party but remote from the state, as if to affirm an autonomy that it retained at least until it was integrated into the "Principal Security Office of the Reich" (*RSHA*) in 1939. The Security Service provided the big chiefs, first and foremost its own, with information about the internal life of the party and public opinion in general. (We shall return to the value of its soundings of public opinion, which were certainly less scientific than those of modern polls but, like the latter, did lay claim to objectivity). An office of particular importance dealt with questions relating to "Jews, pacifists, false propaganda, and political emigrés." Later, the Jewish question became a large enough priority to warrant a special office of its own: for these intellectual purveyors of information also fancied themselves as architects of the purged German society of the future. With that end in view, and judging as ineffective the brutal methods of those they described as "the extremists of anti-Semitism," they described their objective as the emigration, either voluntary or enforced, of all German Jews. This point marked the emergence of a type of planner until then unknown: his ultimate avatar, the murderous bureaucrat (*Schreibtischtäter*).[18]

One might have thought of the "General SS" as performing all kinds of civil services had not their view of life, like their uniform, been essentially bellicose. We may leave aside the SS managers and cloistered academics bent principally upon discovering some scientific basis for racial theory (when, that is, they were not engaged in satisfying some other fantasy of the *SS Reichsführer*). But it is worth taking a closer look at their hold over the police. Up until 1936 each region of Germany had its own police force, divided into three classic branches: the political (*Stapo*), the criminal (*Kripo*), and the maintenance of order (*Schupo*). But Himmler had already managed to coordinate the first two into a single national and secret organ (*Gestapo*). He then undertook a double process of territorial and professional unification which was crowned in 1939 by the creation of the "Principal Security Office of the Reich" (*RSHA*), which integrated everybody, even the *SD*. This was a unique case of a "denationalization of public life," for all the former state police forces were now no longer governed by the rules of public law but instead depended upon the arbitrary decisions of their supreme head and the application of these by an exogenous hierarchy, the SS. "Whereas in a normal State, the police force is part of the administration and the political police is, in its turn, simply part of that police force, in the Third Reich the reverse was true" (H. Buchheim).[19]

The efficiency of a policing apparatus depends less upon its staff than upon its cohesion, and—in a non-democratic regime at least—upon the terror that it inspires in the population. Every department of the *RSHA* was taken in hand by the Black Corps either by means of appointing SS officers to all important posts or, conversely, by turning high-ranking officials—some of whom were not even party members—into SS officers. The success of this amalgamation was linked to a surprising factor, namely the continuity of police personnel from the end of the Republic to the installment of the new regime. In Prussia for example the purging of left-wingers had been completed as early as 1932, following von Papen's coup d'état, leaving in place only conservative police, and the new masters had been astute enough to keep these on, making the most of their skills, their hostility to "Reds" and "Marxists," and their filing system. The same phenomenon is detectable in Bremen, Hamburg, Munich, Frankfurt, and so on. The loyalty of those high in the police hierarchy was thus rewarded by their being admitted into the SS. The rest were urged or forced to demonstrate at least a modicum of conformism, in other words were made to join the party. As a result, in 1939 the Gestapo itself was perfectly well able to function with a minority of SS, no more than three thousand out of a total of twenty thousand officials.[20]

Should we explain this simply as the opportunism of these "apolitical" individuals, and their need to hold on to their jobs? Or was it perhaps due above all to their attraction to a new doctrine that allotted the police a fundamental role in the transformation of society? In 1936, Werner Best in his classic treatise on the German police wrote as follows: "A modern political police force is an institution that maintains a careful surveillance over the state of the political health of the body of the German people, recognizing each symptom of disease in good time, and localizing and annihilating the germs of destruction." This led it to introducing a program of racial hygiene along with a "progressive and modern" social policy for the "healthy" section of the people. Views such as these were not urged solely upon the agents of the Gestapo. They also filled the criminal police with fervor and politicized it. When the 1939 wave of arrests was launched against "anti-social elements," "professional criminals," "habitual (ie. hereditary) criminals," and "idlers," it filled the concentration camps with thousands of people who were regarded as sub-proletarians whether or not they had stood trial: by one year later they made up over half the occupants of Buchenwald.[21] The political police force had even greater reasons for considering itself to be a new source of law: its job was now not only to eliminate opponents but also to punish them, taking the place of magistrates. The procedures of "preventive detention" or "protective detention" (*Schutzhaft*) allowed it to intern suspects acquitted by the courts and likewise those found guilty who had already served their sentences. Denouncing the laxity of judges as Himmler and Heydrich had, the SS newspaper *Das Schwarze Korps* ironically remarked: "For us, the paragraphs [of the legal code] are not small pieces of bone [relics] to be venerated, before which we should grovel." It was with sallies of coarse wit of this kind that the new elite made a place for itself alongside or above the elites of the past.[22]

To control the population as a whole the Gestapo could thus count on the cooperation of other police forces. It certainly needed to, as its own numbers remained astonishingly low. In 1937 its Düsseldorf office was manned by no more than 126 officials, lower ranks included, to control a town of five hundred thousand inhabitants. In the Gestapo office of Essen the ratio was even lower: forty-three for 650,000; the Würzburg office, responsible for the 840,000 inhabitants of the Lower Franconia district, numbered twenty-two men! Sarrebruck was better supplied, no doubt on account of its proximity to the exiles installed in Lorraine. Furthermore, the central office in Berlin heaped paperwork upon its local agents, leaving them little time for their principal task, the surveillance of opponents. The use of paid informers (*V-Leute*) produced no more than negligible results: whether these individuals were men conditionally released from prison or ex-militant defectors, they were few in number, dishonest, and incompetent, or else "burnt-out cases." But the Gestapo was able to exploit a huge mass of spontaneous denunciations: in Würzburg, 57 percent of the inquiries into "guilty relations between Jews and Aryans" were initiated in this fashion, as were 88 percent of the cases of "bad attitude" (*Heimtücke*) in Sarrebruck. Some informers, party members for instance, possibly acted out of conviction, but what could have motivated the rest, close neighbors, business colleagues, even relatives and in-laws of the victims, both rural and urban, proletarian and bourgeois? As well as sordid little cases of rancor, fear no doubt also played its part, fear the Gestapo itself encouraged. Not until the eighties did the low count of Gestapo agents come to light. Until then everyone from resistants to conformist citizens and even the first postwar historians believed the Gestapo was omnipresent.[23] But thanks to this "society of denouncers" the police force was able to deploy the incredible activity that in its turn fueled the myth of its all-seeing power. In Berlin for example during the month of August 1935 alone, 307 arrests were made: 119 Jews, seventy Communists, the rest for insulting members of the government, plotting high treason, distributing illegal literature, or spreading false rumors of atrocities. In Cologne the few surviving reports for 1934 and 1935 record between thirty and one hundred arrests each month.[24] Once the eye of the Gestapo fell upon these suspects there was no escaping it: it followed them into the camps via the "political section," to which the Gestapo seconded a number of inspectors.

Whether the "SS male" was to work in a police station or a camp, an office or a barracks, he was always of a particular type who first had to be selected then trained. At an entrance examination he would be tested for athleticism, political innocence, a modicum of education (by means of a dictation three lines long!), and the racial purity of his ancestors going back as far as the eighteenth century. On this last point however the examiners could close their eyes in a few dubious cases, provided the individual's character was satisfactory. The SS chiefs, less cynical than Goering, did not proclaim from the rooftops, "It is I who decides who is Jewish" (or Aryan); nevertheless they acted in a similar fashion, recognizing the inanity of the biological criteria. At the end of a year the best candidates—those who had performed well—were propelled in the direction of schools for cadres while the rest passed directly into the lower ranks.[25]

Basic troopers and low-ranking noncommissioned officers alike thus embarked upon their jobs with a two-edged sense of belonging to an elite yet at the same time of having failed. These are the men about whom we would be the least well-informed were it not for the testimony of former prisoners and postwar trials, which relate mostly to the forties but from which it is possible to extrapolate for the preceding period. Eugen Kogon was the first to put together a classic picture of these men: individuals who had failed in civilian life whom the training system seems to have conditioned artificially: their mechanical responses seemed to symbolize their moral rigidity. They nurtured a few preconceptions that barely masked their deep-seated impulses: "an inculcated sadism and a barrack-room masochism" bequeathed by their Prussian-style training (*Drill*).[26] Kogon's attempt at analysis, written on the spot and all the better for that, should not be underestimated. However it is perhaps marked—excusably—by a sense of intellectual superiority. Hans Buchheim, called as an expert witness at the Frankfurt trial of 1961, probed somewhat deeper in his attempt to understand what he called "the SS duty to obey." According to him, for these men it was a matter no longer of military obedience (necessary for everyone's safety) but rather of National Socialist obedience. Their ideological training had certainly been no more than elementary; but their physical and psychological training, itself determined by the philosophy of their leaders, had imparted a perpetual tension to their behavior. In the humiliating exercises to which they had been subjected and to which they subjected those whom they assumed to be their inferiors, they discovered a degraded and perverted form of what Ernst Jünger famously called "heroic realism." And in the last analysis if they never (or very seldom) refused to obey, it was not out of fear or doctrinal fanaticism, but as a result of the ongoing logic of their initial commitment.[27]

The future SS officers continued their studies for two years. These included periods of duty in a number of different departments including information and racial studies; as ever, a great deal of sport; military training, and a light dash of theory. Given that this was purveyed to a culturally heterogeneous audience it was necessarily limited to four hours a week for just a few months and consisted of little more than slogans. For example, the syllabuses and textbooks used in these schools for cadres (*Junkerschulen*) have revealed a caricature of historical sociology that divided the great men of the past and the social groups of the present into bad "atomist-materialists," dubious "spiritualists," and good "cosmic-organic" subjects. But the essentials lay elsewhere, in the ideological impregnation that stemmed from all their other activities: their military training was designed to create not only, as in the army, weaponry technicians and moral role models, but also political leaders, "officers of the Führer." Physical exploits, particularly dangerous ones, were considered the best criteria for selection, just as war service and militantism had been before 1933. When they emerged from this training, all fashioned in the same mold, the new officers could be indiscriminately distributed to any province in the SS empire.[28]

But at this point they entered new circles, the social origins and cultural levels of which were very different from their own. In the "General SS," 50 percent of new officers (those who entered after 1933) were holders of the baccalaureat and most had entered upon further studies, if not obtained a degree. In the older units only one-fifth held baccalaureats. Only one-fifth of the former group had emerged from the working class, while almost half had worked in professions that Anglo-Saxon historians classify as "upper middle class." In the latter units those proportions were well-nigh reversed, to 30-40 percent and 15-20 percent respectively. Even the militarized units were becoming more "distinguished": among the new "Death's Head" officers one-third had passed the baccalaureat examination and one-sixth held university degrees. The plebeian veterans were thus joined by the engineers of the new society, the "educated barbarians" to borrow Robert Pois's description. The fact was that, despite the scorn for *Akademiker* professed by the top leaders, the SS machine in order to function well needed a strong contingent of doctors of law and of medicine.[29]

How could an *esprit de corps* be created in these circumstances? Markedly different policies were adopted in the various SS bodies in question. The commanding officers in "Adolf Hitler's regiment of guards" stressed veneration for the traditions of the Prussian Guards and combined this with a minimum of doctrinal training, lectures by experts, and educational films; in the last analysis they modestly invited "each leader to work on his own toward perfecting his conception of the world." The "Death's Heads" tended to cultivate a revolutionary, antibourgeois, even antimilitarist style. The "deployable" regiments took in would-be training staff who likened themselves to the political commissars of the Red Army; but after a few years a general lassitude led to the abandonment of the courses of history and anthropology that had led on from the lessons of school. After all, had not these men been taught at school that a correct "conception of the world" was to be acquired by dint of character rather than through abstract ideas?.[30]

Nothing reveals the weakness of this ideological structure better than the Nazi leaders' semifailure to dictate the religious and family behavior of their subordinates. The Black Order, which Himmler described as a "National-Socialist and military order, a sworn community of northern clans," took it upon itself to set out new rules for the private lives of its members. The God of the Jews and the Christians was opposed by "the Very Ancient One" (*der Uralte*) who personified Eternal Nature; charity was to be replaced by firmness, moral conscience by obedience, the autonomous family by racially pure marriage and a duty to procreate. However, statistics show that the impact made by these recommendations was very uneven: on the eve of the war, 80 percent of the "Death's Heads" and 56 percent of the "Deployable SS" had left their churches and become simply believers in God (in effect, agnostics), whereas only 20 percent of the "General SS" had done so. If apostates were more common in the military units, that was probably because collective constraints were stronger there. Family life eluded those constraints more easily; that is why hundreds of men got married without permission from their commanding officers, and SS households including those of the cadres produced on average fewer than two children (1.4), far fewer than the four expected of them.[31] A private life of tranquillity and a professional life of excess: the signs of schizophrenia were already detectable.

In the last analysis, the ideology peculiar to the SS was characterized not so much by this woolly metaphysics and undemanding morality as by a frenzy of persecution: beleaguered on every side and internally infected by evil forces, the new society could only be constructed by dint of permanent purges. Reds, Marxists, Blacks, Jews, Gypsies, Jehovah's Witnesses, homosexuals, professional or inveterate criminals, antisocial elements, idlers, trouble-makers, double-dealers, and degenerates . . . : there seemed no end to the list of enemies who were to fill the prisons, the concentration camps, and hospitals. In truth, that list was the product of two different rationales: one of vengeance and security aimed against protesters and political opponents; the other bent on purging the social body and aimed against "aliens in the community." But neither allowed for any limits to be set to the repression, the first because the notion of political opponents was infinitely extendable, a fact that led to the politicization of economic transgressions and the criminalization of manifestations of discontent; the second because the racial criteria for membership in or exclusion from the "Community of the People" were not scientifically established: this—through a remarkable inversion—led to a race of individuals being decided by their social behavior. Even so, as heirs to a scientific tradition of a kind, the theorists persisted in believing "in the possibility of a scientific resolution to social contradictions, through a combination of progress in pedagogic methods and the improvement of hereditary characteristics" (D. Peukert).[32]

THE VICTIMS: THE DISCONTENTED AND THOSE WHO RESISTED

Just as eugenics led to murder, such pedagogy obviously included repression. Even political peccadillos, verbal protestations, disrespectful jokes, etc. were deemed worthy of "Special Courts," and by March 1933 these were set up in every regional capital. Rights to a defense were limited and verdicts were not subject to appeal. Eighteen months later these measures were fixed in a law tellingly known as the "Law against underhand attacks on the State and the Party, and to protect the Party uniforms." In the course of six years, the Special Court in Munich, which served Bavaria and Württemberg, initiated proceedings against close to forty-five hundred people. Initially many of those affected were Communists and Socialists whose illegal activities had hitherto remained unobtrusive (cases of high treason were tried by the People's Court). All the same, two out of three were pronounced guilty and given prison sentences of between one month and one year. Later, cases of ill-will with no political connotation predominated, and these were treated slightly more leniently.[33] But it should not be forgotten that even once these people had completed their sentences they could still be rearrested by the Gestapo.

Between 1933 and 1938 resistance in the strict sense (*Widerstand*) was essentially practiced only by militant Communists, Social Democrats, or left-wing Independents. Other groups— Christians, conservatives, and the military—were mobilizing only individuals or very small teams of dissidents. Admittedly that assertion has long been disputed. Some authors have insisted that "all attitudes, whether active or passive, that manifested rejection of the National-Socialist regime or of part of its ideology, and to which risk was attached" should be described as "resistant"—but would that not be tantamount to accepting the definition of the judges and the police? Others have also laid claim to the label for the churches to the extent that they had "refused to fall into line and had unqualifiedly proclaimed their dogma and their morality"—but had not that kind of principled nonconformism likewise inspired different attitudes of reservation in many other circles? Today a measure of consensus exists on this subject and it is generally agreed that all those attitudes should be covered by a single common term (*Resistenz* according to M. Broszat, "dissent" according to I. Kershaw) and that *Widerstand* should be reserved for political behavior that rejected all aspects of the regime and conspired in one way or another to overthrow it.[34] A large measure of optimism was needed to launch oneself upon such a course as well as quite a few illusions as to the fragility of the regime. Communist leaders regarded the regime simply as the last spasm of doomed capitalism and accordingly launched their troops into revolutionary agitation they believed would ultimately prevail. At first their Socialist rivals made the same mistake; later they sought a historical precedent to provide them with surer guidance and believed they had discovered it in the persecution their fathers had suffered in the Bismarck period: the best strategy accordingly seemed to be that which had succeeded in the past, that is to say a strategy of maintaining their networks of solidarity and propaganda and waiting for the inevitable disintegration of the regime. These hopes were shared by the grass roots militants in both camps. However—and this is why the local monographs are so interesting—the reactions of each cell depended upon its own particular environment, the unequal levels of repression, the nature of its previous struggles, and the age and professional level of its members.[35]

It is hard to say how many of the three hundred thousand members of the Communist Party in 1932 were clandestinely militant. The police, who had in their possession files put together under the Republic, proceeded to make numerous arrests immediately following the Reichstag fire and their auxiliaries meanwhile perpetrated a multitude of assassinations. According to Wilhelm Pieck, within ten months the party had lost sixty thousand of its members as prisoners and suffered two thousand deaths. Relatively few major leaders were among the victims, but many middle-rank officers—for example half the members of the central committee—were. Many of the Communist rank and file no doubt withdrew into their private lives, doing so in increasing numbers as employment became more available. Others joined the SA out of prudence or with a view to attracting new members. Between sixty thousand and one hundred and fifty thousand militants remained, now decimated by arrests, now reinforced by erstwhile prisoners who, once released, returned to their former activities, unaware that the police were keeping them under surveillance. Not all belonged to cells in the strict sense of the term. The greater mass of them were dispersed among parallel organizations, printing presses, trade unions, Red Mutual Societies, youth groups. . . . It is clearly impossible to put a figure to their more risky activities, the lightning street demonstrations, the pasting up of posters, the speeches made outside factories. But there must have been many to judge by the number of tracts and pamphlets seized by the Gestapo: 1.2 million copies in 1934, 1.7 million in each of the two following years, just under one million in 1937, which does not seem to have been a very active year.

Histories of the Communist Party attach great importance to its strategic evolution. It is known that the leadership in exile tended to discourage the International from establishing closer ties with the Socialists (let alone the Christians). Before going into exile in 1935 it had circulated contradictory directions, warning sometimes against "reconciliatory" tendencies, sometimes against "sectarianism." At any rate, the arrests of the internal leadership in March of that year left greater freedom of maneuver to local groups. Paradoxically however, many leaders and militants reacted to this by remaining faithful to the hard line, clinging to their rivalry with the rest of the clandestine Left.[36] And so for a long time it continued: even in full wartime, the deportees from every corner of Europe upon their arrival in the camps discovered the same old sectarianism among Communist veterans lastingly impregnated by the doctrine of "Social Fascism."

A tour of the regions would be very helpful for a study of day-to-day underground life. But we are not well informed on the eastern provinces since the historiography of the GDR (German Democtratic Republic, or East Germany) for the most part[37] limited itself to apologia in praise of Communist leaders and heroic chronicles of the rank and file. In the West, in contrast, once the taboos of the fifties and sixties were lifted, studies in greater depth made their appearance.

In the case of Berlin, once considered by the International to be "a new Petrograd," the initial successes of repression can also be accounted for by the extreme heterogeneity of the party. The façade was impressive: thirty thousand members; a third of the vote in the elections of November 1932; and teams of young members of the League to Combat Fascism were aggressively active. But all this concealed considerable weaknesses; a high turnover rate, incompatibility between adult workers in cells centered on particular factories and the young unemployed in the street cells, and the dismay of leaders faced with the violence of these young individuals.[38] What is surprising then is not the catastrophe of the winter of 1933, but rather that active dissidence so rapidly found its second wind. Some parallel organizations had managed in advance to split into small, separate teams ready to go underground. It is estimated that in 1935 the capital still contained about one hundred of these teams, making up about five thousand members, who were printing and distributing thirty or so twice-monthly periodicals. But by three years later their numbers were reduced to but a few hundred.[39]

In the Rhineland-Westphalia in contrast, the party had evolved a bureaucratic system that was perfect for periods of relative calm but that constituted a major weakness when more testing times arrived.[40] It had been necessary to impose a single common line upon the relatively moderate metalworkers of the Berg region, the unstable and radical miners of the Ruhr, and left-wing unskilled workers, etc. Many local cells, links, and communications had therefore been set up, indeed so many that full-time activists eventually represented a third or even one half of the total membership! Their revolutionary optimism was encouraged by the proliferation of parallel organizations, seventeen in all. These middle-ranking cadres, editors, couriers, etc. bore the brunt of the repression: nearly nine thousand fell in four months. Recovery was inevitably uneven depending upon the extent to which Red localities were undermined by discouragement. The regular membership for the following years is estimated to have fallen to 10 percent of its pre-1933 level in the Ruhr, to much lower in Cologne, and to between 20 and 30 percent in the Lower Rhineland. The leadership's appeals for "mass action" were inevitably ineffective; but the diffusion of the press and—old habits die hard—ongoing administrative work presented a semblance of normality. "The Party was continuing to lose its substance while preserving its form."[41] As a result, after a few years the rank and file began to balk. The more realistic claimed that it was time to abandon facile optimism, study the behavior of comrades who had found work and withdrawn into private life, create unifying trade unions in concert with the Socialists. . . . However by the time new reinforcements arrived from the Popular Front, it was too late: following a new wave of arrests, these were badly distributed and local contacts with the rest of the Left remained limited. In their isolation, individual cells now contented themselves with a "simmering resistance" involving acts of solidarity with the families of prisoners and so on. A certain degree of renewed activity was relaunched from 1937 on, but as we shall see, this was for professional and not political reasons.

The organization and strategy of the Communists of Bavaria were identical, and it is not surprising that their destruction followed a similar course. Here too it had been necessary to build up a solid bureaucracy in order to coordinate artisans, the self-employed, and specialized workers in heavy industry, all dispersed as they were (except in a few large towns) within a Catholic and conservative society. The sweep of arrests in March 1933, carried out under the personal supervision of Himmler and Heydrich, was horribly effective: five thousand middle-ranking cadres found themselves in Dachau for more or less extended periods; only the apparatus in Nuremberg, which had taken greater precautions, to some degree escaped. Once the first freed prisoners returned the party reestablished contacts and also, to its cost, routines: by May, subscription stamps were again being distributed as were newspapers in the streets. . . . So the cycles of arrests continued, in some cases thanks to former prisoners who had agreed or been coerced into acting as informers. It was not until they had twice been forced to replace their staff that the regional secretariats of Munich and Nuremberg at last decided to be more realistic, abandoned their procedural rationale, and made a few contacts with their Socialist and Christian comrades. But around 1935–36 even these discreet activities ceased.[42] Another difficult question for the succession of organizers was the matter of making contacts with groups of young Communists. Less known to the police or more imaginative than their elders, these had survived the first wave of arrests and even set up their own contacts with other countries. Having been out of work longer, they had had a chance to be more active and also it would seem more open, recruiting comrades who were apolitical and even, in Augsburg for instance, Christians. Should they be allowed to retain this autonomy? Party interests prevailed: to fill the gaps they were made to integrate themselves into the apparatus of the adults; they then fell along with them.[43]

These local examples certainly illustrate the double handicap represented everywhere by doctrine and a mania for organization. But, better than the histories of the supreme leadership, they also afford glimpses of a few signs of increasing flexibility as one defeat was followed by another, and also of the perseverance of the small cells of those who survived.

In their lists of opponents the police and the Nazi party made no distinction between "Reds" (Communists) and "Marxists" (Socialists). If fewer of the latter fell victim to the Nazis it was due not to any moderation in the apparatus of repression but, paradoxically, to the shortcomings of their national leadership which forced each small, basic unit to improvise in order to survive. For months the leaders of the Social Democrat party and the trade unions wavered between rallying partially to the regime and organizing protest meetings, and between the policy of maintaining a presence in the new institutions and departing into exile. The price of that hesitation was a series of virulent internal polemics. Disoriented, the rank and file resorted to various contradictory initiatives. Some went off to reinforce the ranks of the Steel Helmets–or conservative Right—reckoning that the latter would soon enter into dissidence. Others, the young in particular, had already begun to organize themselves into isolated teams ready to go underground. But such preparations were condemned by the "old guard." In Berlin the regional secretariat went so far as to purge the office of working-class Socialist youth on the pretext of its lack of discipline and illegal activities. Meanwhile certain "Frontier Secretariats" installed in neighboring countries took to sending their propaganda materials by ordinary mail, thereby accidentally betraying their correspondents to the police. This, too, sparked off a series of polemical clashes between the generations.[44]

The trade unionist hierarchy had likewise passed through a phase of extreme prudence, even recommending participation in the official meetings of May Day. But, being less divided than the party hierarchy, it quickly learned the lessons of the subsequent day's violence, which plunged it into illegality. A number of professional federations set themselves up as a double network: while some leaders traveled discreetly abroad diffusing the underground press, others who knew they were known to the police disguised themselves as traveling salesmen or company representatives and reestablished contact with local teams. One such was Wilhelm Leuschner, an ex-member of the national head office who, no sooner than he was released from prison, began traveling from bar to bar pretending to sell technological brewing equipment and succeeded in reconstituting the *Kneipenkultur* that had proved its efficacy under Bismarck. Similarly, Brandes, ex-president of the metalworkers, despite being detained from 1935 to 1936, managed to maintain his contacts right up until the end of the war.[45]

Within the party the essential work was carried out by "Frontier Secretariats" which, from their bases in Czechoslovakia, Austria, Switzerland, the Saar, France, Belgium, and the Netherlands, sent their publicity to sections in neighboring provinces and received from them reports on the internal situation, the famous *Deutschlandberichte* later to become so precious to historians. However these did not always see eye to eye amongst themselves or with their correspondents. The secretariat in the Netherlands, convinced that the regime could not possibly last, pressed for a secret organization ready for action; in contrast the principal official in Dortmund, a former deputy, was so impressed by the power of the police that he counseled his comrades to limit themselves to informal meetings, with the sole mission of "preserving doctrinal traditions."[46] In Czechoslovakia there were two "secretaries." One of them, Hans Dill, sought only to maintain tradition and "horizontal" contacts between neighbours or workshop colleagues. The other, Waldemar von Knoeringen, who also belonged to the New Beginning (*Neu Beginnen*), suggested combining a "vertical" separation of small cells with meetings for theoretical reflection. But those with whom Dill was in communication, in the Nuremberg region, preferred a vertical organization in conformity with the needs of a clandestine struggle; while those in communication with von Knoeringen, in southern Bavaria, neglected all precautions and were even distributing fifteen thousand tracts at the time of the

1934 plebiscite and keeping on with their horizontal meetings for a whole year without suspecting that they had been infiltrated by informers. Why such inconsistency? The party's social recruitment in the two regions was similar: a majority of artisans and skilled workers, not well-disposed toward either risky heroics or the quasi-military discipline of secrecy. What made the difference seems to have been the political antecedents of the respective groups. Those in Nuremberg were products of Young Socialist groups and the paramilitary organization Banner of the Empire. Those in southern Bavaria, for reasons that remain obscure, appear not to have learned the lessons from the hammer blow of March 1933. But at the level of security, the two modes of behavior led to the same results: a first wave of arrests in the spring of 1934, the creation of a new network in the course of the following year, then a new wave of arrests. Losses, though not as massive as those of the Communists, were high: the Würzburg Gestapo for instance boasted of having captured 40 percent of the militants in 1933 alone.

From that point on these "decent little people," like their parents or grandparents of the Bismarck period, were to be content with a strategy of survival. Some, the better to defend their working comrades, were daring enough to compromise themselves by accepting election to councils of their respective firms. Most of these sought to establish more or less apolitical contacts there in order to maintain links of friendship and to read the underground press—not without success: for a long time the Gestapo remained ignorant of the existence of the *Sozialistische Aktion* newspaper despite its wide circulation. Funerals provided a pretext for silent demonstrations. Young socialists would get together in sports stadiums or on rambles organized by the Friends of Nature, and in this way "values were maintained." In 1945, as soon as the regime collapsed, members were to be seen flocking to the old Socialist local headquarters to pay their twelve-year subscriptions in arrears. An idealist such as von Knoeringen scornfully described such activities as "peripheral." But Otto Baner, a more orthodox leader, was still in 1939 declaring that the essentials were being maintained: namely the party spirit and immunization against the regime's propaganda.[47]

A number of small heterodox groups revolved around the larger organizations. They could never boast very many members: just a few hundred, enough for perhaps a dozen cells. But strict security measures and bolder strategic thinking ensured them relatively long lives, which stood in contrast to the internal misunderstandings and contradictions of their more sizable neighbours. The most remarkable was the New Beginning group (*Neu Beginnen*) launched in the summer of 1933 by Walter Leowenheim, who was known as "Miles." Observing the defeat of the workers' movement and declaring that "Fascism" would be with them all for a long time, he adopted the model of the underground groups created at the beginning of the century by the Bolsheviks and criticized foolhardy initiatives, over-frequent travels abroad, and massive distributions of texts. It was under his inspiration that, in Augsburg for example, defectors from Socialism and Communism, intellectuals, engineers, and workers met for several years to discuss Kant or intellectual liberty. When the name "New Beginning" became rather too well known they changed it to "Revolutionary Socialism." In southern Germany there were about a dozen such groups comprising in total about two hundred militants. Elsewhere the Workers' Socialist Party (SAP) and the International Socialist League to Combat [Fascism] (ISK), which emerged from the extreme Left of the Weimar Republic, were also plotting revolution. In Dortmund the National Bolsheviks led by Ernst Niekisch, gathered together a curious assortment of young Socialists, former SA, splinter-group Communists, and veterans from vigilante corps around an ideology that was at once nationalist and pro-USSR. But after 1938 even the strictest precautions did not suffice and almost all these little teams eventually collapsed. In prison and in court their members met up with friends from other regions whom the police had collected together in order to stage a more spectacular trial.[48]

After four years of roundups political resistance might be expected to disappear. However, Gestapo reports persistently warned authorities to be on their guard against excessive optimism. According to the police every new arrest proved that subversion still threatened. In one Berlin armaments factory the Socialists were still "masterminding" unrest. Elsewhere, in Lüneburg for example, workers were sporting in their buttonholes small "red" rubber beer bottle stoppers. Faced with a shortage of labor, employers were clearly obliged to take on Marxists and obviously the latter were "too wily and too well trained for it to be possible to prove that they were working illegally." Nor was there any lack of recidivists. Among the 4,305 individuals arrested between October 1936 and January 1937 no fewer than 101 were ex-concentration camp prisoners. In short, the twofold peril of seemingly innocuous Socialism and "latent" Communism persisted.[49] This outlook reflected not only the professional obsession of the police but also the extraordinary perseverance of the rebels.

Clearly the Left did not hold a monopoly over persecution. On the side of the conservatives it is Bavaria that seems to have provided the only instance of mass arrests: two thousand militants of the Bavarian Popular Party ended up in prison or in Dachau. Having suddenly tumbled from their respectable posts in a hegemonic party into a world of insults and degradations, they apparently felt deeply humiliated. However, as soon as their leaders agreed to dissolve the party they were allowed to return home.[50] Also in Bavaria, the roundup of 1939 dispatched to similar destinations 125 members of a monarchist group made up of both commoners and aristocrats whose behavior diverged from the customary prudence of such circles, which seldom rallied to protest against the new regime but were simply resentful of it.[51] In the Rhineland the "struggle against the Church" (*Kirchenkampf*) culminated in February 1936 with the arrest of fifty-seven lay and ecclesiastical leaders of the Young Men's Catholic Association, four of whom were given prison sentences for conspiracy. Two years later the literary managers of the central office of the diocesan studies of Cologne suffered the same fate for having written "political" articles in a religious journal. In southern Germany a number of particularly bold parish priests and almoners were detained for varying periods or even sent to camps. As for the proceedings instigated on Himmler's personal orders against religious communities accused of spreading slogans or infringing morality, these were of a different magnitude. Although clearly intended to compromise the Church as a whole, they nevertheless rested upon detailed enough evidence for it not to be possible to integrate them into a history of persecutions.[52]

Similar cases occurred among the Protestants. In October 1934 the bishop of Bavaria, Meiser, was arrested for having flouted the authority of the new ecclesiastical hierarchy; however the arrest was soon rescinded in the face of mass demonstrations by the Franconian faithful. More serious was the arrest of the famous Martin Niemöller, pastor of Berlin-Dahlem who was regarded as the leader of the Confessional Church. He was sentenced to prison but then transferred to a concentration camp. The special section of the Dachau camp was eventually to receive at least two hundred priests and pastors.[53] Although their respective churches regarded them literally as martyrs, neither their courage nor relatively large numbers can justify the idea of a Catholic or Protestant resistance frequently put forward in works of apologia.

To escape arrest thousands of militants, mostly left-wing, fled the country, many of them settling just beyond the frontier. In their wake, purged university teachers and officials as well as writers and artists attacked for being "cultural Bolsheviks" followed the same road, some of them doubly threatened because they were or were considered to be Jewish. No more than an approximate estimate can be made of their number. In 1935, thirty-five thousand, one-third political refugees, were living in France. Austria and Czechoslovakia were probably harboring an even greater number, for when these countries were in their turn threatened, the exiles who were obliged to move on to find a new refuge in Great Britain totaled at least seventy thousand. The initial activity of the left-wing militants, their contacts with those remaining inside Germany, their strategic arguments, and the rivalry between their leaders are all well known. Their future prospects, at first resolutely optimistic, became less bright with the consolidation of the regime and the failure of the Popular Front's efforts. It is known for instance that Socialists living in Great Britain felt considerable exasperation as they read the "reports on Germany" regularly sent to them by friends in underground networks, because these destroyed all their hopes of seeing the German people liberate themselves in the near future. As for the intellectuals with no political affiliations, their history is fragmented into a multitude of individual chronicles. Against the few success stories of scholars invited to Anglo-Saxon universities, bilingual writers more or less fully employed as translators, and world-famous artists, there must have been very many isolated individuals living within their own tiny linguistic world dependent on public or private generosity.[54]

THE VICTIMS:
"THOSE ALIEN TO THE COMMUNITY"

Right from the early days of the regime steps were taken to isolate, prior to eliminating, all "aliens," said to be even more dangerous than rebels because they had infiltrated everywhere and were more or less undetectable to the eyes of naïve citizens. We shall have to resort to the use of many inverted commas at this point, for the categories labeled "handicapped," "mentally ill," "anti-social," and "Jewish" could never for obvious reasons be accurately defined. The most eminent scholars whose help was called upon in this connection limited themselves to keeping quiet about their theoretical reservations, providing approximative taxonomies and training cadres to execute the regime's decrees.

In this way, most psychiatrists became associated with the new "treatment" of the mentally ill, forgetting that the meaning of "treatment" had greatly changed. In the preceding years most of them, like their colleagues abroad, had introduced work therapy, insulin therapy, and electric shock treatment. However, faced with the congestion in their hospitals they declared it impossible to treat all patients by these promising methods. The law of 1933 seemed to provide an opportunity to rid future generations of all this ballast. Two psychiatrists, by no means the least eminent, aided by a jurist, circulated to medical insurance companies a list of "hereditary" pathologies such as schizophrenia, alcoholism, and so on, and strongly urged their colleagues to sit on the "tribunals of hereditary health" for which the law made provision. Those colleagues, who were naturally unable to devise any criteria more rigorous than those suggested by their masters, constructed categories as vague as "mental debility" in order to encompass all deviant forms of behavior, including prostitution and poor housekeeping. They then translated these into psychopathological terms which they used to justify their recommendations of sterilization or abortion. Despite the protests of certain doctors and the reluctance of certain establishments, particularly religious ones, thirty thousand of the 160,000 patients in the care of psychiatric services were sterilized in the course of the following year. The pace then speeded up so that by the outbreak of war this mechanism had claimed hundreds of thousands of victims.[55]

The category of "Jews" was similarly treated: it was only ever defined by the religious allegiance of the ancestors of the individual under consideration, which was a way of avoiding having to recognize the inanity of "racial science." However much the director of the Berlin Institute of Anthropology and Eugenics,

Eugen Fischer, thanked the führer for having made it "possible for researchers into genetics to make the results of research available in a practical fashion in the service of the people," his claims were merely empty boasts. In reality the university world of anthropology was deeply divided over the concepts of a Jewish race, a German race, a Nordic race, and so on. Fischer's disciples and Fischer himself, as "experts on Aryanity," decided the fates of thousands of people simply by looking at snapshots of them. A constant flow of hundreds of decrees laid down a variety of requirements for genealogical purity for the various professions and invented an inextricable body of casuistry to deal with "mixed marriages," with which the Wannsee conference was still preoccupied in 1942.[56] As has been noted above, SS members themselves took little notice of these rules of pseudoscience when they cramped their style.

Once the theoretical difficulties had been brushed aside it was a matter of determining the correct official lines of behavior. There were in fact three lines, recommended by different leaders and rival establishments and coordinated, if necessary, by Hitler himself: instinctive brutality, exclusion by legislative means, and organized emigration. In the spring of 1933 the brutalities and confiscations perpetrated by the SA were in danger of creating "semi-chaos" and reflecting badly upon the regime. On the pretext of satisfying popular discontent but in reality to channel this violence, Goebbels organized the boycott of Jewish businesses on 1 April and the bureaucracy effected a purge, both racial and political, of the public sector and liberal professions. In the summer of 1935 Goebbels adopted the reverse tactic: in alliance with Julius Streicher, the most violent and brutish of anti-Semites, he encouraged a new wave of "spontaneous demonstrations," following which Hitler had the so-called Nuremberg Laws drawn up: thenceforward Jews were to be stripped of their civil rights and classified as second-grade nationals, and all mixed sexual relations were to be defined as harmful to the purity of the race. Over the next three years the spate of legal texts slackened, in deference to world opinion during the Olympic Games in August 1936 in Berlin and to the economic experts in Schacht's entourage; but the harassment continued. Double tactics were again adopted in 1938: in the spring, economic Aryanization was speeded up; that summer brought looting and arrests of "delinquent Jews" under the approving eye of Goebbels; in October the Polish Jews were expelled; on 9 November a "popular explosion" was organized; the situation was finally brought under control by means of a collective fine of one million marks and the dispatch of thirty thousand unfortunate individuals to concentration camps. The ultimate, quasi-official objective was now total emigration, as the special services of the SS had already long been urging.[57]

Thanks to professional and regional monographs it is possible to measure the impact of this triple policy on the daily lives of its victims. For the nine thousand Jewish doctors (3,400 of whom were practicing in Berlin), the first official boycott was simply a prelude to a long campaign of intimidation designed to deprive them of their "Aryan" patients. Some Nazi doctors even personally arranged for their colleagues to be arrested. Next, they were eliminated from public services and barred from acting for health insurance companies, except in the cases of war veterans of whom there were large numbers. Also, as some hospital directors declared that they could not manage without them, about six thousand were still working at the end of 1934. Their private non-Jewish clients remained faithful to them for a while but were eventually discouraged by intimidation. Many doctors with private practices were then obliged to close down or go into exile. The final blow was dealt them in September 1938 (even before the pogrom): their work permits were withdrawn, except in the cases of a scant few hundred, now officially designated disparagingly as "carers" and reduced to a clientele of Jews.[58] Daily edicts and blackmail of a similar kind reduced the number of Jewish lawyers from 3,500 (two thousand of whom practiced in Berlin) to 1,700, and then imposed an equally derisory status of "judicial advisers" upon those who remained.[59] In the world of business it was necessary to proceed more prudently for fear of jeopardizing the recovery of the economy, particularly in the sector of foreign trade. So despite intermittent boycotts and looting, the measures of expropriation were slower in coming. Besides, except in pamphlets, how could bankers and the proprietors of large department stores be lumped together with artisans and small-scale purveyors of agricultural produce? Caught between party zealots and clients who greatly appreciated their Jewish suppliers for their correct business behavior, the authorities were indecisive. As late as 1936 the Gestapo expressed indignation at the sight of Jewish cattle dealers continuing to prosper even in the countryside of Bavaria, which was reputed to be very anti-Semitic. Even Jewish industry and wholesale businesses continued to prosper up to a point: a Hamburg textile store, thanks to the loyalty of its clients; a number of weaving mills, thanks to their orders from the military; and specialist and multilingual representatives irreplaceable in Germany's international markets. Once again the radical turning point of autumn 1938 shattered the last remaining illusions: now levies for the collective fine, arrests, and enforced Aryanization procedures (so far, at least, some had amounted to no more than a shuffling of piles of written declarations thanks to the complicity of officials willing to turn a blind eye) finally combined to produce a "Jew-free" economy.[60]

Those periods of semi-tolerance and the legal texts that appeared to limit excesses go some way to explain how it was that some victims had hesitated to make a definitive move.[61] We should also bear in mind the extreme heterogeneity of their society. Among the half million members of what can hardly be called a community, many who had been converted to Christianity a generation or more earlier simply felt that they were German and only discovered that they were Jewish when they were so labeled. In particular, the thirty thousand or forty thousand war veterans, reassured by clauses that spared them from purges and fired by the same patriotism as their brothers-in-arms, began by proclaiming their allegiance and denouncing the "exaggerations" of the foreign press. Some went so far as to dissociate themselves from the recent immigrants from eastern Europe. Even among practicing Jews, deep divisions separated the Orthodox, the more tolerant Conservatives, the Liberals, and the Zionists. Each group had its own way of replying to the question of whether they were German Jews or Jews in Germany.[62] So it would be foolish to marvel today at the fact that they did not quickly emigrate *en masse*. The first to leave were mostly university academics, intellectuals, and artists, perhaps because they saw things more clearly, perhaps because they reckoned they could easily find work in exile. More humble folk could not rely upon such international prestige; the elderly clung to the framework of their habitual lives; the most orthodox almost congratulated themselves upon their persecution ("Wear the yellow star proudly" was the exhortation circulated like an order from on high). After all, did not the Nuremberg legislation at least guarantee them a status and hence a measure of security? So it was that only thirty-seven thousand left Germany in 1933, and even fewer the following year when some even dared to return to their German homes. Between 1935 and 1937 about twenty thousand emigrated each year, but from villages where life had become untenable another type of migration had begun, an internal one toward the big towns. Yet in 1938 this number still did not exceed forty thousand. However, after the pogrom all illusions were shattered, and besides the SS had set up a system that financed travel for the poor by levies made upon the rich: the number of emigrants leaped to seventy-eight thousand, the majority bound not for Palestine but for Britain and the United States, which had recently increased their immigration quotas.[63]

The majority thus remained in Germany. Those who were still fairly well-to-do or who at least possessed certain cultural assets organized Jewish solidarity with the approval of both the Gestapo and the *SD*. The fact was that the latter wished to avoid the formation of a poverty-stricken sub-proletariat, the cost of which would fall upon the state and which might arouse general commiseration. They were also hoping that within these Jewish groups the influence of the Zionists would predominate and this would speed the Jews' departure in the direction of Palestine. Thanks to American, British, and local funds, the (Jewish) Central Committee for Aid and Edification managed to finance a whole survival system. The most pressing need was to re-create a schooling apparatus: primary and secondary school students were increasingly—but, it is true, unevenly, depending on the institutions where they were being educated—incurring the hostility of teachers and classmates: in 1938 the eldest of them even lost the right to sit for the baccalaureat examination. It was therefore necessary to set up religious, primary, and secondary schools to cater to up to twenty-six thousand pupils in what were very difficult circumstances: over-large classes, disagreements over religious education, over secular culture, over Zionism, and so on. For the less highly educated and even for some pupils of classic secondary education the Zionists set up technical schools with special courses (in agriculture, building, etc.) that matched the needs of Palestine. This was an entirely new experiment and one that gave the lie to the clichéd image of "the little Jewish tailor" incapable of prolonged physical exertion. The assistance provided for the needy and the sick was of a more traditional nature, but the task of maintaining it became increasingly difficult. By 1934 there were over thirty thousand indigent Jews in Berlin alone. Furthermore, the economic recovery brought no relief to the Jewish unemployed, and the Aryanization of businesses accelerated the pauperization of employers and employees alike. A comparison with the rest of the Germans speaks volumes: in 1936, official winter social security came to the aid of one-fifth of the "Aryan" population, and the Jewish security system helped a more or less equal proportion of Jews; by 1939 those figures were respectively one-tenth and one-quarter.[64]

In contrast the cultural activity of the Jews, if not specifically Jewish culture, was dazzling. Despite the departure of so many famous writers and artists, the Cultural League of German Jews managed to offer its twenty thousand supporters an incredible number of plays, operas, concerts, and lectures: when the Reich's Chamber of Culture canceled the membership of Jewish authors, artists, and actors (whereas the Chamber of Music, at the instigation of Richard Strauss, showed much greater tolerance), all participation in national cultural life became impossible. Then a crucial question arose: would an all-Jewish repertoire now be favored, or at the very least works by Jewish authors? It was resolved by the authorities, who prohibited the league from presenting even Goethe, Mozart, and Beethoven. Never mind, there were always Shakespeare, Scribe, Courteline. . . . The more assimilated sections of the audience at this point refused to allow themselves to be "ghettoized" and ceased to attend. The League nevertheless continued to put on one success after another, attracting as many as fifty thousand to its concerts, its philosophical lectures . . . and even the shows of its cabaret singers: one faithful member of this audience wrote in to say, "Do be really funny; we have quite enough worries at home." In contrast, for reasons not entirely financial, the market for books declined. After an initial period of high sales the public became "saturated with purely Jewish themes" and publishers as well as booksellers were soon plunged into the common poverty. But the League for its part persisted in its efforts, even after the pogrom of November 1938 — on the injunction of the watchful SS.[65]

Using contrasting methods, brutal anti-Semites and rational anti-Semites between them thus succeeded in depriving the Jewish minority of its most dynamic elements — the wealthy, the scholarly, and the young — who left to go into exile or for the Promised Land, and confined the rest in a tightly closed mental world until such time as veritable physical ghettos could be created. The fact is, throughout their offensives the anti-Semitic groups had benefited from if not the favor, at least the inertia of public opinion. In this connection the reports produced by prefects, procurators, the *SD*, and Socialists all describe the contradictory attitudes that coexisted in all individuals and circles. In country regions, frequently mayors with the support of party members took the initiative in introducing vexatious rules, insulting labels, and measures designed to turn away passing Jews. From 1936 on they were relieved by the Gestapo which, while condemning gratuitous brutality, initiated countless investigations to ferret out "racial pollution" or even plain "friendships with Jews" and thereby put the seal on their isolation. However, the peasant population remained passive and continued to maintain commercial relations with Jewish buyers of cattle and sellers of agricultural materials, even in regions particularly known for traditions of anti-Semitism such as Protestant Lower Franconia, and Bavaria and the Trier region which were strongly Catholic: "It is most alarming to note that the peasants lack any race consciousness" confessed the Munich Gestapo in 1937. Not that that stopped them from gathering in front of the billboard displaying the *Sturmer*, the rabid news sheet produced by Julius Streicher; but if some found it shocking, it was more on account of its obscenities than its anti-Semitic virulence. For the larger towns the only information was provided by accounts of periodic outbursts of violence sparked off by particularly over-excited or manipulated SA or party members masquerading as "hooligans" or "terrorists." On such occasions it was a concern for order that prevailed; neighbors would call in the regular police force, and the official reports, not without embarrassment, would even contain a few expressions of pity for the victims. Socialist militants themselves condemned the ambiguous attitude of their working-class comrades who, while criticizing the brutalities, "were to a certain extent in favor of the rights of the Jews being curtailed and their being isolated from the German people." Some remained loyal to their habitual shopkeepers but were nevertheless not prepared to oppose the regime persecuting them.[66] So the Nuremberg Laws were given a favorable reception. The general hope was that they would put a stop to the disorders. Only a few of the "better circles" (*sic*: the administrative way of referring to bourgeois society) feared an unfavorable foreign reaction.[67]

This passivity mingled with anxiety, also manifested when

the pogrom of November 1938 took place, calls for some explanation. We must beware of the over-facile psychology of "eternal Germany" even if it is once again becoming fashionable. To attribute to an entire people hereditary tendencies of anti-Semitism, and destructive anti-Semitism at that, is to fall through antiracism into a form of racism.[68] Police terror may well have intimidated people; but in that case how was it that those same faithful Catholics and Protestants demonstrated *en masse* when it was a matter of coming to the defense of their pastors or continuing to display the crucifix in schools? It is more justifiable to draw attention to the prudence of the hierarchies of the two churches. On the Protestant side there was a strong tendency toward nationalism, and hence considerable indignation at the attacks of the foreign press. The day after the boycott of April 1933, Bishop Dibelins of Berlin addressed his American brothers on the radio, warning them not to believe the venomous lies of their journalists. Thereafter, despite the indignation of a few individuals with exceptionally strong moral scruples there were no collective protests in favor of the Jews on the part of either the bishops or the synods, except where converts to Christianity were concerned. In the eyes of those high-ranking figures the principle danger lay in the ambitions of the German Christians, and it was best to keep on the right side of the authorities. The Catholic episcopate for its part was above all concerned to protect its Catholic "good works." Furthermore it was divided: in Munich, Cardinal Martin von Faulhaber, in his Advent sermons which attracted considerable attention, roundly condemned racial hatred (at the same time accepting the state's right to protect the German race); but in Breslau his colleague Bertram consistently refused to utter any solemn condemnation, and the rest of the episcopate fell in behind him. The lower clergy in general emulated these examples of prudence and, in this domain, "abandoned its educative function and its leadership role." Even priests—who at the time of the "battle against the Churches" (*Kirchenkampf*) truly did perform an act of resistance—seem to have been inspired more by the defense of their Church than any solidarity with the persecuted Jews.[69]

THE CONCENTRATION CAMPS

At first the concentration camps "received" (in a manner that constituted the first of many daunting trials) principally political opponents, sometimes for a stay of a few days, sometimes for months or years. By the end of July 1933, when the political situation seemed stabilized and the "wild" camps had more or less disappeared, an official statistic still indicated 26,7000 detainees. One year later that figure had fallen to eight thousand, and by 1936 to five thousand. In 1937 it rose to eight thousand again, and by the following summer it had reached twenty-four thousand, following the hardening of political and religious repression and a roundup of thirty-five hundred "professional criminals" and ten thousand "anti-socials," vagabonds, prostitutes (of both sexes), Gypsies, and unemployed. Following the November pogrom these were joined by thirty-five thousand Jews for a few weeks (not that these were the first, for many Jews had already experienced the rigors of the camps on political pretexts or for alleged infringements of common law). On the eve of the war there were twenty-two thousand detainees, half of them political, half criminals or "anti-socials." There was thus a busy flow of arrivals and departures: between 1936 and 1937 the criminal police (*Kripo*) and the political police (*Gestapo*) announced twenty thousand arrests, many of whom probably ended up in these camps. Yet as we have just seen, the total number of detainees only rose from five thousand to eight thousand. Similarly the Dachau camp recorded 18,681 arrivals during 1938, including 10,911 Jews in November. Yet in the summer of 1939 only five thousand were still present.[70] The percentage of Germans who experienced more or less long periods of detention in the camps was thus considerably higher than is suggested by the periodical statistics. In this manner the first objective of the camps was achieved: although the discharged were sworn to secrecy once they returned to normal life, a sense of terror inevitably surrounded them wherever they went. The second objective, reeducation of the guilty, was a pure formality. Their classification into three categories according to their potential recuperability was soon abandoned. At the most the idea of reeducation served as a pretext for bullying, military drill carried to absurd and inhuman excesses, and corporal punishments. The camps were supposed, if possible, to be to some degree profitable, because the SS, while performing public service duties, also drew on private resources. Technicians and investment funds were scarce, but labor was available and renewable, and this accounted for the "indissoluble link established between labor and annihilation" which satisfied both the ideology and the interests of the masters. Some camp jobs, in the kitchens and in organization, seemed to hold a possibility of less hardship than most, and these attracted a rush of candidates with real or false claims to suitable qualifications for them. Other jobs soon led to death from exhaustion: clearing the Dachau and Diesterwege marshes, working in the Mauthausen quarry in Austria, and, despite anodyne appearances, tending the Dachau garden of medicinal plants.[71]

The official documents obviously record no information on the daily life of the detainees, their secret behavior, or their mutual relations. Among the accounts produced in later years, not many of which relate to this prewar period, let us refer to that by E. Kogon since he was the first to attempt not only an analysis of the SS system but also a psychological classification of the detainees. According to him "psychic adaptation to the camp was not primarily a matter of origins or social standing, but depended almost entirely on strength of character and the presence or absence of religious, political, or humanitarian beliefs." The Communists thus appear to have held up under their trials because they were unwavering in their beliefs and maintained their links of solidarity. Likewise, but to a lesser extent, the Socialists. The rest were divided up between the "robust" without scruples, true religious believers, loners, and the bewildered masses.[72] However, the historian Falk Pingel has criticized this classification for being elitist and for discounting the past lives of the detainees, that is to say their experiences during their years of liberty which must have affected their ability or inability to maintain a successful strategy of self-defense. He then constructs as it were a scale of fragility, corresponding to unequal lengths of survival. The harshness of the initial reception seems to have particularly traumatized conservative politicians and the petits-bourgeois sentenced for minor transgressions who had naively expected to receive slightly preferential treatment. The Jews, victims among even the victims, constantly brutalized and assigned to the hardest labor, manifested scant solidarity with other prisoners or even among themselves. Among the new arrivals of November 1938 there were many deaths, cases of madness, and suicides. They had clearly been undermined by the six years of persecution. The "anti-socials" might have exploited their long experience of wretchedness, but they did not, remaining among the most despised of all; and among them, too, mortality was high. In contrast, the Jehovah's Witnesses, steadfast in their refusal to do military service, won general admiration. Finally, at the other end of the chain of power, battle raged between two equally dynamic groups, the "criminals" and the Communists, for control of the top posts in the internal hierarchy: those of secretaries, nurses, heads of dormitories and huts. To begin with, the SS, always keen to humiliate political prisoners, favored the "criminals," first in Buchenwald, then in the other camps except for Dachau and Sachsenhausen. Their violence and corruption clearly did not shock the guards, but they soon proved themselves incapable of filling technical posts, so the time came for the political prisoners to savor their revenge, partially at least. For a long time the Socialists refused on principal to act as auxiliaries, and even when they changed their minds they remained underrepresented. The Communists, some of whom had even before 1933 experienced prison and operated as an underground, had no such hesitations. It is hard to tell whether they abused their powers to favor their friends and put their opponents at a disadvantage. The evidence is too contradictory for a historian to decide, and that will no doubt remain the situation for some time to come.[73]

That is certainly not the only lacuna in the research on this subject. This seems a suitable point to quote a survivor from Buchenwald who, shortly after his liberation, said to Jorge Semprun: "I imagine that there will be many witnesses to provide evidence . . . And then there will be documents . . . And later the historians will collect everything . . . It will all be true . . . but the essential truth will be lacking, for no historical reconstruction can even approach it."[74]

However, at the time public opinion for the most part did not perceive that this apparatus of repression constituted the very core of the system. Just as persecution of the Jews did not shock the population of comrade-Christians (*Volksgenossen*) so long as it was in line with law and order, similarly the social elites, whether or not they were linked with the regime, without protest allowed the latter to crush the Left. This was because they had come to regard the former as "alien to the Community" or marginals, and the latter as troublemakers provoking disorder.[75] The time has come to seek an explanation for this general inertia.

NOTES

1. For example: Bracher K. D., *Dictature*; id., Sauer W. and Schulz G.; Frei N., *L'État hitlérien*.
2. Examples: Argeles J.-M. and Badia G; Broszat M., *L'État hitlérien*; Hildebrand K.; Thamer H.-U. Obviously these choices have nothing to do with schools of history loyalties.
3. Schoeps H.-J., 1970 text cited (and approved) by Fédier F., preface to Heidegger M., *Ecrits politiques, 1933–1966*, French tr., Paris, 1995., p. 13. Here on the other hand it certainly is a matter of a school of thought.
4. *Mein Kampf*, French tr., p. 539.
5. Rosenhaft E., p. 6, 19 f., 120, 164; Fischer C. J., chap. 3, 5, 6; Bessel R., pp. 34–45.
6. essel R., pp. 45–89.
7. Peukert D., *République de Weimar*, p. 102.
8. Abel T., passim.

9. Jamin M.; Fischer C. J., chap. 3, 5 – 8.
10. Stollmann R.
11. Bessel R., p. 98 f., 105, 117; Klein U.; Gruchmann L., *Justiz im 3. Reich*, pp. 344 – 345, 380.
12. Fischer C. J., chap. 3 – 4.
13. Latest accounts: Frei N., *L'État hitlérien*, chap. 1; Philippon J. (particularly detailed).
14. Bessel R., p. 143; Fischer C. J., p. 44 f., 98, 131; Jamin M.
15. Wegner B., pp. 79 – 83.
16. Wegner B., p. 86 – 112 (Höhne H., for a long time a classic work, has now been superseded).
17. Wegner B., p. 102; Kimmel G., pp. 349 – 67; *Dachauer Volksblatt*, April – July 1933, cited by Becker J. and R., 57 (fourteen articles); Pingel F., p. 35, 61 – 65; Billig J., p. 176 – 298, draws an artificial opposition between the Gestapo and the guards; recent synthesis: Drobisch K.
18. Wildt M.
19. Buchheim H., part 1, in particular p, 107, 116; see also Arendt H., *Systéme*, pp. 157 – 71.
20. Gellately R., pp. 51 – 71; Herbert U., *Best*, p. 125.
21. Herbert U., *Best*, p. 164 f., 173 – 76; Gruchmann L., *Justiz*, p. 719.
22. *Id.*, p. 583 f., 658 f.
23. Peukert D., *KPD*, p. 93, 116; Gellately R., p. 45, 58; Mallmann K. M. and Paul G., "Gestapo."
24. Huiskens M., *73*, p. 22; Kulka O. D., p. 612.
25. Wegner B., p. 135 f.
26. Kogon E., p. 305 – 18; Wormser-Migot O., p. 53, paints the same portrait.
27. Buchheim H., part 2 and conclusion.
28. Wegner B., p. 149 f., 167.
29. Ziegler H. F., *SS Leadership*, p. 113 f. (more precise than the two articles by Boehnert G. C.); Pois R. A., p. 34.
30. Wegner B., p. 185 f.
31. Wegner B., p. 41 f.; Höhne H., pp. 99 – 101; Ziegler H. F., "Pronatal Policies"; Steiner J. M.
32. Peukert D., *Volksgenossen*, pp. 142 – 43, 255 – 64.
33. Hüttenberger P.
34. Kershaw I., "Widerstand" (historiography); Repgen K. (Catholic point of view).
35. Broszat M., "Sozialgeschichte"; Droz J., passim, in particular p. 82 f.
36. Peukert D., "Arbeiterwiderstand"; Duhnke H., pp. 101 – 05, 117, 145, 191 – 94, 201.
37. For example, Bramke W., "Westsachsen"; *id.*, "Proletarischer Widerstand."
38. Rosenhaft E., passim.
39. Duhnke H., p. 203, 224.
40. Peukert's book *KPD* proves that even a clandestine organization may leave behind abundant documentation.
41. Ibid., p. 137.
42. Mehringer H., "KPD"; Hetzer G., p. 150 f., 168 f.
43. Klönne A., *Jugend*, p. 144 f.; id., "Jugendprotest," pp. 554 – 60; Hetzer G., p. 170 f.
44. Matthias E., p. 158 f., 242 (doc. 31), 267 (doc. 37).

45. Beier G.
46. Klotzbach K., p. 126 f.
47. Mehringer H., "Bayerische SPD"; Hetzer G., p. 178 f., 187 f.; Klönne A., *Jugend*, p. 149 f.; Allen W. S., "Untergrundbewegung."
48. Droz J.; Mehringer H., "Bayerische SPD," p. 391 f.; Hetzer G., p. 200–205; Klotzbach K., p. 138–51.
49. Mason T., *Arbeiterklasse*, doc. 28, 29, 34, 44, 48, 95.
50. Schönhoven K., p. 576.
51. Aretin K. O. von, p. 562.
52. Hehl U. von, *Erzbistum Köln*, p. 92 f., 158, 174; Hürten H., p. 390 f.; Fröhlich E., p. 387 f.
53. Kershaw I., *L'Opinion*, p. 159 f.; *60*, p. 96; Broszat M., "Sozialgeschichte."
54. Köllmann W., pp. 35–38; Thamer H.-U., p. 461; Droz J., pp. 86–87 (political and racial exiles); Palmier J.-M.; Scholdt G. (intellectuals in exile).
55. Müller-Hill B., p. 28, indicates from 350,000 to 400,000 sterilizations up until 1939; Blasius D., 200,000 to 350,000 up until 1945; see also Bock G., "Racisme."
56. Pollak M., "Une politique scientifique"; Massin B., p. 210, 238 f.; Conte E. and Essner C., chap. 2, in particular p. 352; Müller-Hill B., p. 30.
57. Burrin P., pp. 37–52; Wildt M. (on the *SD*); Kulka O.D.
58. Kater M., *Doctors*, p. 185 f.; Plum G., "Wirtschaft," p. 278 f., 287.
59. Chaim H.-G. and Plum G., "Wirtschaft" give contradictory figures on the pace of the initial purge.
60. Plum G., ibid., p. 268 f., 297, 303 f.
61. See among others the intimate diary of the woman doctor Nathorff H.; and that of the writer Klepper J., *Unter dem Schatten*.
62. Benz W., "Prolog"; Plum G., "Deutsche Juden oder Juden in Deutschland?."
63. Wetzel J., pp. 412–17; Wildt M.
64. Vollnhas C., "Selbsthilfe."
65. Dahm V.
66. Gellately R., chap. 4 and chap. 6 p. 164 (Lower Franconia); Broszat M., "Ebermannstadt" (Franconian Jura); Kershaw I., *L'Opinion*, pp. 281–348 (Bavaria); *65*, doc. 54–58, 60-63 (Trier region); 72, Bd. XI, doc. 2492 (Hanover); Stöver B., pp. 246–56 (workers).
67. Kulka O. D., p. 602 f.
68. Cf. Goldhagen D., and Husson É.'s critical comments.
69. Kershaw I., *L'Opinion*, p. 328; Scholder K., *Kirchen*, Bd. 1, pp. 326–54.
70. Pingel F., p. 15, 42 f., 65-85; Kimmel G., p. 372.
71. Pingel F., p. 35 f., 65; Kimmel G., pp. 368–72.
72. Kogon E., p. 277, 323–29.
73. Pingel F., p. 11 f., 51–60, 85–106.
74. Semprun J., *L'Ecriture et la Vie*, Paris, 1994, p. 136.
75. Broszat M., "Sozialgeschichte"; Peukert D., Volksgenossen, p. 89.

2—The Myth of the People's Community

Volksgemeinschaft is one of those woolly concepts that serve a precise policy; it is a myth. That term "myth" should of course be understood not as a deceptive fiction, but as a collection of themes of a kind to spur crowds to action, themes that are always treated symbolically in speeches, images, and rituals. Raoul Girardet has picked out four principal concepts that held that power over the centuries and throughout the continents. They are the concepts of Conspiracy, the Savior, the Golden Age, and Unity.[1] Nazi propaganda, an example of the art of myth-propagation, founded anti-Semitism upon the first, the cult of the führer upon the second, and the promise of a people's community upon the last two. As it untiringly promoted these ideas, it was responding to the hopes of a society in disarray.

Exactly what type of society was it? Hannah Arendt regarded the German people of the twenties simply as an example of "a shapeless mass of furious individuals, bound together by a terrifyingly negative solidarity, . . . people incapable of integrating themselves in any organization founded upon the common interest."[2] That view, inherited from all the prewar literature on the "era of the masses," nowadays appears somewhat simplistic. Many studies on the disintegration of society during the Weimar Republic have shown that, on the contrary, far from allowing themselves to be reduced to separate grains of sand, its members came together in autonomous collectivities, as age-groups, as sexes, as neighbors . . . In short, to return to a concept of Anglo-Saxon politics, this society had become "sectional"; but faced with the inadequacy of these incomplete solidarities, everybody was then carried away by a passion for unity. Women, who had at first been won over then disenchanted by the model of "modern woman," now took more notice of reactionary concepts of the family. Young men, either war veterans or those humiliated at not having fought, took to cultivating an ideal of bellicose virility. Technicians, employees, and cadres who had hoped to play a significant role in the rationalization of the economy now discovered themselves to be its victims. For this they blamed not so much the capitalists but the politicians, and they dreamed of a synthesis of technological progress and tradition. Health and social workers, overwhelmed by the rise of poverty, began to distinguish between the "deserving" and the "undeserving" or "ineducable." Young peasants, revolting against the civilization of the great towns, proclaimed the superiority of Blood and Soil. Politicians as uncharismatic as former chancellor (1923) Gustav Stresemann and future chancellor (1930–32) Heinrich Brüning deplored the absence of a Leader. On all sides there was a burning desire to fuse into a great Unity.[3]

And National Socialism seemed likely to fulfill that desire. Its response to "sectional" interests was to offer catchall programs and create specialized units. To those nostalgically longing for Unity it promised to found or refound a genuine Community. Its Leader presented himself to these orphans bereft of their Emperor and King as their long-awaited Chief. To vote for the party's list of candidates or to join its militant supporters was thus not necessarily to approve of every article in its program. It was simply a way of rejecting the existing situation and joining the only phalanx capable of changing it for good: a monarch with his train (*Gefolgschaft*) of faithful followers. Hitler "knew how to put into words what his listeners subconsciously wanted";[4] he even knew how, when necessary, to relegate to the shadows themes that were particularly dear to him, such as hatred of the Jews and the dream of a vital German living space. Once the Führer and his party were presented with the realities of power, they needed only to transpose the methods that had so far brought them such success.

THE STRATEGY OF COMMUNICATION

Hitler had intended to set out the rules of propaganda himself in his book *Mein Kampf*.[5] But instead he had simply expressed scorn for the masses and praised the efficacy of a small number of well-honed slogans: these were the methods of an eating-house orator, spiced with memories of French sociologist Gustave Le Bon. When it was a matter of addressing the nation as a whole, the strategy became more complex thanks partly to his own personal intuition and partly to the initiatives of his companions, above all Goebbels, propaganda minister, orator, and organizer whose capacity for rationality was as great as his Leader's was limited.

"When I heard Hitler for the first time," wrote one Gauleiter, "the scales fell from my eyes. He expressed exactly what I would have liked to say." One could cite dozens of similar accounts of conversions, even coming from much less lumpen figures such as the generals who would enter his office with one proposal in mind and reemerge quite convinced that its opposite was preferable. But to invoke the magnetism of Hitler's personality was, at the most, an excuse to surrender one's own responsibilities. As an explanation it is worth no more than an assertion of the soporific powers of opium. The Weberian concept of charismatic power also boils down to a simple verbal exercize when understood in the banal sense of a mysterious attraction. Fortunately, I. Kershaw has recently reminded us of the true meaning of "charisma": charisma "depends upon the heroism and greatness that a group of followers attribute to a proclaimed 'leader' who believes himself charged with a 'mission.'" It is not an innate gift of nature as is proved by the fact that it may fade as the result of a series of setbacks or of being mentioned in too routine a fashion. Thus the construction of the Hitlerian myth resulted from a combination of autosuggestion, deliberate fabrication, and a quasi-universal acceptance. The mediocre aspects of his personality, as enumerated in Thomas Mann's essay curiously entitled *Hitler as a Brother*, were represented as so many signs of greatness. The failed artist was transmuted into the architect of the universe, the deranged ascetic into a saint on a stained glass window, and his entire spasmodic biography as a model of social elevation. How could such a figure, at once distant and intimate, have cut himself off from the people, however many intermediaries came between them?[6]

The rallies truly were, quite literally, meetings between the führer and his people. Hitler's triumphs as an orator are incomprehensible if one simply summarizes the content of his texts, without taking into account the structure of the discourse, his gestures, and their impact upon the public. Purists could be astonished by his vulgar accent and grammatical mistakes. Political commentators could profess disappointment in his strings of emphatic assertions, trivialities, boasts, and lengthy passages of dogma in these speeches virtually empty of informative content. And theologians could be scandalized by his invocations to Providence and liturgical echoes such as the following: ". . . the new German Reich, a State of greatness, strength, honor, nobility, and justice, Amen." But the audience was swept away. After having its impatience whipped up for hours, at last the little man dressed in brown had appeared on the rostrum. His first few quiet sentences were halting, But as soon as the first burst of applause came "the dance began." The posturing of a puppet, exaggerated — so as to be visible from afar — and the bursts of shouting were greeted with wild applause; but eventually there was a return to calm. The parabolic movement of the speech symbolically reproduced the movement's entire history: an emotional evocation of the years of struggle, execration of its enemies, then calm satisfaction with the present successes.

There have been many analyses of this rhetoric. René

Schickelé and Thomas Mann at the time, and Joachim Fest in his famous biography, have represented these meetings as sexual orgies between the male dominator and the female crowd, but that is little more than a metaphor. Linguists have taken the vocabulary to pieces. For V. Klemperer, who described himself as a "philologist," a lover of language, this *Lingua Tertii Imperii* was no more than a hodgepodge of pompous, mechanistic, organicist, pseudo-religious, feudal, pedantic terms . . . but even so it generated a contagious atmosphere of a kind to "carry away primitive men and turn those capable of thinking a bit into primitive animals." His more methodical successors have picked out a number of recurring grammatical ploys: epithets taken from nature, adverbs superimposed upon adjectives, superlatives of superlatives, a whole array of ornamentation splashed on top of ideas no doubt reckoned to be too abstract. Finally, analysts of discourse such as J. P. Stern have noted that, in the course of these exchanges between orator and crowd a whole "perlocutory" process took place, when the grandest and most noble words were perverted into crime stimulants: "the audience was invited to play a role, and its performance created history".[7] Once direct contact was broken the führer's flow needed to be recycled so as to permeate every level of society; this was the primary mission of the media. Replayed over the radio, his speech lacked impact. In print, it became boring. As those in the publicity business had long known, the progress made by photography and the talents of assiduous artists made for a far more effective translation of that original dynamism. In the days of its rise to power the party did not hesitate to recruit avant-garde painters of posters, but later the regime preferred drawings and photographs in two styles contrary both to one another and to abstraction: caricature and classicism. The first reflected a violent hostility toward the Jews, who were portrayed as ugly, rapacious, and nomadic, and later on also toward Anglo-Saxon plutocrats. There was no subtlety to it. In contrast, representations of the great, those who had worked "either with their heads or with their hands," and the young appeared at first glance to obey only the canons of classical beauty. Yet cold analysis could detect—and the subconscious of the beholders would be affected by—its political undertones. The führer would be stretching out his hand either to the sky or to the masses. The vertical banners of the party festivals would stand out against the gothic and baroque curves of ancient buildings. The Hitler Youth members would either be marching along in orderly ranks or scattering in sympathetic disorder — disciplined but at the same time indulging the fantasies of adolescents.[8]

The tasks of cinema were clearly defined by Goebbels. They were: to educate moviegoers politically and also aesthetically; but to avoid preaching, for "propaganda ceases to be effective the minute its presence is detectable"; and to make money. Even today critics are hard put to discover any message at all in these films full of entertainment, waltzes, and romance, which in truth accounted for nine-tenths of production. Historical films, lessons in patriotism, and panegyrics of great men had already been much favored by filmmakers of the Hugenberg *Konzern*; their successors seemed to follow a similar line, but put more emphasis on Manichaeism: pure scholar Robert Koch up against politician Rudolf Virchow (and the microbes . . .), Mary Stuart or Kruger against the English, and so on. Social problems were seldom tackled, with one exception: a film made in 1941 about euthanasia, which constituted a more or less veiled apologia for contemporary crimes. Where definitely-Nazi films are concerned, *The Jew Süss* is always cited along with a few dramas in which the obvious hero belongs to the SA or the Hitler Youth organization. But there were not too many of these. The National Socialist ethos was diffused principally in documentaries. Technicians learned how subtly to use composition and a variety of camera angles to arouse collective hatred or enthusiasm. Such manipulation of the apparent reality of images is even more evident in the newsreels and in the films made by

Leni Riefenstahl: stage-managed representations of the stage-management of the party.[9]

In truth, the greatest manifestations of popular art were the organizations of public festivities. From 30 January, the political anniversary, through to 25 December, the pagan Christmas, each year was punctuated by twelve solemn celebrations designed "to awaken in each comrade the need to live and relive those solemn hours when he expressed his faith" (Goebbels). Experts such as architects, set designers, artistic directors, and lighting specialists could all draw upon a rich German tradition. The national movement had always celebrated its great ancestors from Arminius down to Schiller with spectacular demonstrations in which processions alternated with speeches, religious services with sporting events, night with day. A number of historical sites had been reconsecrated in this way and turned into symbolic spaces, with a temple dominating the esplanade. Wagner then decided to carry this art of festivity to perfection in his "total art-works," and one of his disciples even produced his operas in the open air to enable the masses to enter into communion with them. The army for its part regularly organized processions and torch-lit retreats—but in these the public, by definition, remained passive. In the face of the army and even in reaction to it, the workers' movements had invented the political festival for the masses, complete with an entry-march, sung and spoken choruses, and a dialogue between orators and those in the auditorium.[10] All that remained for Hitler and his advisers to do was complete all this ceremonial with technical improvements, masses of concrete to accommodate larger crowds, microphones and loudspeakers to diffuse words and music, and light-projectors to embellish the night. The quasi-immutable form taken by the Congress of Nuremberg festivals provided the model for thousands of local ceremonies: an entry with banners followed by hymns, speeches, and the swearing of oaths. Critical minds detected overtones of the Latin Mass in all this: an *introit*, a *gloria*, a sermon, and a *credo*. Furthermore, Hitler ascended the rostrum as he would an altar:

the funeral ceremony of 9 November was reminiscent of a mass for the dead, with banners consecrated by contact with the blood of martyrs. With the passing of time these similarities between the two liturgies fostered many interpetations of Nazism as a secular religion: the führer-prophet announced to the distraught masses the possibility of salvation through purification and the advent of a world free from conflict and threats, the "thousand-year Reich." However, if the sacred orator frequently allowed himself to be carried away by such mystic flights of fancy, there is scant evidence that his entourage followed him. An element of mimetism may be undeniable, but it is simpler to regard the high masses of the Third Reich as a kind of "magic," a "manipulation" that "treated reality in accordance with certain imaginary representations and affirmed the reality of this symbolic world by organizing spectacles" (K. Vondung).[11] As for the real impact of these festivals on the morale of the participants, contemporaries were unanimous in their judgment: every individual present at Nuremberg departed as a fanatic, although local imitation, festivals, of which there were too many and which were frequently badly prepared, soon became a bore.

Because it interposed an extra filter between the deliverer of the message and its recipient, reading—printed matter—might well have been relegated to a position of secondary importance. However, account had to be taken of the habitual behavior of the Germans, who were great newspaper readers, and it was necessary, too, that Nazism as well as its opponents could make a show of their intellectual works. But the party's press had never kept pace with its electorate: in 1932 it produced no more than 750,000 copies. The new regime could clearly neither approve pluralism nor brutally eliminate organs respected the world over. Max Amann, the director of party publications, patiently launched a series of attacks on rival newspapers, beginning with those whose directors were not in a position to refuse the Nazis anything (Hugenberg). Then Amann targeted those that were the most fragile financially and exerted pressure on their publishers through the Press Chamber. In three years of using these means he eliminated between five hundred and six hundred rivals. Eventually, he would seize upon the slightest opportunity: in 1935 a campaign against the "scandals press" engineered the disappearance of five hundred magazines, . . . many of them Catholic. It was hoped that those deprived of their usual reading matter would now turn to the right (Nazi) papers. These however lacked talented journalists, and in a servile manner merely reiterated official comments or at the local level the prose of little local potentates: this was known as a "combative style." The results of this monotony are reflected in statistics for Bavaria: between 1934 and 1938 the number of newspapers fell from 170 to eighty (the figures are rounded up), but the number of copies printed also diminished from 350,000 (one-third of which were Nazi) to 320,000 (two-thirds of which were Nazi), proving that only a part of the readership had converted to Nazi reading matter. The record of the *Völkischer Beobachter*, the national party organ, was more encouraging (circulation rose from 130,000 to one million), but that increase was largely artificial since, as the party newspaper, it had to be purchased if not read by every party member.[12]

To bolster its cultural pretensions the party and affiliated organizations founded reviews in which intellectuals were required to make deep studies of the "world concept." The choice of theoretical texts published by Joseph Wulf makes it possible to appreciate the unrelieved nature of this official thinking: for the most part it amounted to no more than verbal bombast. Virtually every contribution reproduced the ternary structure of the master's discourse: the decadence of the past, the appearance of Hitler, and the splendid present or—in some cases—the last obstacles to be eliminated. On the other hand they all worked at refining the vocabulary, particularly when it was necessary to be dogmatic over the racial question. One patient lexicographer has thus picked out thirty derivatives from the word *Rasse*, sixteen from the word *Art* (species), which cropped up increasingly frequently, and twenty-seven from the word *Blut* (blood). This proliferation was not as spontaneous as might be thought, for Goebbels also laid down the law for words. In 1935 he decreed that "Aryan" should be replaced by "of German blood" and "non-Aryan" by "Jewish," thereby sweeping aside major bones of contention among anthropologists. Soon after "the Third Reich" disappeared to be replaced simply by "the Reich": an effective way of making the point that History had now been set in the mold of Eternity. As for daily newspapers, the success of the two most virulent cannot be passed over in silence: the *Schwarze Korps* produced by the SS, and J. Streicher's *Stürmer*. The former was founded in 1935 to confer an intellectual aura upon the SS; in the event though, it too fell into the style of the other hate-filled broadsheets, the only difference being that its attacks targeted not only Jews (to be eliminated by fire and sword) and Catholics, but also judges, the state bureaucracy, even party mandarins. As for *Stürmer*, its obscenities disgusted even an unfastidious anti-Semite such as Goebbels. On several occasions the authorities considered banning it, but given that it was displayed on public billboards its disappearance would have constituted a kind of confession, so it was allowed to continue to provide laughs for imbeciles and the repressed. The fact that both of these papers had as many as 500,000 copies printed (two-thirds of which, in the case of the latter, were sold) proves that the reassuringly "normal" appearance of this society during the prewar years masked a persistent latent death wish that was relatively widespread.[13]

The radio seems to have been more successful in reaching a wider audience. In 1933 its mission was purely political: "to drum up the 48 percent of supporters that the government needs," as Goebbels declared. Totally committed to the party line as it was, it became a branch center for the training of militants. However, since radio receivers were still relatively costly, most listeners were members of the middle and ruling classes. When Goebbels' propaganda became too tiresome they could turn the dial to foreign stations. Goebbels realized that radio was being mismanaged and embarked on an effort to increase both demand and supply. Thanks to the manufacture of a new "popular receiver," the number of households possessing a radio increased from four to nine million. And the minister for propaganda changed his tactics: the aim was still to amass listeners, but now they were to be made up of "the People's Community, one big family." In other words, seduction was to replace indoctrination. Classical music and drama once again found a place, alternating with so-called light music and "radiophonic plays," a genre highly rated by listeners. And given that good writers were in short supply, semi-supporters and even nonsupporters were able to get their plays accepted until they were ousted by rivals or the police. In 1936 all listeners, provided they paid their dues to the Winter Assistance Fund, earned the right to listen to the music of their choice at certain hours, and this à la carte concert met with huge success. But that was about as far as tolerance of the consumers' plebiscite went, as was shown by the great "jazz affair." Authentic American jazz had been banned on the grounds that it was Judeo-Negro. To please visitors to the Olympic Games, the jazz radio station was reopened but limited to "German jazz," which young connaisseurs found insipid, and a few American orchestras consisting solely of whites.[14] This semi-laxity has led an entire current of historiography, known as the "modernity theory," to depict German society in the late thirties as an American-style consumer society. But in truth the most that can be said is that for a time the Third Reich managed to create that illusion.[15]

The superficial nature of the literary and artistic critics made to fall into line by the cultural bureaucracy has been noted above. The principles of Nazi art must be sought elsewhere, from Hitler himself. To his way of thinking, encouragement for the arts was never a simple accessory to the great Nazi policy, but lay at its very heart. Just as in his autobiography he had established a continuity between his ambitions as a young painter and his vocation as the Savior of Germany, similarly he regarded the construction of the community as an aesthetic task in which authors, painters, sculptors, and architects should collaborate, for the same reasons as workers, peasants, and soldiers, since "art . . . constitutes the force that most actively shapes the popular masses."[16] These abstract but fundamentally terrifying ideas were to serve as guides to writers and artists. If we forget about them we abandon any kind of historical perspective and are reduced either to derision in the face of such bad taste or to admiration for such a carefully disinfected "grandiosity."

What exactly was a "National Socialist writer"? Not necessarily a member of the party, as Klaus Vondung explains, but at least somebody perceived as such. In a sample of fifty official authors of this kind he discovered no fewer than thirty-eight university graduates. So their submission to the aesthetic dogmas of the authorities cannot be ascribed to the social ambitions of self-taught petit-bourgeois. They belonged to the educated bourgeoisie, whom the crises of the twenties had left without resources or orientation and who had sought refuge in all kinds of "anti-" ideologies. Their ethos seemed to offer virtually nothing new, but gravitated imperceptibly toward the very worst policies: regionalist novels thus increasingly featured Jewish, Gypsy, or degenerate antiheroes; war novels glorified the virtues of not only past heroes but present and future ones too. Poets, modeling themselves on the führer, laced patriotic sentiments with religiosity, believing themselves to be so many latter-day Novalises, as V. Klemperer puts it. Their public success was uneven. The works that ran into the most editions tended to be those of the eldest of them or even of nonconformist "internal exiles." But their ambitions were satisfied: out of the forty-five included in the sample, nineteen received paid posts in the political apparatus and fifteen were made members of the Academy.[17]

Whatever the interest in analyses of the ideology underlying the works of the painters, we need not linger over them. The caricaturists were the most successful at expressing hatred; the photographers the best at suggesting pulsations of violence behind the formal beauty of bodies and figures. Following the unpopularity of the last of the expressionists, the market was dominated by uninspired painters who found nothing better to do than rework endless variations on well-known themes, which ended up either on the great bare walls of public buildings or as reproductions in family drawing rooms. At the huge exhibition of German Art (Munich, 1937), visitors were oppressed by 150 portraits, fifty of which were of Hitler, three hundred landscapes, sixty scenes of agricultural life and craftsmen at work, and so on. Strangely enough the glories of the past, industry, and war were underrepresented: it was as if the selection committee had been anxious to steer clear of both history and modernity. The visiting crowds were sparse. As a matter of taste, or out of curiosity or disaffection, people preferred to visit a local gallery where the authorities had had the grotesque idea of putting together a collection of "degenerate" art. The same pattern was then repeated in Berlin and Düsseldorf.[18] Architecture, comparable to the organization of public festivals and closely linked with such spectacles, was the major Nazi art form. Hitler now regarded himself as an architect and town planner, and spent hours with genuine architect and future arrangements minister Albert Speer, examining models of Nuremberg, Berlin, and—harking back to Hitler's childhood—Linz. Tearing down old, reputedly insalubrious town quarters and building gigantic monuments in their place seemed the best way to symbolize his efforts for society. Even the slaves were ready to be used, as the necessary materials would have to come from—indeed already were coming from—the quarries and brickyards of the concentration camps. In concrete terms there were three branches of architecture, each with its own style: monumental, functional, and regionalist. The first was reserved for buildings that would represent public power: the party headquarters and the House of Art in Munich, the Zeppelin Space in Nuremberg, the Olympic Stadium and the Chancellory in Berlin. Their general style was inspired by the eternal values of classicism, but the severity of materials and rigidity of forms were designed to create an impression of "pitilessness" (as one commentator wrote of the sculptures of Arno Brecker). Indoors everything was sacrificed to the monumentality of entrances and corridors, while those who worked in these buildings were crammed into uncomfortable nooks and crannies. Like so many mini-führers, the gauleiters set about planning triumphal approaches and immense halls for their own regional capitals, not forgetting to build palaces for themselves. The functional style, an extension of the avant-garde designs from the beginning of the century, was used for factories: the industrialists were still of the opinion that beauty and rationality went hand in hand. The same style also took over a new domain, that of the motor roads. Both economically and strategically their usefulness turned out to be limited. Their construction never provided employment for more than a few hundred jobless men, and during the war the army preferred to use railways for transporting troops. However their harmonious lines, which respected the contours of the countryside, and the rigorous design of their works of art symbolized a reconciliation of technology and nature; and their network throughout first Germany, then Greater Germany—and the great open spaces of the East—constituted the framework of an infinite and eternal Reich. Hitlerian Utopia was in this instance given concrete, durable form. A legacy of the "Blood and Soil" ideology, the utopian dream was to break up the large towns into "residential quarters" where each ordinary family would have a little house and garden. In this half-urban, half-rural setting, the forms of the peasant house were to be preserved, the effect of which would be to reconcile the working class to tradition. However, the project was hampered by economic constraints. As the economic situation declined, people from the countryside flocked to the industrial centers in such great numbers that it proved necessary to build blocks of flats of the type so much decried in the past. When it came to favoring either ideology or economic needs, the choice was quickly made. So in this domain as in others, the policy adopted was "modern" out of necessity, not for reasons of principle. And furthermore it was a failure: the shortfall of popular accommodation (1.5 million homes in 1936) was never made up.[19]

Clearly the channels of communication from on high to below did not always function perfectly. But the party was there, the party which, with its massive strength and leadership, would have the vision to plan ahead for the Community and hasten its advent.

THE PARTY: WAS IT A PREFIGURATION OR A CARICATURE OF THE COMMUNITY?

The contrast between the situation before 1933 and that after 1933 is stark: the dynamic movement that had won power became a system to exploit the power won by commonplace rival clans. This decadence, a common feature in all revolutions, came about all the more rapidly because the seeds of it were already present in the structure that Hitler himself had imposed upon his party.

Right from the start, the *Führerprinzip* had not only legitimated the omnipotence of the supreme Leader, but served as the rule according to which every level functioned. Every department was centered upon a single individual, with no form of interdepartmental consultation. The staff that was available to these individuals were encouraged not so much to use their own administrative skills as to manifest their loyalty as vassals. Despite the existence of central institutions of inspection, jurisdiction, and economic administration, etc., conflicts over powers and involving personalities could thus only be resolved at the top: only Hitler was in a position to hold the system together.[20] During the "years of struggle," this system, or rather this absence of a system, which stood in strong contrast to the sclerosis (or "mandarinocracy") of the Social Democratic party, not only made it possible for the Leader to get rid of his rivals but also proved effective at grass roots level, where it accommodated the frenzied zeal of its militants. Local studies reveal the almost incredible hyperactivity of the party sections and the SA, particularly at the time of the electoral campaigns. In the little Westphalian town of Northeim, renamed Thalberg by William S. Allen, the first forty party members managed to hold twenty-four public meetings in the course of 1931 alone, and the rhythm then speeded up to three a month; not to mention the punitive expeditions mounted against the workers' movement, and more discreet interventions aimed at infiltrating various trade union and youth assocations, etc. It should be added that the initial weakness in numbers was made up for by their extreme mobility: in emergencies the sections of neighboring towns would be brought in by the lorryload to swell the numbers of party supporters. Exploiting the mistakes of opponents and the dramatization of national crises, the party in Northeim won 28 percent of the vote in the spring of 1932 and 62 percent the following July.[21]

Electoral sociology has made great progress since the fifties, when it was customary to simply classify the thirty-three major constituencies according to their percentages of Nazi votes.[22] Over the subsequent decades, about fifty works have appeared, many in English, using methods of calculation more or less sophisticated but invariably based on samples. By and large they agree on the following points: the flow toward the Nazi lists began with former voters for the liberal parties, followed by those from the conservative right, abstentionists, and first-time voters, and even a few from the Communist party. From a social point of view the victims—or those who believed themselves victims—of the economic crisis predominated: rural debtors, the unemployed, small-scale entrepreneurs; and more female electors than male ones. All kinds of theoretical explanations have been constructed on the basis of this data: "central extremism," the atomized masses, and so on. But since the eighties, with the help of computers, statisticians have been able to survey all (close to one thousand) the basic constituencies and proceed to operations more complex than simply calculating the correlations between two variables. Without altogether subscribing to their ironical critique of the whole of the earlier literature, one can certainly accept their conclusions. Unfortunately, these are for the most part presented in the form of extremely subtle theses and can only be summarized by dint of considerable simplification.[23]

In political terms, the balance sheet of votes transferred to the Nazi lists over the five years from 1928 to 1933 turns out as follows (in rounded-out figures): 7.5 million from the "bourgeois" Protestant block (right-wing and center-right parties), six million from abstentionists, two million from the Social Democratic party, 600,000 from the *Zentrum*, and 350,000 from the Communist party. The principal new element, which did not emerge from the earlier studies, is the volatility of the Socialist electors. The distribution of votes according to sex produces another discovery: "there is no question of a mass of female voters switching over to Adolf Hitler"; the most that can be said is that the number of votes of female Protestants rose. This brings us to the denominational factor. Throughout the entire range of constituencies a very strong correlation is noticeable, positive in the case of the Protestant percentage of votes, negative (up until November 1932, at least) in that of the Catholic votes. It is something that even contemporary observers seized upon intuitively. Geographically the differences between rural areas and small and large towns are more or less insignificant and diminish with each new poll. It would therefore be very exaggerated to speak of the "ruralism" of the Nazi electorate. Finally, when one moves on to examine the various social groups, one finds very few marked correlations, either positive or negative, between the variations in the electorate as a whole and variations in the Nazi votes. A slightly negative correlation is detectable for salaried employees, who thus "showed no particular receptivity to Nazism"; a barely positive correlation for civil servants; a stronger positive correlation for peasant-landowners, particularly those with debts; a very weak correlation in either sense for workers (except in a handful of "Red citadels"), and even a slightly negative correlation for unemployed workers! If we add in the votes classified as those of "housewives" and "retired people" belonging to working-class families, it is possible to calculate that 40 percent of voters for the Nazi party came from this social category: so the "Workers' Party" label was not totally unjustified. All in all, "attempts at explanation based on class or social strata are hardly pertinent" (J. Faller). If the detailed electoral map resembles "a leopard skin," that is because no single factor, apart from religious denomination, played a decisive role at a national level. Statisticians accordingly modestly refer their readers to the local studies, which reveal here a particular political culture, there an early conversion on the part of influential social figures and their newspaper, and in many localities considerable dynamism on the part of militants. Where local sections saw their memberships increase, they would be successful in the next elections, and those successes would in their turn produce another rush of new members.[24] W. S. Allen's conclusions on the little town that he studied (which soon became a model case) can thus be extrapolated at the national level.

All the same, the social distribution of party members did not coincide exactly with that of party voters as a whole. With its membership rising from 130,000 to 500,000 in five years, the party welcomed in many workers, particularly agricultural and unemployed ones. It furthermore offered mere sympathizers the services of its Organization of Cells of Enterprise (*NSBO*), the membership of which shot up from forty thousand to four hundred thousand during the same period. Nevertheless, the working class remained underrepresented among party members (one-third) and also among Nazi voters (one-quarter) in relation to its share of the active population (almost half). Salaried employees and minor officials, typical of the "modern middle classes," were on the contrary strongly overrepresented among party members as a result of propaganda targeted particularly at them. The same applies to "independents," the heads of small or medium-sized firms, and members of liberal professions.

Finally, it seems likely, if not proven in detail, that many peasants, retired people, and members of various elite groups also voted for the party, but without joining it, either out of prudence or under professional pressure to do so.[25] We know, for example, that jurists, large-scale landowners in the East, industrialists in Saxony . . . and others, too, placed themselves at the service of the Nazi movement and helped it by canvassing for it in their units of corporative defense, without ever sporting Nazi insignia or uniforms. These elites were already accomplices, albeit not yet official members.[26]

But much of this research rests upon the implicit thesis that the political decisions of individuals are determined by their class or their profession, that is to say in the last analysis by the defense of their material interests. This paradigm of social history may account for the successes of the various satellite lobbies with which the party surrounded itself and also, in all likelihood, for the behavior of some of its electors. But it does not take account of the essential mechanism of seduction, which operated by diffusing and identifying with a number of persuasive great myths. It so happens that we are in possession of a number of the autobiographies of "veterans," party members dating from the years of struggle, which illuminate the psychological— some would say psychopathological—aspect of their conversions. They were written shortly after the seizure of power and are of course not reliable on all points. For instance, when one autobiographer evokes his professional setbacks, bankruptcy, unemployment, or loss of independence, he tends to portray these as a consequence rather than as a cause of his joining the party: according to him, it was on account of his political courage that he was persecuted, but he then made the most of his enforced leisure to consecrate himself totally to the cause—and now he was hoping to be rewarded. But the action that clinched their decision to join the party is always described in detail. The party program did not have much to do with it, not even its racial policy. At the most they were influenced by the apparent complicity between politicians, Jews, and the wealthy. Above all, many had drawn a bitter lesson from their earlier contacts with extreme right-wing movements, where they had acquired a taste for violent brawling but had also discovered and suffered from the arrogance of Junkers, officers, and bourgeois up until the moment the party had presented itself before them as the microcosm of an egalitarian, fraternal society with a Leader who, for his part, "looked you straight in the eye." Whether or not she was familiar with these self-portraits, the sociologist Lucie Varga, an exile in France, deduced an exactly similar synthesis when, a few years later and for the benefit of the readers of *Annales*, she applied to the known facts certain concepts of religious sociology. Joining the Nazi party, she explained, was a phenomenon of "vital, collective experience" (*Erlebnisgruppe*): a "dynamic despair" and the mirage of a Golden Age had been diffused among the social classes that felt cheated and, out of the possible saviors at hand, these lost souls had chosen the most Manichaean and heroic.[27] Their leaders' accession to power inevitably disappointed them and incited them to revolt, to vent their growing violence upon scapegoats or to seek sinecures.

In the course of 1933 alone the Nazi party acquired 350,000 new members. This figure leaped to a total of 2.5 million by 1935, following which new membership was for a while limited to young members of the *HJ* (Hitler Jugend, or Hitler Youth) then eventually made available to all in 1937. By the eve of the war membership had reached the considerable figure of 5.4 million. Its social composition tended automatically to approximate the national average, except where women were concerned, for they never accounted for more than 17 percent. Waves of elites flocked to the party: high-ranking officials as early as 1933, and then again in 1937 when applications for membership were reopened; members of liberal professions and artists arrived at the same rhythm, except the doctors, who were particularly zealous (and at 300 percent were over-represented!). Salaried employees and minor officials were attracted right from the start by the jobs and careers available in all the public and semi-public departments; but in the end, three-quarters of this group remained outside the party, even if they were not outside its professional annexes of which they became members quasi-automatically as part of their jobs. Peasants joined in alternating phases of reticence and massive enthusiasm depending on the ups and downs of agricultural policies. Artisans and small shopkeepers sulked for quite a while, disappointed by too many vain promises, and only came around in large numbers from 1937 on. Finally, workers regularly accounted for between 30 and 40 percent of the new members, and even more on the eve of war. Professional obligations, ambitions for promotion, protection from rivals, patriotic convictions . . . : motivation varied according to individuals who elude us and according to different levels in the social hierarchy which will be examined in later chapters.[28]

These new "Martian casualties"[29] represented a twofold threat to veteran militants: a dilution of their warrior ideal amid this inert crowd, and greater competition in the rush for party jobs. Examples are provided by the SA who having seized administrative posts for themselves were subsequently sacked from them for incompetence; and jobless workers who having been given employment by the *NSBO* then found themselves back on the street when that organization merged with the Labor Front. Such bitterness found expression within the political apparatus through repeated complaints and denunciations, and even through withdrawals from militant action. In 1936, for example the *Gau* of Hesse-Nassau asked one thousand of its earliest members why they no longer attended meetings. Two hundred thirty-four replies were received, a good third of which were variations of the following: "Nobody seems to need us veterans any more!"[30] Originally attracted to a movement that appealed to their vindictive extremism, they now found themselves swamped in a mass organization that made it quite clear that its elite would henceforward be selected on the grounds of competence.

This was a conflict that for some time had even been dividing the national leadership. Robert Ley, who headed the Labor Front, had always held that the party needed to absorb the whole of society, that its task should be mainly educative, and that consequently all it needed was convinced propagandists. In the views of deputy führer Rudolf Hess and future Party Secretary Martin Bormann, who by reason of their very functions within the party secretariat were more interventionist, the party on the contrary needed not to absorb but to control society by means of a hierarchical and technically well-organized apparatus. Hitler wavered constantly between the two strategies. First he would declare, "It is the work accomplished outside the State departments that is decisive," then that the party ought to strengthen the state (which encouraged individuals to accumulate a whole series of responsibilities). Eventually, for example while addressing the congress of September 1933, he would return to the priority of "the moral and intellectual education of the German people." He had passed in full circle from Ley to Hess and Bormann and then back again. In the meantime, the number of party officials with nothing to do had risen from 200,000 to 370,000, and this figure was to double in the following year. In fact, inflation must have been even more galloping than these figures suggest, since by the time the coup of 30 June was over about forty thousand had been sacked.

So what in the last analysis was their purpose? At the lowest level, hundreds of thousands of "heads of isolated branches" kept their neighbors under surveillance and spread propaganda among them. They only worked part-time for the party, meanwhile continuing to practice their own trades or professions. The same in general was true of the immediately superior level, the "heads of cells," which eventually grew to include ninety thousand people. Moving up the scale, the "leaders of local groups" (between twenty thousand and thirty thousand of them) belonged to the category of full-time permanent staff. These already, in fact if not by right, possessed the redoubtable power to issue political "appreciations," certificates indispensable to anyone seeking employment in the public sector, a marriage loan, or even a student grant for his children. The 827 "circle chiefs," those responsible for small administrative divisions, often combined this position with that of subprefect—at least they did until 1937, at which point Hess stripped them of this extra prestige and source of income. Their principal mission was to organize festivities, fund raising, and countless propaganda campaigns (in 1937, these took up fifty-five days!); as well as these duties, they intervened constantly in appointments and decisions made by their state sector. To judge from a sample of Bavarians (eight cases) who appeared after the war before the denazification court, their individual behavior varied from tolerance of sufficiently discreet opponents to complicity with the Gestapo. Finally, the thirty-three "regional chiefs" (*Gauleiter*), some of whom combined state responsibilities as leaders of their *Land*, were extremely well-paid little sovereigns, with twenty or so special services and a court of "faithful" followers at their disposal, who were powerful enough even to resist directions issued by the central authorities. M. Broszat goes so far as to declare that "the essence of the Hitlerian State was this juxtaposition of State centralism and the domination enjoyed by particular individuals."[31]

This territorial hierarchy accounted for perhaps half of the personnel engaged in political work. Adding in the specialists working in offices at every level, from social clubs all the way up to the chancellory, all the little clerks and all the important figures associated with the Labor Front (forty-four thousand), the professional organizations concerned with social assistance, leisure activities, the SS, the SA . . . and so on, the figures would amount to a dizzying total. It would appear at first sight that Ley's doctrine triumphed, and the party really did seem to absorb the whole of society. On two occasions in 1937, Hitler reminded a handpicked audience that the essential qualities for a political leader were blind obedience, physical courage, and authority, and he set his listeners on their guard against the spirit of bureaucracy, by which he meant priority for administrative talents. Meanwhile, the personnel management services were for their part proclaiming that the sole criterion for promotion was the quality of leadership (*Menschenführung*), thereby encouraging the hopes of upward social mobility nursed by the uneducated. However, the constraints of management and social pressures proved the stronger: the hierarchy of party cadres continued by and large to reproduce the hierarchy of their classes of origin. At the lower levels such as that of the "heads of local groups," former workers remained definitely underrepresented (11 percent), to the advantage of members of the lower middle class, ex-employees, minor civil servants, and owners of small businesses. At the middle levels and among department heads, the balance was tipped in favor of the upper middle classes thanks to the arrival of many university graduates. And the two dozen national leaders (*Reichsleiter*) included six former high-ranking officers, eight holders of university degrees, and seven others of more modest origins, but none from the working class: admittedly, at this level selection depended upon the master's whim rather than social distinctions of any kind.

The situation was characterized by frustration on the part of ambitious "plebeians" (to use the scornful and on the whole inaccurate expression of anti-Nazi politician Hermann Rauschning); repeated clashes between rival clans and representatives of the two apparatuses, party and state; an aging team of cadres despite an injection of younger men from the *HJ*; and corruption. In 1935 the national treasurer announced no fewer than 2,350 corruption cases which were discreetly handled by internal courts. In Nuremberg, Gauleiter J. Streicher was enriching himself in such a scandalous fashion that it proved necessary to bring him to trial—but not until 1940. Elsewhere the interpenetration of regional cadres with those from the "economy" (the business bosses) led, in more subtle fashion and under the cover of interventionism, to various collusions of interests. In Thüringen, Fritz Sauckel, another gauleiter, and his principal economic adviser collaborated with the trade union of business proprietors and the military armament services to promote the industrial development and appropriation of Jewish firms. Managers of a new breed were thus making their appearance: half-politicians, half-technocrats. The party was disintegrating into lobbies.

Should we conclude along with M. Broszat that the only way to resolve these contradictions was to make use of the safety valve of internal violence and external aggression? The anti-Semitic actions of the summer of 1935, "spontaneous expressions at the grassroots level," certainly do seem to have been prompted by the lower echelons of the hierarchy in order to give its troops something to do. Was it similarly in order to divert a suspected underlying discontent toward other targets that Hitler, in the following year, launched the "struggle against the Churches" and embarked upon his series of diplomatic poker games? The extent to which the internal and external domains interacted remains a matter of hypothesis. At any rate, the sense of malaise was unmistakable: in their new bulletins the SS, the more agile rival of the party elite, dwelt on that unease. And on this point at least they did reflect general public opinion.[32]

HOW THE MYTH WAS RECEIVED
BY PUBLIC OPINION

It is always difficult for a dictatorship to assess the impact of its propaganda. Even if it traces its progress right down to the level of the most modest of the faithful, how can it hope to catch an echo from public opinion, given that—by definition—that opinion is no longer public? The administrative apparatus of the Third Reich was supplied with reports from its prefects and procurators general, and the political apparatus received reports from the Security Service (*SD*). The former category of reports, when not written by timid courtiers, was capable of presenting a realistic picture of the situation month by month. The second category tended if anything to err on the side of pessimism; not even the slightest evidence of discontent was passed over in silence. But how to decide upon a line of propaganda on the basis of all those thousands of local, instantaneous observations? The Socialist militants who for their part were sending off similar reports to their friends in exile were well aware of the difficulty: "Not only does public opinion no longer exist," they wrote, "there is no longer even such a thing as group opinion . . . The enforced gathering of all and sundry into a single organization in truth means that judgements have been atomized." To define this fine dust composed of individual reactions, they preferred to use expressions such as "apolitical opinion" or "the popular mood" (*Volkstimmung*). The *SD* for its part and such lucid propagandists as read its reports resolved the problem by drawing a distinction between "mood" (*Stimmung*), which was emotional and unstable, and attitude (*Haltung*), which was more durable and formed by inherited character and education. While it seemed impossible to keep moods constantly under control, it was essential to endeavor first to inculcate and then maintain the correct attitude. The trouble was that while moods were observable on a daily basis, attitudes were only revealed in the long term.[33] Ultimately this distinction, which may have been invented in order to minimize circumstantial discontent, turned out to be quite useful to historians: for behind abrupt swings of mood they too can sometimes detect something more constant.

Loyalty to the führer was the most noticeable of those constants. Of course he also had his disloyal adorers, such as one young bourgeoise in Hamburg who, having decided to vote for him on 1 March 1933, wrote as follows in her personal diary: "Only he fills me with real enthusiasm because, even without a program, he wants exactly what I want, yes, without a program: Germany!" Later however, upon rereading her words, she was to comment bitterly upon reality in the margin of her earlier remarks. However, throughout the ups and downs of the peacetime years and well beyond them, the majority remained his to command. In this respect the Bavarians, closely observed by I. Kershaw, are altogether representative even though, being individualists and for the most part Catholics, it was only in March 1933 that they decided *en masse* to vote Nazi. Immediately after this however there followed a wave of political denunciations, which showed that the anti-Marxist slogans had hit their mark. Countless municipalities, even before being purged, proclaimed Hitler an honorary citizen. In April his birthday was widely celebrated as a first step toward his glorification. In July the "German salute" was generally adopted: only a few nonconformists remained faithful to the expression "God bless you." At the end of the year the plebiscite on Germany's withdrawal from the League of Nations and the simultaneous election of a new Reichstag constituted clear evidence of the nation's consensus: even in a bastion of opposition such as the working-class quarters of Augsburg, only 13 percent of the ballot papers carried negative votes as compared to 7 percent in the bourgeois quarters. The results were no doubt partly fixed, but even Socialist observers, summing up echoes from all over Germany, confessed that the official figures "by and large corresponded to real public opinion and to the ongoing process of the Fascistization of society."[34]

The only moment of doubt came in the spring of 1934. The economic promises had still not led to results, the interventionist measures taken against the major stores were reckoned to be timid, and those taken in the domains of agriculture and in relations between employers and workers were deemed excessive. Public fund raising efforts produced fewer donations, fewer people joined in the public festivities, and denunciations declined. Workers no longer gave the German salute, and disrespectful jokes and critical sermons were making a reappearance. Goebbels produced a string of insults aimed at "wreckers, doom-merchants, alarmists, and other adverse critics," the only effect of which was to suggest that he was hostile to the people. Even the person of the führer was not spared. Caught as he was between a reawakening of conservatism and the revolutionary claims of the SA, where would he turn next? All the same, So-cialist reports prudently refrained from reading into these signs anything greater than a phase of sulking. The forceful action of 30 June justified their caution: the revelation of the turpitude of the SA leaders aroused the indignation of decent people, the liquidation of the organization satisfied their call for prompt jus-tice; and Hitler consolidated his contradictory image of su-preme judge and little man standing alone against the political mandarins. A number of non-Nazis, convinced that this beto-kened the end of abusive privileges, adopted the slogan "Up with Hitler, down with the party!" And the plebiscite of 19 Au-gust, which assigned him the combined functions of chancellor and head of state, proved that only a small fraction of public opinion refused to swallow the *fait accompli*: the previous 90 percent of yes votes was only reduced to 85 percent.[35]

Thereafter regular foreign policy successes compensated for the hardships of daily life. However, the SD, still pessimistic, continued to detect discontent and even despair among towns-people who had difficulty finding enough to eat, and people liv-ing in the countryside where farmhands were hard to come by, who were exasperated by all the interventionism. The Socialists were pessimistic too, but for the opposite reasons: they detected more lassitude than opposition among the workers ("the think-ing workers are today no longer able to guide the unthinking"), and among the peasants an abiding fear of Communism which, all in all, made the semi-expropriation they suffered preferable. So there was nothing political about all this discontent. The grand policy was to force a revision of the Treaty of Versailles, and most people who had not read *Mein Kampf* believed this to be the ultimate aim of the führer. The plebiscite in the Saar in January 1935 produced a shock for the Socialists, for they could not deny the total liberty in which the campaign had been conducted. The reintroduction of universal military service in April left public opinion more divided: some welcomed the idea of a new grand army while others feared a return of the Prussian-type "drill." With the remilitarization of the Rhineland doubts soon gave way to enthusiasm, and when the time came to elect a new Reichstag, 99 percent of electors—and never less than 92 percent, even in the most hostile quarters of Augsburg—turned out to vote for the official candidates. Every violent success was thus followed by a period of euphoria, with everyone convinced that Hitler had restored the country's greatness and was at the same time preserving peace. The faith shown in him was not without its inconveniences for the führer: he later admitted that by striving so hard to appear pacific he had rendered his people too pacifist.[36]

As early as the sixteenth century Etienne de la Boétie had spotted the problem: "For the troubles that they suffer people are prone to blame not the tyrant but those who control him."[37] Translated into plain twentieth-century German, that neat observation produced the oft-repeated slogan, "Ah! if the führer only knew!" Those "controllers" constantly under fire were not so much state representatives as party cadres. The first attacks targeted mainly the SA, who would draw the line at no kind of corruption provided there was money in it for them. When the SA was rendered harmless by repression, the "gilded pheasants" next came under fire—dignitaries with highly-paid posts who enjoyed such an extravagant lifestyle in strong contrast to the simplicity of the life of the führer. The scandal was even greater when it implicated leaders of the Hitler Youth organization, who were expected to provide models of asceticism for their troops. As the minister for internal affairs admitted in one of his three-monthly reviews, "It must not be forgotten that National Socialism achieved its principal successes by drawing the attention of the people to the contrast between the theories of the traditional parties and the private lives of their leaders." Hitler, still attached to his militant comrades of the difficult early days, even when they savored their revenge too openly, made a clumsy attempt to defend them at the 1935 congress: "Among the bourgeois (sic), it is often said, 'Yes, the Führer is one thing, the party is another matter!' My reply to that is 'No gentlemen, the Führer is the party, and the party is the Führer!' " Goebbels, more subtly, suggested to the press that it should not dwell in too much detail upon official receptions, as that "might create an impression of new class or caste divisions being created, which would be both objectively and subjectively false." He even forbade publication of any photographs of Goering's hunting parties.[38]

The preferred themes of such "malevolent spirits" are well-known thanks to the archives of the special court in Munich. Many of them came from popular circles and were prone to express themselves in dialect, which was something of an embarrassment to their judges, who were endeavoring to classify their disrespectful remarks in a juridical fashion. Their transgressions were of many kinds: gossip about the *mores* of top leaders, insults directed against officials of the *HJ* by parents jealous of their authority, naive predictions of the regime's imminent collapse, lamentations over economic difficulties, taxes, fund-raising exercises . . . Yet there was little trace of any political opposition among these folk of minor standing. It was the court itself in its judgments that made the whole business political: an irreverent remark viewed with indulgence in 1933 now, two years later, was a sign of "hostility toward National Socialism." Somewhat counter-intuitively however, the rate of guilty verdicts dropped from 60 percent to 40 percent (as opposed to 70 percent for openly political opponents): no doubt the judges reckoned that those few anxious hours of interrogation and appearing in court would be enough to curb the tongues of gossips.[39] These minor cases might be dismissed as laughable, yet they reveal the very darkest aspects of the Nazi regime for most had been initiated by denunciations. Accused and accusers alike belonged to the same popular circles; the only difference between them was that the former included a higher proportion of "asocial" individuals, easy targets for more settled citizens. The latter may have assumed that their victims would be let off lightly. But that was not the case where Gestapo informers were concerned. As has been noted above, the Gestapo was understaffed, and without the help of such informers would have been unable to operate efficiently. The Gestapo police, more methodical than regular magistrates, interrogated their auxiliaries about not only the information they were supplying but also their personal motives for doing so: in a quarter of the cases those motives were claimed to be ideological, and in a third they were of a private nature. However, that distinction seems very artificial, for underlying many conflicts between neighbors or even relatives there lurks a suspicion that anti-Semitism constituted the prime motivation. So it was that during these reputedly tranquil years all those who had not rallied openly to Nazism lived in fear, particularly at night. Many of their nightmares, including those collected by Charlotte Béradt and Reinhart Koselleck, speak volumes. Suffice it to cite just one case: that of a woman from Berlin who dreamed she was arrested at the opera for having thought automatically of Hitler at the sight of a scene of devilry, while her neighbors remained "inexpressive." On another occasion the same woman dreamed that her chimney sweep, dressed in SS uniform, presented her with a bill, saying: "Your guilt is beyond doubt." "Public opinion" was thus not composed purely of the lukewarm and the imprudent, but also of both fanatics and anguished doubters.[40]

One more barometer of the morality of public opinion is provided by the demographic behavior of households. With its appeal for numerous children, the regime turned procreation into a kind of ongoing plebiscite. The reponse of the public, as reflected in the statistics, is thus extremely revealing: its members were lacking in zeal, despite spectacular measures of encouragement. Associations that looked kindly upon birth control were closed down, and abortions (except of course for eugenic reasons) were severely punished. One 1933 law introduced installation loans for newly married couples on condition that the wife would not go out to work; furthermore, it was made clear that each new birth would secure the annulment of one quarter of the sum owed. By 1934 a third of newlywed couples were beneficiaries of this law, but thereafter the proportion fell to one quarter. The reason for this was that, given the possibility of going back to work, most young women preferred to return to or acquire a profession. The upshot was that the restrictive clause had to be abolished. Family allowances, reserved for families on low incomes or with more than two children, were also given. On top of the introduction of pre- and post-natal services, the whole setup was crowned by the issuing of Medals for Mothers, presented annually in the course of a solemn ceremony.

The results of this strategy were widely publicized and seemed magnificent. Over five years over one million loans had been granted, the rate of marital fecundity had risen from 5.9 percent to 8.5 percent and that of reproduction as a whole from 0.7 to 1. However, demographers have not been taken in by these appearances. They point out that the rise in fecundity had been due to women across the board, whether or not they were beneficiaries of the famous loan and whatever their ages. Furthermore, beneficiaries of the loan had on average produced no more than one child in six years; by the eve of the outbreak of war, out of one hundred couples married in 1933 or 1934, forty had still not produced any children and forty others had produced only one; moreover, in the contingent of mothers awarded medals, the older generation predominated. So the sole achievement of what was hailed as a resurrection of national energy was in truth to have — only just — made up for the shortfall that accumulated in the course of the twenties and the Great Crisis; the rate of fecundity in 1939 was still below that of 1922. The explanation for this relative inertia emerged clearly from a public debate that took place at the beginning of 1937, when the *Angriff*, the party's Berlin newspaper, launched a competition of articles by its readers on the theme of "the fear of a third child." Two-thirds of the contributions received simply reiterated the official line on the birthrate, but the rest explained the reticence of families by their inadequate incomes and the high cost of rented accommodations. When the editors judged it wise to respond by publishing an extremely optimistic analysis of family budgets, it started up a new wave of arguments reported even as far afield as the Ruhr. "In this domain, as in others," British historian Jill Stephenson concludes, "the Germans mounted no open opposition, but continued quietly to follow their own desires."[41]

One comment in a Socialist report ran as follows: "Those who complain the most about the situation are the very ones who roar the loudest when the Nazi organizers enthuse them by laying on some demonstration or other."[42] As well as reflecting the bitterness of its authors the observation raises a very real problem. In day-to-day life where did the centre of gravity lie? In the workplace, in the local bar, in family homes, or in public squares decked with bunting and the more or less sumptuous local party headquarters? Or to put that another way, in 1936-37 was this regime that sought to fuse private and public life into an ever more totalitarian community on the way to failing, or succeeding? Many historians have reflected upon the ambiguous situation in which this "people of comrades" was then living and suggested a number of concepts to explain it. The idea of schizophrenia is attractive, but to appreciate it fully requires more than a layman's understanding of psychiatry. As has been mentioned above, discussion has centered productively upon the term "dissent" proposed by I. Kershaw, and even more so upon the expression "refractory dissent" (*Resistenz*) borrowed from medicine by M. Broszat.[43] Both suggestions constitute ingenious attempts to describe without passing any value judgment various ways of thinking that have little to do with resistance or fanaticism. It remains to be seen whether they can be pertinently applied to a range of different elites, to the middle and working classes, and to the various age groups.

NOTES

1. Girardet R., passim.
2. Arendt H., *Système*, p. 31.
3. *53*, p. 105; Peukert D., *République de Weimar*, pp. 102-236.

4. Broszat M., "Soziale Motivation"; Peukert D., ibid., pp. 239–43; Bracher K. D., *Auflösung, pp. 106–27.*

5. Hitler A., *Mein Kampf*, vol. 2, chap. 11.

6. Bramsted E. K., chap. 8–9; Kettenacker L.; Kershaw I., *Hitler*, pp. 26–31; id., *Hitler-Mythos*, passim; Mann T., "Bruder Hitler."

7. *56*, p. 46 f.; Scholder K., *Kirchen*, Bd. 1, p. 280 f.; Fest J., vol. 1, pp. 387–96; Klemperer V., passim; Volmert J.; Stern J. P., chap. 4.

8. Hinkel H.

9. Courtade F. and Cadars P.; Delage C.

10. Mosse G. L.

11. Pélassy D.; Thamer H.-U., p. 418; above all Vondung K., *Magie*; Bédarida F. (on the concept of secular religion).

12. Frei N. and Schmitz J., p. 37, 81, 96 f.; Frei N., "Provinzzeitungen," p. 89; Tenfelde K., pp. 254–55 (the local press in Upper Bavaria).

13. Doc. in *51, 62, 64, 71*, passim; Berning C., *s.v. Arier, Art. Blut, Rasse; 61*, p. 149, 219.

14. Frei N. and Schmitz J., p. 83 f.; Reichel P., p. 157 f.; Kater M., "Jazz."

15. In particular Sch fer H. D., "Das gespaltene Bewusstsein"; the critique by Könke G.

16. Cited by Michaud E., p. 61. I came across this work too late to be able to use all its analyses to enrich this chapter 2, but for the most part I agree with them.

17. Vondung K., "Der literarische Nationalsozialismus"; Richard L., p. 57, 88 f.; Scholdt G., chap. 3; Reus G.

18. Guyot A. and Restellini P.; *51*, p. 363 f.; Arndt K., p. 435.

19. Petsch J.; Reichel P., p. 262 f., 283–84; Engeli C. and Ribbe W., pp. 994–95 (Berlin); Arndt K., p. 457 (Munich); Könke G. (tradition and modernity); Rabinbach A., p. 72 f. (factories).

20. Broszat M., *L'Etat hitlérien*, p. 67 f.

21. Allen W. S., *Une petite ville*, pp. 48–159.

22. Bracher K. D., *Auflösung*, p. 647.

23. Examples of longstanding classic studies: Hamilton R. F.; Childers T. Critical studies: Falter J., "Wer verhalf?"; id. *Hitlers Wähler*, pp. 42–66; Manstein P., p. 167 f.

24. Falter J., *Hitlers Wähler*, passim; id., Lindenberger T. and Schumann S., p. 83, 156–70, 230–31; id. and Hänisch D., "Anfälligkeit"; Manstein P., pp. 11–89.

25. The tables provided by Falter J., *Hitlers Wähler*, p. 288 (electors) and Manstein P., p. 163 (male members) are not entirely compatible. Hence an element of imprecision in the above comments.

26. Kater M., *The Nazi Party*, pp. 51–71, 153–165; Mommsen H., "Verschränkung," p. 164 f.; Manstein P., pp. 90–101.

27. Abel T., pp. 115–200 (an analysis of about six hundred replies, 1934); Schmidt C. (seventy-four autobiographies, Hesse-Nassau, 1936–37); Varga L.

28. Kater M., *The Nazi Party*, pp. 72–115; Mommsen H., "Verschränkung," p. 170 f.

29. *Märzgefallene*. Word for word: "March victims." This is an ironic reference to the (real) victims of March 1848. The only way to translate it faithfully is to create a neologism such as "Marchites," "Marchians," or possibly "Martians" . . .

30. Stöver B., p. 383 f.; Arbogast B. and Gall B., pp. 163–69; Schmidt C., p. 38.

31. Orlow D., passim; Kater M., *The Nazi Party*, pp. 190–212; Rebentisch D., "Poli-

tische Beurteilung"; Feit B.; Thamer H.-U., pp. 356–59; Broszat M., L'Etat hit-lérien, p. 151, 171.

32. Orlow D., pp. 163–74, 214–30; Kater M., *The Nazi Party*, pp. 190–212; John J. (Thüringen); Broszat M., *L'État hitlérien*, pp. 240–43.

33. Stöver B., p. 104; Steinert M. G. *Hitlers Kreig*, pp. 23–24 (on the war, but also valid for the preceding years).

34. 57, doc. 19 (Hamburg); Kershaw I., *Hitler-Mythos*, pp. 46–58 (Bavaria); Hetzer G., p. 137-141 (Augsburg); Stöver B., p. 307 f.

35. Frei N., *L'Etat hitlérien*, chap. 1; Kershaw I., *Hitler-Mythos*, pp. 60–79; id., "Al-ltägliches"; Stöver B., p. 168; 72, X, doc. 2387.

36. Kershaw I., "Alltägliches"; Stöver B., pp. 173–76; Hetzer G., p. 143 f.

37. La Boétie E. de, *Discours de la servitude volontaire* (1574), ed. Goyard-Fabre S., p. 170.

38. Numerous texts, for example: 72, IX, doc. 2163, 2166; X, doc. 2471; XI, doc. 2491 (Westphalia and a national synthesis); 53, p. 251–52 (Hanover); Kershaw I., *Hitler-Mythos*, pp. 81–89 (Bavaria); 68, pp. 91, 95–96 (Goebbels).

39. Hüttenberger P., "Heimtückef lle."

40. Id.; Gellately R., chap. 5 (Gestapo); Béradt C. and Koselleck R. (dreams). On the frequency of denunciations, see above, chap. 1, p. 00.

41. Klinksiek D., pp. 87–92, 158; Stephenson J., *Women*, pp. 42–47, 68–70. Bock G., "Gleichheit"; Marschalck P., p. 78 f.; Glass D. V. (the most precise); Thal-mann R., pp. 109–10; Ruhl K.-J. (Bavaria); Mason T., *Arbeiterklasse*, doc. 27 (the third child).

42. Cited by Kershaw I., "Widerstand."

43. See above, introduction, pp. 11–12.

3—The Illusions, Collusions, and Disillusions of the Elites

Franz Neumann was the first to detect behind the facade of the Third Reich a network of rivalries and alliances between four powers, each led by an elite: the state bureaucracy, the army, industry, and the Nazi party.[1] Under Weimar the first two of these put up no more than a pretense of serving the Republic, the third waged a war of attrition against it, and the fourth clashed head-on with it. How could the leaders of the first three—selected by birth, wealth, or education and forming semi-autonomous bodies—accept or in some cases even encourage the accession to power of the fourth, which practiced demagogy, called for a fusion of the classes, and produced an elite of a new type at once "open and authoritarian"?[2] Some have sought to explain the illusions of these groups by their common nostalgia for the imperial period and attraction to a regime of order; it has been suggested that all three groups made the fundamental mistake of believing the rise of their totalitarian rival would presage purely and simply a return to authoritarianism. But these historians overlooked the fact that the homogeneity each group laid claim to was itself no more than a facade. Within each of those old elites a radical minority was already developing, determined to do away with all their respectable traditions and figureheads. This made it much easier to make bureaucracy, army, and industry "fall into line" in 1933–34.

DOUBTS OF THE LEADING SOCIAL GROUPS

The absence of nobility from the above list may surprise some. But in truth its role had become purely ceremonial and it was furthermore deeply divided. Its values—religion, paternalism, and monarchist loyalty—still predominated in Bavaria, where they were fostered by the Catholic Church and a number of mass organizations. For a long time these deterred the people of Bavaria from succumbing to the blandishments of Hitler, and besides, in Bavaria no more than a handful of nobles were Nazis. The political distance separating the Bavarian nobility from the Junkers of the East was as great as the geographical distance between them. Those Junkers also continued to favor an archaic kind of discourse that relied on references to "Prussianism, the army, the deep roots of the elite leaders, and a vassal type of loyalty." But as a group they had for some time already, been behaving simply as a lobby for major landowners, exploiting their remaining connections with the higher echelons in the administration to secure grants, permission to take over areas of open land, and even to lobby for renewal of the "push eastward." Hindenburg was the man for them; they loathed Brüning, who was proposing to expropriate bankrupt properties, and likewise Kurt von Schleicher—interim chancellor before Hitler—who was threatening to take the lid off a number of scandals. The majority of nobles—a few tens of thousands of families—lived parsimoniously as small landowners, subaltern officers, or on assistance from the Friendly Societies for the German nobility. Like all middle classes that had lost their social standing, they compensated for their humiliation by railing venomously against the modern world, the Republic, Jews, and so on. When the presidential election in 1932 made them choose between Hindenburg and Hitler, most voted for the man whom the old Marshal called "the Bohemian corporal." Some had even joined the Nazi party and were pursuing careers in the SA or SS, where their titles still retained a certain cachet.[3]

High-ranking civil servants with their university degrees and competitive selection no longer maintained close ties with the nobility. Unlike it, they had always formed a deliberately constituted body steeped in the ethics of public service. Most of them thus preferred to believe that they served the state, not the

Republic, and despised any colleagues who had "defected" to the Social Democratic Party (these were in truth less numerous than claimed by right-wing polemicists). Initially, Brüning won their sympathy by recommending policies unburdened by ideology (*sachlich*), but he then lost it by cutting their salaries. Conversely, the Nazi party, which had over a long period annoyed them with its attacks on bureaucracy, captured their interest when it emphasized the revision of the Treaty of Versailles, and hailed as martyrs those few of their number punished for openly criticizing the Young plan. Their proclaimed apoliticism did not prevent them from glimpsing the possibility of a new political regime that would do without a parliament and parties, relying solely on the national right wing and "thinking" Nazis. Besides, the Lutheran theology of both these orders, with which many of them were familiar, predisposed them to accept new authorities of whatever ilk, particularly if they proposed to restore the authority of the state.[4]

Meanwhile the officer corps felt trapped in an impasse. The Treaty of Versailles had reduced it to four thousand individuals, and the high command had used this as a pretext to dispense with the veterans of vigilante groups. Officers thus lived in "their own little world" in their barracks, far removed from the civil unrest (with which the police were expected to deal) and also remote from parliamentary rivalries. Soon however the staff office set about elaborating rearmament plans that presupposed a large increase in the number of cadres, and hence called upon those who identified themselves as "political soldiers," adventurers who either openly or clandestinely acted as militants for the far Right, particularly in the SA. And how could German youth be persuaded to sign up or even accept a return to military service given the wide gap between the military and the masses at that time? Many young officers, even among those serving in the staff office, were tempted not to join the Nazi party, which they were not at liberty to do anyhow, but to establish official links with it.[5] The Potsdam garrison mess, the *crème de la crème* (and future matrix of the 1944 conspiracy), on one occasion invited Goebbels to address them and gave him a great welcome.

The relationship between major business bosses and National Socialism is a subject of extensive literature, even discounting the two opposed oversimplifications of this theme: on one hand the Dimitrovian theory of fascism, on the other the apologias of the postwar period. For a long time the question was reduced to its purely financial aspect: to what extent did captains of industry contribute to party funds or help finance such or such a party leader reputed to be sympathetic to their interests? Now that so many documents have come to light we know the answer to that question. At the time of its modest beginnings the party turned to a number of patrons in Munich. Later it managed to become more or less self-financing up until the Great Crisis. There are records of a number of direct donations in 1930 (from Thyssen), and indirect ones through the intermediary of the "Keppler circle," but there is no evidence of massive support from "the Ruhr." Hitler's speech to the Düsseldorf Industrialists' Club, in which he exalted the role of business proprietors, itself produced few material results: Flick and *IG Farben* made donations but at the same time showered contributions on the other political parties all across the board, from the Right to the Social Democrats. Schacht complained about the situation: "Heavy industry is proving very heavy to move." Massive and exclusive donations to the *NSDAP* (Nazi party) date only from early 1933. No doubt as more monographs on business firms appear, they will reveal other instances of complicity: recently for instance, gifts from the motor firm Daimler-Benz to the Munich party headquarters, to Goering, and to industrialist–Nazi party go-between Walther Funk came to light. However, all in all it would be unjustified to claim that financial support made Hitler a client of the business bosses.[6]

Where political sympathies and contacts are concerned, it is important to distinguish between most of heavy industry and the Reich Federation of German Industry, the *RDI*. The latter gathered together industrialists of a new kind who were involved in world markets and consequently anxious not to incur the hostility of not only foreign public opinion but also members of heavy industry such as Krupp von Bohlen and Silverberg (lignite mines). This shatters the once generally accepted theory of "contradictions between the two sectors," heavy and light industry. Confronted with Brüning, heavy industry opted for a strategy of catastrophe and even suggested that the Nazis should take over the government. Meanwhile the *RDI* for its part preferred to support the chancellor, along with the Social Democratic Party. At the presidential election some industrialists from the Ruhr openly supported Hitler, while Silverberg spoke up for Hindenburg. Then over the next two weeks links with the extreme Right were slackened: Franz von Papen's government enjoyed support from both sides while the Nazi party, with bad timing, chose to publish its "emergency economic program," which was extremely interventionist and discouraged the sympathies of business proprietors. As for the famous letter to the head of state, asking him to summon Hitler to the chancellory — frequently represented as the sign of massive rallying to the party by business proprietors — it was in truth an initiative limited to a few agrarians and heads of firms who were already Nazi converts. In the end the *RDI* and even a number of Ruhr industrialists sided with Schleicher with the exception of Silverberg who, in contradiction to his entire past (and despite being a Jew) supported the Nazis. In short, "Hitler's arrival in power was hardly to the liking of most of the business chiefs."[7] Nevertheless, there can be no justification for all those complicated maneuvers. In the days of Republican power, the body of major business proprietors had no compunction over destabilizing the regime by attacking its "interventionism," provoking social crises, and allying itself with the Right. When it found itself weakened and even in panic as a result of the worldwide economic depression, it split, part of it supporting and part of it opposing the succession of governments, and by doing so it contributed to their collapse. Whether the business proprietors wanted it or not, the Third Reich was what awaited them.

The only criticism that can be leveled at F. Neumann's authoritative analysis is that it overlooks a fifth body of power, what German historians call "the cultural bourgeoisie." This, too, had long regarded itself as the key to the nation's destiny, and it, too, had been both materially and spiritually let down by the Republic. It was generally agreed that the purveyors of further education headed the hierarchy, with teachers of the classic universities placed higher than those of the technical universities, and professors with named chairs (*Ordinarien*) higher than those with nonnamed chairs and their assistants: a huge crowd leaning against the doors that led to prestige and power. These professors truly were incorporated, and doubly so: both in their disciplinarian associations and in the universities, where they wielded virtually autonomous power. They had repulsed as so many "political" interventions all attempts at reform made by ministers responsible for the supervision of education, particularly in Prussia. But this apoliticism was easily reconciled with a nostalgic monarchism: every year on 18 January an academic ceremony was held to celebrate the founding of the Second Reich, when one of the professors would deliver if not a speech in praise of monarchism at least a eulogy of its values, contrasting them to the sad spectacle of the existing divisions and winding up with a call for the appearance of some great savior. As the servants of pure science it was with some alarm that they viewed the evolution of an increasingly technological society quite alien to the troubled values of humanism; the more so given that their alma mater itself was not spared from unrest. The number of students was increasing and they came from more modest circles. Worried about career prospects, they were switching from conservatism to extremism. One after another, student committees (*Asta*) were being taken over by Nazi organizations, starting with the technical universities and classic universities in eastern Germany. At the national congress of 1931 the Nazis even won a majority. All the more reason for professors to distrust the demagogic and unruly Nazi movement. Only eight professors had joined the party before it came to power, and about fifty or so signed its electoral appeal in 1932.[8]

Secondary schoolteachers, themselves former students and many of them holders of a doctorate—the true qualification of academic nobility—still considered their vocation to be to train future elites by initiating them into high culture. So they were extremely sensitive to the suppression of posts, falling salaries, and lack of employment for young colleagues that resulted first from inflation and then from the depression, which they blamed on the parties in power. So strongly did they feel that their principal association, the *Philologenverband*, formally recommended on the grounds of apoliticism that they not defend any Republican institutions in their classes. However, they also did not approve of the anti-intellectualism in Nazi propaganda, and very few of them (unlike primary schoolteachers) joined the party. The holders of "engineering diplomas," likewise university products, convinced that they embodied a new form of German genius and who banded together in a prestigious association of their own, suffered similar ups and downs despite the fact that they had loyally supported their employers in campaigns for industrial rationalization. Some began to dream of a new social order which, by giving modern elites their rightful place, would relaunch technological progress. However, for the moment it did not occur to many of them that National Socialism might be the answer to their hopes.[9] In short, the various sectors of the intelligentsia were hoping for national rehabilitation, but had very little idea of how it might come about.

GETTING EVERYONE TO "FALL INTO LINE," 1933–1934

Gleichschaltung was the order of the day during the first two years. In French it is usually translated as "la mise au pas." In English perhaps the expression "falling into line" will serve. It conveys the sense of discipline the new masters now imposed that was more or less willingly accepted by various preexisting groups, although it loses the technological connotations of the German term. Reflecting during the war on the then-current use of the German word, V. Klemperer was to remark: "You can hear the click of the switch that is flicked in order to impart to human beings a particular uniform and automatic attitude or movement"; and he went on to say that if after a while that switch was no linger flicked, it was "for the simple reason that very soon all those kinds of automatic conditioning procedures had already been performed."[10] More precisely the term evoked the electrical industry or mechanical engineering, as can be seen from an article published in the *Völkischer Beobachter* in 1936: "The economic policy of National Socialism corresponds to the technological age; it allows capitalism to function as an engine, but it is National Socialism that changes the gears."[11] These are important metaphors: they remind us that even as it summoned up archaic fantasies the regime never ceased to proclaim its adoration of technology. Perhaps "synchronization" or "normalization" would be the most appropriate translations for *Gleichschaltung*, but "falling into line" has become a current colloquialism so we may as well stick with it.

Getting individuals to fall into line was achieved by terror, intimidation, or blandishments. Where countless institutions, group interests, friendly societies, and—particularly delicate—major power groups were concerned, a more subtle strategy was adopted. It has been well analyzed by Konrad Jarausch. Within each community the authorities exploited rivalries between its subgroups: former left-wing leaders, seldom determined to fight for their jobs and for the most part resigned; conservative nationalists, prepared to take over from the former during a transitional phase in order to use anything salvageable; and Nazis, ambitious and vengeful. The latter exerted internal pressure while the political authorities operated from the outside. Everywhere the handover of powers passed through the same stages: an initial declaration of rallying and loyalty; access to the managerial organs allowed to a few Nazi colleagues; and the elimination of all Jews. Where the lack of goodwill was too blatant, the state or the party intervened: the SA went along to disrupt meetings, or the administration appointed a "commission" with full powers. Eventually the objective would be achieved: the group in question would either be smoothly integrated into a "front" (legal, educational, technological . . .), or purely and simply absorbed by one of the party's parallel organizations.[12] Rather than set out a monotonous list of these capitulations, let us concentrate on a few typical cases.

Of the counter-powers that had curbed the authority of the first two Reichs and threatened to do so for the Third, the municipal authorities of large towns seemed the most tenacious. Their "principal mayors" (*Oberbürgermeister* or *OB*) were quasi-sovereign and elected for an extended and renewable term, which assured them of freedom of action vis-à-vis the central administrative powers and political parties, even those to which they were close. As for the municipal councils, the Nazis held at best no more than relative majorities there, even after the elections of 12 March 1933. So they took control either by means of juridical tricks or simply by force. In some towns the mandates of Communist and later Socialist or centrist councillors were annulled. In others the council was reshuffled to reflect the results of 5 March (the Reichstag election), which had been more favorable to the *NSDAP*. But there was no ready formula for the sacking of mayors, so to force them to resign the party resorted to campaigns of defamation, SA eruptions in town halls, and sometimes even physical violence. The mayors were then replaced by commissioners: out of fifty-three towns of over one hundred thousand inhabitants, only eight non-Nazi mayors survived. Of those who replaced the non-Nazi mayors and councillors, some, the party "veterans," rapidly proved incompetent and were in their turn replaced; the rest, well-tried administrators who had opportunely become "Martian casualties,"[13] settled in on a more or less long-term basis. Everywhere, municipal policies now adopted aimed to be innovative, reassuring, and dynamic. It was easy to change street names, purge libraries, and balance the budget by slashing unemployment assistance. But purging the municipal personnel, which in many towns ran into thousands, turned out to be a more tricky matter when the intention was to eliminate all Jews, Communists, and any of their "untrustworthy" colleagues. While Berlin succeeded in getting rid of a third of its employees, other towns such as Leipzig and Munich managed to unload barely 10 percent. Even at the modest level of low-grade jobs, Nazi militants proved as incompetent as their leaders already had in posts at a higher level. Municipalities then reallocated these losers as doorkeepers or street sweepers, and reappointed some of those dismissed or at least those who had in the meantime become converts.[14]

Upper echelons of the public sector were treated with greater circumspection. Hitler detested bureaucracies, and many of his companions urged a radical purge. But Wilhelm Frick, minister of the interior, and Goering, director of the administration of Prussia, were in favor of dealing delicately with these pillars of the state. Under the cover of a "revolution from above," Frick was able to publish a directive that seemed rigid but would accommodate a wide range of interpretations. The law of 7 April 1933 "for the reestablishment of professional public services" decreed the sacking or downgrading of Communists, Jews (except war veterans and those who had served more than ten years), incompetents, and finally "those whose unreserved commitment to the national state could not be guaranteed, in view of their past political activities." It thus authorized every kind of excess. However, litigious cases took a long time to examine, and final decisions varied enormously by ministry and region. The five Communists and thirty Jews employed by the Ministry of Finance were forced to leave, but four-fifths of the "politically unreliable" were retained; on the other hand the law provided a welcome chance to get rid of a large number of "incompetents." The Prussian Ministry of the Interior was more radical: here, where despite an earlier purge ordered by von Papen a number of Socialists and/or Jews remained, 28 percent of the high-ranking officials were eliminated. But the corresponding ministries of other *Länder* were less severe. In Bavaria, there were not many losses among high-ranking officials. In contrast, a new service to create jobs such as the National Agency for Employment opened up a breach that swallowed up many jobless party members. On the whole, at the cost of accepting the sacrifice of a few colleagues for whom, in any case, they felt little sympathy, high-ranking administrative officials preserved their positions and even rationalized their services.[15]

The purging of departments of justice also fell to the individual *Länder* until the system was centralized in 1934. The procedure was the same: a combination of terror from below and an imposition of order from above. Yet under the Republic the courts were more lenient to the extreme Right than the extreme Left, and so might expect a measure of gratitude from the new regime. However, these courts had also sentenced militant Nazis to prison sentences or fined them for common law infractions. So judges and lawyers reputed to be left-wing, particularly if they were Jewish, came under violent attack from the SA, and this forced prosecutors general and ministers to send them away "on leave," "to avoid trouble." For many of them that leave became definitive following the law of 7 April, which in this domain was applied extremely vigorously: when former war veterans who believed themselves officially protected tried to return to the courts as judges or barristers, the authorities delayed coming to a decision on their cases until a second law was passed in 1935 which decided the matter against them. Even so, not all of those who still held their positions allowed themselves to be meekly brought into line. Some it is true did agree to preside over special courts, where as Minister of Justice Franz Gürtner put it they were expected "in these revolutionary circumstances, to abandon formal judicial procedure here and there, without renouncing the principles behind it." However, others in contrast stood up to the SA and SS and managed to snatch a few prisoners from their clutches, even occasionally bringing accusations against their murderers: they did not

achieve many results, but their behavior was certainly honorable. But even if their efforts had led to sentences for the guilty,
these would have been canceled by the three major amnesty
laws then passed: that of 21 March 1933, which exonerated over
eight thousand individuals, that of 3 July 1934, which covered
the events of 30 June; and that of 7 August 1935, which annulled
twelve thousand sentences of current prosecution cases.[16]

The officer corps remained virtually intact, physically if not
from the point of view of morale. Right from the very early days
Hitler had struck a sensitive chord here by promising to not involve them in political questions. A few isolated individuals,
mostly prompted by religious scruples, openly expressed indignation at the party's violence. Others overcame their misgivings
by telling themselves that it would not last: "We are living
through a revolution," said General Ludwig Beck, "and in such
periods, the shit always floats to the top in the early days"; and
certain armored car enthusiasts such as Heinz Guderian were
won over by plans for motorization. Already though, the more
politically-minded officers were coming forward, ready to make
any concessions demanded in order to preserve the army's
place in the system. Future Field Marshal Walther von Reichenau declared: "We are in a revolution; whatever is moldy in
the state must go, and terror can make that happen." Minister of
War Werner von Blomberg for his part openly repudiated the
tradition of apoliticism in a letter addressed to the officers and
invited them to become partisan. As the conflict with the SA
grew increasingly serious they decided it was necessary to demonstrate their zeal. In April 1934 all Jews (seventy individuals in
all including seven officers) were sacked, even without any
prodding from the party. Also in April the troops were encouraged to attend sessions of political instruction where National
Socialism was represented as essentially "soldierly." The coup
of 30 June, plotted principally by the staff office and carried out
with material assistance from the army, seems to have sealed this
policy of compromise. Among all the generals and colonels only
one protest was made against the racial purge, two against the

assassination of their brothers-in-arms Schleicher and Bredow, and one against the oath to the führer. Yet already the first aspects of the downside to all this were emerging: in September 1934 the army had to accept the organization of the "Deployable SS" into four regular regiments and provide weaponry for them.[17] Officers from noble families were also given food for thought over the fate of their Friendly Society: when Hitler suggested that it should purge itself in order to do full justice to its "genetic stock," those who ran it did as they were bid and ejected 250 "Jews"—who must of course have been converts to Christianity—without noticing that this materialistic racism totally contradicted their own "moderate" anti-Semitism.[18] After the war the heirs to the army of the Reich claimed that by preventing the SA and even the party from interfering in military affairs, the army had preserved its political virginity. But since then a new generation of historians has shown that those initial compromises ultimately led to many others. In short, if the officer corps had not been forced into line, it was simply because it fell in of its own accord.

The "Economy"—as groups of business proprietors were pompously called—was probably the most difficult body to integrate into the new institutions. Not that its leaders were moved by any spirit of resistance, but they knew they were indispensable for the realization of Hitler's two fundamental programs: rearmament and full employment. Where rearmament was concerned the steel producers could count on the support of the army officers; and as for full employment, here exporters were working closely with the party's liberal economists. Was it necessary to move directly toward state interventionism, to prepare the way for a war economy, or would it be better to rely initially on market forces, that is to say private initiatives, and thereby reestablish the overall equilibrium that would stem from an atmosphere of restored confidence? Hitler himself was in two minds about the contradictory arguments; on the one hand those that praised the great business "leaders," on the other those that looked forward to a rigid corporatism to benefit the middle classes.

The first phase followed the usual pattern of bringing things into line. A few bosses joined the party as individuals, half the business proprietors in the Ruhr, for example. Collectively the *RDI*, after a few weeks of playing a double game when it called simultaneously for union with "everyone rallying to the nation" and for a return to liberalism, was forced to toe the line. In early April its directing committee eliminated all Jews and, in conformity with the *Führerprinzip*, handed over full powers to its president, Krupp von Bohlen, who now officially accepted the very projects he had recently been opposing, namely corporative organization, self-sufficiency, and controlled inflation. Two months later that same *RDI*, without changing its acronym, became the "National Corporation (*Reichsstand*) of German Industry." These concessions provoked a number of dissenting reactions. Steel producer Emil Kirdorf circulated an open letter in which he wrote: "I have not lost all hope of living in a renovated, pure and proud Germany," and described the anti-Semitic campaign as a crime. Another, the vice president of the *RDI*, rejected the idea of any compromise on the Jewish question "if we wish to preserve our moral standing." But the general spirit of submission seemed to be rewarded by the law of January 1934 "on the organization of national labor": each entrepreneur now officially became a *führer* with a staff reduced to the standing of "faithful followers" (*Gefolgschaft*).[19] Social relations were in practice removed from the responsibilities of the Labor Front and instead entrusted to "curators" who were closer to the business proprietors. However, immediately after this an unexpected change was introduced, inspired by the interventionist wing of the party and by the new minister for the Economy, Kurt Schmitt. A second series of edicts reduced the role of the *RDI* to that of a mere facade and brought the economy as a whole within the framework of an extremely complex grid of "national groups" (commerce, industry, etc.), which were then subdivided into "principal groups," the heads of which were to be appointed by the minister. Fortunately for the business proprietors Schmitt was soon obliged to relinquish his post to make way for Hjalmar Schacht, who while preserving the imposing organizational plan, transformed it from within to allow the proprietors' unions to be integrated and headed by their own elected leaders. The end result was a system of two-fold controls exercised on the one hand by the state and on the other by the business bosses, a system characteristic of the ambiguities of this regime. Hitler as usual got around the situation with a pronouncement of his own: "The Ministry of the Economy fixes the tasks, industry carries them out; but if it reckons that it cannot do so, the National Socialist state will be perfectly capable of filling that role." The first phrase suggested a return to interventionism, the second represented this as merely a last resort in times of crisis.[20]

Unsurprisingly, this compromise has since given rise to contradictory interpretations. As early as 1942, F. Neumann, who had not forgotten his past as a Social Democrat, regarded it as a straightforward confirmation of the theory of organized capitalism: "An organization of businessmen that excluded the workers was controlled by the state and performed certain administrative functions." It is true that the cooperation of businesses at every level in the system was obligatory, a fact that appeared to strengthen state supervision. But in truth "all economic activity [fell] within the network of arrangements under the direction of the industrial magnates"; reform of the cartels was no more than a "democratic mask" which left the larger firms free to crush the smaller, domination further strengthened by the 1937 law on public companies, which weakened the shareholders' influence. The bosses, whether proprietors or managers, definitely remained the real *führers*. The body that they formed could be described as "sovereign and authoritarian, endowed with executive, legislative, and judicial powers," and the internal history of the Third Reich was simply that of its alliances and conflicts with the three other bodies, the army, the bureaucracy, and the party. The finishing touches to these somewhat incomplete theories were added in 1964 by Arthur Schweitzer, who recalled Schacht's philippic against the "ideologists": "Cannons and all that is necessary for national defense are inconceivable without highly developed capitalist industry." Schweitzer preferred to describe this economic system as "largely organized capitalism" and the corresponding political system as "partial Fascism." More recently however another economist, Abraham Barkai, has proposed a completely different interpretation of the same data. He perceives no victory for the major industries in the system elaborated by Schacht, but instead a predominance of state control: "curators of labor" were state officials, cartels had to obey the policies of price controls, and the administration dominated foreign trade and the management of savings. In short, the system certainly was based on "dictatorial state interventionism, [but] affected neither productivity nor profit stimulants."[21] In any event however, whether capitalist with a dash of state control, or state controlled with a measure of corporate autonomy, the system was not viable: when the first crisis arose it fell apart, and along with it the cohesion of the body of business proprietors.

Bringing the university community into line required no intervention from external demonstrators: Nazi students were already on the spot. Campaigns of intimidation and spectacular operations such as burning banned books were organized— now by the National Socialist League of Students, closely connected to the SA, now by the German Student Community, reputed to be apolitical but protected by Goebbels; now by the League of Teachers composed of staff without tenure. For students, membership in one of the first two groups was more or less obligatory and was only dodged—as was military training—by a cunning few who enrolled at a different university each semester.[22] Again state power intervened to supervise these "spontaneous" movements, but the measures it took were not all appreciated by its protégés. The "law on the overstaffing of higher education" established a *numerus clausus* of five percent for Jews and 10 percent for women; another imposed ten weeks of Labor Service for students already taking courses and six months for their successors. As for the sacrosanct autonomy of teachers, it was simply abolished: henceforward university "rectors" (presidents) would be appointed by the minister, heads of faculties would be appointed by those rectors, and university councils were greatly reduced, in particular losing their power to recruit new colleagues. Racial and political purging was as severe as in other less prestigious corporations: in two years, 15 percent of university teachers and 11 percent of the *ordinarien* were sacked or forced to retire. But those figures represent national averages, and in universities reputed to be left-wing the disciplines in which Jews were most numerous were truly downsized: by 32 percent in Berlin and Frankfurt, 24 percent in Heidelberg, and 22 percent in Breslau, as against 11 percent in technical universities, eight percent in Munich, and even fewer in Tübingen and Rostock; around 20 percent in physics, mathematics, law, and medicine, decidedly fewer in "philosophy" (human sciences).

Within this tottering ivory tower reactions were inevitably incoherent. Of those purged, some engaged in appeal procedures, others resigned as noisily as possible, and the most famous — already well-known abroad — chose to go into exile. In this way German science lost around a score of Nobel prize winners and future Nobel prize winners, virtually the entire Göttingen schools of physics and mathematics, the Frankfurt Institute of Social Studies, and many more. Most of those who remained were reduced to attempting to reconcile their safety and scruples on a day-to-day basis. An individual who signed a declaration of loyalty might at the same time be bargaining in order to preserve a Jewish colleague. University councils were faced with similar dramatic choices. During the winter of 1933, when they still enjoyed the right to select personnel, they chose rectors and department heads acceptable to the government but not too compromised by partisan agitation. In the spring they confronted a serious test of conscience, the projected auto-da-fé of books: should the professors, many of whom were close to the condemned authors, attend the book-burning? In Cologne for example, once the council had secured an understanding that the university library would be spared, its members resigned themselves to attending the ceremony and enduring the Nazi orators' speeches attacking the mandarins.[23]

The process of bringing the Protestant Church into line presents another typical example of the Hitlerian method—the expression is particularly apposite here, since in this case Hitler made it his personal business. The method adopted yet again consisted in exploiting the internal splits within the elite of the group to be destroyed, that of Protestant pastors, bishops, and theologians. The violence of the polemics that tore this group apart came primarily from an influential group that had emerged relatively recently: the German-Christians.[24] Their extremist theses had so far influenced no more than a handful of scattered parishes, so their organization of a national congress in April 1933 caused a sensation. The congress attacked the existing bishops and called for the creation of a "Reich Church" headed by a "Reich bishop"—a considerable innovation, this—who would promote the endeavor of national renewal, beginning by ejecting all Jewish converts: at the theological level this implied that the *Volk* was a divine creation and that in the heart of each and every individual, Race was more important than Grace. In every parish there then followed a campaign of sermons and publications centered on the themes of renewal, youth, and the People's Community. Hitler himself, although personally originally Catholic, openly supported it, and in July grass roots electors gave the party a clear majority. Inevitably the whole institution was brought into line: the synod of Prussia, which the most zealous fanatics attended wearing the party uniform, gave itself a centralized constitution that contained "the Aryan paragraph." Its example was followed by other provinces with the exception of Bavaria, Württemberg, and Hanover, which declared themselves "intact dioceses." The twenty-third of September saw the solemn enthronement of the first "Reich bishop," Ludwig Müller, who proclaimed, "One people, one State, and One Church."

The ambiguous reaction of the orthodox pastors mirrored that of the conservative circles to which they were linked. As nationalists they welcomed national renewal; as theologians they recalled the necessity for charity. This semi-rejection of party involvement was considered too timid by a number of young pastors in Berlin, not through want of patriotism (their spokesman, paster Martin Niemöller, was a war hero), for their indignation had been aroused by what they called the "*Völkisch* heresy." In one Berlin parish two parallel church services were celebrated: one for the SA, another in which the preacher took as his theme the New Testament sentence, "You have made of my house a den of thieves." In September these protesters laid the foundations for a national organization called the Pastors' Emergency League (or the League of Distress). The conflict was becoming three-sided.[25]

The divisions proved to be serious enough to undermine official policy. Although Müller dismissed many pastors, appointed a number of openly racist bishops, and introduced an obligatory oath of allegiance to the führer, he was outflanked by an even more extremist wing which scandalized public opinion by insisting on a total break with the tradition of the Old Testament, "its Jewish morality, and its stories about cattle-merchants and pimps." At this point Hitler withdrew from the quarrel under pressure, both from diplomats who drew his attention to the misgivings of British Protestants and also from party atheists who looked askance at this strengthened alliance between state and the church. Eventually the more conformist pastors and faithful, once the initial frenzy had died down, also began to balk. In the Rhineland the Reformed Church, traditionally hostile to all centralization, set up its own authorities in opposition to the party hierarchy. In Westphalia, a longstanding stronghold of Presbyterianism and pietism, half the communities backed the Emergency League. In April 1934 this body proclaimed itself the "Confessional Church," "the legitimate evangelical Church of Germany (not 'German Church')," and in the following month its synod in Barmen issued six fundamental theses declaring the primacy of the rights of God and the church, and rejecting the totalitarian state. Meanwhile the third party had not disappeared: the three "intact" dioceses had, by dint of maneuvering, preserved their autonomy. So when an envoy from Berlin supported by the *Gauleiter* dismissed the bishop of Bavaria, he triggered a formidable reaction of *furor protestanicus*. One official report ran as follows: "The peasants of Franconia have but three ideas in their heads: the Führer, faith, and the land, and do not wish to relinquish any one of them." The comment faithfully reflected reality. In the midst of persecution, people continued to appeal to the Leader against his bad counselors, and even the leaders of the Confessional Church did not ever think of blaming the political regime.[26] The latter was thus in a position to back down without seeming to capitulate. Although its protégé Müller disappeared from the scene, a new minister for ecclesiastical affairs reduced the activities of the ministry's services to surveillance pure and simple.

Faced with the Catholic hierarchy, any attempt at division would meet with futility. It is true that a few theologians had produced acrobatic commentaries on Saint Thomas, endeavoring to show that the Holy Spirit communicated itself to men through the blood. And meanwhile the decline in *Zentrum* votes and votes for the Bavarian Popular Party in the March 1933 elections certainly revealed the fragility of a certain "Christian political culture." But this was not enough to enable the authorities to prepare a strategy of internal subversion. The cohesion of the hierarchy seemed unassailable, and many of its members, even as they applauded the national renewal, did not conceal their hostility toward National Socialist doctrine and, in particular, biological racism. Hitler then had the idea of getting around them by approaching the Vatican with the complicity of certain Centrist Church leaders. This resulted in the text of the Concordat which, with its apparent concessions on freedom of worship, associations, and its equivocal pronouncements on the latters' "purely religious functions," was only presented to the hierarchy once the negotiations were over. Some Catholics interpreted this as a success for the church, but their eyes were soon opened by the attitude of various Nazi authorities: the police continued to carry out searches in theoretically protected localities, the Hitler Youth Organization continued to debauch members of confessional movements, and the Labor Front continued to attack workers' associations. Then, when it came to deciding upon defense tactics, the bishops themselves became divided. Some counseled taking a prudent and conciliatory line to preserve what was essential, that is to say freedom of worship, even if it meant silencing the criticisms of the young among both their priests and the faithful; others considered that beliefs of a theological nature were most essential—a domain in which no compromises could be contemplated. The latter could count on many of the faithful agreeing: when Cardinal Faulhaber, archbishop of Munich, declared on Christmas Eve, "We are redeemed by the blood of Christ, not by German blood," the faithful fought over possession of the pamphlets in which his sermons were printed. But eventually the desire for unity prevailed, and the annual Fulda lecture, which all the bishops attended, took to producing only carefully balanced texts in which repeated assurances of loyalty were mixed with lists of their complaints. These were brought to the notice of the authorities and sometimes even the führer, and in 1934 serious negotiations were begun on the status of Catholic associations and mutual tolerance. But then, during the great purge, the SS assassinated Erich Klausener, who had just gathered together sixty thousand Berlin Catholics for their annual congress. So certainly a rift existed between the authorities and the church, but it was kept discreet. From his exile in Switzerland the Catholic journalist who signed himself Waldemar Gurian addressed the bishops with the following words: "We are waiting for a voice to declare that murder is murder." But like the army high command, the body of bishops remained silent.[27]

A whole body of postwar controversy exists on this subject, all the more passionate because it threatened to undermine the political role of the church in West Germany then being reconstructed. After a phase of virulent polemics even between Catholic authors, a number of publications made it possible to establish a cooler balance. It is evident that the bishops, unlike many conservatives in other walks of life, harbored no illusions concerning the fundamental nature of National Socialism, as can be seen from their doctrinal condemnations of it. At the same time however, an undeniable compatibility existed between their political aspirations and the anti-Communist and authoritarian aims the regime paraded in its early days. If they put up any resistance at all, it was "resistance in order to maintain their own autonomy, not on behalf of Right itself" (K. Sontheimer).[28]

Of all the major bodies whose indifference or hostility had so much weakened the Republican state, only the army now appeared to remain more or less intact. The top echelons in the administration, the universities, and the Catholic Church still believed that they might remain outside the political arena; business leaders continued to play their game of maintaining a balance between the forces in power, the judiciary was fighting a rearguard action; local government had already capitulated; and the Protestant Church was in ruins. *A fortiori*, the less prestigious or less organized pressure groups were not strong enough to mount an effective resistance. There is therefore little point in enumerating the delaying maneuvers, the concessions made to the masters in power, and attempts to win the support of supervisory ministers which the associations of teachers, engineers, and members of the liberal professions, etc. all used, and their either swift or delayed disappearances. Suffice it to apply to them collectively the conclusion reached by a historian of the "pseudo-liberal professions": the process of bringing them into line was not simply a measure taken by the authorities, nor was it a purely opportunistic rallying to the party; rather it resulted from a resigned acceptance of what was represented as fusion with the People's Community.[29]

Now let us turn to another elite group, the writers and artists who imparted such a brilliance to Germany during the Weimar Republic. Here it was no longer a question of group *esprit de corps* or even representative institutions, for artist's histories are largely individual stories. In politics, contrary to what is implied by the classic expression "the Weimar culture," they had seldom demonstrated any solidarity with the Republic, for the militant minorities were positioned on the outer edges and most of them preferred to remain "outsiders," as individuals.[30] But individualism was precisely what the Nazi polemicists attacked them for, along with its correlative "Jewish" internationalism, modernism, and negativism. It is important not to underestimate the impact of this vindictive propaganda: the political movement directed by veteran party stalwart Alfred Rosenberg, which ironically called itself the "League to Combat Cultural Bolshevism," boasted no fewer than 250,000 members. Major figures connected with literature, the press, and the arts were deliberately or simply in fact cut off from the public. Some regretted this, and that is one explanation for the diversity of attitudes in 1933.

The affair of the Prussian Academy of Arts provides a good illustration. When writer Heinrich Mann and artist Käthe Kollwitz launched an appeal for resistance, Minister of Science and Education Bernhard Rust dismissed them and then invited the rest of its members to make their commitment clear. Three resigned and three wrote letters refusing to commit and were excluded, along with four Jews. A few weeks later the minister specifically addressed those elected to membership at the time of Socialist governments, giving them a choice between resignation and reelection: two resigned and seven others, some in fawning terms, declined to declare their intentions: they were hoping to gain time and, indeed, for some the moment of decision did not come until 1937. All that remained was to supervise those who stayed, their new colleagues, and a new administrative office. On the day when the minister arrived to announce his list of nominees, all but two members were present.[31] In the meantime—a sign of the entanglement of responsibilities, this— Goebbels had intervened, for was it not his mission as director of propaganda to "enlighten the people" (*Volksaufklärung*)? However, Goebbels also fancied himself an arbiter of taste in painting and sculpture. Hence the ambiguous policy that he adopted which further increased the artists' confusion. He patronized an exhibition of expressionist painters, and then one of Italian futurists, a ploy designed to demonstrate the harmony that existed between fascism and the avant-garde. Rosenberg made a great fuss and Hitler as usual, refused to take sides: in his major cultural speech to congress in September 1934 he condemned first the modern "corrupters," then the "nostalgic" traditionalists. But Goebbels too was speaking with a forked tongue, for by creating the National Chamber of Culture—a huge controlling apparatus with subdivisions for every discipline and profession—he had made sure that no writer or artist could thenceforth publish or exhibit without providing proof of party loyalty. Perhaps the thinking underlying the strategy of bringing everyone into line had never been expressed so clearly: "Creators must feel within themselves the sense of a united whole."[32]

Many letters both private and public as well as personal diaries testify to the atmosphere of these uncertain months. They reflect confusion, optimism "despite everything," and more rarely indignation (for the serious opponents of the regime were already either in prison or exiled). Two examples of the latter describe two individuals of very different degrees of fame. The first was the very well known orchestra leader Wilhelm Furt-wängler, who in an open letter to Goebbels defended his Jewish colleagues threatened with dismissal. It is worth citing at the very least the following carefully balanced sentence from it: "If the struggle against Jewry is aimed principally against rootless and destructive artists who aim for effects in bad taste [*Kitsch*] and gratuitous virtuosity, etc. that is understandable . . . but when this battle is also directed against true artists, it is not in the interest of cultural life." Goebbels' reply, rejecting such casuistry, was brutal: "Art in the absolute sense, as understood by liberal democracy, ought not to exist."[33] The other example is much more modest. Jochen Klepper, a Protestant married to a Jewish woman and the author of novels and plays for radio that enjoyed a measure of success, kept a personal diary. One day, after being sacked from radio as a result of denunciations, he contemplated suicide. A few months later his new novel was well-received by official critics, as was a screenplay on the life of Frederic-William II, and he was even accepted by the Chamber of Writers. He now discovered possible "points of contact with the predominant ideology" of National Socialism. However, he could not accept its attacks against the Bible. Eventually, disgusted by the killings of 30 June 1934, he ceased to turn out to cheer on festival days and voted "no" in the next plebiscite . . .[34]

Defensive tactics were invented every day. Previously influential figures learned how to exploit any cleavages between the state and the party, and between different echelons in the party and its various branches. The more modest endeavored, by making small concessions, to win what has since been called "a small living space" or a "niche"[35] for themselves. Just how excusable this behavior was is a matter for moralists to decide, or perhaps their descendants. Historians simply note that it was founded upon the illusion that the regime was amenable and, once this illusion had become a person's way of life they clung to it as long as possible.

"CONTINUE TO FUNCTION" AT LEAST, 1934-1938

"Function or conspire" is the alternative Klaus-Jürgen Müller applies to the military,[36] and it may be extended to cover all elite groups. Conspiracy, even in the widest sense of police understanding of the term, was an option taken up by very few and only then once they had discovered that "normality" and personal dignity were incompatible. To function meant to work every day as a cog in the machine, adopting as one's supreme value efficiency, performance (*Leistung*), for this was the ideal that the system now proposed to enthusiasts and the semiconvinced alike in place of the old, outworn slogans. It meant living in a state of ambiguity. As noted by one aristocrat, enraged by his children being forced to join the Hitler Youth Organization, "we are obliged to become organically integrated in National Socialism and, consequently, in the new state, but we must never give up being ourselves, on pain of losing our dignity."[37] One might, perhaps, discount that kind of double-talk and attribute it to an archaic class in disarray. But exactly the same behavior can be found in the definitely realistic and modern circles formed by, for example, the managers of *IG Farben*. Their historian explains that each of them, confined within his own particular sphere of technical or financial responsibility, considered himself "professionally" obliged to collaborate in policies of aggression without ever envisaging the eventual consequences of such behavior.[38]

According to F. Neumann, government administrators were "neither Nazis nor anti-Nazis, just ministerial pro-bureaucrats" who left their subordinates and younger colleagues free to compromise themselves further. For a long time they believed they could preserve their autonomy by sheltering behind Frick, minister of the interior, but he was constantly losing ground to the offensives of the party chancellory, that is to say Hess and Bormann. In 1935 their last remaining Jewish and "politically unreliable" colleagues were sacked. Even Frick was obliged to prove his zeal by, for example, ordering a check to make sure that all remaining administrators had voted in the 1936 plebiscite. Political appointments multiplied. The very most these bureaucrats could do was limit speeded-up promotion to cases of particular "merit" and cling to their right to not have to join the party. In any case they had lost real power in most areas of administration: policing and propaganda had eluded them from the start; half the mayors of large towns, despite having acquired their position as a result of earlier purges, now had to step aside for ambitious younger men, some of whom were not even qualified as Doctors of Law; on top of all this, Hitler's mania for endlessly creating "plenipotentiary" posts with exceptional powers to resolve problems in the many overlapping departments created a new category of upstarts.[39]

In some cases even their supposed neutrality was transformed into complicity. The most distressing cases were those of the "apolitical" jurists who drew up the decrees necessary for the application of racial laws. In their later attempts at self-justification the same arguments crop up over and over again: the anti-Jewish policy had revealed its ultimate objectives only gradually; each step was but a tiny one that would not justify a refusal to collaborate on their part. They had done their best to outwit the authorities by inserting loophole clauses into the edicts put before them; and besides, it was surely desirable to stand in the way of the most rabid anti-Semites. In short they allowed themselves to be corrupted, meanwhile muttering regretfully about the concessions they had just made.[40] Complicity by diplomats was of a similar ilk; for they were auxiliaries in a policy that became increasingly aggressive as the years passed. It would not be an exaggeration to say that it was a collective conspiracy since in 1933 they were all, bar one, still serving in the same posts. The most senior men in the hierarchy, Secretaries of State Bernard-Wilhelm von Bulow and his subordinate Ernst von Weizsäcker, elaborated a subtle strategy "to preserve the influence of the part of the bureacracy that was still intact" and thwart that of the troublemakers in Hitler's entourage: it consisted of constant references to external constraints and the risk of shocking worldwide opinion and provoking the creation of a new coalition of hostile powers. Reassured as they were by the absence of purges in their ranks and the presence of conservative Foreign Minister Konstantin von Neurath at the head of the ministry, they in effect behaved as the agents of Hitlerian "revisionism." Some even impelled it forward: for example the telegrams of one ambassador were prone to evoke the Germany imagined by the nationalist poets of the past, "the Germany stretching from the Meuse to Memel and from the Adige to the Belt."[41]

The judiciary was more deeply nazified but at the same time produced more nonconformists: its sacrosanct professional conscience, elsewhere invoked in order to dismiss scruples, in some circumstances led to resistance of a kind. At the national level the National Socialist Association of Judges, and at the regional level the *Gauleiter*, were constantly intervening against magistrates considered too lax and pushing forward more militant candidates. Where top posts were concerned, the effect of this was radical: by 1939, 80 to 90 percent of ministry directors, procurators general, presidents of courts of appeal, and presidents and procurators of courts of the first instance were party members who had joined before 1933, in other words convinced Nazis. Special tribunals and the terrible People's Court (*Volksgerichtshof*) had for their part been composed of fanatics from the time of their creation. But judges lower down the hierarchy did not all fall into line. About half of these certainly did provide more or less formal proof of their loyalty by joining either the party or one of its less showy satellite organizations such as an assistance agency, etc. But among these halfhearted or false supporters were some brave enough to lead inquiries into concentration camp deaths, pass sentences on policemen found guilty of crimes involving torture, or pass lenient sentences on some of the accused fortunate enough to appear before them. The judicial hierarchy gave these outsiders no more than grudging support in the face of Gestapo protests and only extracted from the latter somewhat less than honorable compromises: the police would promise to not rearrest suspects acquitted by the courts . . . until once they had left the courtroom; or they would allow the presence of a doctor during "forceful interrogations,"—in gratitude the ministry in effect gave its OK to such practices.[42]

The officer corps had for a long time passionately desired the re-creation of a large army. They now got their wish, but at the cost of traditional cohesion. In the space of four years the four thousand existing officers of the *Reichswehr* were joined by eighteen thousand new comrades, some of whom had risen through the ranks, others who had served in the imperial army and then adopted an assortment of temporary careers in police barracks or civilian professions. As a result, former caste characteristics became less prominent: the proportion of officers from the nobility fell from 22 to 15 percent, that of officers' sons from 51 to 30 percent. The remainder, about half, of this massive recruitment was composed of cadets who, after one year of training, presented themselves in accordance with tradition before their colonel and submitted themselves as candidates aspiring to join the regiment's body of officers. But all this was regarded as no more than an old-fashioned formality by these young men, many of whom came from the Hitler Youth Organization or from a period of preparation within the SA. Although still not allowed to join the party, these officers were politically minded: for example, their style of relating with their men was more cordial than the icy stiffness of their seniors. This threat of subversion from below was matched by another from on high, for the two high commands dispensed contradictory advice. The territorial army (von Fritsch, Beck) dwelt upon the values of the corps—"this Order (*Stand*) of internally free individuals"— purveyed advice for the troops' moral training, and even at the height of the clash between the state and the churches, urged not only its men but also its officers not to abjure their faith. In total contrast, the leaders of the armed forces (von Blomberg, von Reichenau) threatened to get rid of officers who could not comply with the demands of the National Socialist state both outwardly and inwardly. They dismissed all half-Jewish men and recommended that officers develop links of camaraderie between all units and with corresponding echelons of the party.[43]

Nevertheless, seen from outside the army still had the air of a refuge of a kind for non-politicized young men: an annual questionnaire directed at newly qualified school-leavers on the subject of their future plans showed that on average half hoped to go to university, 15 to 20 percent to enter the army, and . . . one percent to enter the party services.[44]

The common interests shared by the various branches of business and also by the state were disrupted by the 1936 crisis, when it became necessary to choose between the needs of rearmament and those of foreign trade. The War Economy Office (Colonel Thomas) suggested overall planning for the entire economy in preparation for a long war. He was opposed by Schacht, who was extremely worried (the *Reichsbank* held only enough cash to last one week) and argued in favor of encouraging exports, which necessarily implied slowing down rearmament. Hitler, uncharacteristically, for once himself put pen to paper, rejecting the first proposal as being too unpopular and the second for running contrary to his own plan for creating "the largest army in the world." His orders were above all to speed up the production of synthetic raw materials, petrol and rubber, "regardless of cost." To this end he entrusted Goering to direct a new administrative apparatus superimposed upon the military armament offices and also upon civilian "economic groups." This was pretentiously dubbed the Four-Year Plan. Implicitly it represented a strategic U-turn: preparation for a long war with "in-depth" armament was replaced by plans for a lightning war by means of "extensive" armament.[45] The bloc formed by the business leaders was in danger of being split by this decision. The favored sector was clearly going to be the chemical industry, represented by the gigantic "Community of colorant interests" (*IG Farben*), while the steel industry reckoned it would be sacrificed. One classic thesis (by D. Petzina) insists that *IG Farben* in collaboration with the territorial army seized control of the plan's apparatus by infiltrating a go-between—one of its engineers, Carl Krauch—whom it had delegated to represent it.

The investigation carried out by the American Peter Hayes is more circumspect: according to him, once Krauch started working for the new state services he became the plan's man rather than a Farben representative; and the latter for its part did not cooperate fully in planning for the tasks proposed for it, reckoning them to be less rewarding than manufacturing more traditional chemicals. The notion of an "IG Farbenization of economic policy" thus appears to be a myth. All the same, Hayes recognizes that the firm's formidable rate of expansion (a 50 percent increase in its business affairs and a 70 percent increase in profits in three years) did stem more and more directly from the intensification of rearmament, and that it willy-nilly "became a state instrument and partner in expansionism." But some feel this conclusion underestimates the analytical abilities of the firm's directors and hints at a kind of plea in their favor when it attributes a measure of naivete to them.[46]

Petzina's more classic thesis also claims that heavy industry was the loser in this operation: despite its close connections with the territorial army's armament offices, he suggests that its share of the internal market declined in the face of Goering's rising power and that politically it withdrew into a reserve position. True, it did clash head-on with the administration of the plan when it refused to exploit the low-bearing iron ores of Lower Saxony, a move Goering responded to by setting up a vast steel-producing *Konzern* that bore his own name. The asperity of discussions between the president of United Steelworks, "a cultivated aristocrat with many international contacts," and the representative of the Hermann Goering Factories, "a brutish ideologue of proletarian origin," testifies to the rancor felt by the classic business world in the face of this rise of a new breed of politicized manager. However, this skirmish between private and state sectors did little damage to the former, which continued to profit from the orders of the territorial army and the navy, and achieved rates of growth comparable to those of the chemical industry.[47] On balance the major businessmen in chemical and metallurgical products were neither absolute masters of this new policy of self-sufficiency nor its victims, but more or less its convinced collaborators. The macroeconomic results were anyway uneven: after three years the objective of self-sufficiency was 50 percent achieved for wool and 40 percent for gasoline, but only 23 percent for iron ore and five percent for rubber. But that was not due to any go-slow tactics on the part of those in charge of these two influential industries.

Were they representative of the German business world as a whole—to the point of justifying later claims that industry was collectively responsible for the outbreak of the war? The two following examples, one of zealous collaboration, the other of reticence may help answer that question. At Daimler-Benz, manufacturers of trucks, tanks, and aircraft engines, the chairman and the majority of the board of directors had joined the party soon after its accession to power although, as the firm's official history somewhat naively remarks, "the question that remains is whether this was out of personal conviction or for the good of the business." "Aryanization" was rapid at the top, but less so at lower hierarchical levels. Contacts with ministers and even with Hitler in person, who had always been fascinated by the Mercedes trademark, were maintained by the firm's Berlin agency. "The good of the business" was certainly affected: it enjoyed favorable credit conditions, exemptions from regulations governing the siting of factories, and so on. Its level of business is said to have increased sixfold in six years.[48] At the opposite end of the spectrum, Bavarian business proprietors found many ways to show their dissatisfaction. Their association protested against the census of Jewish employers. Small and medium-sized businesses, numerous in the region, complained about government controls and quota-fixing, the forced closure of unprofitable factories, and the elimination of Jewish representatives whom they considered irreplaceable. Managers of a truck factory in Augsburg (MAN) also declared themselves against the military and in favor of maintaining a higher level of exports, as they were convinced that orders from the army would soon dry up! Businessmen had many grievances. Some sought to resolve them by joining the party. Others, despite the risks, persisted in sheltering a politically suspect staff, which proves that the behavior of at least some business proprietors was not inspired solely by a desire for profits. They also had respect for certain values.[49]

The abandonment of professional conscience in the downward slide into political submission, which many industrialists slipped into almost without realizing it, should on the other hand have seemed an impossibility within the medical community. Yet 43 percent of its members joined the party — the highest proportion in any profession — and seven to nine percent even joined the SS. What can explain this exceptional enthusiasm? In the case of the youngest of them, innovations introduced into their university training is sometimes invoked: even more than other students, they had had to attend lectures on "raciology" and take "political training" courses. Indeed, schooling of this kind had monopolized so much of their time that, at the end of their studies, examiners complained of falling standards in their professional knowledge. Among an older age group, some — for example all doctors working for medical insurance firms — were under constraint. Many were glad that unemployment was a thing of the past in consequence of the purging of their Jewish colleagues and the creation of new posts in the army and major business firms. On average their earnings recovered to pre-Depresssion levels, and the lowest paid — those with country practices — even received an extra allowance from the state. Finally, the flattering role now officially attributed to them must also be taken into consideration. The general practitioner was held up as one of the pillars of the People's Community, as it were "the leader of a biological island" (M. Kater). He was expected to encourage a healthy birthrate in his community and report all venereal and "hereditary" diseases as his contribution to eugenicism.[50] The contribution expected from psychiatrists was clearly even more direct, as they were required to select patients, or those said to be patients, to be sterilized. The massive success of this operation shows that most of them perceived no contradiction to deontology in their actions.

University teachers sometimes have short memories. After the war, professors for years continued to claim that, except for a handful of over-excited or careerist colleagues, they and their masters had continued to serve science alone. However, such smug claims were subsequently swept away by two successive waves of disrespect: first, the virulent criticisms from students during the late sixties; then a few years later the works of a new generation of young researchers into the history of scholarship, works even more embarrassing because they were better documented, for where their spiritual "grandfathers" were concerned these young people were totally liberated from the complexes that had paralyzed their "fathers."[51] Thanks to them, the history "at the top" of the universities, covering their major policy decisions, was now complemented by a history "at the bottom" of individual academic disciplines and institutes.

Higher education's official policies emerged from the interplay between three partners: the Ministry of Science and Education, Nazi student and teacher organizations, and the body of professors. The academics tried to defend themselves from the politicians by sheltering behind the ministry, which amounted to sanctioning the legitimacy of the latter's interventions. The first purges had affected on average 15 percent of university posts. Over the next five "normal" years, 45 percent again changed hands, some after lengthy battles between local professors and centralizing officials. Similarly the creation of new ideological courses was imposed from above. However, purely consultative procedures were respected, and some rectors or university heads, although now appointed rather than elected, deliberately turned a blind eye to the internal life of their respective institutions. The real reason for this—seldom perceived by the interested parties—was that the regime no longer considered secondary schools and universities suitable training grounds for the country's future elites, but instead regarded them as leftovers from an archaic system that would progressively be wiped out to make way for its own training schools for cadres. At the very most it took an interest in specialist fields relevant to public health and military defense. The effects of this indifference were compounded by a number of coincidental developments (underattended classes, military service, rising industrial unemployment) that speeded up the fall in student numbers, which decreased from sixty thousand to forty thousand in six years. The range of jobs available to them which had widened under the Republic, narrowed again, and graduates from the working and lower middle classes were increasingly replaced by the offspring of cadres and business proprietors. Paradoxically the number of female students rose, even though a restricted quota of 10 percent had been fixed for them: in 1929 they made up at least 20 percent of the student body. This tolerance by supervisory authorities indicates that, as they saw it, the male youth of the country in whom the Reich placed its hopes, was to be trained elsewhere.[52]

The professional body reacted to the blows dealt to its prestige and autonomy by a "tripartite crystallization" (K. Schwabe). A minority, mostly those working in the narrow category of "new sciences," adopted as their mission the tasks of expounding racial doctrine or justifying expansionism. Some were neither party members nor even convinced supporters of its theses. It is worth mentioning the two best known of these, whom successors have represented as non-Nazis or even secret resistants: the geopolitician Karl Haushofer, who is said to have become "very depressed" once he understood how Hitler planned to use his theory of the great expanses, and who did indeed fall under suspicion; and the jurist Carl Schmitt, who having legitimized the murders of 30 June 1934, decided to transfer his special skills to theories of international relations. At the other end of the spectrum, a few academics who opposed the regime showed their displeasure by pointedly absenting themselves from major celebratory occasions and forming small discussion groups. Although disgusted by the spectacle of the regime's daily brutalities, many were still impressed by Hitler's external successes: Friedrich Meineke, citing German writer Theodor Fontane, had indignantly exclaimed, "It is as though the great revolutionary motor was now to be found in the evil rather than in the good in human nature," yet in July 1940 the very same man expressed his delight at seeing Strasbourg, where he had once taught, returned to Germany. In between these two groups lay the apolitical majority, "a gray zone difficult to illuminate."[53] A study of a selection of university disciplines may help shed some light on this group.

In between the Nazi Walter Frank at one end of the spectrum and the resistant Gerhard Ritter at the other, how were most historians living? Reminiscing on his youth, the medievalist K. F. Werner recalls the "sheltered" atmosphere of seminars packed with students seeking a director of conscience. In these, the textbooks used were always old ones and discussion centered on foreign reviews or even certain German periodicals such as the glorious *Historische Zeitschrift*, which would compare a few articles written in the taste of the day with a more numerous collection of others of a decent scholarly standard. Does this mean that the attempt to force intellectuals to toe the line had failed? Not exactly. For "it was not uncommon for certain scholars who, as we had seen, had safeguarded their intellectual liberty, to express [in their publications] opinions by no means distant from those of the Party." One typical example is provided by the debate that raged around the figure of Charlemagne: in response to Nazi attacks on this "killer of Saxons," the boldest medievalists exalted his Roman character; but the more accommodating defended him by representing him as profoundly Germanic, thereby so to speak accepting the field of controversy dictated by their opponents. The exhumation of ancient Germanizing themes and ambiguous concepts such as *Volk*, *Reich*, and *Mitteleuropa* forces one to "recognize that the doctrines upon which acts of madness were founded were also

to be found in scholarly books written by scholarly authors."
The step from such accommodating behavior to positive contagion was thus unconsciously taken, particularly by academics
specializing in marginal areas. The Bonn school elaborated a
theory of cultural "Rhineland ethnicity" (*Volkstum*), which repudiated biologism but nevertheless could be used as a basis for
territorial claims. In Breslau the directors of "Eastern research"
(*Ostforschung*) introduced themselves using language that was
uncomfortably reminiscent of that used by anthropologists: "It
has been our good fortune to live at a time when the results of
scientific research have become an effective part of the collective
consciousness." Here too the Germans' superiority over the
Slavs was supported only by their culture, but it still served to
justify expansionism.[54] In short, these scholars allowed themselves to be used.

At the risk of sacrificing many nuances, let us pass rapidly
over the other human sciences. Their teachers all resorted to a
more or less similarly elastic defensive strategy, in some cases
not without selling out to one or another faction in power. Ger-
manists for instance were keen to promote their subject to the
rank of a "national science," "an organ of the German consciousness."[55] Ethnologists supported the idea of a "spiritual"
hierarchy of the human races.[56] Geographers were more or less
loyal heirs to Professor Friedrich Ratzel and his vision of the
great expanses.[57] Sociologists were divided, the more pragmatic
of them moving into extra-university institutes of "applied social science," the more conservative such as Hans Freyer
switching from enthusiastic support of the regime to veiled criticism.[58] Then there were the psychologists[59] and jurists,[60] already considered above, and so on. Even mathematicians
hiding Jews in their institutions told the ministry that their calculations might be of service to genetics or aeronautics.[61] Of
course this brief catalog unjustly leaves out many who adopted
conflicting positions that cost them their jobs, just as it ignores
plenty of instances of groveling that led to advantages or promotions.

However, it is worth pausing to reflect on the famous affair of the physicists. The champions of "German physics," Philippe Lenard and Johannes Stark, were by no means mediocre scientists (Lenard was awarded a Nobel prize in 1905), but both were marginal figures in the university world and obsessed with anti-Semitism. Their correspondence shows that they were not even in agreement over their so-called "German physics," a physics purged of all its Einstein-type "Jewishness." They judged it clever to rely on Nazi theorist Alfred Rosenberg, as opposed to the ministry which supported the disciples of relativity and quanta. However, they lost this battle because their opponents' strategy was even cleverer: the signatories to the famous memorandum composed by German physicist Werner Heisenberg represented themselves as defenders of the only true science, but they did not shrink from also using more utilitarian arguments based on the application of their theoretical research to the domain of armaments: this won them the combined support of industrialists, military experts, and even certain SS leaders, in comparison to Rosenberg, who carried very little weight. After the war they were represented as a political opposition, but in truth their riposte was nothing more than a maneuver in a field of lobbyists. Their success enabled them to continue their research, taking in its applications to the atomic bomb. Although they failed in the end to realize their project, it was only because they did not manage to win over the military — not because they harbored any scruples (the latter was yet another myth).[62]

All the historical works on the sciences, or rather the histories of these scientists, make free with terms such as "adaptation," "compromise," or even "complicity." But it is pointless to brandish anathema and to psychoanalyze them as individuals. The kind of flaccid loyalism that characterized their actions is above all explained by the nationalistic atmosphere in which they had learned their discipline and communicated it to others. We should bear in mind K. F. Werner's warning cited above: "Their convictions . . . resulted from a historical process, — not simply from their evident cleverness, blindness, foolishness, or malice."[63]

Once the left-wing newspapers and Jewish journalists had been eliminated, Goebbels judged it wise to tolerate a handful of semi-free dailies for a while. It is true that they had to give the names of all their collaborators to the National Press Chamber, which continued to accept a few nonaligned journalists who were, however, under permanent threat of exclusion for lack of pertinence. Instructions issued each day by the Ministry of Propaganda and many local party officials amounted to an extraordinarily meddlesome precensorship (an estimated eighty thousand to one hundred thousand directives each year!), but this made the game of hide-and-seek all the more exciting. The editors of the two traditionally democratic dailies, the *Frankfurter Zeitung* and *Berliner Tageblatt* as well as those of the conservative *Deutsche Allgemeine Zeitung*, endeavored to "continue without collaborating," as one of them put it, that is to say maneuver between the distrust of the officials and the perspicacity of readers, who prided themselves on their ability to decode allusions. References to events embarrassing to the regime were disguised as dispatches from foreign agencies (and so were expressed in indirect speech). Brief reports of miscellaneous news items were designed to leave an impression that all was not going as well as as it might be in the country. But it was above all the daily cultural chronicle that served as a refuge for what was a veritable opposition by maintaining the high stylistic and analytical qualities of first-class literary and artistic criticism. This stood in total contrast to the pages of home politics, the form and content of which were dictated by the models imposed from on high. Faithful readers were well aware of the situation as were unsympathetic readers, such as one author of a very officious treatise on the tasks facing the German science of journalism, who admitted that "even the most profound article on the racial question loses its value when (right alongside) artistic criticism passes judgment on pseudo-works alien to our race according to the same criteria as those applied to the creativity of German artists." With hindsight, the journalists who survived and their historians continue to wonder whether all those cunning ruses really undermined the regime by reinvigorating readers who were unenthusiastic or opposed it, or whether in truth they had not on the contrary helped it to maintain a facade of "normality."[64]

Whether or not they contributed to the articles mentioned above, non-Nazi writers and artists invented their own tactics for "continuing without collaborating." Who were they? First and foremost were those who refused to diffuse then-fasionable themes such as Blood and Soil and heroic history. On the other hand, anyone realistically detailing social conflicts or the favorable aspects of democracy risked being immediately banned from publishing. But in truth, the authors of the younger generation—at least those who had remained in Germany in "internal exile"—felt little nostalgia for the left-wing or the Republic. Many fell back upon classic forms and ideas. Sonnets enjoyed a new lease on life: easy to compose and recite from memory, and they also helped some prisoners get through the night. Bucolic novels free of all racist connotations were also popular: those by Ernst Wiechert ran into several editions; allegorical novels too—the most famous of this genre was E. Jünger's *The Marble Cliffs*, which readers were prone to dissect in order to detect political allusions the author had possibly never intended. At the same time, those intellectuals one might expect to retreat into their own internal worlds certainly kept up with modern productions. In the cafés of Berlin they discussed Proust, Kafka, American novelists, and even Thomas Mann, to the fury of those who kept them under surveillance and felt too much modern literature was being translated. Hitler himself in his two "cultural" speeches of 1937 called for more severity; and Wiechert among others was forced to experience the trials of life in a prison camp.[65]

"Fellow-travelers" (*Mitläufer*) who went along with the official line on art were more numerous and mostly older: musicians, theater directors, choreographers, writers, etc. Along with certain university lecturers mentioned above such as H. Freyer and C. Schmitt, they shared a common conservative or possibly "revolutionary-conservative" heritage, a common initial enthusiasm in 1933, and thereafter followed parallel paths, beginning as fellow-travelers but ending up in disgrace. Composer Richard Strauss, despite being president of the Reich's National Chamber of Music, persisted in commissioning opera librettos from Austrian "Jew" Stefan Zweig. When attacked by Rosenberg he resigned, addressing a somewhat pedestrian letter to Hitler. Furtwängler, who always conducted works by Mendelssohn or Stravinsky, carried audaciousness to the limit when he published an article praising ultramodern composer Paul Hindemith, whom Rosenberg considered typical of the "degenerate" avant-garde, and disingenuously wondered: "Where should we be if political denunciation were applied to art?" He too was obliged to resign but was then allowed to return to his conductor's podium provided he wrote a public letter of apology. The simple explanation for these two cases of leniency is that the regime could not do much about such famous figures without damaging its image. On the other hand, Goebbels did sacrifice his protégés, the expressionist painters: despite all their protestations of loyalty to "German art," they were forced out of the Prussian Academy. To keep going, theater directors in Berlin and Munich strove to meet the contradictory demands of both censors and the public by putting together programs of many different facets or alternating ideological plays, great classics, "innocent naiveties," and occasional works by banned authors under cover of a pseudonym.[66]

Between the "Browns" in power and the "Reds" (or occasionally "Blacks") who mounted some resistance there thus lay a broad gray expanse where former elites took refuge. The historical literature touching upon this subject often includes expressions suggesting alternatives: "between complicity and opposition," "between accommodation[67] and abstention" . . . or an evolving situation ("from . . . to . . ."). The first two of these expressions are used to discuss both individual dilemmas and collective maneuvers; the third describes instances of individuals coming to terms with their consciences. Up until 1938 the latter, except in a few high-profile cases, were not of a spectacular nature, but they were to occur more and more frequently as the regime became more radical.

NOTES

1. Neumann F., part 3, chap. 1.
2. Struve W., chap. 13.
3. Aretin K. O. von; Vilmann E., "Agrareliten"; Kleine G. H.
4. Mommsen H., *Beamtentum*, pp. 13 – 30.
5. Müller K. J., *Heer*, p. 37; id. "Armee."
6. Trumpp T.; Hayes P., pp. 60 – 68; Roth K. H., pp. 108 – 116.
7. Neebe R., *Silverberg*.
8. Sontheimer K., "Universitäten," p. 29; Kater M., Studentenschaft, pp. 173 – 99; Roegele O. B., p. 139; Faust A.; Ringer F. K.
9. Jarausch K. H., pp. 17 – 92; Enger J., pp. 208 – 22.
10. Klemperer V., pp. 204 – 05, and note 2 by the translator É. Guillot.
11. Cited by Baldwin P.
12. Jarausch K. H., pp. 124 – 25.
13. For the meaning of this joke, see note 29 of chap. 2, p. 98.
14. Matzerath H., *Selbstverwaltung*, pp. 61 – 97; id., "Oberbürgermeister"; Engeli C. and Ribbe W., p. 935 (Berlin); Hanko H. M., pp. 370 – 99, 428 f. (Munich); Schönhoven K., pp. 552 – 82.
15. Caplan J., pp. 178 – 80; Broszat M., *L'État hitlérien*, chap. 6 and 7; Mommsen H., *Beamtentum*, pp. 39 – 60; Silverman D. P., "Nazification"; Schönhoven K., pp. 618 – 34.
16. Gruchmann L., *Justiz*, pp. 124 – 66, 320 f., 434; id. "Bayerische Justiz."
17. Müller K. J., *Heer*, pp. 37 – 136; Salewski M., pp. 48 – 81, 361.
18. Kleine G. H.
19. A somewhat archaic term. The most exact translation would be "retinue."
20. Neebe R., "Industrie"; Schweitzer A., chap. 6 – 10; 57, doc. 150, 182 (protestations).
21. Neumann F., pp. 227 – 32, 260 f. (orig. ed.) and part 3; Schweitzer A., chap. 6-10; Barkai A., p. 124, 150 f., 209.
22. Roegele O. B., p. 139 f., 163.
23. Maier H., pp. 80 – 85; Beyerchen A. D., pp. 15 – 54; Bracher K. D., "Universität"; Fischer K.; Golczewski F.

24. The hyphen and capital letters are intended to translate the emphasis of the German term: Christianity inseparable from Germanness.

25. Scholder K., *Kirchen*, Bd. 1.

26. Id,, Bd. 2; Van Norden G., "Kirchenkampf" (Rhineland).

27. Scholder K., *Kirchen*, Bd. 1.

28. Sontheimer K., "Einleitung," *59*, pp. vii–xxi; the stages in this controversy are followed in: Hehl U. von, "Forschungsüberblick."

29. Teachers: Küppers H.; Jarausch K. H., pp. 117–30; Erger J.; lawyers and engineers: Jarausch K. H., ibid.; doctors: Kater M., *Doctors*, p. 18 f.

30. Gay P. (original subtitle *The Outsider as Insider*).

31. Richard L., p. 37, 61, 85 f.; *51*, p. 31 f.

32. Richard L., p. 61, 113; Brenner H., chap. 1.

33. Letter cited in *64*, p. 86-88.

34. Klepper J., *Unter dem Schatten*. The same distinction between what is acceptable and what is not is made in Binding R. (cited in 57, doc. 30; 72, doc. 2204 b), Ebermayer E (57, doc. 32, 113, 138) and even in Barth K, in 1933 (57, doc. 9).

35. *Nische*: as in the niche for a statue, clearly.

36. Müller K. J., "Militärelite," p. 285.

37. Cited in Kleine G. H., p. 123 f.

38. Hayes P., pp. 377–383.

39. Neumann F., p. 366 f, (orig. ed.); Mommsen H., *Beamtentum*, p. 35–91; Matzerath H., "Oberbürgermeister"; Rebentisch D., "Oberbürgermeister."

40. Mommsen H., "Verschränkung," p. 176.

41. Krüger P., pp. 190–217.

42. Gruchmann L., Justiz, pp. 207–16, 263–70, 645, 704.

43. Bald D., p. 72, 90, 115 f.; Kroener B. R., "Auf dem Weg," p. 657; Müller K. J., *Heer*, pp. 148–96; id., "Armee"; Messerschmidt M., p. 21, 80.

44. Scholz H., p. 184 ff.

45. Petzina D., *Autarkiepolitik*, p. 30 f.; see also Eichholtz D., Bd. I, chap. 1 ("softened" Marxism); Schweitzer A., chap. 11.

46. Petzina D., *Autarkiepolitik*, passim; Hayes P., pp. 125–211.

47. Mollin G., pp. 61–110.

48. Pohl H. et al., pp. 18–45 (barely an apologia); Roth K. H., pp. 165–206 (polemical but documented).

49. Blaich F., "Die bayerische Industrie." On the respective roles played by economic interests and political or moral ideas in business circles, see Turner H. A.

50. Kater M., Doctors.

51. In Germany, the director of a thesis is familiarly known as the *Doktorvater* of the candidate.

52. Maier H., pp. 86–94; Jarausch K. H., p. 157; Kleinberger A. F., p. 21; Stephenson J., *Women*, p. 130 f.

53. Schwabe K.

54. Werner K. F., *Geschichtsbild*; id., "Machtstaat," p. 345 f.; Schreiner K.; Schönwälder K., passim, in particular p. 99, 106; Philipp W., "Ostwissenschaften."

55. Lämmert E; Voszkamp W.

56. Conte E., "Völkerkunde."

57. Korinmann M., chap. 10.

58. Muller J. Z., *Hans Freyer*, pp. 254–99; id., "Enttäuschung."

59. Prinz W.
60. Grimm D.
61. Mehrtens H., "Angewandte Mathematik."
62. Beyerchen A. D., pp. 83–148, 198–207; Kleinert A.; Renneberg M.; Walker M.
63. See above, introduction, p. 4.
64. Frei N. and Schmitz J., pp. 14–96; Frei N., "Provinzzeitungen"; Nazi quotations in *51*, p. 127, and *68*, pp. 217–218.
65. Schäfer H. D., "Nicht-NS Literatur"; Richard L., p. 75; Kater M., "Jazz."
66. Corino K., "Nachwort," and various biographies in the same volume *20*; Richard L., p. 71; Euler F. (Munich); doc. on *51*, pp. 348–49 (painting); *64*, p. 85, 194 (music); *71*, pp. 47–48 (theater).
67. The term "accommodation" is used by Burrin P. in *La France à l'heure allemande, 1940–1944*, Paris, 1995 (or *Living with Defeat, 1940–1944*, London, 1966; or *France under the Germans, 1940–1944*, New York, 1966).

4—The Conquest of the Masses

B y the late twenties the party was faced with the need to diversify its electoral propaganda and attract sympathizers who were balking at open and compromising membership. To this end it created organizations specially designed to cater to different professions, age groups, sexes, etc., which made no secret of their allegiance (most of their emblems bore the initials NS), but which also sought to demonstrate to each subgroup of this *sectional* society that Nazism was also defending their particular interests. This soon produced internal rivalries and even strategic U-turns, as can be seen from among other things the alternation of at least two economic programs, one more interventionist, the other more liberal. When the party took power these organizations attached to it did not disappear but, on the contrary, expanded to absorb their former rivals. Not only did their memberships swell with an influx of those resigned to the situation and a few would-be clever opponents who thought they could set up cells within them, but each organization acquired a hierarchy and administrative apparatus of its own. Their function should have been to politicize the apolitical masses. But, in fact, the careerist attitudes of their organizers, narrow views of their bureaucracies, and pressure from members oriented their dynamism not from above to below but the other way round or, even more, horizontally, setting one against another in defense of their respective interests. These interest groups are frequently described as "lobbies."[1] Meanwhile part of their clientele retained spontaneous reactions, sometimes of dissatisfaction at the meagerness of the results obtained, sometimes even of rejection and withdrawal. The fact is that some of these organizations founded to defend archaic traditions capitulated in the face of demands made by more powerful modernizers, while others which represented youth and modernity, shocked plenty of people who remained attached to the old values. The double nature of the regime, at once retrograde and revolutionary, both nationalist and socialist, led it into dead-end situations and prevented it from achieving its objective of winning total control over society.

WERE THE MIDDLE CLASSES REWARDED?

Down with the petit-bourgeois! An anthology of the authors who turned them into scapegoats would run into many volumes. In the field of electoral sociology alone, Jürgen Falter has listed at least a dozen works, only one of which took the trouble to support its thesis with a few correlating calculations. It was in fact by dint of examining those calculations in greater detail that Falter managed to reveal the inanity of the accusation.[2] In their attempts to fathom the subconscious of Nazi supporters and militants, famous psycho-sociologists, psychoanalysts, and Marxists produced many collective portraits of salaried employees, shopkeepers, artisans, and peasants, all lumped vaguely together as the "lower middle class" (or the *Mittelstand*) who are said to have shared common fears and as a result were more attracted to Nazism than the true bourgeois or the true proletarians. With less scientific methodology, antifascist writers have also invented scornful formulae: "The petit-bourgeois masses that went mad" (Thomas Mann), "an ideology elaborated by mediocre men for the needs of mediocre men" (E. Vermeil).[3] Traces of such arrogance are even to be found in the research of recent years: following a passage of scholarly analysis, one suddenly comes upon "the petit-bourgeois mentality with its propensity for half-truths founded on folklore," or a reference to the lower middle-class origins of Hitler, said to account for his megalomania.[4]

In truth, here the critics themselves deserve to be criticized. In the introduction to his pioneering study of electoral statistics, Richard F. Hamilton points out that the three major explanatory theories on the Nazi party's success—centrist extremism, the proletarization of the middle classes, and the massification of society—were imported into the United States by left-wing German intellectuals more accustomed to manipulating concepts, particularly Marxist ones, than making rigorous calculations. Other authors, more maliciously, have detected in such theses signs of the scorn felt by intellectuals for people of little importance combined with a desire to whitewash the working class.[5] Today there exists a measure of consensus to avoid the term *Mittelstand*, borrowed in the first place from the interested parties themselves who had long had it emblazoned on their banners despite the fact that the term covers a range of widely differing categories of activities and attitudes. As early as 1932, Theodor Geiger called it a "non-concept" and proposed drawing a distinction, still regarded as classic, between the old middle classes—the artisans and small tradesmen—and the new—salaried employees and minor civil servants.[6]

When representing or caricaturing the lower middle class, sociologists of the prewar years usually had in mind only the two traditional sectors of artisans and retailers. It is true that these, or at least their spokesmen, may have encouraged that classification. They regarded themselves as the principal victims of the Great Crisis, overlooking the fact that, although their incomes had diminished, most had been spared bankruptcy. Their leaders, traditionally favorable to an organized economy, had first rallied to the corporatism of Austrian economist Othmar Spann, who was proposing a collection of structural and moral reforms that would produce a vast "popular economy." But as early as 1931–1932 the grassroots majority chose to turn toward National Socialism, for reasons to do with style, rather than on account of its program. For while the plan for a corporative state was sidelined by Hitler, what won over the artisans, especially those in rural areas and above all the small retailers, was the agitation fostered by the "Combat League for the Professional *Mittelstand*" against their major competitors, the over-clamorous salaried employees and Jews. In this context small businessmen rediscovered their role as natural leaders, the central pillars of society. In their press, anti-Semitism was conveyed by the increasingly frequent use of the epithet *völkisch*. As early as 1932, while leaders of the artisans' movement were still recommending that people vote either Nazi *or* German-National, their counterparts the retailing shopkeepers were to leave the way free for declared Nazis.[7] In a way this constituted an anticipatory falling into line. But should we on that account conclude that these small business proprietors were as much the pillars of the Nazi electorate and party as they believed themselves to be the central pillars of society as a whole? Statistics show that their contribution of Nazi votes was hardly greater than that of other socioprofessional categories, and that their over-representation among party members was short-lived.

Did they subsequently become the regime's favorites or its dupes? Were they an "indispensable *Stand*" or a "superfluous *Stand*"? Some historians take the pessimistic view that these traditional middle classes were sacrificed on the altar of big business and rearmament; others more optimistically believe that they, or at least their aristocracy, came out of it all very well. The former point out that, after a few months of agitation against the big department stores and Jewish tradesmen, the "Combat League" was taken in hand by the Labor Front and encouraged to concentrate on the tasks of civic training, which even included a measure of self-criticism: a specialist newspaper wrote as follows: "For half a century, the *Mittelstand* manifested no comprehension of the wretched plight of the workers. When it was its own turn to suffer, it adopted an egoistical policy of self-defense that was as gross as it was ridiculous." When master artisans and retailers expressed their disappointment, they were fobbed off with solemn promises that granted the former control over the juries for professional examinations and the latter assurances that their Jewish competitors would be eliminated. But the matter of examinations sparked a ridiculous guerrilla war against the Labor Front, which aimed to modernize programs —a conflict that was not settled until 1939. As for the Aryanization of the retail trade, all it succeeded in doing was to create a new form of competition which this time favored the new "Aryan" proprietors who had managed to acquire their businesses by taking advantage of extremely advantageous conditions. Even more serious, the increasing need for labor in the munitions factories caused the services responsible for finding it to draw upon the reservoir of artisans: in 1936, twenty-eight thousand workshops were "combed," in other words officially closed; and each of the next two years saw a further sixty-three thousand shut down. Among the malcontents in Bavaria, those the *SD* labeled as troublemakers, it's no surprise that small business proprietors were the most vociferous.[8]

The optimist school's response to this interpretation is that it is a mistake to consider workshop proprietors as a whole as survivors from a bygone age who became victims of the policy of modernization. In many branches a number of them had already become impressive business owners perfectly capable of serving the munitions industries as subcontractors, who made up for the larger firms' poaching of their work force by economizing production methods. They also controlled the Chambers of Trades and drew up the lists of workshops to be eliminated by labeling them (using an antiquated vocabulary that was not too hard to reconcile with technical innovations) as "wasters" (*Pfuscher*). Finally, the number of closures amounted to little more than 10 percent of the 1.5 million businesses, and that marginal decrease in the competition, combined with orders picking up, restored prosperity. Lists of subscribers to large loans show that there was an abundance of liquid cash among all these tailors of uniforms, builders of barracks, and mechanical engineers producing small parts, for example. It is true that at the same time the rate at which they were joining the party fell slightly, from 13 to 11 percent, which may be interpreted as a sign of unease; but it is an overall figure that reflects two contrary developments: an influx of well-to-do artisans, and withdrawal by those considered rejects. We are less well informed about the concrete situation of small shopkeepers. The "combing" policy hit the food sector particularly hard, but others such as tourism enjoyed a boost at the time of the Olympic Games, and all must have benefited from the restored purchasing power of consumers. Here, the high rate of party membership, 24 percent, is certainly an indication of satisfaction. It is true that workshop proprietors and shopkeepers frequently figure among the malcontents listed in reports on public opinion; but their number is negligible among the political opponents arrested by the police.[9]

These "traditional middle classes" that were benefiting at least partially from modernization stood in contrast to the "modern middle classes," whose hopes were not always fulfilled. Since the late nineteenth century industrial concentration and state interventionism had brought into being two parallel hierarchies of salaried employees and private technicians on the one hand, and public officials on the other: under the Third Reich the former numbered about four million, the latter one million, not counting permanent party officials. In the lower and middle echelons of the hierarchy, people had long been confident of upward social mobility which was guaranteed by a statute that differentiated within the private sector between employees (*Angestellten*) and workers, and within the public sector between officials with tenure (*Beamten*) and other employees. But the waves of rationalization in the twenties followed by the Great Depression, had shown them that they were in truth protected neither from unemployment nor falling incomes, which were decreasing at rates admittedly slower than those of workers but were nevertheless regarded as signs of proletarization. The major trade union organizations, still oriented to the Right, quite soon fell into the hands of the Nazis and in 1933 aligned themselves of their own accord, without any fuss. As has been noted above, these classes were slightly underrepresented in the electorate but relatively numerous in the party. It must be said that the party never encouraged their hopes by anything more than the vague perspective of a "world of workers using either their hands or their minds," which many feared heralded fusion within an enlarged working class. Only the most reactionary ever imagined they might be offered a leading role in this new social amalgam.

At first the hopes of this group seemed to be realized. Within the Labor Front their own professional organization remained autonomous, and the distinction between senior employees and their subordinates was maintained. But disillusion soon set in: not only did that administrative autonomy vanish in the space of a few months, but in 1935 slogans about the unity of workers made a reappearance as did polemics against the caste-consciousness of nonmanual workers. These were given concrete form when workers were given benefits such as paid vacations and social assistance, in the past reserved for employees only. In offices the return to fuller employment and pre-Crisis wages came about more slowly than in manufacturing workshops. Furthermore, the rationalization of administrative work increased the amount of repetitive tasks and reduced the number of posts of responsibility. In department stores the work force, for the most part women, continued to be exploited under the approving eye of the authorities, probably with a view to making job offers in industry seem more attractive. In short the old division between white-collar and blue-collar workers was tending to be eroded. Only the minority group that comprised technicians, foremen, and manufacturing engineers was able to hang on to its privileges. Once these men were appointed *führer* of a team or workshop they organized productivity campaigns, acting as the avant-garde in a new society that placed performance (*Leistung*) above all other virtues.

Yet employees remained loyal. Official and clandestine reports alike seldom mention expressed discontent among them; in fact, the Socialists reckoned they were even more Nazified than the workers. They certainly took more advantage of the excursions and cruises organized by the *KdF* (Strength through Joy) and were more prone to send their children to the party's secondary schools. Perhaps as Michael Prinz suggests they really did appreciate having acquired "new chances as consumers and for upward social mobility, at the cost of their exclusive privileges." Although that is pure hypothesis where employees in the private sector are concerned, it is an explanation that becomes far more likely for minor officials in state and para-state sectors. The former benefited from the creation of posts in new ministries such as propaganda and aviation; the latter benefited even more in the offices of the party, the Labor Front, the Hitler Youth Organization, etc., once the incompetence of the "veterans" lodged there en masse had been recognized along with the need to replace them. People employed in these offices even had the right to special advantages such as immunity to the wage freeze—not to mention possibilities to acquire other resources of a more unmentionable nature. Were their aspirations toward upward social mobility as well-satisfied as their material appetites? *De facto* if not *de jure* advancement to higher echelons was always blocked; in both state administrations and even party services the barrier represented by diplomas, which coincided with a social frontier, remained more or less impassable. Although certain statistics do indicate more rapid social mobility in the twenties and the thirties, they probably relate only to promotion from the lowest to the middle ranks. However at the time, when these figures were not known, people were easily affected by all the egalitarian slogans: a small tradesman financially ruined and a student seemingly destined for joblessness, who were now provided with employment and even a uniform, could believe in their success and hope for an even better future for their sons. The myth of "Hitler's social revolution" entered into their minds if not into reality and so affected their modes of behavior in real life.[10]

Throughout the so-called stable years of the Weimar Republic the rural world had been in a state of constant unrest, with the cultivators of small and medium-sized plots of land among the most violent. Bad harvests alternating with plummeting prices, heavy taxation, and wage costs had progressively aggravated their wretchedness, even if the high cost of credit, the principal scourge of large landowners in the East, affected them less. Recognizing the impotence of their professional associations, they had in some regions decided to "help themselves," for example by refusing to pay their taxes. In Schleswig-Holstein, an old tradition of hostility toward the state, Socialists, Jews, and modern civilization in general persisted in the shape of the "Rural People's Movement," which held giant meetings in 1928 and had veered toward terrorism. But this seemingly spontaneous and apolitical movement was secretly organized by former members of vigilante groups that later went over to Nazism. Elsewhere, politicization proceeded amid a certain confusion. In 1929 an attempt to set up a Green Front, which was already calling for a nonparliamentary government, made no headway. Whereas the "Rural League" dominated by the large landowners of the east was split between the national Right, a number of small parties, and National Socialism, the "Peasant Associations" of the west and south for a while managed to preserve a semblance of unity. Organized politically by the *Zentrum*, spiritually by the Catholic clergy, and paramilitarily—in Bavaria at least—by militias, they were relying on Brüning to restore a corporative society in which peasants would hold pride of place. However, they by no means wielded the monopoly to which they aspired: while their aristocratic leaders were, like their counterparts in the east, shifting toward the extreme Right, the young peasants were flocking to Nazi meetings, attracted there by a festive air that was a welcome change from the routine of their elders. These defectors were sufficiently numerous to assure the party of its first electoral successes in Protestant Franconia and even in Catholic Swabia. An even greater number were eventually to swing over to Nazism in March 1933, deserting the *Zentrum* and its satellite, the party of the Bavarian People. Two very different local monographs, the one on a poverty-stricken area in the Franconian Jura, the other on a village in Hesse dominated by well-to-do peasants, show that the business of bringing people "into line" was not problem-free. In the former, members of the Bavarian militia had to be arrested; in the latter SA commandos, brought in from the surrounding neighborhood were pressed into use. However, by the end of the year, general behavior in the countryside could arguably be said to reflect a "passive loyalty."[11]

The misunderstanding that then arose between the regime and the rural middle class stemmed from the juxtaposition of an agrarian ideology that exalted the virtues of the peasant and an agricultural policy that deprived him of all initiative. Walther Darré, who simultaneously exercised the functions of head of the peasants and minister of agriculture, was able to implement his program without delay. A large number of medium-sized farms were to be promoted to the status of "hereditary properties": the head of such a farm would be given full powers over the work contracts of his laborers, and the land would be inalienable, to be passed on only to the eldest son. The operation was designed to create peasant lineages that would be masters of their own fates in the same way as the *Junker* dynasties were. At national level the "Corporation for Food Supplies," a huge apparatus that integrated agriculture, trade, and the processing industry, was responsible for orienting types of production, fixing minimum delivery quotas, and setting prices. The literature devoted to promoting it described this as crowning the aspirations toward corporatism, that old agrarian dream. And in the years that followed, official optimism was indeed supported by eloquent statistics: the privileged 700,000 "hereditary farms" represented one-fifth of the total number and one-third of the usable agricultural surface area; in the remaining farms mechanization was speeded up, a massive use of fertilizers was introduced, average incomes rose (more rapidly in some years than others), and indebtedness was eradicated. For the nation as a whole, all this indicated success in the battle for self-sufficiency.

However, those principally involved were considerably less well-satisfied than the economists. Because the "hereditary farms" were inalienable, their heads no longer had the right to borrow. The danger of a blockage in investments was avoided by public grants, but these then gave rise to jealousy on the part of less fortunate neighbors. The price policy, intended to be harmonious, instead reinforced inequalities. In an attempt to reduce imports it favored cereals at the expense of cattle raising, which was practiced in the main by small-scale peasants. The two-tier prices for cereals (minimal for the obligatory quotas, higher for produce over and above them) brought further rewards for the large-scale cultivators. The manic interventionism of the bureaucrats exasperated the entire rural community: farmers lost the right to process their own products and choose their buyers; if they remained loyal to their traditional Jewish clients, as happened in many regions, even those reputed to be anti-Semitic, the police intervened. The problem of labor was even more serious: hundreds of thousands of agricultural laborers and farmers' sons were drawn by the rising wages in industry, and nothing — not even official prohibitions — could stem the rural exodus. Young boys and girls sent out from the cities in their stead by the Labor Service were understandably unequal to the task, and the weight of the extra work fell upon the peasant women left behind. What of all the promises of real corporatism, to ensure collective stability and at the same time liberate individual initiative?

By 1934 the authorities were already becoming alarmed by the first manifestations of indiscipline: failure to deliver the obligatory quotas, black marketeering, and so on. In the Bavarian countryside large numbers of electors abstained from voting in the August plebiscite. Propaganda efforts, inadequately sustained by the "peasant leaders" of the villages and the mayors, only 10 percent of whom were committed Nazis, were largely ineffective and besides were then canceled out by the launching of the campaign against the churches. In 1935–36 in the Trier region, the same lassitude was evident along with the same disinclination to break off commercial relations with the Jews, the same irritation at the quotas, the fund raising, the meetings . . . Mutters of "All this organization will be the death of us" were reaching the ears of the sub-prefects. However, once again it would be mistaken to assimilate this dissatisfaction into political opposition. Like their rival purveyors of bitter jokes among the urban middle classes, the peasants were certainly not absent from the courts responsible for stamping out "ill-will"; however, they were rarely to be found among those accused of genuine resistance. All the same they were fed up with politics in every form, even when it claimed to be integrating them into the People's Community. On the eve of the war, the *SD* and the Ministry of Propaganda, synthesizing all the regional reports, summed up public opinion in the countryside in two words: revolt and resignation. Some peasants did still belong to the party, about eight percent on average, but now the only high rates of membership related to the holders of "hereditary farms" and village leaders.[12]

The unity of the *Mittelstand* had never been anything more than a rallying cry to disguise the contradictions that divided city dwellers from country folk, producers from middlemen, and independent workers from wage earners. Satellite organizations attached to the National Socialist movement were therefore assigned the task of harmonizing all these diverse groups; and when these groups persisted in playing their lobbying games, a series of measures integrated them forcibly either into the Labor Front or the Food Supply Corporation. But the clash of interests was still not dispelled. To make matters worse, the need to rearm and achieve self-sufficiency encouraged the rise of small aristocracies in all sectors. These were allowed a modicum of autonomy and the profits that stemmed from it in return for enforcing the general discipline, like so many mini-*führers*. They were the only people in a position in which it was possible to believe in the open society they had been promised, and they manifested their gratitude through a variety of signs of loyalty. Far from recovering the supposed equilibrium of former times, the middle classes and each of their particular components were subjected to a process of differentiation.

A DISINTEGRATING WORKING CLASS

The expression *Arbeiterklasse*, often used, even unavoidable, in left-wing texts, calls for a few explanatory comments—in the first place because the word *Arbeiter* covered a far greater collection of people than just the workers in heavy industry. In 1933, 17 percent of those designated by the term by statisticians were working in agriculture, 17 percent in service industries, and 27 percent in businesses employing fewer than ten wage earners.[13] The word *Klasse* for its part seems to imply a homogeneous collective consciousness; yet quite apart from the opposition between Socialists and Communists, electoral studies have shown that the three sectors on the periphery of the working class—agriculture, service industries, and artisan circles—had been more deeply affected by the Nazi party than the very core of the working classes, the industrial proletariat.[14] The party, which only referred to the concept of *Klasse* in order to reject it, on the contrary made abundant use of the concept of *Arbeiter*, the capital letter of which appeared in its acronym *NS-DAP*, and even extended its meaning virtually *ad infinitum* by having it include "those who work with their minds" as well as "those who work with their hands." Not that this meant that it had given up the idea of conquering even the citadels of the proletariat. Hitler was haunted by memories of November 1918 when, as he saw it, the military collapse had been provoked by the betrayal of the masses led by their Red leaders. In his view, before the greatness of Germany could be restored it would be necessary to use terror to destroy the revolutionary cadres and integrate the grass roots of the working class into the People's Community. Many of both the initiatives and retreats of the regime can be explained by the anxious attention that it paid to working-class public opinion.[15]

The winter and spring of 1933 provide examples of the combined two approaches the party adopted: intimidation and seduction. So long as the SA concentrated on running to ground the militants in the left-wing parties, the trade union leaders believed they might be left alone. In the elections of March and April, they were still able to put forward candidates for the business committees and demonstrate that they retained the confidence of their grass roots supporters. Naively, they even encouraged the latter to take part in the great demonstrations of 1 May, . . . only to find on the very next day that their local headquarters had been seized, their organizations dissolved, and that they themselves were under threat of arrest. This was a triumph for the radical wing of the Nazi movement, the "National Socialist Organization of Business Cells" (*NSBO*).

This group was typical of the excrescences produced by the Nazi apparatus that were constantly threatening to elude the control of their initiators. At this point *NSBO* membership was still weak—fewer than four hundred thousand—and extremely heterogeneous: rootless youths, old conservative workers, Berlin tramworkers . . . ; and furthermore it was not particularly loyal: three hundred thousand members had already defected. It was strongest in regions where the party was relatively weak, but its methods of recruitment were similar, involving the defamation of opponents overlaid by inflated demagogic rhetoric. The apparent success of 2 May presented it with a seemingly impossible task, that of absorbing one million members of the now dissolved trade unions. Its leaders imagined that an ingenious way to integrate this mass of people would be to relaunch the class struggle within individual firms, including some whose bosses belonged to the Nazi party: the organization's newspaper attacked "the mandarins and the barons." The bosses reacted vigorously. The director of one Augsburg factory growled, "Now you are coming to us with the same nonsense as those other gentlemen [the former trade unionists]. If you do not trust the management, we shall have to prepare for battle." Party leaders were also alarmed by this unrest, which they attributed to an infiltration of the *NSBO* by disguised "Reds" whose vocabulary was strangely similar to that of the SA revolutionaries. The "law to impose order upon labor relations" (20 January

1934) brought this period of anarchy to an end. The mission of the new curators of labor was to make sure that conflicts of interest did not degenerate into class struggles and at the same time to respect the prerogatives of the business bosses who were to be the only *führer*: the work force (*Belegschaft*) was to become an entourage of faithful subjects (*Gefolgschaft*). In the meantime the *NSBO* had been subordinated to the Labor Front, and no more was heard of it.[16]

It was meanwhile generally understood that the regime would be judged first and foremost by its employment policy. The fortuitous turnaround of the second semester of 1932 had brought the total number of unemployed officially down to five million, really to 6.7 million. But by February the customary winter layoffs and political uncertainties had caused those figures to rise to six million and 7.8 million. By the spring the first government measures and a return of optimism among employers had brought about no more than the beginnings of a fall in those figures, which speeded up somewhat in the course of the rest of the year and then, following a new slump in the following winter, led to the triumphant announcement in June 1934 that only 2.5 million people were still jobless. As well as celebrating his victory over the SA, Hitler could thus congratulate himself on his victory over economic difficulties.[17] No doubt the official figures had been deflated by the elimination of temporary—in effect, part-time workers—and by the four hundred thousand young men required for Labor Service,[18] but evidence shows that at this date the two curves, the official and the real, truly were tending to converge. Skeptics also invoke the party's campaign for women to return to their housewifely duties, which probably greatly diminished the number of unemployed women. It is true that the radical wing of the party was stigmatizing households with two salaries, and the state was dismissing female officials, encouraging the employment of domestic helpers, and insisting that in order to qualify for marriage loans women should give up their jobs. But these measures only affected a few hundred thou-

sand women; and when employers discovered that their posts in
workshops and offices could not be taken over by unemployed
men, the female work force eventually crept back up from 4.6
million to five million in the whole group of branches paying
social insurance. It was, however, a slower increase than that of
the male workforce.[19]

We therefore need to seek more convincing explanations for
the so-called employment miracle. Over those two years expen-
diture on munitions still represented only a minute percentage
of the national product and played no more than the role of an
extra stimulant. The voluntary or enforced employment of jobless SA sometimes led to spectacular results (in Saxony, a 96
percent success rate in one year), but it created just as many new
unemployed as jobs. The first "Reinhart Plan," copied from
projects elaborated by previous governments, mobilized the unemployed for agricultural labor and motor road construction;
and the Second Plan put them to work on the construction of
homes. The efficacy of these plans was very uneven. In East
Prussia, where the *Gauleiter* was on good terms with Goering, it
was remarkable; in Berlin it was poor, for there was no coordination with the surrounding districts; in Bavaria the plans
achieved no results at all, as business proprietors even refused to
accept the public credits linked with taking on the unemployed,
and besides, the Ministry of Finance, fearing deficits and inflation, was reining back as hard as it could. The most likely explanation for the overall success is one that takes account of all these
factors: the official programs, the follow-up to the autonomous
fortuitous improvement in the situation, and the gamble taken
by certain employers who foresaw orders for munitions coming
their way. But this return to fuller employment was accompanied by tough conditions: at Daimler-Benz young workers had
to submit to being investigated by the Hitler Youth Organization; in the principal *Konzern* of Krupp, Siemens, and *IG Farben*, and in coal mines, there were longer working hours and
wage cuts, and most of the workers' pay depended on piecework. National statistics clearly do not reflect the evolution of

the increasingly divergent incomes of individuals; however, they do indicate that in 1934 the average weekly wage was still one-quarter lower than that of 1929, although in the meantime the cost of living had also sunk lower than ever before.[20]

The morale of the workers was given a chance of expression by elections to "confidential business councils" which took place in 1934 and 1935. It has long been accepted that these constituted a setback for the new regime, which then drew its own conclusions and decided to put a stop to them. However, further examination of the archives of the firms in question suggests a less clear-cut situation. Participation in the elections was massive but may have been forced. But many electors made use of the only liberty left to them by voting for nobody or crossing particular names off the voting list. At Krupp's two years running, 20 percent of the voting slips were either left blank or entirely crossed out, and 10 percent had the names at the top of the lists, that is to say those of the orthodox Nazis, crossed out. Conversely, the most favored candidates were members of the *NSBO* who had advertised their anti-capitalist opinions. In the chemical industry sector, at Hoechst's, there were very few blank voting slips, a fact that the Socialists' secret reports attributed to the terror that reigned on the shop floor; but at Bayer's, the name heading the list obtained far fewer votes than those following it. Overall, in the large firms in the Cologne region, participation in these 1934 elections was high, and discrimination among the candidates was even greater: 35 percent of the lists were partially crossed out; branches most vulnerable to contingent conditions such as textiles and food products, and those where the most workers had been laid off and recovery had been slowest produced the most nonconformist votes. In the following year the Labor Front prepared its campaign more thoroughly, eliminating the more incompetent candidates, but the reaction of the electors was almost identical. The authorities pretended to be delighted by the interest shown in their new institutions, and Socialist reports noted nothing but a general indifference, while the Gestapo on the contrary detected proof of general discontent. What should we believe? Specialists reckon that there was no political vote involved here, rather a genuine choice of representatives capable of standing up to management on day-to-day issues. And in truth, in some large firms, the workers' newly elected representatives did take their task seriously and passed on many complaints about the accelerated rhythm of work. It may have been precisely the fear of seeing the rise of a new kind of trade unionism that prompted the Labor Front, at the suggestion of the bosses, to suspend the whole operation.[21] The workers' little window of autonomy was slammed shut.

The acceleration of rearmament in 1936 caused those responsible for employment policies to make significant changes in the official slogans: the phrase "creating work" was replaced by "mobilization for work." By opting for a kind of "extended rearmament," that is to say by developing a number of key sectors as a matter of priority (chemical, steel production, electricity, and mechanical engineering), the regime was hoping to avoid the complications of "in-depth rearmament," in other words an economy planned right across the board together with all the sacrifices this would demand from the population. But at a macroeconomic level that priority caused a profound imbalance between the various sectors: in the space of three years the index of production goods, armaments included, leapt from 114 to 148 (1928=100), whereas that of consumer goods, civilian buildings included, lagged behind, falling from 108 to 98.[22] It was furthermore discovered that the labor available was not indefinitely extendable: by the summer of 1937 full employment had been achieved for the first time in living memory (only five hundred thousand jobless remained).[23] In the daily life of the workers the battle for employment gave way to the battle for productivity, and the population as a whole was subjected to a kind of "hidden austerity": the market in foodstuffs was increasingly limited to native products, fewer homes were being built, and small businesses folded.[24] Affected by the new constraints and yet sometimes encouraged by the new perspectives, the workers reacted now with demonstrations of discontent, now by exploiting such margins of negotiation as chanced to present themselves.

The saturation of the labor market led to an even more rapid increase in the female labor force than in the male one. The subordinate jobs in which traditionally young women used to stop work when they married or produced their first child were now generally taken by women who continued to work throughout their lives (no doubt the inadequacy of their family budgets had something to with this). They also now filled posts hitherto exclusively masculine, thanks to the introduction of production line work. As a result the lowest paid sectors such as agriculture, domestic service, and the textile industry were deserted and found themselves undermanned. The official ideology was obliged to adapt to the new situation. The leading women's journal, *Frauenwarte*, which in early 1935 had still been urging women to remain at home, was three months later stressing the nobility of professions such as typists and nurses, and the following year announced that women were "needed in every domain." The *führerin* of German women, Gertrud Scholz-Klink, addressing an audience of business proprietors, roundly repudiated the old anti-feminism: "It is unthinkable that women should continue to be considered in that archaic fashion, . . . that the best thing to do is to keep them shut up at home, in the kitchen or the nursery." The Labor Front went so far as to call for equal pay for the two sexes, an idea that the ministerial offices hastened immediately to block, pointing out the "unfortunate psychological consequences" that would result. But new tasks brought new rules: the women workers, like the men, had to submit to strict discipline and docilely accept advice on hygiene or even sterilization that their firm's social assistants offered them. In order to retain the services of this unstable labor force, management for its part, at least in the larger firms, offered maternity leave, crêches (day care), and so on, but only—of course—for "healthy" mothers and families.

This certainly represented improvement compared to previous conditions for women working in factories.[25]

Propaganda trotted out impressive sets of figures to show that workers were benefiting greatly from the relaunched economy. Overall, with no category distinctions, the hourly wage was said to have increased 11 percent between 1935 and 1939 and the weekly wage by 17 percent, whereas the cost of living had remained virtually stable with a mere 1.4 percent increase. In truth, in order to calculate the true average wage, it would have been necessary to deduct taxes, subscriptions, and quasi-obligatory contributions to public fund raising, all of which would probably amount to 18 percent, and to use a more realistic price index, say four percent higher. The increase arrived at would then have been no more than seven percent for the real weekly wage, which would bring the national average for 1939 down to roughly the pre-Great Crisis level. Above all, it would have been necessary to evaluate the figures region by region, branch by branch, and according to qualification levels. Wages were higher in the West than in the East and in the munitions industry than in textiles. The improvement over four years was great (17 percent) for professional workers and for males with special skills, considerable (11–12 percent) for unskilled men and professional women, slighter (eight percent) for unskilled women. Including bonuses and overtime a Siemens electrician could each month earn as much as a salaried employee, something that had never been possible in the past. But a steelworker at Krupp's was earning barely as much as before the Crisis, and even he would be envied by a coal miner who earned far less. This last example, taken from a sector that was, after all, of capital importance for rearmament, proves that there was hardly any national wage regulation and that decisions relating to wages were simply made by individual firms or at the very most by sectorial organizations. So it seems somewhat arbitrary to attribute to state authorities—as some authors do—a Machiavellian desire to differentiate between the respective wage packets of different categories of workers as much as possible in order to weaken working-class solidarity.[26]

The urgency of orders and the shortage of manpower caused business management to embark on further rationalization of production methods. There were two ways to do this: either with technical innovations accompanied by a measure of consensus, or simply by an intensification of work accompanied by threats. The first of these two methods was adopted by *IG Farben* in the chemicals industry, by Siemens-Halske in electricity, and by Krupp in mechanical engineering. Contrary to one classic thesis it did not lead to any massive disqualification of the production staff: below the small elite of maintenance workers with four years of training behind them a new category of supervisors was developing, still classified as specialized workers but whose training was completed in two years and who benefited from special promotion conditions. In contrast, coal mining underwent hardly any modernization and depended mainly on longer working hours in order to meet production objectives. Meanwhile, relations of pure force reigned in all kinds of firms from the most archaic to the most modern. On the motor road construction sites and those of the Labor Service, the militarization of the language adopted betrayed the incompetence of the cadres: disguised under the label "impulsion to work," bullying compounded by inadequate lodging, poor food, and lax safety precautions created a detestable atmosphere. At Daimler-Benz, despite the firm's great prosperity and its position at the cutting edge of technological progress, customary rewards such as extra pay for piecework and social advantages seemed insufficient to discipline the staff. So management created a whole policing apparatus, operated by heads of sections and cells, and social assistants responsible for surveillance.[27]

"Productivity" and "performance" were also key slogans for the Labor Front, along with "workers' assistance." The Labor Front employed forty-five thousand permanent staff and its budget was three times that of the party. But its director R. Ley, perpetually hesitating between keeping his workers under control and defending their interests, managed to satisfy neither the business bosses nor the workers. His representatives to the various firms, who were kept out of wage negotiations, tried to pass on complaints about the organization of labor and tone down the punishments for undisciplined behavior. But for the most part these skirmishes achieved nothing, and there was a hollow ring to all the grandiose pronouncements on unity in the production battle. For example, how was it possible to believe that "its truly socialist task was to keep all those who work in good health," when the stated objective was to reduce days of absence from twenty-two to eight per year, and the firm's doctors declared even semi-invalids fit for work? Even Social Protection cynically advertised its policy as "health interventionism."[28]

The perpetual balancing act between appeals to individual initiative and reminders of collective discipline is neatly illustrated by the uneven success of the "National Professional Championships" organized annually by the Labor Front. The individual competitions or "Labor Olympics," combined professional and sporting contests and eventually attracted millions of competitors. But competition to win "the model National Socialist Business" award made but a limited impact. Competing firms had to prove they were taking part in the battle for armaments and improving productivity as well as their social good works. The panels of judges also took into account the political loyalty of the firms' respective directors. As a result the only firms to show an interest were small businesses hoping to land a few public orders. The larger firms did not deign to compete, perceiving no interest in obtaining official recognition of the paternalistic social policies they had long been practicing anyway at no inconsiderable cost.[29]

The Front proved more successful in its campaign for the "Beauty of Labor": if workers were to take pride in the nobility of their tasks, they had to be given an agreeable environment. On this score the bosses did satisfy expectations: by 1935, twelve thousand firms had become associated with the movement, and by 1939 it included sixty-seven thousand of them. No doubt they were attracted by the fiscal advantages and also by a skillful propaganda campaign that dangled before their eyes the gains to be made in productivity. But they were also responsive to the aesthetic theories that inspired the campaign. The Central Organization Office directed by Speer was run on modern lines inherited from the functionalism of the twenties. It encouraged not only decorative details to enhance the environment but also better lighting and acoustics on the shop floor, a rational arrangement of offices, and construction of sports facilities and playgrounds on any surrounding open land available. For new buildings it favored projects reminiscent of the Bauhaus style, to the fury of Rosenberg and the delight of the business bosses who had long been won over by architectural rationalism. The improvements did to a certain extent result in better working conditions for the work force, even if the rather cold modernistic settings were rather a shock at first.[30]

The Front's leisure service was called "Strength through Joy" (*Kraft durch Freude, KdF*). Even rest periods were supposed to be devoted to furthering the greatness of the nation. However, that was not quite how the beneficiaries saw it. Even before the paid week-long holiday became general, in 1937 they were flocking in their millions on weekend excursions and to sports clubs. The Front thought this enthusiam signaled reconciliation between the social classes. But Socialist observers who wrote reports on the situation were alarmed: "They [the beguiled workers] refuse to see that what is represented to them as pleasure and joy is ordered and directed by Fascism just as are the tax-forms that they will recieve the next day." Both the optimism and fears were ill-founded. Members of the *KdF* were quite simply behaving as consumer-clients. The sporting associations tolerated reunions for former members of left-wing movements ("You hardly ever hear a 'Heil Hitler!'"). The excursions satisfied a longing for fresh air on the part of many who had never before ventured outside their home town. But the cost of such outings, although modest, had to be taken into account: workers never made up more than 40 percent of those who took part in the three-day-long trips or more than 17 percent of the passengers on the famous sea cruises which caused the press to go into such raptures. Even the employees and civil servants who made up the majority of passengers looked to foreign observers more like tourists than militants. "What is needed is more Strength and less Joy," was Goering's ironic comment.[31]

If observers of all kinds resorted to ambiguous formulae to describe worker morale, that was because there was no trace of collective reactions. One demonstration calling for better conditions would be mounted by professionals who knew that they were indispensable, another by groups of exploited workers with very little hope of success. On top of this the agents of the authorities in power tended to exaggerate the scale of such incidents so as to make their own mission seem more important, while Socialists working secretly would denounce the passivity of their comrades, the better to excuse their own impotence. Small wonder historians have since been divided as to how to interpret all the documentation.

A tour of the various regions turns up countless examples of contradictions. In the eastern provinces the policy of decentralizing rearmament sparked off migrations that were catastrophic for the older industries. Miners in Silesia and construction workers in Saxony and Thuringen flocked to the huge new factories of *IG Farben* in Leuna and the Hermann Goering complex in Salzgitter, while their comrades who had remained behind put in claims for equivalent advantages. In the metallurgy industry of the Saar, an ill-conceived rule that blocked interfirm mobility resulted in lower production across the board. On the motor road construction sites, indiscipline could only be brought under control by the police, who then sent the supposed ringleaders off to "camps of education for work" that were almost as harsh if not as deadly as the concentration camps. In the major Nuremberg factories (MAN, Zündapp, Siemens), the extension of daily working hours was followed by a leap in absenteeism, which could only be reversed by an offer of new advantages. Messerschmitt's in Augsburg was proud to have been awarded the title "Model National Socialist business"; wages there were high but spying was rife. In the textile and construction industries throughout Bavaria in contrast, wages remained low and there were even periods of technical unemployment; the poorest families would then be sent off to draw Winter Benefits, which humiliated them, while a number of agitators would be dispatched to particularly unpleasant work sites along the "Eastern Wall" which fortified the frontier. The Special Court in Munich was overworked: the number of those accused of "malevolent criticism" trebled between 1936 and 1938. The exhausted miners in the Ruhr reacted by adopting the old "go slow" method; the Labor Front accused the leaders of behaving as though they were back in the Weimar Republic, and the *Gauleiter* intervened—to no avail: the business bosses, despite being short sixty thousand men, agreed to raise wages only if they received a state grant to do so. Could these be called strikes? In high places that word was never breathed, but punishment for the guilty was considered advisable. However, on the day when 262 Opel workers in Frankfurt openly stopped work it became impossible to continue to deny reality. In the general panic that followed the only solution found was to create a crisis cellule composed of both Gestapo and Labor Front agents . . . along with a special statistics service. To this we owe the few relevant figures available: 179 strikes in 1936, seventy-two in 1937, seldom lasting more than one day, and seldom involving more than one hundred strikers, one third of whom were said to be politically inspired.[32]

But "should it be left to the Gestapo to decide whether or not a strike could be defined as Resistance (*Widerstand*), for that would surely provoke great unease" (G. Morsch). It is a question that has provoked a vast debate among historians, a debate more discreet but also more instructive than many others the public press has seized upon. It was opened in 1975 by English historian Tim Mason who, using documentation mostly of an official nature, drew attention to the very numerous manifestations of working-class discontent. Without confusing these workers with a veritable political resistance, he detected growing tension between 1936 and 1938 and something like a return to class warfare. Since then half a dozen researchers have investigated the matter in more depth by consulting the Socialists' reports and a number of both public and private archives, and all have reached conclusions that are convergent (albeit expressed in different terms): all of them reject the legend of a workers' resistance. In the meantime the initiator of the controversy, with rare honesty, had rallied to the general consensus, acknowledging that he had exaggerated the importance of those acts of indiscipline and had underestimated the regime's capacity for integration.[33]

On the basis of this ongoing research the behavior patterns of the workers may be divided into three kinds. Former trade union and left-wing militants exemplify the first. Having avoided arrest or already suffered it for varying lengths of time, they were taking fewer risks than before. Now skeptical about the chances of a rapid collapse of the regime, they were exploiting the discontent of their comrades rather than arousing it by means of propaganda. Some of them, qualified professionals well respected on the shop floor, had managed to retain their posts, where they dispensed information and advice. At the time of the most recent illusions, a few under pressure from their workmates had even allowed themselves to be elected to "confidential councils." Other members of this professional elite proved more susceptible to the attractions on offer. Conscious of being indispensable to the work of maintenance and the supervisory offices, they used their strategic position to obtain bonuses and other advantages. They did not necessarily approve wholeheartedly of Nazi ideology, but did at least relish the exaltation of manual labor and technical achievement. As patriots they cheered the launching of a new aircraft, tank, or submarine engine, all symbols of work well done, "German work." A minority among this minority, promoted to the category of technicians, were led to believe that the regime had done away with social barriers and in their wake a few skilled workers in their turn became professionals. The majority finally maintained an ambiguous attitude, now keeping their distance from the official world, now making the most of the advantages that it offered. Doctrinal training sessions organized by the Labor Front bored them, but they were more willing to attend the firm's parties, at which all levels of the hierarchy were supposed to meet. They used the Hitlerian salute as little as possible, boycotted informers, teased the over-exalted partisans, and sometimes even refused to contribute anything to the fund raising attempts of the Winter Assistance. But they admired Hitler for the successes of his foreign policy. They ranked lower in their employers' esteem than the two categories mentioned above, but all the same they did as well as they could for themselves by dint of cunning in the manner of the "Good Soldier Schweik," sucking up to their immediate superiors, taking days off, or agreeing with a group of friends to slacken their output. In short, if they resisted at all it was not in order to bring down the regime, but simply to limit the Nazification in their daily lives. The expression "refractory behavior" (*Resistenz*) introduced by M. Broszat might be applied to them, although some historians upon whose research the present comments are based avoid it. Alf Lüdtke for his part prefers to detect in their behavior the traditional "desire for autonomy" (*Eigensinn*), that secular workers' stubbornness that always had prevented the state and bosses alike from altogether controlling life on the shop floor. All the same, the increase in acts of defiance, deliberate or otherwise, alcoholism, sickness, and accidents at work all suggest that they were now failing to preserve that equilibrium.

Curiously enough, postwar inquiries of oral history revealed that the collective workers' memory did not retain too bad an image of those years, and contrasted them to both the misfortunes of the earlier Crisis and also those of the 1939–48 decade. However, those interviewed did seem to remember that their center of interest shifted from the factory to the family home and neighborhood, which offered more sheltered refuges from the pervasiveness of the political world.[34] One particular form of retreat into the private sphere was that adopted by Catholic workers, who were particularly numerous in the Rhineland and Westphalia and in southern Germany. Although never as large as the great Socialist battalions, by the early thirties their church associations had already attracted several hundred thousand members. Deprived of their secular arms by the dissolution of parties and trade unions sympathetic to them, they had obeyed the rules of the Concordat, which forbade them any incursion into the political domain and, in order to avert suspicion, had even sacrificed their traditional autonomy and placed themselves under the supervision of the hierarchy. But all to no avail: the police persisted in regarding them as an avatar of the political movements that had been dissolved, while the Labor Front was so convinced that they were its dangerous rivals that it went so far as to prohibit double membership. This caused a few dropouts, but only about 10 percent. And the loyalty of the members of these church associations continued to manifest itself through massive attendances at pilgrimages, in which they could melt into "the Christian people" as a whole. Should this be seen as something more than a reaction of protest, as a political opposition? There is no evidence to prove that it should, if—that is—we again reject the categories used by the Gestapo. But these Catholic workers did at least feel that in their parishes and at such gatherings as were still permitted they still belonged to a community.[35]

Plenty of expressions are used to encapsulate the general situation of the world of the workers: "segmentation," "individualization," "a dissociated consciousness," and so on. But is it legitimate to speak of *a* working class? Does not the diversification of statuses preclude any reference to a single proletarian condition? Does not the weakness of resistance movements on the eve of the war indicate that class consciousness had disappeared? Nevertheless, Michael Voges, referring to the works of Edward P. Thompson on the origins of the British working class, has pointed out that class is not something that either does or does not exist, rather "it appears [in the present context one might say that it reappears after having disappeared] as men and women experience situations that are determined within the complex of social relations as a whole, with all their cultural heritage and expectations." Underlying day-to-day behavior, a nonconformist working-class culture, quite distinct from the more highly elaborated culture of the militants, does seem to have blocked totalitarian ambitions. At any rate the regime, instead of integrating this hostile class within its Community, succeeded only in bringing about its disintegration.

THE CONQUEST OF WOMEN AND YOUNG PEOPLE

The National Socialist program assigned contradictory roles to on the one hand women and on the other young people. Abdicating all professional vocations, women were expected to concentrate all their efforts upon family tasks, looking after their men, producing and educating their children, as devoted auxiliaries in the service of the People's Community. But to young people the political battle was presented as an ongoing struggle of new forces against fossilized traditions, so it was up to them to prepare for the fight by pouring their youthful dynamism into their own special party organization: it was certainly not by chance that this bore the Leader's name (*Hitlerjugend, HJ*), flaunting it like a banner. However, this privilege implied that they, on their side, should distance themelves, if not break completely, with the early framework of their lives composed by the church, their schools, and even their families.

The first item of business was to eliminate women from positions they had recently won within the elite of public officialdom and the liberal professions. This offensive presented the double advantage of pleasing their male colleagues, alarmed by their competition, and of sending back into private life over one hundred thousand people who were proud of their achievements and so were for the most part emancipated and politically to the left. The campaign was developed on two fronts: early training and employment. To staunch the flow bringing more and more girls into further education, the Ministry of Education banned Latin classes in the first five years of their schooling and science classes in the last three years, replacing them with domestic training and modern languages. But the girls' desire for education was too strong: many went off to attend secondary schools for boys. An extra deterrent was then introduced to stop them entering universities. It took the form of a quota of 10 percent. This was not always effective: the proportion of female students in faculties of medicine only fell from 20 to 17 percent. Elsewhere it sparked off protests: in law and literature the proportion of women fell so rapidly that feminine party organizations worried that they would soon be unable to recruit cadres.

Sexist discrimination among the generations already at work was frequently unsuccessful for analogous reasons: the determination of women to continue in their professions and the lack of men to replace them. The organization of assistance for mothers and families created many jobs clearly reserved for women, and as a result the number of women doctors increased and so did even the percentage of women in the medical profession. The association of women doctors was now integrated with that of the men: was this a sign of alarm on the part of the authorities, or did it indicate their recognition of women as partners of their male colleagues? Similarly the dismissal of two thousand women teachers led to a shortage of teaching staff that had to be repaired by a new recruitment campaign. Only in the apparatus of the judiciary were women completely eliminated, no doubt because they were suspected of being too lenient. Hitler himself intervened to keep them out of courtrooms and away from the bar.[36] Military mobilization followed by the war, was to cause these artificial constraints to crack.

Was the party misogynist? During the years of confrontation, the SA and SS, virile leagues by definition, had admitted women only so that their heroes could be fed and nursed. The "Women's National Socialist Organization" (*Frauenschaft*) created in 1932 devoted itself to the teaching of domestic skills, which brought it a number of sympathizers but implied no overt political commitment. After the party came to power it became just one more huge, politically impotent organ among many others. In principle it was supposed to produce a new type of militant female, ideologically sound and so suited to guide the feminine half of society. But of its two million members only seven thousand took part in the doctrinal courses, for how could a girl take promises of promotion seriously knowing that at each step up the hierarchy she would always be subordinate to her male counterpart? In contrast, the "German Women's Work" (*Frauenwerk*) correctly carried out its task of providing domestic training. Mothers of families—at least those passed as "healthy"—flocked to courses on domestic economy, gymnastics, and music, but absented themselves at the announcement of a session on theory, let alone at a hint of antireligious propaganda. Ordinary women thus behaved as their husbands did, as consumer-clients.

Yet some women must have been committed supporters of Nazism, for otherwise the press photographs and newsreels would not show so many women's faces in the cheering crowds. In 1933, when the party decided to admit anyone who wished to join, it was hoping to increase the proportion of women to five percent of its membership but could not even achieve that. When it opened up its membership for the second time, in 1937, its appeal to "eliminate prejudices" obtained a much better hearing. Women members rose to 10 percent, then to 17 percent. This was the period when the economists were urging them to take up or return to a profession, demographers were explaining that maternity and professional work were not incompatible after all, the party's newspaper was defending girl students against the insults of their male classmates, and Goebbels was condemning as exaggerated the purists' campaign against the use of lipstick. Were women now becoming appreciative of the attractions of this party that at least seemed to be recognizing their emancipation? If they were, disillusionment was soon to follow. Despite the egalitarian claims of G. Scholz-Klink and her intellectual followers, theorists of the stronger sex were still proclaiming the principle of "the particular nature of women"; and psychologists working for the employment service went so far as to justify steering women exclusively into dead-end posts, asserting that they were more suited to unrewarding and monotonous tasks since family life provided them with emotional compensations. As for girls who at first volunteered for Labor Service and those later forced into it, it is doubtful whether they considered their six month stay in the countryside as a liberating experience: the educational and sporting part of each day was increasingly sacrificed to the production battle and they were constantly made to chant the slogan, "You are nothing, the People is everything."[37]

On balance it seems reasonable to suppose that most of the convinced female militants had emerged from the "German Girls' League" (*BdM*), which was more successful at molding hearts and minds than the adult organizations. Its initial activities were nothing if not totally conformist: physical education with no thought of setting any records, housewifely education, and preparation for maternity (with strictly no information about sexuality). But the Wednesday evening "At Home" receptions reserved for fifteen to twenty-year-olds laid the emphasis on culture in its reputedly most feminine aspects: music, poetry, and drama. Saturdays were devoted to sport, and in the summer the girls went off for a week's camping—quite an innovation. This idealistic atmosphere was not so opposed as it might be thought to the virile virtues that reigned in the masculine organizations, for among the girls too, forceful and energetic personalities were appreciated and, as well as a "particularly feminine" spirit of self-sacrifice to one's daily duties being promoted, submission to the group as a whole and its leaders was encouraged. The title of the cultural organ that arranged these evenings, "Faith and Beauty," could even be interpreted as a discreet appeal to neo-paganism. And plenty of traditional families were worried at seeing their daughters wearing uniforms of too emancipated a nature.[38]

There were two possible means of winning over young people. One was by way of the schools, the state route, the other by way of the Hitler Youth Organization (*HJ*), the party route; and the two sometimes ran parallel, sometimes diverged. Some Nazi pedagogues started from the principle that the new man would distinguish himself through his ability to act rather than through his learning: "The only way to become a National Socialist is through the camping life and marching in line." In their view, schools ought to play no more than a complementary role. On the other hand, the offices of the Ministry of Education reckoned that to integrate young people into the Community the best strategy consisted in politicizing the schools, while the Youth movement's contribution would be to organize the leisure hours. As nobody could resolve the problem, in the early years the two systems followed parallel paths: schools, especially primary schools, were rapidly Nazified, while the *HJ* for boys and the *BdM* for girls recruited massively, in theory at least, on a voluntary basis. But in 1936 the youth of the party became the youth of the state, that is to say a single if not obligatory movement, and received definitive primacy in all educative tasks. Primary education was materially sacrificed, its prestige damaged by this unpopular reform. Secondary schooling was diversified: it was as if the regime was seeking to divide the future elites.[39]

The body of primary schoolteachers seems to have set out to guarantee that from infancy onward, children would be educated along correct lines. Although not many of these teachers joined the party before 1933, they were very prominent among "those who rallied in March." Within a few months a quarter of them had joined the party; and that proportion then rose to be the highest of all the professions except doctors. Opportunism certainly played a role here, but even more instrumental was the desire for social recognition: hitherto, schoolteachers had been considered people of little importance, burdened with many supplementary tasks and strictly controlled by the Catholic or Protestant Churches. The party now offered them unhoped-for careers as "political leaders" (as heads of cells or larger groups), cadres in the SA and SS, or instructors in the Hitler Youth Organization. New recruits to the teaching profession looked even more promising: in the "Advanced Training Schools for Teachers" set up in the countryside they were groomed to form a new layer of leaders with courses in German and general and local history, all deeply steeped in ideology. For those left in their classrooms however, disappointments were in the offing. Their salaries remained lower than the average wage of workers, the Advanced Schools did not train enough teachers to make up for those leaving the profession, and the number of pupils per class, already very high, continued to increase. The teachers organization (*NSLB*) itself complained of the drop in the scholastic standard of pupils, attributing this to too many extra activities, in other words laying the blame on the *HJ*.[40]

The remedy seemed ready to hand: by dint of amalgamating the Catholic and Protestant schools of each locality into a single "community school," classes could be divided up more rationally and would set a good example of national unity: "One People, one Reich, one Führer, one School!" was the slogan that was launched in several regions by pupils' parents who were members of the party, and this was then diffused officially if with some delay (for it clashed with certain articles in the Concordat). From 1936 on a referendum in favor of the reform was held on the first day of every school year, accompanied by many pressures and much electioneering as on the eves of plebiscites. In Bavaria and Württemberg the Protestants submitted without much fuss, apart from members of the Confessional Church. The Catholic hierarchy protested as a body and got the Vatican to intervene, but was forced into silence when the administration threatened to forbid entry into the schools to priests accustomed to visiting them for catechism classes. After two years the percentage of votes in favor of the community schools had reached the desired 96 percent. In the Rhineland, the opposition was better organized. The clergy set up counter-referendums for the maintenance of the church schools, aided by a multitude of mothers against whom the Gestapo had to confess itself powerless, and the status quo was preserved. This massive reaction (two million signatures) shows that it was possible to thwart the regime's ambitions where they ran counter to a tradition that was all the more deeply entrenched, since it could congratulate itself upon an earlier victory against Bismarck.[41]

In contrast, secondary education has often been represented as an oasis of tranquillity. Not that the ministry and the Teachers' League had given up the idea of transforming it. As they saw it, however strong the priority to be given to physical and moral abilities, the future elite could after all not be raised in a total cultural desert, even if it was important for it to escape the debilitating humanism diffused by the essentially conservative body of secondary school teachers. The favored solution was the creation of *Oberschulen*, a sort of upper primary system in which the basic disciplines were complemented by modern languages and which led to a passing-out diploma that did not give access to the universities. As for the secondary schools proper they, along with the universities to which they led, were now considered merely relics of the old privilege-based society. Their number decreased sharply and their teaching staff was systematically complemented by auxiliaries. The fact that their pedagogical instructions did not reach them until 1938 may have been a sign of embarrassment, or possibly disdain. These instructions began by lauding the types of teaching that were "close to life," that is to say housekeeping matters for the girls and the philosophy of National Socialism for everyone. Then came advice directly counter to tradition as to how to apply this to the various disciplines. "Raciology," until then a subject studied in special courses, was now to be diffused in all disciplines as a matter of fundamental principle; and, as if it were feared that students who were dark and small might feel excluded, it was expressly pointed out that the essential criteria to determine race were not physical but psychological: "It is one's psychic attitude that reflects one's nordic heredity."

Did the reality conform to those instructions? An examination of textbooks gives a picture that exactly reproduces that of the teaching body: a minority of nonconformist works that happened to survive the purges; a few doctrinal catechisms; a majority of neutral texts that were permitted publication in return for a few compromises. Clearly teachers could make whatever use they chose of these seemingly innocent textbooks, giving them either a militant or simply a patriotic interpretation. Their situation preserved all the ambiguities of the old conservative values upon which the *Philologenverband* had been nurtured. If we are to believe their activity reports, teachers of German in the secondary schools of Berlin devoted 16 percent of the hours of their courses to Goethe and Schiller and only three percent to specifically Nazi authors. So there are grounds for concluding, with K. H. Jarausch, that "by maintaining levels of competence, the system had created an apolitical refuge." However, they also devoted 12 percent of their teaching time to the vague collection of works known as the literature of war, both colonial and *völkisch*: here apoliticism gave way to the inevitable allusions to the current renewal of national greatness. In similar fashion teachers of mathematics could produce perfectly neutral exercises from their textbooks, but likewise others of a racist or even criminal nature. If we believe that teachers do to some extent influence their pupils' way of thinking, it is worth remembering the results of the annual questionnaires on school-leavers' future plans: about half of them hoped to go to university, increasingly with a preference for the exact sciences, one-sixth were aiming for the army, and only one percent for a post in the party apparatus. Science and the army: secondary schooling seemed to be guiding students toward the two "niches" supposedly free from politics.[42]

Realizing either with resignation or satisfaction that the children of former elites were thus being marginalized, the regime set about forming a new elite with a wider social base, in its own schools. But the ministry and the party respectively adopted two different strategies. The ministry, using the relatively neutral label "establishments of political and national education" (*Napola*), tried to reconcile three models, the youth movement of the early years of the century, the cadet schools of old Prussia, and the British "public schools." It was a triple heritage not at all to the liking of Baldur von Schirach, head of the Hitler Youth Organization, but it was viewed more favorably by the SS on account of its aristocratic pretensions. Fifteen of these establishments were created and each year recruited about thirty new pupils following a very stiff physical and intellectual selection process. Their clientele was indeed wider than that of the secondary schools, with a majority of sons of officials and salaried employees and a scattering of peasants' and workers' sons. The boys' literary and scientific education were complemented by periods spent working in industry and agriculture and by ceremonials modeled on major official festivals. Schirach and Ley for their part devised a type of training of a more popular and politicized nature: in their *Adolf Hitler Schulen* the criteria of selection were mainly physical, teaching concentrated on Nazi literature, and little or no attention was paid to real scholarship: the schools were clearly designed to produce only minor cadres. For the eighteen to twenty-one-year-olds, "Fortresses of Order" (*Ordensburgen*) were supposed to resuscitate the communities of old Teutonic knights. However, the first of these institutions made an unfortunate impression, chiefly due to the contrast between their grandiose neo-medieval architecture and the absence of motivation and low intellectual caliber of the students.[43] Nazi elitism was thus faced with a dilemma. Either it was creating an aristocracy cut off from the masses, or it was offering the true sons of the people no more than a caricature of promotion.

* * *

The real success, possibly the only one among all these projects to encourage social revolution, was the Hitler Youth Organization, although—as a result of its very triumph—it alarmed many traditionalists whom the authorities still needed. Its popular, even proletarian, origins and the speeches of its head, Baldur von Schirach, had engendered in the *HJ* a sharp hostility toward the "bourgeois," that is to say intellectuals, teachers, particularly those of secondary schools, and the churches. It considered itself better suited than them and even many parents to teaching children and adolescents patriotism and class reconciliation, in accordance with the slogan, "Youth must be guided by Youth." By making the most of the elimination of the Young Socialists' and Young Communists' movements, absorbing the right-wing leagues (*Bünde*), Protestant associations and Youth Hostels, and attracting young people who belonged to no organization, within the space of a few months in 1933 it had accumulated five million members. Only the Catholics, protected by the Concordat, kept their distance. This rapid growth was not achieved without running into problems. In particular, former members of the youth movement and the Leagues, noting, not without reason, that the *HJ* was copying their own activities—camps, meetings, and patriotic ceremonies—as well as their favorite themes of "Soil and Blood," the Community, and the führer, for a time held on to a remnant of autonomy then tried to infiltrate the *HJ* leadership. But their aristocratic style and exotic taste for Lapp tents and Russian dances were profoundly irritating to the proletarians of the early *HJ*. Schirach declared them to be "enemies of National Socialism," and spirited polemics ensued. Eventually most of these organizations knuckled under, and a purge eliminated those that clung on, making them illegal. The scare had produced such heated reactions that the police set up a special department devoted to wrecking their meetings, and anything reminiscent of their "Asiatic culture" was condemned as high treason.[44]

No sooner were they rid of these opponents than the little *führers* of the *HJ* found themselves others, this time in the form of the teaching community. Initially the *HJ* had been allowed to gather the young together only on Saturdays for open-air activities, handiwork, and doctrinal training. But soon they were organizing more and more evening meetings and hindering completion of the school homework that was traditional at least for secondary school pupils. Then they got themselves appointed to parent-teacher committees, where they criticized the content of school courses and prevented the administration from forcing their own politically zealous but intellectually inadequate comrades to repeat school years. Despite all the minister's attempts to intervene and find compromises, the two cultures continued to clash. In 1937, Lieutenant-Colonel Erwin Rommel, appointed to supervise the military training offered by the *HJ*, in publicly taking up the defense of the teaching body (as the dutiful professor's son that he was), clashed with Schirach and had to resign from his post.[45] But far from upsetting those principally affected, the young, this conflict simply increased their enthusiasm for the movement. As early as 1931, Protestant educators had been alarmed by the attraction that Nazism exerted upon certain adolescents, detecting in it "something irrational, infectious, that makes the blood beat in the veins." Four years later, Socialist observers were in their turn noting that young workers were delighted to be told that school and family mattered less than their own community and had taken to imagining perspectives of advancement up the hierarchy opening up before them at the mere sight of their physical prowess and enthusiasm. They were heard to exclaim, "The People's Community is better than belonging to the lower classes!" These young people no doubt understood very little about ideology, but they allowed it to seep into them, making them feel that they were no longer mere children, . . . some even considered themselves "lords." Finally, here is a confession from Hans and Sophie Scholl, young "White Rose" Catholic resistants: "[In the Hitler Youth Organization] we were taken seriously, remarkably seriously, and that filled us with a particular energy . . . We felt that we were part of a process, a movement that was turning the masses into a people."[46]

In 1936 the *HJ* was declared to be the sole state youth organization, and unenthusiastic young people were subjected to increasingly heavy pressure to join. These efforts were only moderately successful: the membership figure of eight million reached in 1939 was certainly impressive, but it represented only two-thirds of the age groups concerned. Hence the decision in the spring of that year to make membership compulsory. The leadership structure had also been expanded: at the lowest level there were 750,000 team and section leaders only a couple of years older than their troops: youth certainly was being "led by youth." But it was above all the apparatus of eight thousand full-time leaders that gave the Hitler Youth Organization the air of the society of the future: these were recruited increasingly according to racial and ideological criteria; eventually they were even required officially to abandon their churches; and the diversity of their social origins showed that class fusion was by now more than just a slogan: the 50 percent of past or future baccalaureat holders were flanked by 20 percent of workers and 25 percent of salaried employees.

Having won the battle against the young people's teachers and parents, the movement could now encroach heavily on school hours, taking over as much as two and a half days a week. Camping and handicrafts were no longer enough—and besides, they were beginning to bore the adolescents—so the *HJ* introduced "national professional championships"—that rewarded the most adept with their hands—and above all military training in the form of shooting practice, field maneuvers, courses for radio operators, even gliding and sailing. At this point the social cleavages that were supposed to have disappeared made a reappearance: the units that provided naval and aviation training mostly attracted "bourgeois" pupils from secondary schools, following the example of their fathers who were flocking to the "National Socialist Air Corps" and the SS cavalry, refuges of an elegant lifestyle. The essential task however was to prepare these young people to be loyal followers of the führer. There were many ways of demonstrating commitment, many optional activities to engage in, and many ways to prove one's devotion, but they were not particularly uplifting: collecting funds in the streets, helping to bring in the harvests, swelling the crowds at party demonstrations. And one wonders whether evening classes on ideology followed by an examination and diploma really inspired this generation with the "fanaticism" of which Hitler dreamed. What we know of their favorite reading matter prompts a certain skepticism: they preferred military information sheets to the movement's own special magazines, and war novels to the lives of Nazi heroes. Even the official collection of songs included only a few overtly partisan texts, the remainder being shamelessly borrowed from the old anthologies of *bündisch* groups. However, the work of conversion was carried on not so much through ideas as through live experiences and constant appeals to excel, which "camouflaged the harshness of the system by seemingly satisfying the youthful need for dynamism" (A. Klönne). The courses on raciology did not necessarily produce racists full of theories but rather men convinced of the right of the strongest and the "boxers' ethics" denounced by E. Wiechert (who was then sent to a concentration camp for his pains). The SS, who understood that active complicity led far more inevitably to absolute loyalty than any theoretical teaching, seized the opportunity to create an elite in their own image: in 1938 they set up within the *HJ* a "patrol service" whose task was to keep new recruits under surveillance. It was now a matter of youth not only guiding youth but spying on it.[47]

However in 1936 half the children and adolescents of Germany eluded this control, and in 1939 a third of them still did. They were the faithful of the two Christian churches and nonconformists of every kind.

From a purely administrative point of view the young Protestants represented an intermediate case, as their groups had been absorbed into the Hitler Youth Organization as early as 1933 by order of "Reich bishop" Ludwig Müller, whose authority many of them refused to recognize. Astonishing scenes resulted in certain localities where religious cohesion was strong, and *HJ* detachments flocked to church services in force. But elsewhere anti-religiosity prevailed, and clashes and fighting often erupted. Protestant pastors organized parish almoner services, but without any organizational connections so as not to be accused of reconstituting the movements previously dissolved. During the calmer months of 1935–36 it was even possible for regional meetings to take place at which preachers commented on the Bible, contrasting it implicitly at least to the official dogmas. In these "small vital spaces" the authorities predictably detected seeds of opposition.[48]

In 1933, organized Catholic youth constituted a much more imposing mass. one and a half million boys and girls made up twenty-eight different groups. The largest were the Association of Young Catholic Men and that of Catholic Girls, but they were flanked by scout bands more or less in the *bündisch* tradition, professional groups, students' corporations, and so on. Their leaders, although answerable to the hierarchy, laid claim to a certain autonomy, particularly where politics were concerned, and this manifested itself during the March electoral campaign in a number of violently anti-Nazi pronouncements such as the following: "What is happening before our very eyes is national corruption . . . Bolshevism is appearing in a national guise." Brutal reactions soon followed: in Munich the Congress of Catholic Companions was dispersed by the SA and the police made a number of arrests. For a while Catholic leaders and their followers believed themselves protected by article 31 of the Concordat, which guaranteed the existence of their associations, without noticing that one restrictive clause, a ban on all political activity, lent itself to any and every kind of interpretation. Soon the offensive resumed, carried out by the Hitler Youth Organization, here and there with the support of the *Gauleiter* or even the prefects if these were particularly hostile. The objective was to demonstrate practically, and possibly also by issuing administrative edicts, that membership in the Catholic Church was incompatible with that in the *HJ*. On top of all this, pressure was exerted upon the parents and employers of recalcitrant young Catholics, followed by physical intimidation and, in 1937, the arrest of fifty-seven national Catholic leaders. The defense was further hampered by the bishops, who were constantly assuring authorities of their loyalty and recommending prudence to their flock. "We are martyrs without a mandate," young militants were heard to complain. Inevitably the grass roots base began to crack: the Young Men's Association lost one hundred thousand members in the space of a few months, but at the same time its journal gained two hundred thousand new readers, which shows that those resignations had been forced.

When their public meetings, collective outings, uniforms and insignia were banned, the Catholics fell back upon strictly religious activities just as the Protestants had. Nevertheless it would not be fair to say that they really let themselves be forced into line, as the atmosphere of their meetings remained overtly oppositional. One Bavarian leader wrote as follows in his personal diary: "We, the young, who are not Nazis, still for the moment, have our liberty. The old, particularly teachers, officials, and so on are all going over to the Nazis in order to hang on to their salaries; but what about us?" The younger generation thus felt it had a role of its own to play, not only in defending religious tradition, but even in a renewal of bible and liturgical studies with the help of priests of the same age.[49] But even if such behavior cannot be described as a simple retreat, can it really be called resistance? The later memories of one man who was young in those days provide a clear answer: "It was not a great opposition that set out to liberate the country from the tyrant. But we did want to [defend] our rights and freedom, including religious freedom, and despite great fear we derived a youthful pleasure from this life as an independent and adventurous group."[50]

The Hitler Youth Organization clashed even more violently with gangs of young people in the major towns. This was no new phenomenon. In the Berlin of 1930 hundreds of such gangs had indulged in many kinds of activities ranging from innocent strolling around to harassment of the Scouts, whom they sought to rival in discipline, obedience to their leaders, and uniforms. For the most part they followed no particular political line but simply expressed their loathing of the established order. When the *HJ* began to claim a monopoly, their numbers fell slightly but not their activism. The Leipzig "Hounds," the "Edelweiss Pirates" of Cologne, and the Munich "Rabble" took over particular streets and systematically provoked the Hitler Youths. The police regarded them as a resurgence of Communist Youth or else labeled them "asocials," which justified arresting them. But in truth they were completely out of touch, as is proved by the way they assimilated these kinds of gangs with others that were totally different, being extremely middle-class, such as the "swing" clubs of Hamburg and Frankfurt. All they could see were groups who were similar by being heterogeneous and sexually liberated—a sign of depravity that both the police and *HJ* condemned out of hand.[51]

The whole world was invited to the 1936 Olympic Games in Berlin, and the whole world allowed itself to be impressed by the façade put up by the Third Reich, which portrayed Germany as both pacific and united. Pacific it certainly was not: the very next year in committee, Hitler was to set out his plans for expansion. Nor was it united, as was proved when the games were over and repression resumed. Contrary to the story the *SD* and the Gestapo were purveying, there was no serious threat of an uprising, since the regime had been more or less successful in depoliticizing the masses, and demonstrations of discontent only targeted the minor masters of the hour, not their Leader. Nevertheless they did indicate that entire sectors of the population continued to elude overall control, which were bound to be the ultimate objectives of any regime with totalitarian ambitions: those people who still had a private life of their own.

NOTES

1. Hüttenberger F., "Interessenvertretung"; Kater M., "Sozialer Wandel," p. 48; Noakes J., *53*, p. 220.

2. Falter J., *Hitlers Wähler*, pp. 194–98.

3. Ayçoberry P., pp. 216–29.

4. Kater M., *Nazi Party*, pp. 216–29.

5. Hamilton R. F., p. 423; Scholdt G., p. 641.

6. Geiger T., in particular p. 24, 124; more recently, the same criticisms are to be found in Wegner B., p. 236, n. 81, and Peukert D., *Volksgenossen*, p. 42.

7. Winkler H. A., *Mittelstand*, chap. 7 and 8.

8. Id,. "Mittelstandsbewegung"; id., "Der entbehrliche Stand"; Schweitzer A., chap. 3–5, had already presented the same argument; similarly, Kershaw I., *L'Opinion* (Bavaria); Stöver B., p. 251 (Aryanization).

9. Saldern A. von, *Mittelstand*; id., "Alter Mittelstand."

10. Prinz M., *Angestellten*; id., "Der unerwünschte Stand"; Kocka J., chap. 6 (in collaboration with Prinz M.); Caplan J. (State officials); Falter J., *Hitlers Wähler*, pp. 230–34; Peukert D., *Volksgenossen*, p. 42 f. (ideal of the *Leistung*); Schoenbaum D., chap. 7 and 8 (social mobility).

11. Bergmann J. and Mengerle K.; Broszat M., "Ebermannstadt"; Wilke G.

12. Schweitzer A., chap. 3; Saldern A. von, *Mittelstand*, pp. 67–88, 113–33, 174–81. Bavaria: Kershaw I., *L'Opinion*, pp. 59–84; Wiesemann F; Schönhoven K., p. 174. Trier region: *65*, p. 85, 125, 290. *SD* synthesis 1939: Steinert M. G., *Hitlers Krieg*, p. 64.

13. Figures recalculated following Falter J., *Hitlers Wähler*, p. 199.

14. See above, chap. 2.

15. Mason T., *Arbeiterklasse*, pp. 1–16.

16. Mai G., "NSBO"; Hetzer G., pp. 96–111; Mason T., *Arbeiterklasse*, p. 22; Herbert U., "Arbeiterschaft," pp. 320–29.

17. Falter J., Lindenberger T., and Schumann S., p. 38.

18. Mason T., *Arbeiterklasse*, pp. 46–61; Petrick F.

19. Klinksiek D., pp. 100–103; Stephenson J., *Women*, p. 88; Winkler D., p. 49.

20. Mason T., *Arbeiterklasse*; Silverman D. P., "Work-Creation Programs"; Zollitsch W., *Arbeiter*, pp. 72–107; Roth K. H., pp. 140–44.

21. Zollitsch W., *Arbeiter*, pp. 218–27; id., "Vertrauensratswahlen" (Krupp); Rüther M. (Cologne); Stöver B., p. 309 f.

22. See tables in *70*.

23. Mason T., *Arbeiterklasse*, p. 55 f.

24. Kroener B. R., "Ressourcen," p. 702 f.; Blaich F., "Wirtschaft und Rüstung."

25. Hachtmann R.; Stephenson J., *Women*, p. 100 f.; Klinksiek D., pp. 104–08; Winkler D., pp. 56–77; Sachse C., pp. 239–54 (speech of S.-K.)

26. Mason T., *Arbeiterklasse*, p. 61, 100–119; Siegel T., pp. 104–34; Zollitsch W., *Arbeiter*, pp. 85–103.

27. Zollitsch W., ibid., pp. 19–71; Herbert U., *"Arbeiterschaft,"* p. 41; Mason T., *Arbeiterklasse*, p. 598 (mines); Roth K. H., pp. 148–56.

28. Mason T., *Arbeiterklasse*, p. 78, 84–86; Mai G., "Arbeitsfront"; Geyer M. H.; Reulecke J. (competition).

29. Reulecke J.; Zollitsch W., *Arbeiter*, chap. 3.

30. Rabinbach A., pp. 58–69.

31. Mason T., *Arbeiterklasse*, p. 84; Mai G., "Arbeitsfront"; Spode H.; Stöver B., pp. 271–91.

32. Mason T., *Arbeiterklasse*, p. 288, 340, 606; Kershaw I., *L'Opinion*, pp. 85-121; Hetzer G., pp. 111-30; Wisotzky K. (Ruhr); Morsch G. (strikes); Voges M. (strikes, giving lower figures).

33. In chronological order: Mason T., *Arbeiterklasse* and *Sozialpolitik* (1975-77); Voges M. (1981); Mason T., "Bändigung" (1982); Peukert D., "Arbeiterwiderstand" (1986); Herbert U., "Arbeiterschaft" (1989); Lüdtke A., "Rote Glut" (1989); Stöver B. (1993).

34. Niethammer L., Hg., *"Die Jahre weiss man nicht, wo man die heute hinsetzen soll." Faschismuserfahrungen im Ruhrgebeit. Lenensgeschichte und Sozialstruktur im Ruhrgebeit 1930 bis 1960*, Bd. 1, Berlin and Bonn, 1983.

35. Stehkämper H.; Hürten H., pp. 276-77, 565; Hetzer G., p. 216 f.

36. Stephenson J., *Women*, p. 118 f., 152 f.; Winkler D., p. 49; Thalmann R., p. 84 f.; Kater M., *Doctors*, pp. 89-98; Klinksiek D., p. 45.

37. Kater M., "Frauen"; Stephenson J., "Frauenorganisationen"; Klinksiek D., pp. 48-51, 90, 123-30; *66*, quotations from the *VB*, December 1935, and from Goebbels, January 1936; Peukert D., *Volksgenossen*, p. 212; Miller G.

38. Klaus M., pp. 55-58, 72-90.

39. Scholz H., pp. 47-99.

40. Breyvogel W. and Lohmann T.; Kershaw I., *L'Opinion*, pp. 144-46; Ottweiler O.

41. Sonnenberger F. (Bavaria); Hehl U. von, *Erzbistum Köln*, p. 140 f. (Rhineland); Thierfelder J. (Protestants of Württemberg).

42. Scholz H., p. 62, 86-92, 184 f.; Flessau I., pp. 92-210; Riemenschneider R. (history); Hopster N. (German); Dithmar R. (German); Weiss S. F. (biology); Lehberger R. (English); Mehrtens H. "Mathematik als . . . Schulfach"; Jarausch K. H., p. 169.

43. Koch H. W., pp. 269-300.

44. Stachura P. D., *Nazi Youth*; id., "Jugenderziehung"; Klönne A., *Jugend*, pp. 8-24, 105 f.; Kater M., "Jugendbewegung."

45. Stachura P. D., "Jugenderziehung"; Koch H. W., pp. 254-58.

46. 1931 text cited in *53*, p.108; Socialists cited by Scholz H., p. 66; H. and S. Scholl cited by Thamer H.-U., p. 405.

47. Kater M., "Jugendbewegung"; Klönne A., *Jugend*, pp. 56-130; id., "Jugendprotest," pp. 535-51; Stachura P. D., "Jugenderziehung"; Scholz H., p. 83 f.; Koch H. W., p. 162, 205-38.

48. Klönne A., *Jugend*, pp. 164-75; id., "Jugendprotest," p. 564 f.

49. Schellenberger B.; Hürten H., p. 565; Klönne A., *Jugend*, pp. 185-97; id., "Jugendprotest," pp. 571-74 (Bavaria); Kleinöder E. (Eichstätt); Hehl U. von, *Erzbistum Köln*, pp. 54-61, 79 (Rhineland).

50. Cited by Klönne A., *Jugend*, p. 197.

51. Rosenhaft E., p. 131 f.; Klönne A., *Jugend*, p. 228 f.; id., "Jugendprotest," p. 589 f.; Peukert D., "Alltags," p. 550.

5—Radicalization, 1938-1939

P. Milza has noticed that all the fascist authorities, after a few years of tolerating erstwhile allies and nonconformist minorities, entered an increasingly rigid phase when they aimed for total control over the entire population.[1] If the Third Reich provides such a remarkable illustration of this rule, that is because, spurred on by the impatience of its leader and the extremism of his subalterns, the rhythm of spectacular decisions was constantly speeding up. In order to pursue an aggressive foreign policy, rapid rearmament was essential. This precipitated the country's economy into tight situations that could only be resolved at the cost of further sacrifices. Would not these sacrifices seem easier to bear if the triumphs abroad continued? However, as the risk of war became clearer, that hope became increasingly unrealistic. It therefore became necessary to strengthen the repression of all opponents or lukewarm onlookers and at the same time satisfy public opinion by a hunt for scapegoats.

That logic accounts for most of the decisions of 1938-39. However, there is one other aspect to this hardening policy that it does not altogether explain: namely the battle against the churches, which had just been resumed.

THE BATTLE AGAINST THE CHURCHES

Kirchenkampf: to Catholics at least, the term was reminiscent of the *Kulturkampf* of Bismarck's day. But the means of applying pressure available to the political authorities had evolved: instead of proceeding by passing laws and then using force to implement them, they would now first let loose their most zealous subordinates in order to test the solidity of resistance. At this, it became customary over the years for their opponents to take the only course open to them: protest to those same authorities, thereby on each occasion manifesting recognition of the authorities' legitimacy.

1935 saw changes that seemed to offer some hope of a *détente* between state and church. So what was it that prompted Nazi leaders to launch a new offensive? The two cases of Protestantism and Catholicism need to be studied separately.

The conflict of 1933–34 had left the official Protestant Church humiliated, its opponents the Confessional Church and the Catholic bishops stronger, and its toughest wing, the German-Christians, under threat from extremists in the "Movement of Faith," the name of which was the only Christian thing about it. A last attempt to bring the different tendencies together within regional and national "ecclesiastical committees," suggested by the Minister Hans Kerri, got bogged down.[2] At that point, when various ways of forcing people into line had failed, the last resort seemed to be an appeal for desertions. Now the institutional battle became well and truly a religious one. The party radicals, Ley, Rosenberg, Schirach, and the SS, for once in agreement, took the Movement of Faith under their protection and encouraged the members of their respective organizations to stage an official "walk-out from the Church" and simply become "believers in God," in other words to proclaim themselves agnostics. In all, this category seems to have included 2.5 million people in 1939, to whom should be added the 1.2 million who chose to be classified more discreetly as "with no faith."[3] But given that the Catholic Church, which kept more accurate records, recognized rather fewer than one hundred thousand defections per year, it seems reasonable to conclude that most were nonpracticing Protestants whose numbers had been rapidly increasing ever since the end of the nineteenth century.

In the face of these attacks, the defenders of religious liberty were still presenting a by no means united front. The three bishops wily enough to avoid being forced into line, those of Bavaria, Württemburg, and Hanover, encouraged their pastors to swear allegiance to the *führer* and in some instances dissociated themselves from the actions of the Confessional Church. Even within the latter, not everyone emulated the audacity of Niemöller and his companions. His parishioners in Dahlem (in west Berlin), composed mainly of high-ranking officials and highly educated bourgeois, along with just under half of his fellow pastors in the capital, were prepared to risk arrest by going to listen to him or distributing his writings. Recalcitrant *nuclei* also survived elsewhere: in the Rhineland, where 180 pastors out of eight hundred refused to the very end to swear the oath; in Württemburg where seven hundred out of a thousand insisted on adding a clause of conscience; and throughout the south and the southeast, where at every step they defended the Confessional Church against the mayors, teachers, certain parents, and those of their own colleagues who favored the "German-Christians." But the leaders of the Confessional Church, its "council of brothers," sometimes wavered. In June 1936 they sent Hitler a list of complaints that even included a denunciation of the concentration camps. But the text of this document was published only in the Swiss press, and the authors were only able to extricate themselves by asking the police to trace the source of the leak. The next circular, read out from the pulpits in the manner of Catholic bishops, combined protests with assurances of loyalty—although that did not prevent the arrest of Niemöller the following year. During the Sudeten crisis that same leadership drew up a service of prayers for peace arranged around the biblical quotation, "Your name is insulted among the people." The SS newspaper let fly, accusing the Confessional Church of complicity with Karl Barth, and his "brothers" were obliged to dissociate themselves from their master. Finally, like so many others, the Protestant leadership kept silent after the pogrom of 9 November 1938, and this is what has earned its members the most cutting reproaches from posterity. However, it is only fair to point out that at his date there was a whole host of reasons for nonaligned pastors to be discouraged: their parishioners were divided, the "German-Christians" were harassing them, and their little Bible-reading meetings were eventually banned. In these circumstances the vocational crisis was bound to worsen: in the space of six years the number of students of Protestant theology fell from just under six thousand to just over one thousand.[4] The Protestant pastorate, once a pillar of society, was now in danger of disappearing altogether, and with it the administrative and military elites with which it was so closely associated.

In the task of weakening the bishops and directors of Catholic good works a certain measure of initiative had been left to local authorities, some of whom now threatened and made life difficult for the Catholic leaders while others bided their time. The campaign for "community schools" was thus conducted with varying degrees of force in different regions, and further restrictions on the religious orders were now speeded up, now slowed down. Hitler himself had kept silent and so continued to appear as a possible defender. It was an initiative from Rome that precipitated the hardening of tactics. The encyclical *In Burning Anxiety*, published in March 1937 and then disseminated by priests speaking from their pulpits and by what remained of the Catholic press, was no longer content to denounce the state's violations of the Concordat but went so far as to expressly condemn the racist doctrine: "God cannot be imprisoned within the frontiers of a particular people or a particular race." But while priests and journalists were being subjected to threats or arrested for having circulated the encyclical, the hierarchy produced a restrictive interpretation of it according to which it was the state's ideas, not the form of the state, that were the target of the Pope's text. The hierarchy accordingly continued to acclaim the successes of the Reich's foreign policy: immediately following the *Anschluss*, Cardinal Innitzer, archbishop of Vienna, loudly exclaimed, "Heil Hitler!" but was soon to regret this when he himself became a target of Nazi violence. In the long run this tactical adaptability proved ineffective. Enraged by the encyclical letter, Hitler himself issued a directive to resume the offensive against the religious orders (which were accused of currency trafficking, immorality, and so on). The charges were of course all trumped up, although in some cases there turned out to be real grounds for them. At this signal the more hostile *gauleiters* and state officials proceeded to intervene in a domain the faithful had always considered sacrosanct: crucifixes were removed from classrooms, to be replaced by portraits of the *führer*, and it was forbidden to mention the Old Testament in catechism classes. Some centers of Catholic theology were closed down. Such measures provoked protests which in their turn provoked measures taken at a national level. By the eve of the war all Catholic youth groups and associations of workers had been dissolved.

The cohesion of the body of bishops now began to crack. The bishop of Berlin, von Preysing, wrote: "The time has come to distance ourselves from 'as if' policies and to abandon subtle diplomacy"; and the bishop of Münster, von Galen, even urged his flock to act in concert with the Protestants and unbelievers who defended human rights. This was a completely new move, both tactically and theologically, for by tackling human liberties in general, not just the religious liberty of Christians, the church might have been led also to take up the defense of the Jews. However, on that it score it continued to remain extremely prudent: no more than one or two cases are known where priests helped persecuted Jews or suggested that parishioners should pray for them, one being that of Lichtenberg, preaching in the Berlin cathedral. At the time of the pogrom of November 1938, the church, as such, remained silent.[5]

As usual, persecution intimidated the lukewarm and increased the fervor of the faithful. The annual number of "departures from the Church" rose from thirty thousand in 1933–35 to first fifty thousand, then over one hundred thousand; then fell slightly. This represented no more than 0.5 percent of officially registered Catholics, but that national total conceals considerable regional differences. It is possible to be more specific about the number of Easter communicants, a good indication of religious fervor: in a homogeneous diocese such as that of Eichstätt in Bavaria, it increased by 10 percent, in the more mixed diocese of Cologne it decreased by 10 percent, in diaspora it also decreased, by seven percent (Meissen) or as much as 15 percent (Berlin). The defensive movement was thus clearly more robust wherever "Christian society" with all its religious, political, and cultural traditions was more deeply rooted. Processions and pilgrimages, formerly the most impressive of all Church demonstrations, were now ruled out and it became necessary to fall back upon "sacristy Christianity," sessions of meditation, masses made more "communal" by the use of German instead of Latin, and doctrinal study groups in which, with targeting that was slightly off-beam, the theses of Rosenberg were laid open to criticism. In such meetings, attended mostly by young people, both laymen and priests, the catacomb-like atmosphere that prevailed encouraged every kind of audacity including condemnation of the prudence of the bishops. The latter reacted in as many diverse ways to internal criticism as they did when confronted by the authorities. The bishop of Fribourg advised the catechists to pass over the history of the Jewish people in silence "in view of the circumstances"; the bishop of Cologne entrusted thirty-two-year-old priest Joseph Teusch with editorship of a defense bulletin with the bellicose title *Abwehr*, but preferred that a brochure entitled *Truths of the Catechism*, of which several million copies were printed, should not be reprinted by his own diocesan new sheet. . . .[6]

Thus even an organization as strongly structured as the Catholic Church tended to dissolve into a collection of microsocieties. Although atomized by the joint offensive of a number of official apparatuses and linked only by their modest broadsheets, these nevertheless reacted with remarkable unanimity. M. Broszat stresses the ambiguity of this *Resistenz* which, except in the cases of a few individuals, cannot be described as a political resistance (*Widerstand*). Catholic solidarity with the Jews was limited to converts, their defense of religious schooling was limited to maintaining the status quo, and their condemnation of antireligious leaders spared Hitler himself. In these respects the deepest feelings of the faithful seemed to tally with the vain subtleties of many of their bishops, as is confirmed by one Bavarian father who wrote as follows to his son: "I shall pray . . . for the preservation of Christianity in Germany, for the union of Churches, for the *Führer* to see the light, for him to find collaborators to serve God . . . It is with these sentiments that I now sign off, writing the words 'Heil Hitler!' from the bottom of my heart."[7]

Hitler was by now committed to ventures of an increasingly risky nature, but thanks to his charisma he could still drag into national union the very people whom his entourage—with his approval—were each day hunting down.

MARCHING AS TO WAR

If war had broken out at the time of Munich, the Allied blockade would soon have gotten the better of the German economy.[8] The sequence of spectacular decisions taken within the space of eighteen months, between the spring of 1938 and the autumn of 1939, betrays the nervousness of the German leaders, their disagreements, and the inefficiency of a system that combined state impulsion with a free market. The way out of these difficulties was obvious but easy, namely to put new, more resolute leaders at the head of the conservative elites. But was the risk of alarming public opinion too great?

To release more sources of labor would require coordinating the actions of the curators of labor, business proprietors, the Labor Front, and the Four-Year Plan. Hitler complicated the "organigramme" even further by setting above all these "a plenipotentiary for the mobilization of a labor force," the *Gauleiter* Fritz Sauckel. A number of decrees now fixed maximum levels for salaries, requisitioned workers from "superfluous" sectors, made the obligation of Labor Service more stringent for both boys and girls, and limited the possibilities for nomadism among workers moving from one firm to another. But the market was hard to regulate and individuals were recalcitrant. No longer able to entice staff with higher wages, munitions factories contrived to poach each other's skilled workers by promising a special social support system, housing, and overtime. Seen from a distance these advantages were alluring; but in the day-to-day reality, longer working hours and the pressure to increase production caused more accidents and absenteeism. One example cited was that of a manager who, in order to cure his workers of "Opel sickness" (constant requests to be treated in the same fashion as at that model firm), sent them on a visit to the factory in question from which they returned horrified by the rates of production expected there. In the Ruhr coal mines, a decree issued by Goering in person ruled that wages were to be increased by 10 percent in return for one hour's extra work each day. But all in vain: overall production was to remain at the same level up until 1945. As for the four hundred thousand men forcibly sent to work on the "Western Wall" (the Siegfried Line), they like their predecessors continued to manifest what the Gestapo termed "camp psychosis" characterized by brawling, alcoholism, and a general lack of discipline. As an ultimate resource, the *Anschluss* authorized the transfer of thousands of Austrian workers to the "old Reich," but they proved incapable of maintaining the pace of work. Implicitly the regime recognized its impotence; meanwhile the police arrested "ringleaders," but propaganda remained extremely discreet on the score of all these problems, no doubt because its major argument, the imminence of war, might well have rebounded against the regime.[9]

At the other extreme of the social scale it now became necessary to ensure not merely the neutrality of leading figures but their unreserved collaboration. In the short space of a few weeks (November 1937 to February 1938), conservative ministers and generals were sacked and replaced by men loyal to the regime. Wine merchant Joachim von Ribbentrop went to foreign affairs, Walter Funk to the economy, and Generals Wilhelm Keitel and

Alfred Jodl to the high command of the armed forces. What was less apparent to international observers was the simultaneous nazification of the major elite bodies.

On the face of it the diplomatic corps seemed less affected than most. The presence of Weizsäcker at the General Secretariat and the incompetence of the newly appointed minister allowed many of its members to hang on to the illusion that they could still exert a moderating influence: "One does not give up on one's country just because one has a bad government," one of them remarked. The Munich agreement (which Hitler for his part regarded more as a concession) seemed to confirm their view, although there were already some who suspected that expansionism would not prove limitable and were telling their foreign colleagues so — the first step toward "treason."[10]

Similarly, the traditional officers drew comfort from noting that, beneath the Staff Office of the armed forces (*OKW*), which was entrusted to party "lackeys," that of the territorial army remained in the hands of more independent figures, first Generals Walter von Brauchitsch and Beck, then Brauchitsch and General Franz Halder. Brauchitsch ventured only to limit the party's more flagrant interventions in his domain, meanwhile soft-soaping his "easygoing" chief. Beck for his part did go so far as to suggest exerting pressure on Hitler by threatening a collective resignation of all the generals; but the plan he set out in July 1938 boiled down to a set of contradictory slogans. The very first two were significant: "Up with Hitler! Down with the Gestapo!"; these were followed by a number of claims favoring freedom of opinion and religion, deploring the SS, who were called a "Tcheka," and agitating for the improvement of civil budgets. The last slogan exclaimed, "Prussian simplicity and cleanliness!" When Beck was dismissed, his successor Halder simultaneously prepared an order for operations against Czechoslovakia and a putsch to be launched if war was declared. Historians given to hypothesizing will continue to wonder what would have happened if Chamberlain and Daladier had not backed down on Munich. But the greatest problem for the Prussian tradition the generals dreamed of restoring was that, among their own subordinates, it was undermined by initiatives of the *OKW*. The latter forbade officers to adopt any position on religious matters, authorized "departures from the Church," and dismissed all pastors of the Confessional Church from their positions as almoners. It sent its lecturers to spread among army garrisons the new ideal of an officer: a political leader charged with propagating ethical values (*Volkstrum*) among his men and explaining that the future war would be an ideological one. This maneuver of subversion from below counted on the younger generation of serving officers, many of whom were trained by the Hitler Youth Organization. And as it clashed with the principles of apoliticism upheld by staff officers, an order was circulated withdrawing the latters' right to present written comments on the orders of their superiors, which had always constituted a special feature of the Prussian army. Discouraged by these attacks and no doubt also by the vanity of conspiracy, these defenders of the ethical tradition kept silent when the pogrom of 9 November took place, whereas a number of individual protests came from the air force and the navy, even though these were reputed to be more supportive of the regime.[11]

The freedom of maneuvre enjoyed by major business bosses, or at least those proprietors who were "their own masters," also suffered a number of blows. After the sacking of Schacht, the leadership of the Ministry of the Economy was entrusted to political managers. At the Four Year Plan, C. Krauch extended his "plenipotentiary powers" to cover munitions, and in relations with his original firm *IG Farben* pursued an ambiguous policy that has been described by some as a privatization of economic policy, by others as a nationalization of the chemical sector. In the steel industry the balance between public and the private sectors remained indecisive. On the one hand expansion of the "Hermann Goering Factories," which were favored by every advantage, absorbed the possessions of Thyssen (who had fled into exile), a large proportion of the Austrian steel industry, the coal mines of northern Bohemia, and the Skoda munitions works in Czechoslovakia. On the other hand, the private *Konzern*, Flick, Röhling, and Mannesmann made similar acquisitions as a result of Aryanization and conquests abroad. What weakened the body of business proprietors even more than competition between these *Konzern* was the appearance of a new type of "party card-holding industrialist": no longer an entrepreneur who became a party member as a matter of precaution or an incompetent "old veteran fighter" installed in a lucrative post, but a manager making a career at once in the economy (whether private or public mattered not) and in the party or SS hierarchy. The rise of such men was characteristic of this whole system, the nature of which would be difficult to classify. Is nationalization or capitalism the better description? A compound expression such as "monopolistic state capitalism" hardly helps solve the problem. Whatever the correct description, these groups of businesses with all their internal rivalries, also collaborated in the expansionist policies that would lead to war.[12]

High-ranking officials, staff officers, and a number of businessmen, some in semi-disgrace, others still in harness, would meet in the salons of Berlin and in their country retreats. The diary of Ulrich von Hassell, distanced from active diplomacy since 1937, records a number of their conversations during the period in between Munich and the war. Confident rightly or wrongly that these intimate circles harbored no spies, they made no bones about criticizing party climbers or even Hitler himself. Some placed their hopes in Goering; others noted the increasing popular unrest. Many were hoping for a catastrophe, a war that Germany was bound to lose which would bring an end to the detested system. But all were resigned rather than combative. Some it is true were beginning to think in terms of a coup and the "new Germany" that might emerge from it. But so long as they were not pushed into resigning, all this did not stop them from working in ways that promoted laws and plans of aggression. Inevitably, daily accommodations of this kind were reflected in their own plans for the future. Even for those hoping to get rid of Hitler the future Reich was to retain its extended frontiers and, within them, an authoritarian constitution: in short, it would simply be "an improved Third Reich."[13]

It is not often enough noticed that the pogrom of 9 November 1938[14] came hard on the heels of the diplomatic success of Munich: Hitler could now afford to disregard the indignant reactions that anti-Semitic violence would not fail to produce in public opinion. Nevertheless we need to track further back in time in order to trace its origins. Once annexed, Austria provided a new field in which to test the twofold anti-Jewish policy already tried out in 1933 and 1935: a policy basically violent with its brutalities, arrests, and looting, it was also apparently rational when seen from above, with the rich financing the emigration of its victims. This policy was forthwith transferred to the territory of the "old Reich." Official harassment resumed with breathtaking speed, as was recorded daily in the notebooks of victims: fortunes had to be declared, Jews had to take a second forename (Israel or Sarah), their identity cards had to be stamped with a "J," and the work permits of Jewish doctors were withdrawn with the exception of seven hundred physicians derisively labeled "carers." At the same time the police were turning a blind eye to a new wave of physical violence: in June in Berlin; in early autumn in Munich and the Franconian countryside (where inhabitants had earlier risen in defense of their bishop); Goebbels dispatched 1,500 Berlin Jews with police records to concentration camps and in October seventeen thousand Polish Jews were expelled from Germany and forced to vegetate in poverty on the frontier while their country of origin refused them entry. All these actions were harbingers of violence on a larger scale, which now only needed a pretext.[15]

The assassination of German embassy secretary Ernst von Rath in Paris by a teenage Jewish refugee from Germany on 7 November 1938 provided it. Again it was Goebbels who seized the opportunity. The sequence of events is well documented.

After a press campaign attacking the "worldwide Jewish conspiracy" on the seventh and eighth, "spontaneous" episodes of violence erupted while the police received orders not to intervene. Then came the terrible night of the ninth, with one hundred deaths and more than seven thousand shops looted; the following day the press was ordered to minimize the damage. Throughout these days other leaders had remained silent. The SS, which would have preferred a massive, well-ordered expulsion, even expressed a few reservations and then made up for their temporary inactivity by sending thirty thousand Jews off to concentration camps, which they emerged from a few weeks later broken by individual brutal assaults. Goering now intervened by virtue of his economic powers and inflicted a collective fine of one hundred million marks on the victims. What motives led Goebbels, the initiator, and Hitler, without whose authorization the operation could not take place, to relaunch a campaign of undisguised terror? They probably sought at one stroke to appease the impatience of their fanatics with a ritual of Jewish humiliation, convince more Jews to emigrate, and also persuade public opinion, which had remained singularly unbellicose during the period of international tension, that Germany remained permanently under threat from the Jewish peril.[16]

For the victims the return to calm was just the beginning of their eventual ruin. All Jews had to sacrifice a quarter of their fortune to pay the collective fine, works of art and even sums the insurance companies paid them to repair damage caused during the riots were confiscated, and jewelry and the last remaining non-Aryanized businesses had to be sold off at giveaway prices. Daily life for Jews in Germany grew even more somber as they were banned from swimming pools, parks, museums, and theaters, and Jewish tenants of "Aryan" landlords were expelled and forced to move into separate apartment blocks. In symbolic fashion the "Representation of German Jews" was renamed the "Union of Jews in Germany." All the signs pointed to the creation of ghettos, a phenomenon already taking place in Vienna.[17]

However, public opinion did not react the way it was supposed to. The few fanatics who had stoked up the flames were outnumbered by the many who protested publicly, some of them evem party members who were avowed anti-Semites. Some were indignant at the destruction and looting in the name of the rights of property. Others, seeing synagogues set ablaze, feared it would soon be the churches' turn. Patriots claimed they were humiliated to see Germany reduced to the level of Tsarist Russia. Weighing up the situation on the basis of regional reports, the *SD* picked out as centers of discontent the mainly Catholic towns in the west and the south, and liberal circles, above all in Hamburg, where the Hanseatic tradition of tolerance and good manners was particularly shocked. In contrast the Protestant and rural north seemed more indifferent. If Goebbels had launched the operation to win over public opinion, he had to acknowledge his failure—and did so by multiplying his polemics against the Jews, arguing that it was "inadmissable that only the state and the party should be anti-Semitic." Of course that was wildly exaggerated, but so was the converse optimism expressed in the reports of Socialists, who saw in the German people's reaction proof that they had not succumbed to the poison. In a more qualified manner, it seems fair to conclude along with W. S. Allen that in their hierarchy of values many Germans still placed respect of order and property and even of religions, whatever they were, above their prejudices against the Jews.[18]

No doubt the public was also alarmed by the threat of war, for the sequence of international crises had been nerve-racking. The first two, the Austrian and Sudeten crises no more than six months apart, aroused the same pattern of emotions: alarm at the initial press campaign and recall of reservists; a measure of doubt regarding the propaganda, with greater attention paid to foreign radio waves; fear of war when the tension was at its peak; relief when the Westerners' backed down (except among the groups of opponents who were counting on the West to stand firm); followed finally by renewed enthusiasm. The second time around though, anxiety was more in evidence, so much so that *SD* reports again took to using the word "psychosis," their usual way of criticizing propaganda's inefficacy. On 27 September Hitler tried to raise the morale of Berliners by having troops parade through the city center, but hardly anyone turned out to watch; and in the streets of Munich at the time of the conference Chamberlain was the man initially applauded. News of the agreement was greeted with all the more admiration for the *führer*, who through his moderation was considered to have saved the peace. However, at this point he realized that this pacific image might rebound against him, so Goebbels ordered the press to adopt a more aggressive tone with respect to foreigners. The annexation of "what remained of Czechoslovakia" in 1939 caused unease, since not many people had read *Mein Kampf* and understood that the revision of the Treaty of Versailles, of which they approved, was to be followed by the conquest of the "inferior peoples" of eastern Europe. However, Hitler's fiftieth birthday on 20 April 1889, celebrated with political meetings and military parades, restored the consensus. And when new claims were made, this time against Poland, public opinion was favorable because Danzig and the Polish Corridor had once been German possessions and were therefore legitimate objectives. Besides, the "filthy Poles" deserved to be taught a lesson. The German-Soviet pact signed in August 1939 strengthened the feeling of optimism: it would certainly intimidate the Westerners, and the peace would once again be saved. Their declaration of war after Germany attached Poland on 1 September thus came as a surprise. Hitler's standing was by no means diminished by this development, as people were still grateful for his efforts to find a peaceful solution. Nevertheless, according to observers,[19] morale was "depressed."

Did Hitler decide to go to war simply in accordance with the program he set out in 1937 in the famous address recorded by Colonel Friedrich Hossbach? Or was he forced into attacking in order to provide an escape from the hopelessness of the internal situation he himself had created, with its shortage of raw materials, inflexibility of the labor market, and unpopularity of all the material sacrifices and religious persecution? Had the "rigid and sickly overorganization in every domain of life" that J. Keppler remarked upon in his diary engendered a series of blockages that could only be dissolved by a new wave of ardor, this time of a bellicose nature? In his early theses Tim Mason asserted that the renewal of the working-class struggle precipitated the sudden decision to go to war; later however he recognized the error in exaggerating the dimensions and impact of that popular unrest. Besides, it was not a short war of a kind to strengthen the cohesion of the people that Hitler had in mind, but the conquest of a whole continental if not worldwide empire. He could count on the obedience of the military, but could not be as confident about the unconditional loyalty of the civilian population. This would continue to worry him.[20]

NOTES

1. Milza P., passim, in particular p. 379.
2. Scholder K., *Kirchen*, Bd. 2, p. 366 f.
3. Conte E. and Essner C., p. 384.
4. Droz J., p. 144 f.; Boyens A.; Confessional Church doc. in *60*, nos. 10 – 15, 19, 109; Klönne A., *Jugend*, p. 170 (Darmstadt); Kershaw I., *L'Opinion*, pp. 159 – 81 (Bavaria); Broszat M., "Ebermannstadt" (Franconia); Thierfelder J. (Württemberg); Van Norden G., "Kirchenkampf" (Rhineland); Klotzbach K., p. 227 f. (Westphalia).
5. Lewy G., chap. 5 – 6; Volk L., p. 66 f.; Hürten H., p. 380, 428 – 433, 446 f.
6. Hürten H., p. 328, 556 f., 571; Hehl U. von, *Erzbistum Köln*, p. 77, 86, 128 – 40; *65*, doc. p. 240, 247 (Trier); Blessing W.K. (Bamberg); Kershaw I., *Hitler-Mythos*, p. 90; id., *L'Opinion*, pp. 183 – 212 (Bavaria); Hetzer G., p. 217 (Augsburg); Maier J. (Baden).
7. Hehl U. von, "Forschungsüberblick"; Broszat M., "Sozialgeschichte"; Frölich E., p. 523 (quotation).
8. Petzina D., Autarkiepolitik, p. 195.
9. Mason T., *Arbeiterklasse*, pp. 135 – 58 and doc. 108, 123, 141, 150, 156; Petzina D., "Mobilisierung"; Blaich F., "Wirtschaft"; Wisotzky K. (Ruhr).
10. Krüger P.
11. Müller K. J., *Heer*, pp. 313 – 48, 381, 415 – 19; id., "Armee"; Messerschmidt M., p. 170, 189, 223 – 34.
12. 12. Petzina D., *Autarkiepolitik*, p. 195 f.; Hayes P., pp. 166 – 80; Mollin G., pp. 110 – 33, 184 – 90, 262 – 66; Broszat M., L'État hitlérien, pp. 434 – 39.
13. Hassell U. von, notes on 1938 – 39, passim; Müller K. J., "Eliten"; Droz J., ppo. 133 – 37.
14. It seems preferable to call it by its real name rather than borrow the expression "night of glass" used sneeringly by the breakers of the windows.

15. Burrin P., pp. 52–65; Plum G., "Wirtschaft"; see the journals of Nathorff H. and Klepper J., *Unter dem Schatten.*
16. Benz W., "Novemberpogrom."
17. Kwiet K.; Plum G., "Deutsche Juden," p. 67 f.
18. Allen W. S., "Offentlichkeit"; Peukert D., *Volksgenossen*, p. 67; Auerbach H.
19. Auerbach H.; Steinert M. G., *Hitlers Krieg*, p. 81 f.; Kershaw I., *Hitler-Mythos*, pp. 111–25; Stöver B., pp. 173–206; Broszat M., "Ebermannstadt" (a reflection of public opinion in a peasant microsociety).
20. Klepper J., Unter dem Schatten, notes on 24 January 1939; Mason T., *Arbeiterklasse*, in particular the introduction; Düffler J.

—Part Two

WARTIME SOCIETY

1939–1945

6 — The Dissolution of Civil Society

The small living units that had more or less survived state and party attempts to take them over now inevitably suffered from the constraints of the war economy and the direct impact of operations — initially from the skies and later on the ground. The cohesion of family units was undermined by the mobilization of fathers, the evacuation of small children to the countryside, and the participation of adolescents and mothers in the tasks of defense. Workshops and stores were liable to be closed down from one day to the next by the authorities, and peasant homes in the countryside compensated for the departure of their adult menfolk by employing strangers or taking in refugees from the towns. In the towns, evacuations as a matter of precaution were more or less willingly accepted. These were followed by massive emergency evacuations that broke up the remaining links of neighborliness and friendship. Only those who worked in munitions factories were supposed to stay but they too were then decentralized and shifted to more sheltered regions. Most individuals thus found themselves cut off from familiar surroundings, constantly having to move on, living amid strangers. Civil society turned into a kind of kicked-in anthill. This atomization resulted from the nation's circumstances, but corresponded too closely with the leaders' plans for them not to seek to exploit it. Meanwhile, those most affected by society's disintegration were devoting all their cunning to minimizing its effects and repairing old ties.

FAMILIES SPLIT APART

As early as 1940 a vast operation called "sending the children to the countryside" was launched. The reason invoked officially was the need to get them away from possible air raids and all the other wartime difficulties bound to arise in large towns. But in truth this was a renewed political strategy: one pedagogical review called it "a truly Socialist and revolutionary undertaking." Control over the schooling system had passed to the Ministry of Education at the Chancellory, that is to say to Bormann and his assistants, and their aim was to detach young children from the influence of their parents and teachers who were too traditional and entrust them to the new formative influences of the SS and the cadres of the Hitler Youth Organization. Crowds of little citizens (figures vary between eight hundred thousand and 2.5 million) were scattered throughout Germany and even the conquered countries and installed in various buildings or in camps. They were taught by their old teachers for six hours of classes daily and the rest of time by *HJ* leaders. The latter had many opportunities to impress upon their students that qualities of character were now more important than book learning, and that ideally one should aim to be not a good pupil but "one of the lads" (*Kerl*). Such encouragements to embrace a false independence were all the better received given that the only remaining teachers were old and easy to despise. The Teachers' League was itself concerned at the situation but no longer had any role to play and was soon dissolved.

In the future that dichotomy between teachers and educators would have to go. Teacher-training institutes were subordinated directly to the *HJ*, no baccalaureat was necessary to enter these, and intellectual culture was reduced to a minimum. There was even a plan to swell recruitment of teachers with demobilized noncommissioned officers once peace returned. Post-primary education was not to escape this revolution either: to select a lower elite from the mass of adolescents, a new type of professional school was introduced, the *Haupteschule*, which was to recruit its students using as criteria (in descending order of importance) "character, physical aptitude, and intellectual ability." Young people destined for the upper elite were discouraged from entering secondary school and directed toward

the *Napola*, nurseries for cultivating new Europeans where the
SS spirit predominated. Their German students, "ethnic Germans," and "Aryan foreigners" were lured in by the prospect of
their future role as leaders and took courses that sent them to the
conquered eastern territories, visits to the ghettos, and so on.
Initially fifteen of these establishments were set up, but their
number soon increased to forty-two: the time for prototypes was
certainly past.

But did German youth really become steeped in the desired
"Nordic attitudes?" Apart from two minorities, the fanatics on
the one hand and anarchists on the other, the children subjected to this camp-living seem to have emerged militarized
rather than nazified. The *HJ* catechism published in 1943 was a
total flop and soon disappeared into the hands of collectors of
old papers. On the other hand the youthful German public were
keen on war stories and particularly interested in technical
weaponry, tanks, submarines, and airplanes. As they grew
older, those who remained in the towns were increasingly drawn
into the war effort, first into tasks aiding passive defense and
later into anti-aircraft artillery operations (*Flak*). Hundreds of
thousands served under the falling bombs in this way. It was a
far cry from the lecture halls, despite the presence of teachers
who lived with the boys on the gun emplacements where they
attempted to hold a few classes. Nor were the young interested
in politics: they were not at all pleased at efforts to make them
wear swastika armbands. One wonders whether the ten thousand others who joined the *Hitlerjugend* division and were later
cut to pieces in Normandy were actually fanatics. Even if they
were, they represented no more than a minority. Hitler and
Bormann, reading the *SD* reports, were alarmed at the disappointing attitude of members in classes 24 and 25 who, it was
claimed, were steeped in "Christian poison" and hostile to all
forms of partisan commitment. When in October 1944 cadets
from that age group were incorporated into the *Volkssturm* militia, they and their grandfathers formed a strange combination:
they no doubt were determined to defend the frontiers, but were

far less interested in the superiority of the German race. A photograph of the *Führer* stroking the cheek of one of these young heroes received wide publicity in the press, but editors were careful to hide another which showed a child-soldier who for all his virile uniform could not hold back his tears. The experience of defeat was life-changing for many of these boys: Hitler, their idol—as he was to many of them—had been brought low, and military heroism was revealed in all its inanity. But it was too late for them to feel any attraction to doctrine. This was how "the skeptical generation" as sociologists were to call them entered adulthood.[1]

In the meantime some of their contemporaries had openly taken to dissidence. As usual the Gestapo had no hesitation in designating as "enemies of the Reich" both the young "swing" bourgeois of Hamburg and Frankfurt who interspersed American jazz sessions with criticisms of the regime and the insubordinate youths in proletarian quarters. Also, these gangs of young "pirates" had no precise political aims. Prewar gangs had evolved out of exasperation caused by the *HJ*'s determination to control them. The effect of the subsequent dislocation was to encourage their delinquency. By the winter of 1940–41, magistrates were already alarmed at the increase in robberies, nocturnal disturbances (despite the curfew), and juvenile prostitution, while the police, to excuse their impotence, complained about the absence of fathers in the homes and "the bad education purveyed before 1933." From 1942 on, disorder became so general that Himmler and Hitler himself were worried. Repressive legislation seemed ineffective; eventually all demonstrations of hostility toward the *HJ* came to be assimilated into a serious political crime, namely the reconstitution of a league recently dissolved. But the magistrates found it hard to pin down violators of that particular infraction. Although some gangs were taking over the uniforms and songs of the earlier gangs of young *bündisch* and the "Hounds" of Leipzig were of Socialist or Communist inspiration, many others could only be described as street gangs: groups of adolescents living on the same street, for the most part workers' sons, themselves apprentices, seeking a collective style of life less military and chaste than that of the official movement, who lorded it over the neighborhood, hustled passersby, and from time to time took off roaming around the country. The police—authoritarian, prudish, and close to the cadres of the Hitler Youth Organization—detested them. By 1941 the police were forcing some youths to serve one month of hard labor (*Arrest*) and dispatching others to retraining camps for young vagabonds. It is hard to say how many of the forty thousand minors sentenced that year and the fifty thousand sentenced the following year belonged to gangs. But locally the police produced some impressive figures: in the Rhineland, for example the "Edelweiss Pirates" were said to have twenty-eight gangs with thirty members apiece. During the last months of the war some boys, by then both morally and materially homeless, took to camping in bombed-out ruins where they met up with army deserters, escaped prisoners of war, and foreign workers on the run. The Gestapo launched veritable military operations against these iconoclasts and executed them just as readily as they did their older companions. Even the civilian and military elites of the Resistance misunderstood the nature of this revolt, as can be seen from the plans laid by General Beck and Carl Goerdeler: had the assassination attempt against Hitler on 20 July 1944 succeeded, the whole of German youth would have found itself gathered into a single movement led by the officers.[2]

It proved harder to mobilize women than their children. The needs of war clashed with the doctrine that continued to assign women the role of guardians of the home, which is why Hitler, while consenting to appeal for volunteers occasionally, for a long time blocked plans for massive female labor requisitioning. When he was eventually forced to accept this, he announced that in compensation they would never have to work in industry again once the war was over. For once, one of his long-term policies corresponded to the desires of the population.

Women who had worked for some time but only taken jobs under financial constraint and new working women who found themselves more or less forced to work continued to be the most intractable to discipline, and those who constituted a reservoir of labor used all their ingenuity to avoid having to work in factories. The results of this general reluctance are reflected in the statistics. On the eve of the war, 14.5 million working women made up 53 percent of the age-group fifteen to sixty; by the autumn of 1944 that number still had not risen to fifteen million and in the meantime even fell to fourteen million, then slowly rose again thanks to the combined efforts of employment and munitions agencies. But even that total is misleading as it results from many more women taking jobs in industrial offices and a few more employed in agriculture, handicrafts, and domestic service, with total stability in the tertiary sector and industrial production. This semi-failure has often been contrasted to the far more rapid increase in the number and percentage of working women in Britain over the same years, and pointed to the conclusion that democratic consensus had proved to be a far more effective motivator than dictatorial constraint. But that thesis unfortunately rests upon a fragile basis: given that the proportion of working women had in peacetime already been much higher in Germany than in Britain, it was inevitably harder to persuade the inactive remainder into jobs. At any rate about three million "available" women of suitable age, unmarried or with one child at the most, for a long time remained at home rather than go out to work, although many proved proved their civic commitment by working, unpaid, for the social services or clearing bombed-out ruins.

How this internal battle was fought throws light upon both the illogicality of the authorities and the persistence of inequalities in this society claiming to be egalitarian. At the beginning of the war employment agencies assumed they could rapidly find women to replace the male workers called up to fight. Legislation to introduce this requisitioning was in place, the Labor Service had at its disposal one hundred thousand eighteen-year-old girls, the organization of the "obligatory year" could supply three hundred thousand more school-leavers, and restrictions on the production of consumer goods liberated many other workers. But the girls were steered into jobs in agriculture and as family home-helps, and women working in textiles refused to move to the centers of the munitions industry — quite apart from the fact that the latter had lost to the *Wehrmacht* many skilled male workers whom few women were qualified to replace. Furthermore, the authorities dispensed relatively substantial allowances to soldiers' wives, and within the first six months of the war five hundred thousand working women eligible for these grants decided to stop working. Those who contined were subjected to very harsh conditions, working up to ten hours a day while coping with many food shortages as well. Their rate of production fell by a quarter, absenteeism increased even further, and industrial managers clamored for energetic measures of coercion. But all the eloquence of the Labor Front and the party went unheeded, and eventually the Gestapo simply refused to have anything to do with women. Military armament offices urged general requisitioning as the only means of salvation, but the political authorities told them "this would lead to too much unrest." Certainly plenty of women were looking for jobs in administrative offices, civilian public services, and military offices, some out of patriotism, the youngest to avoid agricultural labor. But factory work was shunned, and soldiers' wives who had already experienced it remained obstinately at home with the approval of their husbands. One wrote, "I have forbidden my wife to work so long as wealthy wives and girls are not mobilized. I am fighting for those families just as much as I am fighting for my own!" He might have been even more resentful if he had got wind of Goering's remarkable sociological theories: "Women from good backgrounds are the transmitters of hereditary culture and capital, so they should not be exposed to the stupid remarks and insolent mockery of ordinary women."

And girl students, typical representatives of those with "good backgrounds," were indeed spared all obligations throughout the duration of their studies. In order to fill now-open positions in the teaching body, medical profession, and the administration, the ministry even did a U-turn on its policy of imposing female quotas in schools, and by 1943 as many female as male students were attending. But women from the popular strata were not impressed by such realistic justifications and expressed the same resentment against "bourgeois" and "high-class" ladies as soldiers at the front did against those "sheltering" in the rear.

"Mobilization for work" was finally announced in January 1943. As well as nonworking men between the ages of sixteen and sixty-five, women between sixteen and forty-five were required to undergo a census with the exception of girls in secondary school, mothers of small children, and those with two children aged fourteen or younger. But this decree also allowed for so many other exceptions that they became known as the "rubber regulations." Of the three million women recorded in the census, 1.2 million were classified as employable, half of them on only a part-time basis. Middle-class women retained their servants and enrolled for office work or even went off to travel. New female workers, pushed from one firm or workshop to another, received a sour reception from those already employed and even from the heads of personnel, who wanted men even if they were foreigners. By July 1943 half the newly recruited women had abandoned their jobs. Unable to cope, Sauckel, the labor-force plenipotentiary, dismissed all denunciations filed against privileged nonworking women as prompted by "pure jealousy, truly Marxist instincts." He was relying above all on a massive importation of workers, both men and women, requisitioned in the east, and presented this as the miracle solution. But industry's appetite for workers proved insatiable. Goebbels meanwhile was intriguing to become the director of "total war." When he eventually replaced Sauckel in the summer of 1944 his spectacular decisions, such as closing theaters and restaurants, were accompanied by further capitulations before established interests: so as not to "upset the population," they stuck by the much-repeated formula that wives of officials were temporarily exempted from work. Not until the end of that year was this reserve of labor requisitioned, mostly for aviation factories . . . but the following year the factory proprietors confessed that they did not know what to do with the women and asked if they could sack them.

Several explanations may account for this relative impotence of the public authorities. It may be exaggerated to follow T. Mason's assertion that women were treated with circumspection because of "fear of the people": for in this case the "people" consisted mostly of well-to-do families or the soldiers mentioned previously who liked to know that their wives were at home (or in the country). Many industrialists' failure to cooperate also played its part: although dependent on State orders they remained their own masters when it came to policies affecting their staff. Should it be concluded, as do certain authors who stress the "modernizing" effects of the war, that this mobilization of women workers, even if only half successful, may have favored a certain fusion of the social classes and brought at least some improvement in the condition of women? In truth it appears that not many women from "good backgrounds" were seated before a machine tool alongside proletarian girls. The latter no doubt did benefit from the apparatus of social aid and care provided for mothers and infants that was traditional in at least the larger firms. Yet despite all the egalitarian promises, their wages, whether gauged by hours worked or production, remained considerably lower than the pay earned by working men, and their chances of promotion were few and far between. So until the new society materialized, women workers would remain welded to their lot, their sole comfort deriving from a comparison of their lot to that of fellow workers who were Jewish or "from the East."[3]

TOWNS REDUCED TO RUBBLE:
RESOURCEFULNESS AND
NEW SOLIDARITIES

For a while the evacuations of children and the spontaneous departures of well-to-do families affected relatively few people: up until July 1943, Berlin lost only three hundred thousand inhabitants out of over four million.[4] So virtually the entire urban population suffered the consequences of war, which were at first distressing and eventually tragic: material difficulties, the closure of small businesses, air raids.

There is no doubt that the statistical entity known as "the average German consumer" was adequately fed throughout most of the war years. Daily rations, estimated at 3,200 calories before the war, even increased for a while to 3,600 and only fell to 2,800 in 1944–45. During those years the inadequacies in domestic agricultural production were compensated for by purchases (requisitions really) from the occupied countries, which were supplying up to 20 percent of the total consumption. But those figures represent averages only for various regions and different social strata, and include only food. By 1940 textile sales had already shrunk by half. Domestic coal was in short supply for several winter months: with the canals frozen and the railways monopolized by the military, citizens, particularly in Berlin where the authorities usually kept a very careful eye on living conditions, were suffering from the cold and schools had to be closed. Discontent was rife in the suburbs, where people grumbled that residents in the fashionable quarters were enjoying privileged treatment, just as they did in the First World War. Propaganda simply promised better days ahead and claimed that conditions were worse for the English. For a while potatoes were in short supply too, but speeded-up deliveries and produce from small local gardens remedied the situation in the spring. Up until the summer of 1941 reports on public opinion mentioned only a few waves of unrest, when the bread ration was temporarily cut and especially over clothing shortages. Nevertheless consumer confidence persisted for roughly another year, proved by the disciplined way that people entrusted their savings to financial institutions which then reloaned that money to the state. The turning point came in 1942: in the spring a number of rations were cut, with "shattering" effects on morale, and at the end of the year households suddenly withdrew their funds and used them for bulk buying. The black market also expanded. Rumors and rancor were rife: social rancor against the rich, political rancor against the agricultural bureaucracy and judges seem as too easygoing on speculators. After a Christmas without presents, at the time of the bad news from Stalingrad in early 1943, V. Klemperer notes that people started using the verb *organisieren*, "to make do," a verb with very uncivic overtones. Eventually, from the winter of 1943–44 on, official rations were fixed at a barely adequate level and a whole economy based on the non-monetary bartering of services and commodities evolved.[5] No doubt such trials affected all countries involved in the war, but the German people fared better than many others, at any rate far better than those occupied by its armies whose privations helped to maintain a bearable living standard in Germany. But the *SD*'s persistence in spying on the grumbling housewives shows how nervous officials were made by memories of 1917–18.

SD reports also contain allusions, less abundant but equally concerned, to small businesses' misfortunes which threatened to undermine the loyalty of the independent middle class. Mobilization had already closed "for the duration of the war" many workshops and little stores worked by sole proprietors. Some wives of these men tried to struggle on alone but were eventually defeated by the difficulties of daily life. The situation was compounded by the resumption of "combing" operations which uprooted masters and their apprentices, shopkeepers and their employees, and transferred them to industrial jobs more useful to the country's defense. For a long time the selection of these victims was handled by the Chambers of Trades, organizations dominated by the most affluent and modern small-scale business proprietors, so now the remaining corporations found themselves at once fewer in number and economically strengthened. In the building trade for example, the number of construction firms was halved, but the survivors grouped together to get work on the large sites where fortifications were being built. Other branches of activity fared in a similar fashion: by 1940 it was estimated that public orders accounted for two-thirds of the business of artisans' orders. Rising prices for raw materials and higher wages for a workforce now much in demand, which contrasted starkly with the inflexibility of the tariffs paid for public orders, provoked plenty of grumbles, and in these circles many imprecations were voiced against this callous nationalization. In truth however, it appears that the incomes of this little aristocracy were increasing appreciably. Small shopkeepers, once rid of many competitors, also prospered up until 1942, first as a result of more customers and then by selling off their stock. But the Chambers of Trades then lost their precious right to select the businesses to be closed down, and many more medium-sized firms in their turn disappeared. The victims naturally enough returned to their old complaints. In Bavaria they prophecied, "After the war, there won't be a middle class, nothing but the rich and the poor"; and the most aggrieved talked of Bolshevism. As party members held on to their jobs more successfully than others, police observers noted their growing unpopularity with malignant satisfaction. The lack of cohesion between these two official organizations was by no means exceptional: as early as the end of 1939, administrators of annexed territories in the East had suggested settling German artisans there (the very people for whom industry was clamoring!) to take the place of the expelled Jews and Poles, and it received eight thousand applications to join this new-style colonization project. In the end however the SS instead decided to install "ethnic Germans" transferred from the Baltic States and central Europe.[6]

*   *   *

If the cohesion between consumers and producers was not more seriously undermined, it was because more dramatic trials afflicted them from 1942 onward, plunging everyone into identical misery: death or ruination in the air raids.

For two and a half years city dwellers had been left more or less undisturbed by the fighting war, with Britain's Royal Air Force simply dropping tracts and making a few pinpoint raids over Germany to demonstrate that they retained mastery of the skies. That was indeed more or less true: the *Luftwaffe* specialized in supporting ground troops and attacking enemy towns, and only organized a centralized home defense against enemy aircraft in the autumn of 1941. Until then only passive defense had been carefully organized. Suddenly the British changed their strategy, and instead of targeting precise objectives such as bridges, railway stations, and factories they began to carry out "zone bombing," systematically destroying specific urban districts both industrial and residential, adopting the very method their enemy had inaugurated first on Rotterdam, then Coventry. First tried out on Lübeck on the nights of 28 and 29 March 1942 and then Cologne on the nights of 30 and 31 May, the figures involved were unprecedented: 1,140 aircraft dropped 1,500 tons of explosive bombs and eight thousand three hundred incendiary bombs; ten thousand inhabitants were made homeless at least temporarily; sixteen industrial plants were flattened and fifty-five were severely damaged, with 151 partly damaged. Thanks to the collective shelters of apartment blocks, small individual family shelters, and huge shelters of reinforced concrete (*Bunker*) only 460 people were killed. Aid for the victims was prompt and efficient: countless staff members and helpers from the "National Socialist Popular Assistance" (*NSV*) distributed food and clothing, officials speedily dealt with applications for compensation within one month, and seventeen thousand workmen started making emergency repairs. But as time passed those statistics were to seem puny, particularly those relating to loss of life. The British bombers managed to navigate even in bad weather, when the Germans could not give chase. They also used a new type of incendiary bomb, whose combined heat caused a huge blast effect that prevented rescuers from reaching survivors trapped in the shelters. Soon all major towns were each in turn targeted for several consecutive nights. By 1943 American bombers were also attacking in daylight, setting out from either the British Isles or Italy so that southern and eastern Germany were also within their range. During the Normandy invasion in June 1944 there were fewer air raids in Germany, but after a month the offensive started up again and became even more extensive: Dresden, packed with refugees from the East, was flattened on 13 and 14 February 1945 with human losses on a huge scale never precisely established; Berlin suffered 12 attacks in the course of that same February, twenty-nine in March, and twenty-six more in April. In total, civilian losses came to between five hundred thousand and six hundred thousand dead and over eight hundred thousand wounded; an average of 40 percent of all dwellings were destroyed; in Cologne up to 70 percent.

The effect of these bombings on German production appears to have been relatively limited, at least up until 1944 when the British decided once more to target mainly factories producing synthetic petrol and communication routes as the Americans had been doing all along. When hostilities came to an end, the U.S. Air Force tried to calculate on the spot the effect of these strategies and discovered that the German war production had continued to increase right up until the autumn of 1944. German industry had responded to the air raids on large towns by dispersing throughout the countryside and burying itself in quarries and mines. In terms of the indirect consequences on the military operations the score was more satisfying for the Allied air forces: in order to concentrate on antiaircraft defense, the *Wehrmacht* had been obliged to withdraw thousands of men and a third of its artillery units from the land armies, while the *Luftwaffe* itself, concentrating on defense of the fatherland, had been unable to support German ground troops at the

Normandy landings in the West and the Soviet offensives in the East.

But in bringing an unprecedented intensity to this new type of warfare, the principal intention of the British high command was to break the morale of the civilian population; and in this it failed utterly. Essentially those tragic nights and the following days gave inhabitants a chance to manifest their spirit of initiative and collective solidarity which the Nazi regime had tried to wipe out. On the spot the perceived image of the regime was frequently that of a blustering *Gauleiter* and a clutch of paralyzed party officials, or it was represented by Goering, oversized target of a hail of bitter jokes since he was blamed for the defensive air power's weakness. In contrast the organs of passive defense, of rescue, and more generally of civil administration functioned as well as could be expected. As soon as the first incendiary bombs were dropped, one person in each apartment block was appointed to stay in the building and use sand to extinguish the initial small fires. When those incendiaries were replaced by large liquid gasoline bombs, that strategy became ineffective, and faced with the "cyclones of fire," even the professional fire fighters were helpless. When the apartment block shelters were recognized as death traps, the inhabitants flocked to the *Bunker*, huge concrete cubes that had by now become part of the urban scene—except in Dresden, where the *Gauleiter* had forbidden their construction—or else to areas of open land or public parks. As soon as the alert was over, terror gave way to hyperactivity. City dwellers were indignant at the sight of "bigwigs" returning from outlying neighborhoods where they had spent the night and scoffed at the news bulletins that minimized the destruction. But as one Nuremberg inhabitant noted, "The soul of the populace is on the boil, but not boiling over." Aid for the victims was the responsibility of local authorities and the *NSV*, theoretically an organ attached to the party but one which many men and women, young and old alike, teachers along with their older pupils, had joined even though they specifically refused to commit themselves politically. The bombed-out were grateful for its help; and Nazi leaders as usual seized the opportunity to issue one of their typically mean-spirited directives: in January 1944, Bormann ordered that "all activities of the *NSV* must be carried out under the name *NSDAP*" because "the party is forced to undertake so many unpopular tasks; therefore the activities that elicit the most gratitude from the people must be publicly seen to operate under its name." The following July, Hitler similarly decided to subordinate the passive defense services to the *Gauleiters* and *Kreisleiters* despite the fact that many of them were renowned for their incompetence.[7]

What the authorities feared most was a panic inducing hundreds of thousands to flee into the countryside, halting industrial production and overwhelming the services in charge of evacuation. Although that did happen after some heavy bombing, many of those who fled soon returned home. The task of rehousing them seemed insurmountable. Local authorities began setting up huts, then the state announced a grandiose plan to house people in one million basic little tents, which never got further than the drawing board stage. The fact was that inhabitants wanted to return to or hang on in their towns in order to remain "at home," in their own streets and in their own ruined houses. In Cologne, a plan to rehouse fifty thousand homeless people outside the center of town attracted only four thousand volunteers and even many huts set up on the spot remained unoccupied. English radio called this determination to remain in town proof of German fanaticism, but that was altogether mistaken as seen from the diaries of two Berlin women from very different but equally nonconformist backgrounds, Ursula von Kardorff and Ruth Andreas-Friedrich. "Nobody thinks about Hitler when they are hammering in nails," wrote one; the other declared, "With these methods they'll never get us to go under." The author of a recent and more general study of air raids in the Second World War concluded: "Family life and community life were perhaps two forces in urban society that were much more powerful than had been believed by specialists on social matters in the period between the wars."[8]

Nazi utopians were equally misinformed. They intended to break up the large cities into a series of semi-rural quarters after the war. So the immediate chance to send several million citizens to the countryside in the interests of safety seemed too good to be missed. The agency responsibile for organizing the territory elaborated two successive plans with detailed maps for the evacuation of women, children, and old men. Berliners were to be routed to destinations ranging from western Prussia to Thuringen; those in Hamburg were to move either northeast or southward; the people of the Rhineland were to go to Baden and Württemberg, the Saxons to the Tyrol . . . a total exodus of twelve million people. In September 1944 these organizers found themselves planning to accommodate the same number of people fleeing into Germany from Soviet assaults in the eastern provinces (including Berliners previously sent there for "safety"!). The party, always seeking to present itself in a good light, was to be responsible for transporting and then sheltering these outward bound refugees when they reached their terminus. The data collected from the regions that received them indicate that, although not fully implemented, the plan did involve massive migrations: seven million people at least, not counting an extra two million who, as was their right, preferred to follow an itinerary of their own choice. Cohabitation of the refugees with their hosts was not without its problems: "I was better off living in my cellar in Hamburg," one refugee lamented; and on the banks of the Moselle and in the Baden region, refugees from Cologne were given such a disastrous reception ("community spirit is disappearing," one official report confessed) that ten thousand of these unfortunate city people had to be rerouted, this time to Silesia. Understandably then, many people preferred to set out again, and return home to wait for the bombs. So the nationwide heaps of city rubble never did become totally deserted. In the spring of 1944, five hundred thousand inhabitants were still in Cologne, four-fifths of them bombed out, and in March 1945 when American troops arrived there were still thirty-two thousand people living there. In Berlin, "which looks like the Roman forum at the time of the invasions" as one scholarly observer remarked, the population of four million had fallen to 2.8 million by the beginning of 1945, but the exodus was very uneven and varied considerably from one quarter to another: 40 percent from Charlottenburg in the bourgeois west of the city, but only 15 percent from certain lesser-class suburbs. This may have been due to a stronger local community spirit in the proletarian *Keize*, or more likely was because despite official promises travel out of town cost more than poorer families could afford. When military operations finally came to an end, refugees in the countryside hastened to return home. In the Ruhr the new municipal authorities forbade access to the most dangerous zones, but in vain. Nothing could stop former inhabitants from returning to live there as troglodytes.[9]

THE MIXING AND MIGRATIONS
OF RURAL POPULATIONS

The peasants, who clung to their customs, dialects, and community practices, were considerably annoyed by the Food Supply Corporation's repeated interference into their daily activities, and even the holders of "hereditary farms" felt let down. As in all countries the war inflicted two simultaneous and contradictory trials upon farmers. The army needed their young men, reckoning them to be better suited than city dwellers to live the hard life of infantrymen and also care for the army's horses, still widely used for transport despite the progress of mechanization. But in order to supply food for both civilians and the military it was necessary to increase production, and this required efficient, strong men on the farms to run them. Every village saw conflicts over the designation of those who had special dispensation to remain (as *uk*). "Local peasant leaders," many of them appointed by the corporation, thus on top of their job of orienting production took on the job of selecting these men. This task made them all the more unpopular, since they themselves were automatically exempt from armed service and were also accused of favoring the sons of the "wealthy" over the sons of the "poor." But these trials were not without their material compensations: the state allowed a slight rise in basic prices, for which it compensated with subsidies so as not to disadvantage consumers, and the average income of agricultural workers increased considerably. Then it stabilized for a while, while the cost of fertilizers and equipment fell, since industry failed to deliver them. Peasants thus had plenty of liquid money, not counting extra income derived from the black market, but this made inroads upon both their capital and their health. The shortage of labor had been dire even before the war, but now the aged, the young men exempted from military service, and women were obliged to make even greater efforts. In one rural locality in Franconia, in 1942 the subprefect began to worry about the population's signs of physical and nervous exhaustion, even in children, and about their excessive use of medicaments. For that reason, the army agreed to send assistance in the form of thousands of prisoners of war, at first Poles and French, and later—but fewer of them as they were not trusted— Soviets. The fine ethnic homogeneity of the German countryside was in danger from such cohabitation, but the police assiduously kept spying to make sure there were no scandalous intimate relations as a result.

When the refugees arrived from the cities the atmosphere became even more charged, if—that is—the reports of the authorities and information agencies, always more prone to report undesirable incidents than harmonious conditions, can be believed. The people of Hamburg and Kiel, resettled in Franconia, were at first treated with compassion by villagers, who were moved by their accounts of the nights filled with air raids. But discord soon took over for the simple reason that, thanks to their state grants, the mothers of refugee families could live a life of leisure while their hostesses were ground down by agricultural and domestic duties. In Württemberg, rich women from the cities scandalized the locals by lounging around in the hotels for all the world like tourists. The mutual preconceptions of city people and country folk, northerners and southerners, Catholics and Protestants, never flattering of each other at the best of times, became even more hostile as a result of these daily contacts. As the city dwellers saw it, all peasants were privileged, if not speculators. Meanwhile the extremely Catholic peasants of Bavaria criticized their new neighbors from Hamburg for not going to church and thereby calling down retribution, that is to say all those bombs, from Heaven.[10]

Similar examples of friction would be easy to find in other war-torn countries. But the eastern provinces of Germany constituted an altogether exceptional case of a mixing of populations followed by a tragic exodus. At the end of the Polish campaign in 1939 the SS agencies of ethnic cleansing had set out to Germanize the provinces newly annexed to the Reich: West Prussia, Poznania, and Upper Silesia. To replace the five hundred thousand Jews and seven hundred thousand Poles expelled from these areas, they brought in just under four hundred thousand inhabitants from the "old Reich" and 350,000 "ethnic Germans" collected from the Baltic States, the Tyrol, and the whole of central and eastern Europe. The 1.7 million people considered to be "Germanizable" remained from the autochthonous population, including between one hundred thousand and two hundred thousand children who had been removed from their parents; meanwhile, six million Poles were destined to be expelled soon. The "General Plan for the East," elaborated on the eve of the attack against the USSR was even more ambitious: within the next twenty-five years, it envisaged installing four million Germans in "farm-fiefdoms" scattered over the Russian and Ukrainian plains, where they were expected to reign like latter-day Teutonic knights over native populations reduced to serfdom. In those distant lands concrete applications of this plan were reduced to a few protoptypes since hardly any volunteered for the experiment, and because the SS, which probably would have been more energetic, was occupied elsewhere at the time. Further to the west however, between the Vistula and the Oder, the experiment was conducted with all the unscrupulous vigor that this first step toward Utopia demanded. Native villages of both Germans from the Reich and "ethnic Germans" were utterly dislocated, with only the families classed as "highly valuable" being kept together. Nazi ideology was revealing its true objectives. The traditional communities it initially pretended to exalt were to be replaced by "a social structure in which individuals would be totally mobile and disposable" (G. Aly). All these upheavals were compounded by others that stemmed from the evolution of the war, producing an extraordinarily mixed population composed mainly of old men, women, and children: former inhabitants, new colonialists, evacuated Berliners, prisoners of war, and foreign civilian workers. In all it totaled close to ten million individuals, more or less the same as the prewar population, except that young Germans mobilized to fight and the expelled Jews and Poles had been replaced by close to three million displaced persons.[11]

At this point the Red Army launched its offensives. By October 1944 it was threatening eastern Prussia; in mid-January it attacked again everywhere, then the front stabilized along the middle reaches of the Oder with eastern Prussia and the town of Breslau surrounded. The rumors circulating about behavior of Soviet troops—the raping, the massacres, and the looting—were terrifying. Today we know that many were well-founded, even if some units did behave in a more humane fashion. Their attacks westward provoked a huge exodus aggravated by the exceptionally cold weather and the indifference of political cadres. City dwellers rushed to catch the last trains heading west, then when the lines were cut imitated the peasants by loading their possessions and families on horse-drawn carts. Endless refugee convoys, frequently blocked by traffic jams and overtaken by avant-gardes of the enemy forces, were known as

Trecks. The history of this word perfectly reflects Germany's history of the war. Initially the name was invented by the propaganda service to glorify the arrival of German peasants in this Promised Land by resurrecting a Dutch word meaning "migration" applied in the late nineteenth century to the Boers' long march from the Cape to the Transvaal. When Germany's military situation was reversed, so was the meaning of this word which, instead of designating joyful arrival, now meant pitiful exodus. Maps later produced by the Ministry of Refugees in Bonn are marked by long, thick, black arrows leading from East Prussia to Danzig by way of the Frisches Haff and from there by sea, ever further westward, from Poznania to the Brandenburg region, and from Silesia to Saxony and Bohemia. They represent the routes taken by hundreds of thousands of people. In the spaces between them is a confused network of small arrows pointing in all directions, some them even returning eastward, which represents all the convoys that lost their way.

The attitude of party cadres made the catastrophe even worse. In Königsberg, in Elbing in East Prussia, in Brandenburg, and in Breslau, *Gauleiters* delayed the evacuation order on the pretext of not undermining morale or blocked the path of those newly arrived, assuring them that they had now reached the shelter of the old frontier fortifications (which for the most part existed only as a line drawn on paper). When civil administrators again found time to write reports, they condemned the incompetence or even cowardice of the *Kreisleiter* and their subordinates. One subprefect of the "Warthe country" (Poznania) wrote: "The convoys that arrived were not organized by the authorities of their districts of origin, for *they* traveled right at the front instead of at the rear of the *Trecks*." Another commented more forthrightly on refugees' surprise when they encountered one of these political officials still wearing his uniform, for everyone else had by now donned civilian clothes. The mayor of Posen (Poznan) told how his German staff deserted him, while his Polish employees now sabotaged the transport system, now did their best to keep some services functioning. In besieged Danzig the military and Nazis were accusing each other of being saboteurs and accomplices in the assassination attempt of 20 July.

It is hard to calculate how many lives were lost. Following the rather suspect figures suggested by the Bonn Ministry of Refugees, in 1969 the Federal Archives produced a number of more prudent calculations (six hundred thousand dead and 2.2 million "non-resolved" cases) and condemned the exaggerations of an anti-Soviet argument that added those two totals together and arrived at three million victims.[12] At any rate the *Trecks* deeply marked the nation's collective consciousness. It is often forgotten that the famous "historians' quarrel" of 1986 erupted not only over whether or not the genocide was unprecedented, but also because one historian involved had seen fit to discuss "two destructions" in parallel, that of the Jews and that of the German populations in the East.[13]

MILITARIZED WORKERS

Throughout the war the daily life of workers was governed by decisions made by distant bureaucrats who transferred them now from their factories to the army, now vice versa, now from one region to another. Furthermore they had to work alongside inexperienced people unknown to them: women, former employees, and small business proprietors from the tertiary sector, all strangers with whom it was difficult to set up a rapport of solidarity. These repeated changes in workers' geographical and human horizons resulted from the contradictory policies of the military and civil authorities, known as "mobilization for work."

The historiography of Germany's war for a long time accepted the distinction proposed by Alan S. Milward between its two phases: lightning war, which lasted until 1942–43, and than total war. According to this thesis, for a long time, up until the first major defeats, the regime limited its interference in the lives of civilians, food rationing, and sweeping planning of the labor market—a prudent policy that chimed with its general strategy, for, as one commentator wrote, "Dictatorial and demagogic regimes characteristically embark upon wars of pillage in order to avoid internal unrest." T. Mason reinforced that thesis when he noted the surprising weakness of the dictator who, after deciding in the first few days of the war to apply energetic measures to the labor market, rapidly went into reverse when faced with the resentment of the workers backed by the Labor Front. But as we have noted above, certain consumer goods nevertheless were restricted in those early days, and businesses listed as non-indispensable were constantly targeted by "combing" operations. These objections plus a number of others have recently been developed by economist Richard J. Overy, who concludes that the Third Reich did in fact enter into a total war economy right from the start: in one year the proportion of workers assigned to munitions leaped from 22 to 50 percent, and no doubt that concentration speeded up thereafter, if we are to believe Goering, who immediately after the victory over France announced forthrightly: "Now we shall really start rearming."[14]

But those long-term objectives did nothing to ease the difficulties of the present moment. Hitler decided to settle these conflicts of responsibility by creating the post of Minister of Armaments, which he entrusted to Fritz Todt, a technocrat who had proved his worth in motorway construction and fortifications and kept himself relatively distant from personality clashes. But as usual, Hitler also allowed the already existing administrations to continue operating as so many antagonistic pressure groups. The armed forces—the navy, the air force, and the territorial army—all needed specialists, particularly mechanics and electricians to service and repair the modern machinery. But such skilled men were equally indispensable in factories where those aircraft, tanks, radio transmitters, submarines, and so on were made. For despite the rationalization of production lines, all kinds of adjustments and upkeep tasks could only be carried out by these experienced professionals. Colonel Thomas, still in charge of the army's economic offices, spoke of "the battle over skilled workers between the front and the rear," a battle that was to continue for years.

The armed forces' mobilization of September 1939 had taken three million men out of the labor market. But by the end of the campaign in Poland, already, the army realized that its stock of munitions was running down so it agreed with bad grace to release a certain number of its specialists. Within a few months the number of those on "special release" (*uk*) rose from seven hundred thousand to two million. But industry was still not satisfied, for the repatriation of these workers to their homes had created new imbalances between the regions—a serious deficit in central Germany, where many munitions factories had been set up, and a glut elsewhere. A "National Plan of Rebalancement" then forced hundreds of thousands of workers to move to other more or less distant regions. At the same time, victories abroad and police repression at home were providing more new laborers: over a million prisoners of war, almost two million requisitioned or volunteer foreign civilians, and two hundred thousand Jews. But many of these were assigned to agriculture or public works, and of the remainder there were never enough skilled workers. In the summer of 1940 confusion was at its peak: Hitler began to envisage a more or less long world war which would have to be waged above all at sea or in the air, and during which civil production could return to its peacetime level. The army was ordered to dismantle seventeen divisions, all at once and send a new wave of specialist workers with "work permits" home to be employed in the shipyards and aviation factories. But at the very same moment Hitler reconverted to the idea of attacking the USSR and ordered the production of munitions for land warfare to get going again. Meanwhile the industrialists, making the most of the contradictions between Todt's local labor agencies and Thomas's munitions inspections, were playing their own games. A partial inquiry revealed that some factories in theory committed to military production continued to assign a quarter of their staff to manufacturing peacetime goods, and that others despite all the decrees continued to lure the best workers away from their competitors by offering them bonuses. As a result of these demands for manpower from the business bosses and workers stubbornly clinging to their peacetime tasks, the total number of workers on "special release" eventually almost equaled that of men in the armed services. The army that attacked the USSR on 22 June 1941 comprised very few more soldiers than it had on previous campaigns.

The colossal German victories in Russia that summer created an artificial optimism. At first, until the extent of their debilitation was discovered, the millions of Soviet prisoners seemed to constitute a limitless reservoir of labor. Todt was encouraging his partners to economize on labor by forcing up production. But when subjected to increasingly harsh pressures and longer working hours, the workers reacted in the usual fashion with absenteeism and nomadization, despite the creation of internal police forces known as "business guards" and the threat of being sent for a few weeks to "labor training camps" that would make them long to be back at their everyday factory job.

Just at the time of the battle of Stalingrad, the system appeared to become totally blocked. The armed forces, losing 150,000 men a month, estimated their need for replacements at two million. Back in Germany, industry for its part was clamouring for eight hundred thousand workers for munitions and seven hundred thousand for other sectors. The customary toing and fro-ing between the factories and the regiments was no longer enough: the two hundred thousand on special release who were sent back to the fight represented no more than a drop in the ocean; and the war wounded sent to replace them at the workbenches were incapable of making a strong productivity effort. Sauckel, who succeeded Todt as labor plenipotentiary while Speer took over production, was a simplistic and brutal *Gauleiter* who boasted of reconciling ideology and efficiency by "openly exploiting the raw materials and human work forces of conquered zones, for the good of Germany." However, the Ger-

man people themselves were not to be spared extra sacrifices. At
the moment of publication of the decree mobilizing all men between sixteen and sixty-five for labor, Speer, no longer content
to crush all firms considered just "superfluous," decided to
close down most of those that remained. The same mechanisms
once used to defend women's jobs were now resorted to in defending the men's. Goebbels, completely forgetting his speech
on "total war" at the Sports Palace, protested that these closures
and transfers would "annihilate the middle classes, in contradiction to the party program"; and meanwhile the party itself continued to shelter in its offices masses of permanent officials and
employees who were perfectly fit for more strenuous duties. By
the summer of 1944 the situation had pretty well reverted to
what it had been at the beginning of 1943: the army was still asking for 1.3 million men and the industrialists wanted six hundred
thousand, half of them with special skills.

At this point the failed assassination attempt of 20 July took
place and the Nazi leadership as a whole, exploiting the general
feeling of shock, decided to face down the discontent at every
level. Goebbels, appointed "plenipotentiary for total war,"
closed down the theaters. Himmler now undertook to "comb"
military units behind the lines in order to reinforce those at the
front, and Bormann set about overcoming the lack of cooperation of party cadres. Within five months 140,000 people from
the cultural sector, 330,000 state officials and almost as many
public and para-public agencies were reallocated to *Wehrmacht*
services and to factories, while one million workers on special
release departed or redeparted for the army, hardly enough to
fill the gaps caused by the recent battles. Labor policy at last had
coherence: by requisitioning men in unproductive jobs and exploiting slave labor, it was possible to convert a large percentage
of workers into fighting men and to impose upon the rest a
quasi-military discipline by threatening them with the same fate.
Translated into figures, these enforced migrations may be summarized as follows: the overall number of workers remained
more or less unchanged, about eleven million, but their distri-

bution was revolutionized when taking into account levels of qualification, the different branches of industry, sexes, and nationalities. Among German men, almost all specialized and manual workers initially classed as "on special release" eventually lost that status and were sent to serve in the army. So were skilled workers, but a smaller proportion of them. As for the affected branches of industry, those producing consumer goods lost one million people who were redirected into either the armed forces or munitions. The latter sector doubled its number of female workers from eight hundred thousand to 1.5 million, but its number of male workers increased very little, only from three million to 3.3 million. All the above figures relate to German workers. As for foreigners it is hard to say how they were distributed between those two main branches; but assuming that munitions took priority, by 1943 there must have been as many foreigners working in Germany as Germans.[5]

With this heterogeneous and for the most part inexperienced work force, German industry managed to produce five times as much military material in 1943 as it had in 1939, and this was to speed up even further over the next nine months. That astonishing achievement cannot be solely explained by the employers' victory over the military bureaucrats or the bullying of masses of foreign workers. It also resulted from increasingly heavy demands made on German workers. After the führer himself retreated before them at the end of 1939, they enjoyed two relatively easy years. The official wage freeze allowed for many exceptions and, thanks to the plundering of conquered countries, material restrictions and fiscal pressure had been relaxed. But from 1942 on, these workers evidently became increasingly worried about maintaining their "special release" status always temporary anyway, about food supplies, and about the ever more vigorous enforcement of production quotas. Even before being made responsible at the national level, Sauckel in his fiefdom of Thüringen, had experimented with new calculations that obliged people to work faster if they wished to preserve their income level. When he tried to transpose these norms to the metallurgical industry as a whole with the objective of a 20 percent increase in average production, employers at first proved as lacking in zeal as their staff. But the urgency of orders and the shortage of qualified professionals soon forced them to obey the directives. Only the most physically dexterous workers would now be able to earn bonuses and accumulate overtime. As a result a new range of wages emerged. Miners and skilled metallurgical workers saw their wages rise by 15 percent over the five war years, while casual construction workers' wages increased by 10 percent; but women's wages rose no more than two to eight percent, depending on the branch of industry. The gap widened even more for weekly wages, including overtime. All in all, taking account of the simultaneous rise in taxation and in the cost of living, the real average weekly wage (it is not known how it varied from one category to another), after rising slightly during the first two years of war, eventually fell below the 1939 level. The exhausting efforts produced by both political and employers' pressures and in many cases also by patriotism had not been rewarded.

Monographs on individual firms make it possible to imagine the atmosphere on the shop floors. It was often tense but occasionally curiously relaxed. At the Daimler-Benz factories producing cars and aircraft engines, pay was now based on the production of groups of men who worked together (*Kameradschaften*), to force the slowest workers to keep up with the set pace: weekly working hours increased to sixty hours, seventy for foreigners. "New workers," mostly women, went through many stages of rapid training that taught them how to service machine tools while foreigners worked at tasks calling for no qualifications at all. Rates of absenteeism were dangerously high, but it is important not to underestimate the impact that the various promotions and family grants made on German workers' morale. The differentiation between Germans and foreigners was noticeable everywhere. At the Messerschmitt firm in Augsburg for example, the management, thanks to the importance of its fighter planes, employed a large number of special release workers who (according to munitions inspectors) led a relatively easy life "with absolutely no soldierly spirit or feelings of responsibility toward the German people." On the other hand this firm regularly appealed to the police to take action against undisciplined foreign workers: over five hundred arrests were made during the second semester of 1943. In other factories in Bavaria, those inspectors noted the same tranquillity among the autochthonous working elite who "concentrated on the art of the possible," the same fatigue and absenteeism among women, and the same Gestapo interventions against foreigners. At "United Steelworks" in the Ruhr, the number of tonnes produced per wage earner actually fell by one-third between 1939 and 1943 as the proportion of foreign workers increased. But the firm's historian insists that the two phenomena are not proved to be related, implying that the fatigue or lack of zeal felt by the old "core" of workers was also partly responsible. In short, as a critical report by the *SD* noted as early as the end of 1939, those in charge of the war economy looked upon workers as a working force pure and simple, not as "members of the People's Community," and in consequence the latter no longer took an interest in anything but their own material conditions and immediate environment. A collective consciousness and pride in their trade survived only in the aristocracy of professionals exempted from military call-up due to their age and specialized skills. These workers did maintain traditions of loyalty to the "old firm," while hoping to be promoted to foremen. However, it was an aristocracy that ruled over a mass of women, cripples, ex-penpushers, prisoners of war, wretched "Easterners," and concentration-camp prisoners.[16]

Working-class resistance had nevertheless not disappeared completely. Social Democrat teams seem generally to have limited themselves in working-class quarters to actions of solidarity or friendly reunions, and in the work place to encouraging gestures of discontent. Their "reports on Germany" ceased soon after the war began either because of the difficulties of circulating them or because they were discouraged by exiled comrades' criticisms of "exaggerated pessimism." However, a few former leaders of the Socialist party and the trade unions did make contact with the conservative circles determined to bring down the regime. For both sides it was difficult to forget the class prejudices and memories of Weimar and come to some agreement on a program of renovation for Germany, since the authoritarian ideas of high-ranking officers directly contradicted workers' aspirations for emancipation, let alone the plans for socialization of their partners. But the younger officers in the 20 July conspiracy were more open-minded and even insisted that their new allies from the proletarian strata should be given important posts in the future government, for example trade unionist Wilhelm Leuschner as a minister and Socialist Julius Leber as vice-chancellor.[17]

Thanks to their strict security a number of "New Departure" teams had managed to avoid arrest, and we at least know something of the activities of those in southern Germany. Their links with Waldemar von Knoeringen, which had ensured a certain continuity, were broken, which may be the reason they swung into activism. Security precautions were well maintained, even reinforced: the Augsburg group for instance, which included, among others, workers from the MAN factories, decided not to admit any individuals who might attract the attention of the police, such as former Communists or people already arrested once, or even men over age forty. But the object of its meetings, up until then mainly intellectual, now became truly military. Assuming that the USSR would be victorious, they imagined liberation would be accompanied by a revolution of the masses, and to provide leadership for this they planned to organize themselves into "rolling commandos" comprising five men each. The most daring even proposed—without success—that they immediately perform acts of sabotage. Eventually in 1942 the police arrested several of these groups, some in Bavaria and others in Austria, but in the meantime this underground had managed to keep going for nine whole years.[18]

Not all grass-roots Communists had followed the strategic U-turns of the International, in particular where the Popular Front was concerned. If after a few days of stupefaction they came to accept the 1939 German-Soviet pact, it was because it at least liberated many comrades held in concentration camps and gave Communists hope of continuing their activities in a context of semi-tolerance. Their press set about criticizing the Western powers, and following the outbreak of hostilities in Poland it clamored for an immediate peace settlement with Russia, betraying not the slightest embarrassment at this repetition of themes dear to Goebbels. The German army's invasion of the USSR naturally brought this ambiguity to an end. In the interval certain groups had entered into cooperation with non-Communist resistants, and this was strengthened when Great Britain and her commonwealths officially became allies of the Soviets. Successive members of the "central leadership" set the example, Robert Uhrig by welcoming at least one former National Bolshevist, then Anton Saefkow by meeting with the Socialists who in their turn were in contact with the Conservative conspirators. But these meetings, not well camouflaged, ended in a general spate of arrests. These national leaders had in any case not managed to maintain more than spasmodic contacts with local groups, so the latter possessed a new degree of autonomy in deciding on their recruitment, analyses, and tactics. Some thus worked alongside young Catholics and Socialists as in Berlin-Neukölln, with former National Bolsheviks or members of right-wing leagues (the best known of these was the Red Orchestra), with Jews as in the Siemens factories in Berlin, with Socialists, Christians, or even young "pirates" as in the Rhineland, or with members of former vigilante groups as in Munich. However, the best known groups (possibly because attention was drawn to them later by East German historians) aimed for homogeneity in recruitment which, however, did not prevent their adopting wide ranging action. Tracts were distributed (the

Gestapo was still seizing large quantities in 1941) then gradually disappeared; elsewhere resistants were strongly organized in teams of three, action cells or information networks. Even passionate doctrinal and strategic divergences occurred. In the Rhineland, Wilhelm Knöchel, disagreeing with the views of the central committee in exile, noticed the regime's disastrous effects on working-class consciousness and encouraged his followers to work together with non-Communists when agitating for better conditions on a day-to-day basis. But he was arrested at the same time as his comrades of the first central leadership, Uhrig and his team, in early 1943. Resistants in Munich, probably under the influence of new friends from vigilante groups, elaborated a program of national Communism. Conversely, Red leaders in Leipzig persisted in what their critics called sectarianism, refusing to cooperate in any way with "bourgeois" resistants and even planning for a future war between the USSR and the Western powers, contrary to the theme of allied unity the "National Committee of Free Germany" diffused on Soviet radio.

Forewarned by the hard experience of 1933 and subsequent years, the Communists did manage to remain quite active. There is evidence of no fewer than thirty operational cells in Hamburg, thirty in the munitions factories of Berlin (with up to forty or even eighty members), and fifteen or so in Leipzig, and so on. But very few remained at liberty right up to the end, and it is precisely from the records of the victorious Gestapo that we learn of the impressive numbers involved. They announced the arrest of over eleven thousand Communists and Socialists for the year 1941 and close to ten thousand for the first semester of 1944 alone, but without distinguishing these figures by party. For the second three months of 1944 the data is more precise: 4,723 Communists arrested of whom 1,442 were Germans (the rest were probably Soviets), and 328 Socialists of whom 282 were Germans. Extrapolating, it is possible to calculate that Communists represented 10 percent of all Germans arrested under the Third Reich for "offenses" and "crimes" of various

kinds, and they made up one-third to one-half of political prisoners in the strict sense.[19]

"It was when it was in its death throes that the regime was the
closest to achieving its ultimate objective: the fusion of worker
and soldier" (M. Prinz).[20] Lost children, mothers, and workers
were shunted from one end of the Reich to the other, no more
than drops in the human flow directed by bureaucrats and ideologues. Except for those who belonged to a privileged category,
all civilians witnessed their native community of workers disintegrating and thrust into a composite world that for a long time
had not been called the "working class," or even — as in the early
days of the regime — the working-class order or state. It was now
known as the working world, or simply the world of wage-
earners.[21] In his prophetic moods Goebbels announced the
coming of a "radical restratification," and the futurologues of
the Labor Front looked forward to a time when the sole impetus
would be competition between individuals and the sole objective the emergence of a radically pure elite. Yet the upheaval
sparked off by the war and aggravated by the Nazi leaders failed
to destroy certain ancestral loyalties, family solidarities, neighborly links, religious practices, and the *esprit de corps* of small
professional groups.

Besides, the planners who believed themselves the masters of
totally malleable social clay were themselves trapped in a network of rival elites, some on the wane, others on the rise — a de-
formed version of prewar society.

NOTES

1. Scholz H., p. 48, 100–176; id. and Strand E.; Ottweiler O.; Klönne A., *Jugend*,
   p. 54, 288; Koch H. W., p. 201, 228, 284 f.; Steinert M. G., *Hitlers Kreig*, p. 391,
   400; Nicolaisen H.-D.; Schelsky H., *Die skeptische Generation*, Düsseldorf and
   Cologne: 1957.
       In Germany, an age group is numbered according to the year of its members'
   births.
2. Kater M., "Jazz"; Steinert M. G. *Hitlers Krieg*, p. 117, 175; Peukert D., *Volksgenossen*, pp. 183–84; id., *KPD*, pp. 389–92; Klönne A., *Jugend*, pp. 234–48, 283; id.,
   "Jugendprotest," pp. 593–620; Muth H.

3. Petzina D., "Mobilisierung"; Overy R. J., pp. 425 – 32; Hachtmann R.; Winkler D. (essential); *63*, 26 May 1941 and 4 February 1943 (popular opinion); Miller G. (Labor Service); Klinksiek D. (students).

4. Engeli C. and Ribbe W., p. 1015.

5. Petzina D., "Soziale Lage"; Walther S.; Overy R. J., pp. 379 – 411; *63*, 8 January 1940, 21 November 1940, 29 September 1941, 23 March 1942, 20 January 1944; *72*, doc. 2894 (Jan. – Feb. 1940); Müller R. D., "Mobilisierung," p. 581, 588; Steinert M. G., *Hitlers Krieg*, p. 286 f.; Herbst L. (savings); Klemperer V., p. 141 – 42.

6. Saldern A. von, *Mittelstand*, passim; Winkler H. A., "Der entbehrliche Stand"; Müller R. D., "Mobilisierung," pp. 582 – 83; Kershaw I., *L'Opinion*, p. 286; Stephenson J., "Emancipation"; *63*, 8 March 1943, 13 December 1943.

7. Beck E. R., passim, in particular pp. 1 – 9, 162; *55*, Bd. I, pp. 1 – 68 (generalities), Bd. II, 1, p. 85 (Stuttgart), 226 – 407 (passive defense), Bd. IV, 2, pp. 3 – 9, 74 – 83 (Berlin), Beiheft 1, pp. 51 – 66 (Hamburg), 199 – 251 (Cologne), 253 – 73 (Nuremberg), 292 – 320 (Dresden), Beiheft 2, p. 492 (balance sheet); Vorländer H. (assistance).

8. Recker M. L., "Wohnen"; *55*, Bd. II, 1, pp. 11 – 20 (Cologne); Kardorff U. von, 3 February 1944; Andreas-Friedrich R., 3 January 1944; Konvitz J., p. 840.

9. *55*, Bd. I, p. 77 f., 153 – 78 (evacuation plan), Bd. II, 2, pp. 302 – 36 (statistics), Bd. IV, 2, pp. 74 – 83 (Berlin), Beiheft 1, pp. 189 – 251 (Cologne). Engeli C. and Ribbe W., p. 1015 – 21 (Berlin); Recker M. L., "Wohnen"; Brepohl W., *Industrievolk . . . dargestellt am Ruhrgebiet*, Tübingen, 1957, p. 351.

10. Saldern A. von, *Mittelstand*, p. 71, 114, 134; Broszat M., "Ebermannstadt"; Stephenson J., "Württemberg"; *72*, XIX, doc. 3349 b (Lippe); *63*, 18 November 1943 (Bavaria).

11. Benz W., "Generalplan Ost"; Aly G. and Heim S., pp. 125 – 66; Umbreit H., p. 153 f., 269 – 73 (with different figures); *54*, Bd. I, 1, p. 1E – 19E.

12. *54*, Bd. I, 1, p. 13E – 69E; 157E-160E; *43*, p. 226; *72*, XXII, doc. 3588, and XXIII, doc. 3616a; Klemperer V., p. 307.

    N.B. The introduction to the collection of documents *54*, published in the fifties by the Bonn Ministry of Refugees, sometimes betrays a virulent anti-Sovietism; but it is confirmed by collection *43*, which dates from 1985 and collects together scientific articles of a more rigorous nature.

13. See *Devant l'Histoire. Les documents de la controverse sur la singularité de l'extermination des juifs par le regime nazi*, French translation, Paris: 1988 (orig. ed. 1988); in particular the article by Habermas J. of 11 July 1986.

14. Milward A. S., passim; Mason T., *Arbeiterklasse*, p. 158 f.; Overy R. J., pp. 379 – 424.

15. Recker M. L., *Sozialpolitik*, pp. 58 – 81, 155 – 93; above all Kroener B. R., "Ressourcen," pp. 751 – 810, 928 – 50 (for 1939 – 42); Herbert U., *Fremdarbeiter*, p. 237 (1943 impasse); id., "Arbeiterschaft," pp. 351 – 353; Mammach K., p. 14 f. (summer 1944).

    Labor statistics: Overy R. J., art. cit., complemented by Petzina D., "Soziale Lage."

16. Herbert U., "Arbeiterschaft," pp. 345 – 49; Recker M. L., Sozialpolitik, pp. 33 – 58, 193 – 250; Siegel T., pp. 104 – 20 (the most precise salary statistics); Hetzer G., p. 126 f. (Messerschmitt); Kershaw I., *L'Opinion* (Bavaria); Mollin G., pp. 94 – 96 (steel production); Roth K. H., pp. 230 – 48 (Daimler-Benz); Mason T., *Arbeiterklasse*, doc. 234 (*SD* report).

17. Hoffmann P., pp. 238–242
18. Hetzer G., p. 201 f.; Mehringer H., "SPD," p. 404 f.
19. Duhnke H., p. 353, 457–530; Peukert D., *KPD*, p. 326–412; Mehringer H., "KPD," pp. 264–85.
20. Prinz M., *Mittelstand*, p. 238, 307 f.
21. Respectively, *Arbeiterklasse, Arbeiterstand, Arbeiterschaft, Arbeitnehmerschaft.*

7—The Nazi Party and the Social Authorities

The rules of the game observed between the four powers that dominated society, namely the state bureaucracy, the Nazi party, the business bosses, and the army, changed with the advent of war. The powers of the state bureaucracy were increasingly whittled away. The party, in order to justify the continued existence of its permanent staff of thousands and compensate for its decreasing popularity, strove to extend its zones of influence into the administration, the economy, and even the army. The body of business proprietors competed with the army for control of the labor force, but won the battle for control over industrial policy. The high command of the army — considered here as a pressure group — lost ground as the defeats multiplied, and fell behind even more following the assassination attempt of 20 July 1944. Meanwhile, a fifth power, the SS, was in the ascendant.

The two examples that follow will show the extent to which relations between these authorities were entangled. At the level of each region (*Gau*), the struggle against absenteeism was led by the Chambers of Trade and Industry, the curators of labor, the party's Labor Office, the Labor Front, the agency for labor run by the Ministry for Armament, the (military) Inspectors of Munitions, the Chambers of Doctors, the Fund for Sickness Insurance, and the Gestapo, not to mention the heads of individual firms. In the occupied territories of the East, the management of confiscated firms was the concern of two different managerial departments of the Ministry of the Economy, a managerial department of the Ministry of Foreign Affairs, the Office for properties confiscated under the Four-Year Plan, the Commission for the Management of Enemy Possessions, and the *OKW* War Economy Office, not to mention the local authorities, and the German banks and companies seeking shares in them.[1] Every new extension to the empire and every new difficulty complicated this poly-cratic amalgam still further.

THE HIGH-RANKING OFFICIALS: CAUGHT BETWEEN IMPOTENCE AND CONSPIRACY

Before the war, most high-ranking officials had trod a difficult path "along the narrow dike that separated opposition [to dangerous initiatives] and complicity."[2] Their delicate position was further weakened by the mobilization of many younger men, sent off to the services and staff offices of the armed forces. Their professional association requested that the time spent in service under the military flag be taken into account when it came to promotion up the civil service ladder. However, Bormann not only opposed this but even threatened a radical purge of the civil service once victory had been won. The shift of balance in favor of party administrators thereafter intensified, initially in terms of sheer numbers: whereas those on "special release" in the state sector were soon recalled to army service, many of those holding "tenured political posts" (*Hoheitsträger*), that is to say the heads of local groups or those with higher rank, remained comfortably in their posts. The battle was lost in 1943 when Frick had to hand over the Ministry of the Interior to Himmler. But it had not been fought solely in the offices of the capital. Regional and local administrations were now run solely by elderly or crippled men overwhelmed with work and living in dire material conditions that did nothing to spare them the criticism of those in their charge, criticism carefully encouraged by party militants. Secondary school teachers also lost their dignity as they were forced into temporary living quarters that they had to share with their pupils, where they tried to fit their teaching into the few gaps in the timetable left free for them by the Hitler Youth Organization and antiaircraft artillery defense. They also lost their last remaining protectors when the *NSLB* was dissolved in 1943.

Teachers still living in towns were further burdened by a
plethora of extra-school tasks, including social assistance and
passive defense duties.[3]

The judicial apparatus was now squeezed between partici-
pating in the repression, and the attacks of Nazi leaders who
considered it lacking in zeal. Those judging issues of guardian-
ship were faced with a new problem when the mentally handicapped they were supposed to protect were not just sterilized
but actually put to death. Some refused to sanction this and were
forced into retirement. Others, appalled by the rumour that attributed the initiative in this operation to them, turned for help
to Minister of Justice Franz Gürtner, who simply made a few
formal adjustments to confer a semblance of legality upon it. For
a while they continued working at their posts in semi-secrecy,
but protests continued to flood in, and in April 1941 (before
Monsignor von Galen's famous sermons) magistrates had to
face up openly to their responsibilities. In the course of a meeting of appeal court judges and procurators general, delegates
from the Chancellory unveiled their completed plan for "euthanasia." According to one witness the announcement was followed by a deathly silence in the hall. However, even if the
upper echelons of the hierarchy, already mostly nazified, were
won over, some minor judges and lawyers still retained a professional conscience, as is proved by the attacks made on them.
The Gestapo no longer hesitated to execute those given prison
sentences only, and the *SD* justified this by arguing that public
opinion was demanding the death sentence in the case of, for
instance, black marketeers. In April 1942, Hitler addressed the
Reichstag at a special session and enumerated a series of complaints against bureaucrats and magistrates, demanding full
powers to dismiss them—a strange request given that he already
had so many ways to intervene. Soon after this the timid Gürtner
was replaced by Otto Georg Thierack as "justice" minister,
who in the next two years showered a series of twenty-one circulars on the magistrates. In these he severely criticized the
over-lenient sentences passed by ordinary courts for antisocial

behavior, economic offenses, and antipatriotic talk, and contrasted them to the severity of the special courts. Barristers, their number now reduced by 60 percent, lost their last liberties when records of "violations of the code of deontology," that is to say of over-bold pleas, were transferred from their bar to the administrative tribunal. The judges' reaction to these ministerial circulars reveals how divided they were among themselves: some older judges criticized their severity; others, while "remaining on the movement's ground" (translation: while accepting the official comments), deplored the excessive interventionism; the rest thanked the minister for "treating every individual case, not from a juridical point of view, but in a realistic fashion, according to its impact upon the People's Community."[4]

Some from the legal community who were mobilized for military duty found themselves in fighting units. Statistics from the Ministry of Justice for example record that eight percent of prosecutors were killed in action, five percent of the bench judges, and as many as 13 percent of younger lawyers. The army employed other magistrates according to their professional abilities in its juridical services and military tribunals. The fact was that, particularly since the campaign against the USSR, troops were becoming increasingly undisciplined: thefts, absences without leave (as distinguished from veritable desertions), insubordination, and drunkenness gave rise to no fewer than 630,000 trials: about sixteen thousand of these resulted in death sentences, out of which ten thousand according to some, fifteen thousand according to others, were carried out. These figures, finally brought to light after forty years, have provoked stupefaction and led certain authors to conclude that military or militarized magistrates must have gone along with the terror dictated by the high command, in order to maintain discipline to the very last. But in truth they did not act with great severity either against small offenses committed among military men or crimes committed against civilians or prisoners of war. However, their humanity was unilateral: those condemned to prison sentences would eventually be sent to disciplinary units where they could virtually expect certain death.

Administrative officials for their part were often sent off to direct the occupation services in conquered countries. Their role, represented initially as one of purely management, progressively became a cog in the ethnic cleansing policy. Thus the main office for the sequestration of property in the East took over restarting and eventually selling Jewish businesses. Members of the Accounts Court of Berlin in January 1941 gave their expert opinion on the Lodz ghetto and decided that with so many destitute people, it could never be a going concern, so it would be better to "evacuate" them. Were they unaware that all those who could no longer work were sent to Chelmno? Later, these apolitical experts made great efforts to distance themselves from the SS, explaining that their sole concern had been the smooth running of the war economy and that they had even tried to save the lives of all Jews fit for work. Never had the dividing line between a strictly professional conscience and an ethical conscience been so permeable.[5]

Yet within those same circles a current of resistance developed that was to lead to the assassination attempt of 20 July 1944. Its earliest historians — survivors from the conspiracy or its eulogists — represented it as a moral protest against the crimes of the regime. Subsequently, realizing that the first contacts between diplomats and the military went back to before the war, some authors laid greater emphasis on their realistic desire to put a stop to Hitler's mad ventures which were in danger of plunging the country into catastrophe. Finally, when individual portraits of the conspirators were followed by analyses of the various groups and plans involved, it was interpreted simply as the reaction of an elite whose remnants of power and prestige were under threat. The journal of U. von Hassell reveals that these three kinds of motivation — ethical, strategic, and social — were indissociable. In the winter of 1939–40, von Hassell himself, along with diplomats and high-ranking officials who were friends of his, was begging the generals to organize a coup d'etat, invoking the SS atrocities in Poland and the planned Western offensive as reasons. But their pleas were all in vain. In the summer of 1941 he again took to noting news of crimes in which the army was now an accomplice, but at the same time he expressed his alarm at the growing power of the regime's most revolutionary elements. He deplored the SS "Tcheka" both for its inhumanity and undisguised scorn for the "upper class." All the evidence at hand was grist for his mill: the mobilization of secondary school pupils in the *Flak* was, in his eyes, "yet another blow against the ruling class." This morally irreproachable and socially reactionary attitude was shared by his fellow-conspirators except the Socialists and younger officers. Their coming together had been helped by family relations, civilian clubs, officers' messes, and neighborly contacts both in the country and the elegant quarters of Berlin. Despite serious differences of opinion on some points, their various programs all rested upon one assumption—the idea that "as an elite, they represented the Whole" (H. Mommsen). They still considered parliamentary democracy undesirable as they did even democracy in itself, for it reflected a society of the masses. According to them the future society should be founded upon basic communities, families, small rural and urban businesses, and medium-sized towns; above, a ruling elite would be reconstituted, recruited on the bases of merit and birth. There were even certain similarities with a moderate Nazism: the position of Jews in society would be regulated by a special status; youth would be controlled by compulsory work service, and the electoral body by amended universal suffrage (but only for some) and by a single party. Unanimity had by no means been reached even by the spring of 1944: the conservatives and the younger officers disagreed about the roles Socialists and trade unionists would play; in foreign policy, Goerdeler was still yearning for the frontiers of 1938 or even 1939, whereas others accepted that Germany should be smaller provided it belonged to a united

Europe. But all in all, if the conspiracy had succeeded and the Allies had agreed to recognize the government that the elite planned, postwar Germany would have resembled the Reich of 1937–38 but without the terror.[6]

THE AMBITIONS AND THE DISCREDIT
OF THE PARTY

The choice between the two models of a party for the masses and a party for the elite was settled by the war in favor of the former, and membership in the party was reopened. Success was not immediate; the first year (1939) brought in only forty thousand new members. Then the pace increased to two million in the next three years, after which it slowed down again. The total of eight million was barely reached by 1944. That curve clearly runs parallel to the curve of optimism in the population: reticence at the outbreak of war, enthusiasm during the victorious years, anxiety yet tenacity up until the battle for the frontiers, renewed by the assassination attempt of 20 July. The social distribution of the streams of new party members is also significant. The flow of workers was continuous but never matched the proportion of the active population they represented; but it must be said that it is hard to reconcile that reaction with all their demonstrations of discontent and exhaustion, mentioned above. The flow of shopkeepers and artisans slowed down, although it never dried up completely as a result of so many being transferred into industry and the worries of those who remained. Low-level civil servants and—even more—their superiors, along with students destined to take over from them, reserved their commitment, reflecting the reported and daily increasing evidence of decadence in the public services. Among the big businessmen, some continued to keep their distance as a matter of principle or out of a lack of interest; others went along to promote their firms' relations with the centers of power. Overall the party became increasingly popular, if not working-class. But its structure in terms of age groups and sexes changed considerably: with so many young men in the armed forces, a general rise in the age of its civilian members was inevitable; on the other hand, the proportion of women members regularly increased, accounting for as many as one-third of new members and, as most of them were girls from the *BdM*, this helped readjust the average party members' age.[7]

The cadres' duty was to keep up the morale of the population so the fighting men would not be "betrayed behind their backs," as in 1917–18. For example, "the People's Service" went on humanitarian as well as repressive missions. The former might have won back general sympathy for the political apparatus had it not run up against competition from specialized organizations that attracted committed Nazis to their concrete schemes as well as millions of devoted helpers from every part of society: passive defense, Winter Aid, Social Assistance (*NSV*), the German Women's Service (*DFW*), etc. We have already noted the machinations the party used to take over the best known and most effective aid operations in the blitzed towns, a ploy that fooled no one. Public opinion, particularly among soldiers' families, continued to regard all permanent party workers as "skivers." That was a slightly exaggerated view: in 1942, out of eighty-five thousand full-time "political leaders" (heads of local groups, or above), only fifteen thousand were in fact mobilizable but kept their posts on "special release." However, the scandal grew the following year, when it became known that they were also excused from being requisitioned for factory work.[8]

What then were the essential duties that justified such privileges? In the first place, to diffuse daily the propaganda announcements most recently elaborated by the ministry. This involved interpreting war news in conformity with not only the ostentatious optimism of the military (for the *OKW* communiqués saw to that), but also with the "National Socialist view of the world." Whereas propaganda in belligerent countries generally is designed to simultaneously deprecate the enemy and put forward a program for peace, it is remarkable that Goebbels's service nearly always limited itself to polemics. The fact is that Hitler's war objectives were constantly changing—for example alternating between an entente with Britain and destruction of the plutocracy—and the most ambitious of them such as creating a "Nordified" continental empire could hardly be exposed to the general public. The main tasks of the party press and its orators were thus to portray their enemies now as despicable, now as terrifying. The Poles were represented simply as Britain's auxiliaries—but their Jewish fellow-citizens were already shown as subhuman. The French were a people interbred with Jews and blacks. The English, initially treated relatively mildly, then became the tools of Jewish finance as the Americans were later to be. Clearly the war in the West, which historians have interpreted as purely military if not even "a war of chivalry," was in truth deeply impregnated with ideology. But in the case of the Soviet peoples it was much more tricky to decide on a coherent attitude, and here leaders were divided. Were these Asiatic hordes Slavs of pure race dominated by Judeo-Bolsheviks or a mixture of national minorities oppressed by the Russians? When Goebbels wanted to promote the theme of benevolence toward conquered peoples, he clashed with the SS. At this point the front stabilized, then came the first retreats, and propaganda replaced the conquering slogans with appeals to the fanaticism of total war to ensure the country's survival. One observer made the ironic comment that "Strength through Joy" had been replaced by "Strength through Fear," and the Allies confirmed that strategy when they declared that Germany would have to capitulate unconditionally. However, under the rain of Allied bombs this "all the way" attitude could not be fostered indefinitely without some gleam of hope, which is why the permanent myth of Hitler's infallibility was eventually accompanied by the myth of miraculous weapons.[9]

But the radical wing of the party had not lost sight of its other objective, total control over civil society, at the expense of the churches. Urged on by the (rival) directives of Goebbels and "culture" minister Alfred Rosenberg, some local sections introduced a new kind of festival held on Sunday mornings, to clash with Catholic Mass and the Protestant Sunday service. In it, party heroes who had lost their lives in the political struggle and in the war were celebrated in an atmosphere of joy, as the instructions insisted, not of funerary sorrow. After a few selections of music and poetry, a number of quotations from the führer would be read followed by a succession of party songs. The audience was inevitably made up solely of committed Nazis, but the *SD*, despite its reservations wherever initiatives other than those of the SS were concerned, had to admit that these meetings were quite well-attended. On the other hand the neo-pagan ceremonies designed to replace the Christian liturgies of Christmas and Easter, baptisms, marriages, funerals, and the harvest festival were all flops: it seems that expression of political loyalty, even when it involved sacrificing religious practice, was one thing, but ostentatious conversion to the "new faith" was quite another and for many people the step was just too far.[10] The party did not learn from that setback however, but instead launched into a new antireligious campaign with an insensitivity that was astonishing in those times, when national cohesion needed to be preserved more carefully than ever. The offensive started off with some petty niggling: on various pretexts such as the danger of air raids and the priority of war production, weekday festivals were transferred to the following Sundays, the number of Sunday masses was restricted, and Sunday schools were closed. Then the threat of secularization was made more direct. The *Gauleiter* of Bavaria, always avant-garde, abolished morning prayers and the display of crucifixes in schools. Mothers retaliated by threatening to boycott Nazi shopkeepers and write their husbands at the front about it, to make the authorities climb down. But what had appeared at first to be simply an excess of zeal was transformed into an official offensive in the early 1941, when monks were expelled from 123 monasteries and their buildings were confiscated as "places of activities hostile to the state." Meanwhile, the latest diocesan information sheets also were banned. The annual congress of bishops, held two days after the invasion of the USSR, tried to protest against such blows, which struck at patriotic unanimity, but as a result once again of their failure to reach agreement on tactics to adopt, the document it finally produced was much more moderate than many of the faithful had hoped. It took Hitler five months to see that the war might last a long time, and that he would have to give way to public opinion on this point. He accordingly annulled the measures taken against the monasteries and even published an article praising of the loyalty of "the great majority" of Catholics. Many Catholics once again concluded that he had had nothing to do with their misfortunes and continued to project their rancor against his bad advisers.[11]

The conquests in the East provided party ideologues and activists alike with a much better chance to create a new society with a hierarchy based on racial purity and dominated by the most dynamic individuals. In the Polish provinces annexed to the Reich, militant party men and women arrived to lead the "ethnic Germans" and teach them to become true Germans. In the rest of Poland, about fifteen thousand of these people, designated the "General Government," filled all the posts in the administration. But as their superiors in the metropolis had chosen the most mediocre of their staff for these duties in order to get rid of them, the incompetence and corruption of these party "leaders" forced them to relinquish the reality of power to the SS. Still further afield, in the heart of Russia and the Ukraine, they were sent with the title of "commissars" to represent the party and state simultaneously, with the same catastrophic results and the same eventual handover to the SS. As for the society of the future promised to the master-people, the Germans of the Reich in the strict sense, one would have to be very clever to discern its characteristic features from observing the hierarchy set up as its model. Depending on their respective temperaments the *Gauleiters* sought to win over public opinion either by maintaining the status quo or, on the contrary, by provoking it with announcements they considered revolutionary. Thus while in Baden-Alsace the *Gauleiter* supported the protests of hoteliers, shopkeepers, and artisans threatened with closure, the *Gauleiter* of Bavaria explained to the female students that they were wasting their time at university and would do better to fight, work in a factory, or produce babies; he even promised to provide the necessary males.[12]

All these incoherent initiatives were useless: if the civilian population managed to endure its difficulties and sufferings right to the end, it was no thanks to the party. When young men emerging from the *HJ* were asked what kind of jobs they would aim for in peacetime, most mentioned industry or the army, a few spoke of the SS, very few considered working for the party agencies. In Bavaria the most fantastic rumors were rife about the lifestyle of national and local party leaders; it was said that the reason the führer now wore a gray uniform rather than a brown one was that he wanted to distance himself from all those rotten officials. Even party members took to removing the swastika badge from their lapels as it exposed them to sarcastic comments. They also stayed away from lectures on ideology, and if they did attend asked embarrassing questions contrasting the program announced in the early days to the present realities. Questions such as the following were typical: Whatever happened to the great, pure People's Community heralded ever since 1933, now that there are millions of foreigners everywhere, among whom it is hard to find any real Germans?[13]

Conscious that the nation's real heroes were the military, the party exploited the failed coup d'etat of 20 July 1944 for all it was worth. Over and above the traitors themselves a whole campaign was launched against the noble and military caste to which the traitors belonged. Finally, the "gilded pheasants" thought their hour had come, with them heading national defense, when in September Hitler created the "popular draft" (*Volkssturm*) and made the *Gauleiters* commissioners for defense in their respective regions. Newsreels everywhere showed

parades of boys and old men in suits, and at the same time revealed the presence of numerous relatively young adults wearing the party uniform. In a somewhat tardy readoption of
Röhm's ideas, the latter were now designated as leaders of this
new revolutionary army. However, in the unnerving months of
winter 1944–45, the party manifested its incompetence one last
time despite a smokescreen of blustering. We have already
noted the mass desertion of local party cadres in the provinces
threatened by the Red Army, and the catastrophic decisions
taken by the *Gauleiters* of Poznan, Breslau, and Dresden. Their
colleagues in more central areas of Germany who saw the front
creeping closer week by week displayed equally frantic stubbornness. The Stuttgart *Gauleiter* transformed his entire urban
area into a fortress, defying the mayor who wanted to declare it
an open city and ordering his arrest when he learned that the
mayor had contacted the Allies. The Bremen *Gauleiter* forced
the population to resist to the very end, thereby achieving the
town's destruction. The only *Gauleiter* with apparent foresight
was Hamburg's, who in agreement with the garrison's commanding general brought the fighting to an end to spare his
people war's ultimate tribulations. "This war is a national catastrophe for us and a disaster for Europe," he confessed.[14] When
in his last days Hitler accused the German people as a whole
of cowardice, it was the ultimate deception designed to cover
up the collapse of the party he had created and used to seize
power, but which then proved itself useful neither in peace nor
war.

THE MAJOR BUSINESS BOSSES
MOVE TOWARD LIMITLESS EXPANSION

As the victors of 1945 saw it, the directorial teams who ran the
major business *Konzern* deserved to count as war criminals
since they had collaborated in the servitude imposed upon the
people of Europe, even when it led to the most inhumane con-

sequences. That thesis was taken up and amplified by the historiography of the DDR: less interested in the internal life of firms than their hold over economic policy and foreign dealings, it represented them as the principal motivators of imperialism in alliance with the state bureaucracy and political leadership.[15] In contrast, the arguments of those defending the industrialists have been repeated with, it is true, important qualifications in monographs written by Anglo-Saxons and authors in West Germany. Their common thesis is that where these leaders, whether proprietors or managers, erred was in adopting such a narrow perspective: with their eyes fixed on the interests of their firms, they did no more than go along with Hitlerian expansionism. *IG Farben*, it is claimed felt "obliged to protect its interests in the new context [of the conquests in the East]" and only acquired branches in Czechoslovakia in "self-defense" against the ambitions of its rivals; "its economic interests were not the motors of German aggression, but were not indifferent to its consequences"; it "suffered" SS interventions in its internal life and was even threatened with confiscation once the war had been won.[16] Similarly, the directors of Daimler-Benz were unaware of Hitler's long-term objectives and simply reacted to whatever happened from day to day "according to the tendencies of economic policy, the good of the firm, and their personal safety."[17] At Siemens, "the employment of foreign workers, prisoners of war, and Jews from 1940–1941 and, eventually, of concentration camp prisoners from 1942 on did not—initially at least—result from any initiative on the part of the firm, nor, according to subsequent declarations by the directorial board, did they correspond to its views on the correct treatment of human beings"; consequently "it is hard to decide whether or to what extent certain members of the directorial team, inspired by a national but not necessarily National Socialist spirit, took decisions or behaved themselves in an unjustifiable manner."[18] Quite apart from the style of these remarks, it is worth pointing out that a major historical problem is in this way reduced to the psychology or morality of a few dozen individuals.[19] It is however perfectly possible, without neglecting the particularities of the various firms, to detect the major guiding lines of strategy the business bosses used in at least three domains: the production of munitions, the seizure of European industries, and the employment of slave labor.

The first of those domains is the most complex, as it could only be described precisely by dint of studying a series of extremely entangled organizational programs. On the side of the state authorities the situation seemed to become less complex as early as March 1940 when Todt was appointed Minister of Armament and Munitions, as this implied the withdrawal if not disappearance of the Four-Year Plan. It is quite true that the Four Year Plan from this time on became little more than a "publicity ploy," contenting itself with sending "prospectors" to the occupied countries in search of raw materials, war materials, and requisitionable factories.[20] But Goering had not yet lost all influence, as he could count on the aviation lobby, associated industrialists, and his own steel-producing *Konzern*. Furthermore the new minister was not in charge of all branches of industry and was still pressing for this when he was killed in an accident. All the same he had drafted a system to coordinate the public and private sectors, and this his successor Albert Speer perfected. The prices of military materials were now aligned with conditions in the most modern factories, a move designed to force other firms to rationalize their methods. To simplify procedures, the summer of 1940—in other respects a period of great strategic uncertainty—saw the creation of the Commission for Armored Cars, a first attempt to coordinate manufacturers and buyers of the same product under the presidency of first a steel producer, then Porsche, the engineer. The results of the experiment seemed positive enough for it to be imitated by a Commission for Cannons led by a cadre from Krupp's, then by the aeronautical industry which set up a number of "groups," each corresponding to a particular type of aircraft. However, relations between the industrialists and the military on the one hand and individual firms on the other remained at odds until Speer's appointment in the spring of 1942: the officer-inspectors of munitions deplored the lack of zeal shown by certain entrepreneurs and the manner in which prices were fixed, and persistently called for new improvements which slowed down production of a whole series of goods. Meanwhile, specialists in organizing large factories, with their eyes fixed on America, desired on the contrary, to speed up the installation of production lines and reduce less advanced competitors to the role of subcontractors.

It was Speer who engineered the triumph of the principle of "the autoresponsibility of industry." Thanks to the total confidence Hitler placed in him, he was in a position to brush off the criticisms of Goebbels and Ley, who insisted that public opinion was very hostile to "war profiteers," and likewise complaints by the SS, which was keen to create its own munitions factories and condemned "the mammothism of production, which herds men into masses." One year later, Speer was appointed Minister of Armament and the War Economy with powers that extended to managing raw materials, the artisan sector, and trade. He was thus well-placed to set up numerous commissions under different names, each specializing in a particular product. Theoretically these assumed their task of coordination in the name of the state, but their respective presidents were industrialists who imposed their own priorities on all the parties concerned.[21] This once again raises the controversy noted in connection with the Four-Year Plan of 1936: did this mixed economy system represent a triumph for the big capitalists, a sharing of power, or a state seizure of control over the private sector? The list of these all-powerful commission presidents reads like a *Who's Who* of heavy industry: Krupp at cannons, the United Steelworks followed by Volkswagen at armored vehicles, Siemens at machine tools, Junkers and Heinkel at fighter planes, Daimler-Benz at aircraft engines . . . . Did they operate as agents of their firms or of the state? In truth, that is an artificial question, and historians whether Marxists or not prefer to answer it using mixed formulae: one says Nazi imperialism was led by "groups" (*Gruppierungen*) of capitalists and bureaucrats; another that the business bosses invaded the sphere of the Nazi state but in return allowed themselves to be won over by the prospects of expansion it offered them; a third, following Max Weber, speaks of the bipolarity of two types of power, monopoly and command.[22] Whatever the case may be, this "autoresponsibility" of the business bosses was inseparable from ostentatious political loyalty, and the type of "party card-carrying industrialist" who appeared on the eve of the war tended to multiply, particularly at the higher levels. At United Steelworks for example, nine out of the eleven members of the directorial commmission were cardholders by 1944, while among the 517 senior cadres, thirty-two belonged to the SS and nineteen held important positions in the party.[23] Rather than seek out the more or less self-interested motivations that impelled these men to join the party, in other words repeat the postwar denazification trials, let us examine the logical consequences of their actions. For out of these meetings officially required for purely technical reasons developed the industrialists' collaboration with some of the most ravaging aspects of the regime, the exploitation of the material resources of continental Europe and the enslavement of human beings from every corner of the continent.

A few examples illustrate the geographical expansion of these gigantic groups. The most insatiable was without a doubt the *Konzern* that bore Hermann Goering's name. Founded on a technical gamble, namely the use of low-grade ores, its initial specialization proved to be a financial bottomless hole: the production of one tonne of steel cost two-and-a-half times as much as it did elsewhere, and the deficit could only be made good by state subsidies. That congenital weakness no doubt explains its repeated annexations of factories and mines in the East, coal mines in Polish Silesia, steelworks in the Ukraine and in the Lorraine and Luxembourg basins in the West—but the booty had to be shared with competitors who based their claims on rights granted to former (pre-1918) proprietors. This integration from above led to extensions below: the seizure of the leading Austrian engineering firms was followed by an attempt to acquire Skoda, which failed, and other annexations in the Netherlands. All these conquests were openly justified as laying the foundations of the National Socialist empire. While one director came out in support of Rosenberg's ideas about the treatment to be inflicted on the conquered peoples of the East, within industry in Germany itself foreign labor eventually accounted for 58 percent of the total work force: 14 percent were prisoners of war and 44 percent were civilians, not counting fifteen thousand concentration camp detainees. To discipline them, the firms' own police forces were made responsible for punishments and even executions.

Apart from a few individual acquisitions, the steel-producing industrialists of the Ruhr and the Saar showed little interest in the industries of the East, probably having judged them unprofitable. In the north and the west on the other hand, they rediscovered earlier possibilities for expansion. To be sure, here too they faced a number of obstacles. The Ministry of Foreign Affairs prevented them from taking total control of the Norwegian steelworks (so as not to upset British interests) or the iron mines of Algeria (so as not to alarm Italy). But in annexed Lorraine, Röhling was left free to expel French cadres and replace them with Germans while in Belgium, Luxembourg, and northern France F. Flick's representatives shared control with Goering's.[24]

At Daimler-Benz a certain prudence with regard to the East is detectable: the firm limited itself to having *Wehrmacht* vehicles repaired by Jewish workers from Minsk. In the west it opened a branch in Colmar, but could obtain no shares in Renault because of opposition from the military commandant in France. In Austria and Slovakia plans were even more grandiose: they involved creating new factories turning out aircraft engines, using a labor force to be trained in rapid sessions in Germany. However, the results were disappointing, the workers were particularly recalcitrant, and Goering in person went so far as to intervene in the internal life of the firm, sacking the project's directors. No doubt he looked askance at the possible increase of competition in these zones of southeastern Europe, which he regarded as his own preserve. Overall, Daimler-Benz ended up employing 40 percent foreign civilians and 6 percent prisoners of war.[25]

The short-term strategy of *IG Farben* was to eliminate foreign competitors rather than increase its own production capacity. Thus, even before the Munich agreements it bought out a chemical firm in the Sudeten region and immediately set about Germanizing its cadres. In Poland it bought back three paint factories in conditions that ruled out any profit; in Russia it only managed to seize a small share of the "eastern companies" in the chemical sector. In France and Norway it was content to become a shareholder (admittedly a major one) with local partners. It is worth noting in passing that it manifested a similar prudence in Germany itself, even in the high priority task of manufacturing synthetic petrol: the new factories for this purpose were built by the state and only rented by the firm. In contrast, its long-term plans included nothing less than domination over the entire continent: in a "plan for the organization of the future Europe" presented to Goering following the defeat of France, it put in a claim for half the capital of the French and British chemical industries of postwar Europe and urged the closure of a number of its other competitors. Its own direct interests were skilfully integrated into an overall vision of a European economy in which Germany would control the cartel system and even the customs policies of the other countries.[26]

By these different means — including the enforced purchase of all or part of the capital, the German states' repurchase of confiscated companies, the appointment of "commissars" to head nominally independent firms, infiltration of the controlling administrations of occupied countries — the principal industrial groups had by 1942-43 assured themselves of mastery over the entire continent. Their few failures to do so can be ex-

plained by unexpected circumstances such as the inferior state
of the Ukraine factories or vetoes imposed by diplomats or military commanders anxious to deal tactfully with local interests,
or by the superiority of a rival with better contacts among the
top authorities, But they were not alone in wishing to colonize
Europe. In the "General Government," governor Hans Frank,
on the advice of economists in Hamburg, set up fifty or so trad-
ing houses for the exchange of German machines against agricultural produce, a move that prompted one journalist to
comment, "German firms specializing in overseas trade are now
supplying Europe with food; they have succeeded in civilizing
space." In a more critical vein, the staff office of an army of armored vehicles that had just occupied the Donets Basin reported in 1942 the sudden appearance of "a whole crowd of
individuals, commissars, plenipotentiaries, and so on, even
some true knights of industry, but they soon became disappointed and departed."[27]

The employment of concentration camp detainees occasions no
surprise where certain fanatical industrialists are concerned, but
it does in the case of others who claimed to be merely managers,
for it does not seem to have been justified by any considerations
of profitability. Those business executives were subject to three
convergent pressures that may provide an explanation. The first
was psychological, the "precedent argument" so familiar to
rhetoricians. Each of these directors/managers, whether head of
a firm or a factory manager, had already taken decisions that
would have made him recoil in normal times, the inhumanity of
which had been increasing little by little: first, the employment
of prisoners of war and foreign civilian volunteers more or less
protected by their status, then that of Red Army prisoners and
"workers from the East," all starving and underpaid. The acceptance of concentration camp workers was simply one more step
in the worsening exploitation. The second pressure was produced by circumstances: from 1942–43 on, the loss of resources
from occupied countries made it essential to speed up construc-

tion of factories for synthetic products, and meanwhile the munitions industry decided to avoid the bombing by taking refuge underground. This construction work called for a mass of laborers to clear the terrain and also for unskilled masons. Finally, the SS insisted on offering the services of its slaves. Having briefly contemplated setting up its own factories, their employment specialists decided it would be more profitable simply to rake in the rent for every human "head." Of course the above remarks do not totally illuminate the attitudes of the industrialists: did they make those decisions of their own accord or were they forced into a resigned acceptance of them? The case of the *IG Farben* factory at Auschwitz-Monowitz proves that it is vain to try to separate managerial responsibility from manic ideology. The very site is significant: in this region of Poland, which served as a terrain of experimentation in ethnic cleansing, the engineer-in-chief of the project declared, "this industrial creation will be a foundation stone for virile and healthy Germanization in the East." First however, the buildings had to be constructed, and conditions were so harsh that free laborers deserted. But the very existence of the plan had encouraged Himmler for his part to provide the Auschwitz camp with a vast extension where the client-firm could easily draw its labor force, although this would have to make long trips to and fro until an extra camp was set up near the work site. The industrialists' complicity by now was total: in the winter of 1943 one director took part in the "selection" of sick detainees. The balance sheet works out in human terms at twenty-three thousand deaths out of thirty-five thousand detainees; in technical terms at one year to build a partial factory. Like so many other projects, this one thus clearly represented a prefiguration of the future Reich, and the exploitation of camp detainees was a logical consequence.[28]

The no less tragic history of the aviation factories provides another example of this collaboration. The aeronautical industry was one of the first to use deportees in its production workshops, but not without running into friction with the SS who insisted that the detainees should work in separate buildings. Everything came together when the "staff office of fighter planes," which included pilots, manufacturers, officials, and SS, decided to bury the principal factories underground either in already existing tunnels or in others to be rapidly dug, or else in huge *Bunker*. In this instance proof exists to show that the industrialists themselves asked for tens of thousands of deportee laborers, for example Jews from Hungary. The building sites were insalubrious, lacking in equipment, without safety precautions, and functioned throughout the winter of 1944–45. Thousands of deaths occurred as a result, particularly in the improvised camps and underground passages in the Neckar valley. Once production started, some of the deportees found themselves working alongside foreign workers on production lines (many of them women from eastern Europe) and a few German team-leaders. Given that a certain level of productivity had to be maintained and that the SS no longer visited the workshops, their material conditions became less terrible and the death rate fell.[29]

Whether these industrialists were motivated by their firms' interests, the urgency of military orders, or preparation for the Great Empire, one cannot but conclude, along with the historian of the Mauthausen camp, that this return to slavery represented "a veritable degeneracy in capitalism."[30] One of the architects of the Neckar tunnels confessed that he felt he had returned to the times of ancient Egypt. The extension of these *Konzern* into such gigantic dimensions also suggests metaphors drawn from pathology: six hundred thousand workers at the Hermann Goering factories, 230,000 at IG Farben, 250,000 at Seimens, 280,000 at Krupp;[31] were such organizations still manageable? To judge by the continuing rise in production up until the autumn of 1944, the answer has to be "yes." But if the "autoresponsibility" of the business bosses won out over the clumsy interventionism of the military, the bureaucrats, and the party, it was thanks to the iron discipline imposed upon their staff and the decentralization of decisions to the middle echelons (also a good pretext used to whitewash business leaders on the score of "regrettable abuses noted here or there"). At any rate, in this civil society suffering the throes of dissolution at the end of the war, the only structures still intact were those of these semi-states.

NOTES

1. Siegel T., p. 132; Mollin G., pp. 180-81.

2. Krüger P.

3. Mommsen H., *Beamtentum*, pp. 87-90; Kershaw I., *L'Opinion*, pp. 287-91; Jarausch K. H., pp. 170-200 (teachers).

4. Gruchmann L., *Justiz*, pp. 497-534, 675; Steinert M. G., *Hitlers Kreig*, pp. 289-95; Boberach H., "Einleitung," *69*; Jarausch K. H., pp. 170-200 (lawyers).

5. Kater M., *Party*, p. 131 (losses); Schulte T. J., pp. 242-47 and Schieder W., p. 440 (military tribunals); Aly G. and Heim S., p. 65, 300, 307, and Umbreit H., p. 167 f. (occupied countries).

6. Hassel U. von, winter 39-40, 3 September 1941, 21 December 1941, 1 August 1942, 6 March 1943; Broszat M., "Sozialgeschichte"; Mommsen H., "Widerstand"; Dipper C.

7. Kater M., *Party*, pp. 116-52.

8. Orlow D., pp. 262-474; Kater M., *Party*, pp. 213-33; Stephenson J., "Frauenorganisationen."

9. Baird J. W., passim; Herbert U., *Fremdarbeiter*, pp. 238-40.

10. Vondung K., *Magie*, pp. 64-107.

11. Hürten H., p. 479 f.; Steinert M. G., *Hitlers Kreig*, pp. 216-19; Volk L., p. 74 f.; Hehl U. von, *Erzbistum Köln*, pp. 211-22; Kershaw I., *L'Opinion*, pp. 299-318; Blessing P., pp. 46-60 (Bamberg); *63*, 13 November 1941.

12. Orlow D., and Kater M., *Party*, n. 8; Peter R., p. 190 (Baden); Beck E. R., p. 28 (Munich).

13. Kershaw I., *L'Opinion*, pp. 143-49 (Bavaria); Steinert M. G., *Hitlers Kreig*, p. 279 f., 391.

14. Orlow D., p. 474; Beck E. R., pp. 173-96.

15. Eichholtz D., in particular Bd. II.

16. Hayes P., p. 213, 223, 267 f., 322-323, 370.

17. Pohl H. et al., p. 183.

18. Feldenkirchen W., p. 204, 214.

19. However, it is important not to generalize: the works of Mollin G. for example avoid this kind of casuistry.

20. Petzina D., *Autarkiepolitik*, p. 134 f.

21. Müller R. D., "Mobilisierung" (up to 1942); Volkmann H. E., "Grosswirtschaft."

22. Respectively, Eichholtz D., passim; Volkmann H. E., "Grosswirtschaft"; Mollin G., pp. 274-78.

23. Eichholtz D., Bd. II, pp. 12-293; Müller R. D., "Mobilisierung," p. 670; Mollin G., p. 258, 265-66; Pohl H. et al., p. 23 f.

24. Mollin G., pp. 138–258.
25. Pohl H. et al., p. 82 f.; Roth K. H., pp. 217–48.
26. Hayes P., pp. 223–97.
27. Umbreit H., p. 149, 220–38; Aly G. and Heim S., p. 233 f.; Müller R. D., "Scheitern," p. 951, 1011, 1028.
28. Hayes P., pp. 347–58; Sandkühler T. and Schmuhl H.-W. (criticizing Hayes P.).
29. Fröbe R., "Arbeitseinsatz"; id., "Die Verlegung."
30. Fabréguet M., pp. 735–38.
31. Eichholtz D., Bd. II, p. 540 f.; Hayes P., p. 325 f.

8—Toward Utopia
through Terror

Of the five original branches of the SS, one, that of the "Death's Heads," disappeared when it was integrated into the *Waffen-SS*. That macabre name was thereafter only used for one particular fighting division.[1] The "Honorary SS," a network of influence rather than a structured organization, continued to recruit members from the economic and administrative elites, who were happy to don their uniforms occasionally within the framework of their professional activities. The *Waffen-SS* developed alongside the regular army to the point where it formed regular army corps, then armies (in the technical sense of the term). So it seems logical to study the *Waffen-SS* within the context of fighting units as a whole at the risk of impairing the unity of the Black Corps, which always prided itself on its ideological cohesion and practiced a rotation of its cadres up to a point. The "Security Service" (*SD*) continued its work of providing information and analyzing public opinion in the Principal Security Office of the Reich (*RSHA*). Finally, those at first known as the "General SS"—but the term seems subsequently to have fallen into disuse—ran policing, inspection of concentration camps, economic services, offices for racial studies, and "intervention groups" (Einsatzgruppen) responsible for carrying out mass killings: these were the thinkers, organizers, and executors of the nordic Utopia. In this way, within the Greater Empire an SS empire developed in which some tens of thousands of men exercised the power of life and death over millions of people who were excluded or reduced to serfdom.

THE SS EMPIRE

In a system that saw infractions of common law as political opposition, the distinction between a criminal police force (*Kripo*) and a political police force (*Gestapo*) became purely a matter of form. But it was the Gestapo that stocked the fears of contemporaries and held the attention of posterity. Apparently the Gestapo was a considerably larger force than its partner: over thirty thousand men compared to thirteen thousand. But if administrators and auxiliaries are discounted, that leaves no more than fifteen thousand policemen in the strict sense of the term. Many were young men recruited in haste to replace those mobilized, who knew little about methodical techniques of questioning and so were particularly inclined to extract confessions by torture. In its battle against the judiciary the Gestapo had long since assumed the right to seize individuals acquitted or given light sentences and send them off to concentration camps, where they would be received not only by camp guards but also their police colleagues of the "political section." Already by the third day of the war, Heydrich as head of the *RSHA* authorized his services to execute immediately certain of the "guilty" spared by the courts. At first there were not many of these executions, but later they became increasingly frequent, and by the last months of the war were running into such high figures that it has not been possible to determine them with accuracy.[2]

The discrepancy between the relatively small number of SS police and the wide scope of their activities had been striking even in peacetime and became even more so as time passed. The national synthesizing report for the month of December 1941 records 8,398 arrests, 6,412 of them for "stopping work" (that is to say for manifestations of indiscipline in factories) and 927 for "acts of opposition." The remainder were for economic offenses or fraternization with foreigners, religious propaganda, or Jews or finally "Communists and Marxists" (which proves that the category labeled "opposition" must have meant simply grumblers for the most part). Eighteen months later the Gestapo services of the three districts of the Ruhr Basin alone recorded four thousand arrests in July and over sixty-five hundred in August, 60 percent of whom were Soviets. A comparison between the two reports indicates that it would not be an exaggeration to say that police activity increased tenfold during the interval between them. The district of Cologne made as many as two thousand arrests in August 1943: 1,620 foreign workers, 235 assorted deliquents, ninety "reactionaries" (religious?), forty "resistants," and four "Communists or Marxists." Thanks to the documentation that exists, the subsequent activities of these Cologne police, who numbered no more than one hundred or so, can be followed in more detail: surveillance of a local annex of the Buchenwald camp; deportation of 11,500 Jews from the region; an increasing number of arrests of foreigners, now classified as "resistants"; from the autumn of 1944 on, the repression of gangs of youths; in January 1945 the destruction of a cell of the National Committee for a Free Germany, probably Communist. All these operations were meticulously recorded in a mass of obsessively detailed paperwork once they had been carried out amid violence and disorder. In the overcrowded prisons of the town, foreigners, Germans, common-law, and political prisoners were intermingled. To reduce overcrowding the police themselves carried out executions, some of them publicly, to cow the population. After liberation the bodies of 792 victims were discovered.[3]

One question that again arises centers on the Gestapo's sources of information without which it could not have operated on such a large scale. The use of paid agents apparently varied from one regional office to another: the Nuremberg office used only one hundred or so to cover the whole of Bavaria, while the Frankfurt office used twelve times as many. Frankfurt agents included only a few officials and party members, but many foreigners, German workers, and even individuals classed as "oppositional" who were no doubt subjected to blackmail. But the vast majority of denunciations invariably came from voluntary informers who knew the victims. Perhaps the hard times exacerbated conflicts between individuals. Yet Gestapo documents on Düsseldorf, particularly precise on this point, show that in reality the zeal of informers correlated closely with the military situation. It peaked in 1941, decreased up until 1943, then fell off almost completely at the very time when conditions were becoming much harder. Obsessional hatreds die hard, however: in Würzburg denunciations of "guilty relations between Aryans and Jews" continued long after all the Jews had disappeared. In the last analysis it was the brutality of the interrogators themselves that enabled them to uncover so many resistance networks: the first arrests made in a random fashion or prompted by denunciations were followed by forced confessions and roundups of the survivors. This is how the Gestapo created its image of a mysterious body that "knew everything, could do anything, and was everywhere."[4]

Of the three missions assigned to concentration camps—to reeducate the detainees, work them to the point of exhaustion, and exploit them profitably—the first was never any more than a pretext for persecution. Eventually it disappeared altogether from official discourse, as did the category of "educable asocials" who were simply dispatched directly to disciplinary army units or else suffered the fate of "hardened cases." The only criteria of classification now were racial: Jews were relegated to the most humiliating and dangerous tasks and Slavs fared little better, while higher up the scale, in order to recruit various echelons for the internal hierarchy, Germans whether political or common-law prisoners took priority as "Aryans."

At what point was the second objective sacrificed to the third? The turning point is generally fixed around the spring of 1942, when Pohl, the head of the economic services of the *RSHA*, ordered that "the camps should convert their previous political structure into an organization suited to their economic task." The detainees were thus to be "mobilized for labor" just as German civilians as a whole were, except that for the former the objective of productivity would be pursued without scruple, with no limitation set on working hours. Their mortality rate immediately rose so much that even Himmler was worried and prescribed a number of precautionary measures: the camp system, managed like any business, was required to maintain its stock of labor in a rational manner, however limitless it might appear. The *Reichsführer SS*, keen to swell its fighting units, for a while considered building its own factories to supply them with arms. But the ranks in the concentration camps contained too few skilled workers and private industry refused to supply any to the SS, so the project was abandoned. In the end the administrators of the camps chose to reduce their role to that of suppliers of labor, maintaining surveillance over their subjects only outside working hours in return for a contractual sum "per head" (*Stück*). In May 1943, 43 percent of the detainees, about forty thousand men and women, were thus placed at the disposal of the industrialists, so, as can well be imagined, the SS must have made a sizable financial profit. The geography of the concentration camps was seriously affected by this arrangement. Each main camp now became the center of a galaxy of *Kommandos*, some as far distant as several hundred kilometers. Virtually every little town in Germany had at least one small camp set up near it, and each day the prisoners' journeys to and from the factories or building sites revealed how authorities treated their enemies to the local inhabitants, if indeed any were still unaware of it. In 1939 concentration camp detainees had totalled twenty-five thousand. By 1942 the number had risen to sixty thousand, by 1943 to ninety thousand; then at the beginning of 1944 it leaped to three hundred thousand, and one year later to seven hundred thousand. Significantly this acceleration kept pace with that of the Reich's defeats and territorial losses: the greater the threat of catastrophe, the greater became the fear of a slave revolt and the more the SS intensified repression of all forms of real or suspected subversion.[5]

Waffen-SS guards were considered archetypes of the Nordic race, so it seemed fitting to use as many as possible at the front for "heroic" tasks immediately behind the lines, such as massacres of Jews or Bolsheviks. Very few remained to guard the camps, only about forty thousand men. In Auschwitz for example, in May 1944, 2,300 men sufficed to guard sixty-seven thousand detainees. They did not even live in the camp, for their quarters and guard posts were situated outside the barbed wire fence. Inside, administration, food supplies, and even the maintenance of order were responsibilities of the detainees. The situation was identical in Dachau, Buchenwald, and Sachsenhausen. As a result, face-to-face encounters between masters and subjects should have been reserved to an even more restricted minority, the camp commandants and their immediate subordinates. However, teams of workers transferred to work sites close to the principal camps, and the installation of extra camps where that segregation was not so strictly observed, multiplied the occasions of master/subject contact and consequently also opportunities to inflict humiliations and brutalities. Little by little, however, the need to reinforce divisions at the front forced the authorities to replace fanatical SS guards with old reservists, semi-invalids, and men "grounded" from the air force and navy whose behavior was in many—but not all—cases more humane.

The word "fanatical" has just been used above. Did these guards truly conform to the Himmlerian model? The memories of detainees refer so often to cases of corruption that the superhuman ideal appears to be no more than a fantasy. The doctrinal training of these SS guards had not been carried very far, not even in the case of their officers, most of whom were of quite low rank and did not belong to the cultivated and distinguished elite of the corps. It is not even certain that they had sought such a position, impelled by some kind of conviction. For instance, among the Mauthausen guards whose files are available, not one had joined the party before 1931. Equally revealing is the fact that 40 percent of them had never held any previous job. Female guards at Ravensbrück present a similar picture. From modest backgrounds, many were recruited through advertisements and propaganda campaigns, then suddenly found themselves promoted by their new functions to the rank of superior beings. For both male and female guards the two main motives appear to have been a desire for a comfortable life and a need to tyrannize someone, knowing that a few grand Nazi words served to legitimize their power. As for the massacres during the last days in camps threatened by enemy armies and in death marches, they were caused by panic: those killers were certainly no heroes.[6]

It is hard to choose a representative sample of the twenty main camps. The deportees themselves frequently had a chance to make comparisons since, for reasons that remain obscure, they were often shunted from one *Kommando* to another or even between the principal camps. It is still possible to trace the passing of particular little teams with their guards across the chaotic Germany of the last months of the war, as they were tossed from Baden to the Baltic, through Bohemia and Saxony. Although occasionally struck by the particular conditions they encountered in some places (like one group of Sachsenhausen detainees who, after a few days at Natzweiler, wished they were back in their former camp), in general wherever they went they found the same dualist power system and the same kind of behavior on the part of those profiting from it. The choice of the following three models is thus an arbitrary one: Dachau, the initial model, Dora, as it were the ultimate model; and Natzweiler-Struthof, a punitive camp that turned into a fictitious one.

Dachau was under the command of three successive SS officers: the first was sacked for corruption; the second, originally an engineer, applied himself above all to running it as an economic machine; and the third was powerless to control the final confusion when the camp was invaded by transfers from the East and epidemics. At the moment of liberation the national distribution of detainees still reproduced the geography of German Europe as it had appeared at its peak: six thousand Germans, both "common-law" and political, fifteen thousand Poles, fifty-seven hundred French, mostly resistants, thirteen thousand five hundred military and civilian Soviets, thirty-four hundred Italians from Badoglio's army, twelve thousand Hungarian Jews temporarily spared extermination . . .—in all representatives of thirty-seven countries. A special department was reserved for the twenty-seven hundred priests, two-thirds of them Polish.

The total came to between sixty thousand and seventy thousand individuals, but the list of entries registered since the beginning included almost two hundred thousand people, the difference being accounted for by a small number of liberations, innumerable transfers to other camps, and twenty-eight thousand officially recorded deaths. The graph of annual deaths reflected the very history of the institution, from the all-powerful days of the SS system to its utter impotence: between 1940 and 1942 the number of deaths rose from fifteen hundred to twenty-five hundred, in parallel to the rise in the number of detainees and the increasing momentum of "euthanasia"; the number fell to just over one thousand in 1943, when orders were received to preserve the strength of the labor force; it was up to five thousand in 1944 and 15,400 between January and April 1945 (without counting subsequent deaths), reflecting the general confusion in which typhus spread and the guards gave free rein to their murderous madness, particularly on the *Kommando* death marches. The central camp had extended its network of annexes from Austria to the Neckar, sometimes in small groups of men, sometimes in huge masses, as in Kaufering in Bavaria where up to one hundred thousand were sent to dig underground shelters. The "Dachau model" thus evolved from a carefully calculated prototype toward progressive decomposition.[7]

If Dora-Mittelbau in contrast represents the perfecting of the system, it is because here employers and suppliers of labor collaborated in exceptional harmony. It is true that the mission assigned to those running the camp was of capital importance — to oversee production of the supreme weapon, the V-2 rocket. To this end, in the summer of 1943 two parallel societies were set up: one to manufacture the weapons, *Mittelwerk*, a state-owned firm managed by engineers; and one to dig the tunnels where the production lines would be installed, *Mittelbau*, a purely SS enterprise. The site chosen was the Harz, in the center (*Mittel*) of Germany, and its (derisively feminine) code name was Dora. Laborers were provided by the Buchenwald camp, but soon their numbers increased so rapidly (up to twelve thousand at a time) that the *Kommando* received the status of an autonomous camp. Accommodation huts were built at the entrances to the underground tunnels, but to save time the detainees were made to live permanently on the work site amid all the dust and stench, harassed constantly by the SS who, exceptionally, were here able to intervene even in the work place. Once the underground chambers had been dug out (at the cost of seventeen thousand lives), the survivors remained as unskilled labor for the factory or else were replaced by comrades better qualified to assemble the rockets. These, basing their arguments on the need for high production, obtained a few material improvements but continued to be subjected to surveillance and summary arrests and executions by the Gestapo, now obsessed by fears of sabotage in this primary sector. After diminishing for a short while, hunger and disease worsened again, causing six thousand deaths in the first three months of 1945; and as central Germany was the last region to be conquered by Allied armies, in the month of April forty thousand deportees were still in those tunnels. Whatever the individual behavior of German civilians, Dora truly was the laboratory of collaboration between state scientists, bureaucrats, and engineers on the one hand and the SS on the other.[8]

The Natzweiler-Struthof camp had a number of distinct characteristics. Opened during the winter of 1940–41 in the heart of the Vosges for the exploitation of a granite quarry, it was also possibly put there to intimidate the native Alsatian population in preparation for its annexation to the Reich. Its commanding officers and guards were particularly brutal, the climate was harsh, and the steep topography made all movement difficult if not positively dangerous. On top of all this the camp was dreadfully overcrowded. The main camp, designed for fifteen hundred detainees, eventually contained over five thousand. They included many *NN* resistants whom the *Wehrmacht* high command, followed by the Gestapo, had decided should vanish into "the night and the fog." Like other camps, Natzweiler produced offshoots, some in Alsace, some in Lorraine, some on the right bank of the Rhine. But—and this was its exceptional feature—after the Vosges were evacuated as the Allied advance pushed forward, the camp continued to exist administratively speaking with a small team of commanding officers moving from one refuge to another. Right to the very last it thus continued to provide labor for underground factories and work sites in the Baden and Württemberg regions. "Natzweiler, incognito, was present in the midst of daily life, hardly detectable in the chaos of the last months of the war" (H. Vorländer). Some detainees were employed in already existing tunnels manufacturing Messerschmitt planes. Epidemics took such a severe toll here that those in command ceased to send in the customary reports of deaths to the local town hall. Others were placed at the disposal of the Todt organization, to build aerodromes and subterranean shelters in the Neckar valley, and there casualties were so great that one of the camps had to be converted into a reception area for the sick, called a "rest camp" by the SS, a "dying place" by the detainees. Yet others were the victims of one last aberrational fling by the planners: the exploitation of bituminous shale that would supposedly yield small quantities of petrol for aircraft. Hygiene, safety, and food supplies were everywhere so appallingly poor that many died.

Conditions were sometimes aggravated and occasionally improved, by the behavior of the guards. Where the SS were outnumbered by old reservists, gratuitous brutalities diminished. But elsewhere they were allowed free rein and moreover encouraged similar behavior on the part of civilian foremen and the military. As witnesses to these brutalities could not be allowed to fall into the hands of the Allied armies, they were sent back to Dachau, many on foot, leaving the roads strewn with corpses. The SS, never short on plans, still intended to have them work in their "alpine refuge."[9]

The very logic of the system had turned the initial isolated units into a network that circulated the terror diffused throughout German society. The world of the concentration camps became confused with Germany itself. We have seen above how it contributed to the efficient running of industry. But now we must consider its contribution to "racial hygiene" and "public health." Some camps were unquestionably equipped with gas chambers as has been proven at least in the cases of Dachau, Mauthausen, and Natzweiler. Dachau had a small installation that could be used for particularly secret executions, and it was also connected with the larger establishment of Hadamar where, in 1941 for example, two thousand detainees classified as mentally sick, crippled, or Jewish were liquidated. Similarly, in Mauthausen the authorities could carry out gassing either on the spot or using the neighboring facilities of Hartheim. Natzweiler set up its gas chamber in the neighboring farm at Struthof, a name which would eventually loom large in the collective memory. We also know that the distance separating Auschwitz and Monowitz from the industrial installations for murder in Birkenau was extremely short.

Many other camps ran infirmaries that were transformed into laboratories for military doctors and university researchers who were supplied with human guinea pigs in limitless numbers. To help save the lives of pilots, *Luftwaffe* doctors subjected Dachau detainees to low pressure experiments in which eighty of them died. To protect the army from typhus, new vaccines were tested in Buchenwald and Natzweiler regardless of the number of victims. Also in Natzweiler a specialist in gas warfare made his guinea pigs inhale phosgene, then injected them in vain with a counter-poison. Similar practical tests were carried out in Ravensbrück to test sulphamides, in Neuengamme on infantile tuberculosis, and in many other places too. But over and above these utilitarian experiments, some tests were designed simply to prepare for a racially pure society or to verify the hypotheses of the scientists who set them up. In this spirit, one professor at the University of Strasbourg had eighty-seven Jews gassed in Struthof in order to enrich his anatomical collections, and in Auschwitz several gynecologists tried out new methods of sterilization. Others who made the most of the abundance of corpses or, when they needed more, procured them by administering lethal injections, were constructing what they described as "a new biological anthropology that would put an end to the old ideas on humanity" on the basis of material provided by "women unworthy to reproduce," "abnormal children," twins, and dwarfs. . . . Rather than continue with this list, let us seek a few explanations. The most facile, put forward after the war by the German medical corps, is that only a minority of criminals and madmen were involved. But although there no doubt were a few notoriously unbalanced and incompetent doctors among them, many others were simultaneously holding down prestigious jobs in universities and research centers — one of the Natzweiler experimenters was even considered Nobel prize material. Now when the SS suddenly presented them with undreamed of means to advance their favorite lines of research, it seemed an offer almost too good to refuse. Even when Nazi ideology did not provide the direct inspiration for their work, it at least came to their aid by dismissing any deontological scruples: how much did Jewish or Gypsy children, destined for an early death in any case, weigh in the balance against the glorious future of science? One did not even have to be a party militant to see that the answer was "nothing." From that position to participation in genocide took only a few short steps.[10]

HOW TO LIVE WITH TEN MILLION
EXCLUDED PEOPLE

Whether arrested by the police, captured in war operations, or requisitioned by occupation authorities, the unwilling servants of the Great Reich were at first shut away in camps of varying dimensions. But they ended up living in the midst of the population and being seen daily in the streets: in Berlin in February 1945 one correspondent of a Swiss newspaper remarked that Russian was heard more often than German.[11] Only their clothing, old uniforms of striped rags with an arm band or a badge, indicated to passersby that they were people apart, classified in categories that made some even more unapproachable than others. Germans, essentially political deportees, constituted only a tiny minority among them, and it might seem that a book devoted to the German people need do no more than mention them in passing. Yet surely the history of this cohabitation is an integral part of their history.

In the concentration camps and their scattered *Kommandos*, the thought of death was in the forefront of all minds daily. Many deportees were welcomed on the day of their arrival with the terrible joke warning them that they would be leaving through the chimney of the crematorium. After studying the registers of newcomers and deaths, historians of each camp have attempted some calculations: Neuengamme, 100,000 arrivals in all, 50,000 deaths; Mauthausen 230,000 arrivals, over 100,000 deaths; Ravenbrück, 130,000 arrivals, 60,000 to 90,000 deaths; Bergen-Belsen, 90,000 arrivals between December 1944 and April 1945, 50,000 deaths. . . .[12] The figures do not include anonymous individuals executed upon arrival or those who died of disease after their liberation. Perhaps these statistics lose a little of their cold impersonality when they are applied to the different categories of prisoners. The Jews always suffered the highest death rates (100 percent each month in Mauthausen) along with the Spanish Republicans, followed in decreasing order by delinquents torn by the SS from preventive detention in prison, then Poles, politicals, asocials, Soviets, and finally — with the fewest deaths — "professional criminals." This macabre classification reflects not only the different kinds of treatment that the SS meted out to those they particularly hated or favored, but also the behavior characteristic of each category. Solidarity, always weakest among asocials, Polish civilians rounded up as early as 1939–40, and the Jews already weakened by earlier trials, manifested itself more strongly among political resistants and the Soviet military. Obviously, length of survival also depended upon individual circumstances such as age, the amount of time spent in the camp, and the degrees of physical and moral resilience which, according to E. Kogon, determined whether "after three months one was sinking irreversibly or beginning to 'organize' a way of living in the camp." *Organisieren*, the word that meant "scheming to improve their daily lot" for German civilians, had penetrated the international language of the camps to sum up all the techniques of survival.[13]

The camps also have a political history: the history of the acquisition of internal power by more or less politicized international teams. Based on the argument that they could not have succeeded without a long period of clandestine preparation, they are often identified as resistants who continued their former activities. Conversely, deportees who felt excluded from these networks engaged in spirited polemics against them, particularly the Communist teams such as those in Buchenwald and Dora. The controversy was further fueled by the Cold War and continues even today. The only way to pass beyond it is to make a meticulous study of the history of each camp. In Flossenbürg for example a number of political prisoners, German at first, then—quite late on—foreigners too, managed to get themselves appointed *Kapos*, or heads of labor teams, but did not undermine the general domination of the "common-law" prisoners. In Mauthausen the replacement of criminals with political prisoners in the administrative services was favored due to the gigantic size of the installation and the increasing numbers of *Kommandos*, which were in danger of becoming unmanageable without the help of competent clerks. In Dora, posts of internal responsibility were immediately filled by German Communists, "old concentration camp hands" capable of persuading the SS that the work would not progress unless a minimum of material improvements were introduced. They did obtain a few results, but nevertheless then became victims in the massive executions of the winter of 1945. In Auschwitz in contrast, the services of internal order remained in the hands of the "common-law" prisoners, who continued their tasks as loyal auxiliaries of the SS even in the evacuation marches.[14]

On the other hand, the activities of other international committees were totally clandestine. The initiative, generally coming from German and Austrian Communists, at first was taken in opposition to the distrust and internal disagreements between different nationalities: the older prisoners attached to the old methods of the Komintern steadfastly refused to collaborate with their Socialist, Liberal, and Christian co-detainees, while younger activists who had become involved after the 1935 turning point pressed for veritable popular fronts. Agreement was reached in at least five main camps: Dachau, Sachsenhausen, Mauthausen, Auschwitz, and Buchenwald. In the latter the name Popular Front was even adopted along with a plan for a future Germany and preparations for an uprising. In the final weeks of the war some of these committees, weakened by transfers, were unable to oppose total evacuation. But in Dachau, Buchenwald, and Mauthausen they played a useful role in maintaining order between the flight of the SS and the arrival of the Allies. Having been masters of the camp for a few days, they even felt they had liberated themselves by their own efforts.[15]

After that, while former deportees and certain local authorities kept the principal camps open, the traces of most *Kommandos* eventually disappeared. Not until forty or fifty years had passed did calls come from within the German population pressing for some kind of commemoration. At this the embarrassment of the older generations became apparent. They could hardly plead total ignorance, since from 1942 on they had all seen columns of deportees passing beneath their windows or worked beside them in the factories. A more convincing plea was that their general passivity in the face of the Gestapo's omnipresence and brutalities should be excused, and made their few gestures of solidarity all the more admirable. The other retrospective view, that of the deportees themselves, more or less confirms that picture. It is not possible to define an attitude typical of the German civilians. Studies devoted to the *Kommandos* of Dachau at Natzweiler in Württemberg reveal a population now uniformly hostile, now—in more isolated places—compassionate, now indifferent. Some took part in hunts for escaped prisoners, while their neighbors discreetly placed little piles of food along the paths taken by the starving fugitives. Similarly, on work sites and in factories, for every German foreman who insofar as possible looked after his team, there was no doubt one who acted like a galley-slave guard.[16] In a destroyed society, what could be expected other than individual reactions?

The expression "prisoners of war" covered both the western military, protected by the Geneva conventions, and the Red Army, to whom Hitler had denied that right. Contacts between the two groups were forbidden and their living conditions were poles apart. Among the former, the French soldiers were the most numerous, 1.5 million in 1940 and still nine hundred thousand in 1944, not counting twenty-two thousand officers whose status excused them from working for the victor. Noncommissioned officers and lower ranks were at first imprisoned in camps guarded by reservists, most of whom hoped for "collaboration without a fuss," who were only too happy to remain far behind the front lines. Only escapees recaptured as they fled to France had to endure the far harder conditions of disciplinary camps. Later many went to work either willingly or under force on farms and in factories where they lived alongside soldiers and civilians from all over Europe, virtually merging with the German population. Their postwar memories and even more revealing letters from that time describe infinite varieties of behavior by employers and working companions alike. On the whole they were surprised to find that the German population "had remained far more diversified in their opinions than they had expected" and to note frequent signs of their at least tacit oppositon. As for the fabled weakness of German women for French men, the idea stems mostly from fears of the police and barrack-room-type boasts, although a number of cases of intimate relations were brought before military tribunals.[17] Possibly this cohabitation helped revive in French minds the old dichotomy between good and bad Germans, and to correct in their partners' minds the official caricature of the lazy, degenerate Frenchman. At any rate the lot of French prisoners was better than that of the six hundred thousand soldiers of the Italian army who had refused to rally to Mussolini in 1943 and were treated as traitors to the Axis cause: as has been noted above, several thousand were sent to Dachau.

The fate of Red Army soldiers was even more distressing, even if they survived the firing squads and famine in the transit camps. Many were employed on the spot in services behind *Wehrmacht* lines or even as auxiliaries in the maintenance of order (*Hiwis*). But as early as 1941, Hitler decided to move some to the coal mines of the Reich, even though his advisers warned him of the danger of "Bolshevik contamination" for German civilians (the memory of 1917–18 died hard!). They were required to deliver the same level of production as other miners although on much smaller food rations, so that by June 1944 eight percent of those in the Ruhr were hospitalized, mostly with tuberculosis, and an extra 10 percent were in infirmaries. The economic section of the staff office estimated "the monthly consumption of the labor force" (*sic*) at 3.3 percent. Their military status now availed them nothing, for the army had turned over their surveillance to the Gestapo. When certain employers offered them extra rations, protests were made by the party and Speer himself: the method of "annihilation through work" introduced by the SS had thus been communicated to ordinary Nazis, the military, and to technocrats. Some employers, particularly convinced of its efficacy, particularly in the mines of Silesia, even decided to increase production not by improving rations, but on the contrary by cutting those of recalcitrant workers. All in all, on a national average each of these workers cost his employer even less than a concentration camp detainee hired from the SS: 3.75 marks per day as against four to six. Including those sent to work in agriculture or on building projects, etc., 860,000 of these Soviets remained in 1944—but it is not known how many had already been killed on the spot or in the concentration camps.[18]

* * *

Even in peacetime the Third Reich had begun to recruit workers, more or less forcibly from the annexed industries of Austria and Czechoslovakia. The Czechs had even seen legislation passed that ordered the most minor offenses to be punished by deportation to a concentration camp. Then victories in Poland, western Europe, and the Balkans made more massive recruitment possible, voluntary in the West, enforced in the East. By the summer of 1941 the German economy was already employing 1.5 million of these foreigners, one million of whom were Poles. When numerous reservations were expressed regarding the importation into the heart of Germany, particularly in the countryside, of such huge numbers of "Polacks," both men and women, propaganda explained that it was necessary to prevent German men and women from performing obligatory work. But however close the police surveillance, anxiety persisted: complaints streamed in from "peasant leaders," and during the course of the war the SD devoted at least a hundred or so reports to these grievances, expressing their fears that foreigners were attracting the sympathy of German Catholics and corrupting German girls. A whole repressive apparatus was set up to make sure they stayed confined to their status of exclusion: a large P was sewn on their clothing and they were banned from inns and public spectacles, attended masses separate from the German parish masses, were sent to "camps to teach them how to work" if they were lazy, concentration camps if they were rebellious, and were sentenced to death, possibly public hanging, if they seduced German girls. As for workers from other nations—the 50,000 French and 270,000 Italians, etc.—they had volunteered to come but nevertheless caused difficulties by protesting against living conditions they considered inferior to what was promised by contract. The administration thought it could get around all this by racial and political discrimination that favored "Aryans" and "Allies," but this simply accentuated the jealousy between different nationals and discontent among German workers, who could not understand why for instance the Dutch and the Italians, whom they particularly detested, had the right to earn the same wages as themselves. Popular xenophobia did not always coincide with official classifications.

As soon as Russian and Ukrainian territories were occupied, the labor-force services sought volunteers from the East to work in Germany, then proceeded to requisition and later offer them to German industrialists. The latter, who would have preferred German recruits or those from neighboring countries, "resigned themselves" (the term used by steelworks in the Ruhr) to taking them on. Whether volunteers or requisitioned they were subject to the same rules as the Poles and forced to wear a label on their clothing bearing *Ost*, short for the distant East from which they hailed. By late 1942 more than a million of them were employed. Undernourished, ill-lodged in hastily established camps, and monstrously exploited by guards who insisted on a share of even their minimal rations, they were soon falling sick at the same rate as their military comrades. When the worst affected were sent home the effect was catastrophic as the trickle of volunteers dried up definitively, and the last fit and active men disappeared to join the partisans. In the meantime German public opinion on the subject was divided. Every time rations were cut, people cursed all the foreigners in the country eating their bread. But German mothers who had Russian or Ukrainian girls assisting them in the home declared they were satisfied with the help, for the Soviet girls were apparently more docile than German girls. "At very little cost" these German ladies thus acquired "the symbolic status of bourgeoises that reflected a quasi-colonial social order" (U. Herbert). In the factories, opinions and behavior patterns were equally contradictory. In general it was in the interest of German workers to behave correctly with their new partners, particularly in firms that adopted a system where wages corresponded to the level of production of teams of workers, as in Krupp's mechanical engineering factories. In order to improve the wages of each team member, the weakest had to increase productivity to equal the rest of the team, and to achieve this German workers did not hesitate to supply them with extra rations. But what happened after working hours was another matter. The hatred and blows—still at Krupp's—usually came from the factory police, whose zeal could rival that of the political police. In coal mines on the other hand, foremen and miners often committed brutalities against the *Ost* because working teams were separated according to nationality, so there was no persuasive reason for solidarity. In short, the working class turned out to be singularly uninternationalist.

From 1943 on this foreign labor force increased in size more and more rapidly. Within a few months there were one million westerners (two-thirds of whom were French), either ex-prisoners of war dressed as civilians or those rounded up by the STO. However, the young men of France soon learned to escape into clandestinity, and that source of labor also dried up. The Italians contributed their highly involuntary contingent, and above all the *Ostarbeiter* (eastern workers) exceeded two million. Their image and living conditions gave rise to new controversies. Goebbels and the Labor Front insisted that the Russians should not all be confused with the Bolsheviks, and that many diligent and "decent" workers were to be found among them; a number of circulars were sent out designed to improve their lot a little. On the other hand the *RSHA* persisted in warning that "through their very presence in Germany, they represented a danger to the order of the German people." It was a matter of differentiated racism and the battle for production on one hand, and absolute racism and an ideological battle on the other. Even the clique of business bosses was divided. At Krupp's food rations were increased, the productivity of the *Ost* equaled that of the Germans, and some of the former were even promoted to jobs involving leadership. But in the mines of Silesia and at Daimler-Benz, beatings, threats, and denunciations of sabotage remained the only methods for maintaining productivity levels, and in the *Bochumer Verein* steelworks opinion continued to be that the *Ost* were incapable of anything but "purely mechanical and subordinate work."

All these contradictions resolved themselves spontaneously in the period of the final chaos, when men from the East were forced to labor sixty hours a week, women worked all night, and even children of fourteen were used as reinforcements. Without air raid shelters they suffered more bombing casualties than the Germans themselves; in their camps the onslaughts of guards reduced them to a situation that inspectors of labor themselves described as "catastrophic." Through sickness, death, and absenteeism their replacement rate rose continually as did the number of attempts to flee homeward into the forests or no man's lands of the ruined cities. The theoretical distinction between military prisoners and requisitioned civilians was no longer respected, and the more politicized, many of them Red Army officers, set up resistance movements: in September 1944 the Gestapo reported that such cells existed in thirty-eight different towns. The authorities and population then developed a panic-stricken fear of a slave revolt, which the Gestapo fostered by labeling as "Communist" all gangs of young "pirates," deserters, and traffickers, carrying out spectacular raids on suspect localities, and then proceeding to public executions by hanging. The "Russians" had restored their 1941 image, that of innumerable and omnipresent bandits. Innumerable is certainly the right word: the last careful census, in August 1944, revealed the presence on Reich soil of 7.5 million foreigners, close to three million of whom were Soviets; however, soon after the end of hostilities the Allied services responsible for "displaced persons" estimated them at eleven million. The Greater German Reich had turned into Babel.[19]

THE FINAL SOLUTION TO "THE JEWISH QUESTION"

When Hitler ordered that Jews were no longer to be dumped elsewhere but should be annihilated, was that decision the fruit of long meditation or was it a quasi-improvised response to the failure of other solutions and the initiatives of his most dedicated partisans? For a long time that alternative fueled the arguments between "intentionalist" and "functionalist" historians. Nowadays however discussion hardly concerns the exact date, sometime between July and September 1941, when the "Führer's order" was issued. An examination of the circles involved in its preparation and execution makes it possible to set it at the end of the three phases that led up to it: the intensification of measures regulating the lives of the Jews, experiments in mass executions of groups "alien to the Community," and the elaboration of theoretical studies designed to legitimize the genocide. If the "intention" of the Leader was carried out without scruple it is because the system already "functioned."[20] All the shootings and gassings tend to paralyze the means—of comprehension and explanation—historians usually use; out of decency, they shrink from trying to describe them. The only remaining option is to adopt a roundabout way to approach the unfathomable reality symbolized by the name Auschwitz, "the anus of the world."

The status of German Jews was never fixed definitively but became more dire at every stage, slowly when it was still necessary to save appearances and then more rapidly when the impatience of grass roots Nazis had to be calmed. After war was declared there was no longer any need to bother about international opinion, and Hitler was able to announce the Jews' "annihilation" publicly without specifying what he meant. In the meantime, what was to be done with the 180,000 male and female Jews still in Germany who were either unable or unwilling to leave, and the few who had even returned from emigration? Barred from all professional activities, stripped of their possessions, and reduced to famine rations, they now simply constituted a destitute mass. But whatever physical strength they had left could still be used to help the war economy, so at the beginning of 1941 thirty thousand of them were sent to work in munitions factories. This gave little "Aryan" bosses a chance to treat clumsy and shattered intellectuals as pariahs; but these enemies of the state also included a number of qualified professionals, and the interests of production if not a minimum of compassion prompted firms to hang on to them as long as possible. Evenings and the nights were even harder to bear: crammed into buildings or camp huts not yet openly called ghettos, exhausted by their labors and journeys to work on foot, they heard rumors, which from the summer of 1941 became increasingly insistent, about the fate of other Jews in the East. In July their schools were closed and Jewish children were now in danger of being arrested for homelessness. In September they were ordered to wear a yellow star affixed to their clothing, an old symbol of discrimination recently reinvented in the concentration camps and then generalized throughout Poland. A few days later their Cultural League, which had still afforded them a few distractions, was dissolved. Finally on the 18th, Hitler decided to deport them to the East. What did "deportation" mean? Heydrich, commenting on his leader's decision, explained: "a definitive disappearance" (and applied this to all Jews in Europe). But the Jews themselves did not know that. Some, suspecting the truth, chose suicide—as many as three thousand to four thousand mostly elderly bourgeois who had always considered themselves fully German and whose children had managed to emigrate. Tens of thousands, half of them in Berlin, plunged into an underground life of hiding. But the majority packed their bags and lined up in columns to be marched under the gaze of passersby to the railway stations for deportation. Soon no more than fifty thousand, reckoned still to be useful to the war effort, remained. That figure had hardly changed in February 1943, when the Berlin police launched a *Fabrikaktion* in the factories themselves, removing 2,757 at a single stroke. In an excess of zeal, the police even tried to pack off "mixed couples" of Jews and "Aryans" along with them, but that proved too much: the women of the neighborhood rushed out to manifest their indignation and—for once—the police retreated. By now only thirty thousand remained. No statistics on their later numbers exist.[21]

Radical anti-Semites also wanted to settle the problem of "mixed couples," "first-degree metics" (descendants from two Jewish grandparents), and "second-degree metics" (one Jewish grandparent). The latter, forty-three thousand of them, were eventually assimilated to Germans, following Byzantine discussions between experts on the regenerative power of Aryan genes as compared to Jewish genes, which took up, for example, much of the Wannsee conference. The sixty-four thousand "first-degree metics" were on the contrary classified along with "full Jews." As for Aryan partners in mixed couples, they were subjected to pressures of every kind to persuade them to divorce, which would then make it possible to deport their husbands or wives. Thus the linguist V. Klemperer was saved by the obstinacy of his wife, who resisted all SS efforts, while the novelist J. Klepper, after months trying to save his Jewish wife and daughter-in-law, even going so far as to beard Eichmann himself in his *RSHA* den—eventually committed suicide with both of them.[22]

It was not possible for the German population to remain unaware of the departures of deportees, which took place in full view, out in the streets, nor of their ultimate fate, news of which was brought back by soldiers on leave from the eastern front. But the usual reports that are available, which are fairly trustworthy for peacetime, are not very helpful in finding out how the German people reacted to these developments. The Social Democrat militants had discontinued their reports in late 1939; those of the "New Departure" group, which continued to appear a while longer, limited themselves to reporting rumors and noting that informed people were more concerned about the mentally sick than the Jews. *SD* reporters for their part gave the matter no coverage at all except when some spectacular event occurred. When the first yellow stars appeared, they noted a few manifestations of pity, but reported that in general people seemed to be satisfied—an assertion that testifies above all to the zeal of these reporters. A (nonscientific) poll carried out in the autumn of 1942 among party members divides them into 69

percent who were indifferent, 21 percent who favored creation
of a Jewish state (late echoes of the stillborn plans of 1940), five
percent who called for the death of all Jews, and five percent
who rejected anti-Semitism. This may quite accurately reflect
the views of the population as a whole. In the streets of Dresden,
V. Klemperer, wearing his yellow star, was in general ignored
by passersby, sometimes insulted by an SS or "a man with the
look of a tough," and was openly comforted by a distinguished
looking gentleman and a furniture mover. In the elegant quarter
of Berlin-Nicolassee, J. Klepper's wife and daughter-in-law
were shunned by all their neighbors on the day when they dared
to emerge wearing their badges of exclusion. When the air raids
and defeats on land came thick and fast, it was rumored that it
was vengeance from Heaven for the murder of the Jews. But that
reaction could be interpreted either as a return of superstition, a
common enough phenomenon at this time, or simply as a naive
translation of the official line that claimed the Allied armies were
commanded by Jews. On the other hand, demonstrations of
solidarity must have been rare: we know of no collective protest
except that of the Berlin women in defense of mixed couples.
Jews in the capital who survived years of underground living
later recounted encounters with pitiless exploiters, compassionate Christians who tried to convert them, understanding officials, and heroic and disinterested protectors. In short the
masses were moved neither by radical anti-Semitism nor active
solidarity, but were sufficiently neutral not to impede the realization of SS plans.[23]

That neutrality might find a partial excuse in the prudence of
ecclesiastical authorities, who for the most part made no attempt
to defend Jews unless they were converts. Whereas the authorities considered Jewish converts from a strictly racial point of
view, most church leaders whether Protestant or Catholic and
most of the faithful too reckoned that if these new Christians had
been baptized and withdrawn from their original community,
they deserved to be spared; but they had nothing to say about
what the state intended to do with "real Jews." That was always

the position of the majority of Protestants, even within the Confessional Church, and their postwar defenders could only point to two instances when they took up a truly forthright position in defense of the Jews: a circular from the bishop of Württemberg, Theophile Wurm, in July 1943 asked his pastors the following question: "Have we not seen the temples of others disappear in flames [in 1938] and must we not now behold our own temples set ablaze [by the bombs]?"; and in another, produced shortly after the Berlin synod, he stated: "The life of all men, including that of the people of Israel, is sacred in the eyes of God." Similarly, Catholic bishops were for a long time concerned only for their Jewish converts. When the deportations became publicly notorious, Cardinal Faulhaber drew a subtle distinction between the "duty" to intervene in their favor and the "possibility" of intervening for the rest. But the Raphael Association for Aid for Jews soon received enough information about what happened to Jews arriving in Poland to exert pressure on the hierarchy and even on Rome, and the Fulda conference circulated a commentary on the Fifth Commandment, which declared: "To kill is evil in itself, even if it seems to serve the common good," and followed this with a list of the victims, the mentally sick, hostages, prisoners of war, and "people of foreign race and extraction." But only a few isolated believers reacted in a concrete fashion by helping Jews in hiding, or associating themselves for reasons of conscience with the conspiracy of 20 July 1944.[24]

It had taken years to accustom the German people to the segregation of the Jews; but it did not take long to accustom its new elite to their physical destruction, as the number of victims to be slaughtered grew and a new vocabulary came into circulation, seemingly innocent but easily understood by initiates. Some of its expressions only gradually acquired definitive meaning. When Hitler used "final solution" in 1939, it could still signify exile, as well as death for all. Then, when its true interpretation became clear, all too clear, some editors replaced it with "re-

moval" or used the Auschwitz formula "separate billeting."
Eventually Bormann declared that the only expression to be
used was "mobilization of the Jews for work." The euphemism
"special treatment" (*Sonderbehandlung*) was dealt with in similar fashion. When it first appeared in Gestapo circulars in 1939,
for a while it was followed in parentheses by an explanatory
word (*Exekution*); this became progressively superfluous, and
the principal word itself became so transparent that it had to be
replaced by "transportation" or "flushing out." As far as the restricted circles that received these instructions were concerned,
all this was clearly not a matter of security but rather of pallia-
tives designed to calm their remaining doubts. Accustomed to
decoding the ambiguities of official discourse, they felt reassured when they used a vocabulary that appeared to concern
nothing more than organizing conquered territory.[25]

The situation was similar to the initial state murders of the
mentally ill and cripples, which was disguised as "putting to
death out of compassion." A whole series of arguments was put
together to be used by the people involved. The families of the
first children liquidated in this way, as early as 1939, were told
that the injections were part of a new treatment that presented a
small number of risks. When Hitler decided to move on from
sterilization to "euthanasia" for adults, he backdated his decree
to 1 September 1939 to make it appear it was one of the emergency measures taken at the start of the war. Later, division of
responsibility again proved an effective way to calm consciences: members of selection committees were never present
at the murders; and the murderers were merely implementing
decisions made without them. When injections were replaced
by executions using gas, the bureaucrats of section T4 in the
Chancellory, who were in charge of the program, declared the
new procedure was more humane. When the system moved on
from killling only the mentally sick to including cripples, "ineducable asocials," and Jews in concentration camps, the doctors of Auschwitz for example claimed that this "selection"
would ease overcrowding and improve hygiene in the camp. Fi-

nally, the interest of scientific research was invoked as the supreme argument: the young and brilliant researcher Joseph Mengele regularly presented the results of his autopsies to his masters at the Emperor William Institute of Anthropology and Eugenics, and professor Robert Ritter regularly divided Gypsies into "Aryans of value" and "genetically determined asocials" and proceeded either to castrate or gas those in the latter category. In total, about one hundred doctors were involved directly and several hundred indirectly, some of them motivated by the worship of Race, others by the quest for "scientific knowledge," while many did this work as a result of a "progressive chain of compromises" (R. Lifton). Meanwhile, the label T4 had been replaced by 14f13, and its agents had been transferred to the extermination centers of Poland, Belzec, Sobibor, and Treblinka.[26]

Protests came not so much from the medical corps but from the churches, representing the horrified families in their faithful flock. A few professors of psychiatry, administrators, and nurses in Protestant and Catholic asylums tried to save some of the patients in their care — and succeeded without too much difficulty. But the affair could not be kept secret. The ferrying of the sick to the extermination centers and the letters announcing their deaths to thousands of families generated first rumors, then indignation. The bishops intervened, discreetly at first, but in vain. Monsignor von Galen, bishop of Münster, was the first to protest publicly in his series of sermons delivered in July and August 1941. Underpinning his message with a patriotic argument ("the internal People's Community has been unscrupulously shattered"), he denounced first the closure of the monasteries, then the assassination of the sick. The problem then became political: at a time when the resistance of the Red Army was proving more tenacious than expected, was it really well-judged to open a breach in the internal front? Hitler let it be known that he was ordering the operation to be suspended. But in fact it continued in secret and the public was not deceived. When the film *Ich klage an* ("I accuse") appeared in cinemas the following January, many, particularly among the Catholic clergy, condemned it as a covert plea in favor of euthanasia.[27]

But the main operational field of racism was in the East. The Polish population, the first to be conquered, included several million Jews, the *Ostjuden* whom the Germans, even Jewish Germans, traditionally represented as hideous and terrifying people. Hounded from provinces newly annexed to the Reich, they were chased in the direction of the "General Government" where they were concentrated in huge ghettos and the only men and women to emerge were those fit enough to work for the war effort. But by now the practice of massive, immediate elimination had already been inaugurated by SS intervention groups (*Einsatzgruppen*), small units composed of twenty-seven hundred men at the most which indiscriminately massacred all snipers, hostages, Slavs, and Jews. The problem arose again in the summer of 1941 for the Baltic States, Russia, Belorussia, and the Ukraine, and this time the general threats to the Jews were backed up by an official incitement to slaughter. In Hitler's communiqués to his generals, later relayed to the troops, the enemy was systematically described as "Judeo-Bolshevik," turning every Jew into a dangerous revolutionary and every Communist into a member of the race threatening Europe. In particular, one set of orders handed down on the eve of the attack on the USSR had commanded units in the vanguard to shoot all political commissars of the Red Army and to send Jewish prisoners to the rear where SS intervention groups would deal with them. These groups had been reconstituted in the spring and were now composed of between three thousand and four thousand men, divided into four autonomous units. The troops were extremely heterogeneous. Group A, for example, in the Baltic States, was made up of one-third auxiliaries: drivers, secretaries, and so on; one-third *Waffen-SS*, for the tasks of execution in the strict sense of the term; and a last third consisting of police drawn from the Gestapo, the criminal police, and even the "police for the maintenance of order," the ordinary keepers of the peace. It was further supported by thousands of local militiamen assembled for the purpose of hunting down Jews. Its leadership was in the hands of officers of the information service (*SD*) and the Gestapo: the elite of the elite who had always disdained the routine drudgery of the concentration camps and withdrawn to the technical services and study offices of Berlin now had to justify its motto: "The name of my honor is loyalty." Dividing among them the zones of occupation behind the lines all the way from the Baltic to Ukraine, these four flying units executed the Jewish prisoners handed over to them by the army as well as members of all the communities they encountered. According to initial orders issued by Himmler they should have sacrificed only adult men, but the killers, German and autochthonous alike, intoxicated by alcohol and sadism, made no distinction between young and old, or men, women, and children. Deciding, probably in August, that those women and children had fallen simply as a result of the necessities of war, Himmler gave his troops no more than a retroactive warning. In the meantime the army officers, keeping their own hands clean, limited themselves to viewing the spectacle (when some were sickened by it, their leaders made a point of later congratulating them for having stayed at their posts) and periodically writing reports accompanied by statistics. Thanks to these accounts it is possible to estimate the number of victims at half a million. Did these excesses on the part of a killing force, deliberately left free from controls, spark the supreme decision to embark on generalized genocide? On 31 July, Goering, in confidence, directed Heydrich, head of the *RSHA*, to prepare "an overall solution to the Jewish problem in Europe," but still left open the choice between "emigration and evacuation" — another euphemism. Many historians believe that Hitler's own order to exterminate soon followed. Others, such as Philippe Burrin, believe it was not issued until late August or early September. At any rate, gassing centers were open by autumn, perhaps to relieve the "elite" of such demeaning tasks, and no doubt also to distance spectators whose reactions, now cynical, now horrified, was being reported in Germany.[28]

Important though it may be, the contoversy over dates is of secondary importance to the basic problem, which is the question of human nature, no less. Among the thousands of books and articles devoted to this, the most convincing answer is that suggested by Christopher Browning in the conclusion of his study of an "ordinary" police battalion which also took part in these massacres. After eliminating factors such as battle frenzy, fear of punishment, and so on, Browning concludes that the prime factor was the group's conformism, and that sets the responsibility squarely upon their leaders. On the more precise case of the "intervention groups," it should be added that the lowest grade policemen in the execution squads were inured to physical violence while serving in their original commissariats, while their officers constantly elaborated theories in their offices to justify the mass killings.[29]

Those who initiated the extermination of Jews and Gypsies represented it as "the solution to a problem," that is to say as the result of a scientific project prepared by their advisers. At this point the "precursory theorists" of genocide make their appearance and, if we wish to progress toward comprehension of the incomprehensible, it is important to study them specifically as thinkers. They had after all been gathered together in June 1940 for a colloquium entitled "The mobilization of the human sciences for the war." In truth virtually every discipline contributed something to the stages of elimination (deportation, sterilization, execution) and those (selection, colonization) designed to construct the path to Utopia. The names of those past and future, young and old intellectuals matter little. They were sufficiently numerous to warrant classification into different schools, at the risk of overlooking their colleagues who retained their reservations and the handful who actually resisted.

"Research into the East" constituted a remarkable case of interdisciplinary collaboration. Materially it was helped by certain university research centers and the SS study services; and intellectually it benefited from the common use of a number of concepts familiar to everyone. As noted above, universities in eastern Germany had long since set up institutes to study the history, geography, economy, and demography of Poland and the USSR. In 1939 the SS Staff Office had for its part merged with two other offices, one devoted to the study of Germans in foreign countries, the other to race and colonization, all under the umbrella of the "Commissariat for the consolidation of the German race" (*RKF*), a huge planning apparatus that employed thousands of collaborators. The occupation of Poland made it possible to test out the validity of hypotheses there on the spot, then apply them in a first attempt at remodeling populations by expelling Jews and Poles and installing in their place Germans from the "old Reich" and central Europe. Then while the heads of old-style schools pursued their studies in German universities, their disciples would repopulate the universities of Poznan and Cracow, whose teaching bodies were all in prison. There, faced with a student audience of Germans from the local minorities and "Germanizable" Baltics and Poles, they set themselves up as models of a new type of scholar whose task was to provide scientific legitimacy for the actions of the politicians. The *RKF* for its part collaborated with the experts of various ministries in preparation for the invasion of the USSR. The early months of 1941 thus saw the emergence of the "General Plan for the East," which organized the resources of conquered territories in advance and submitted their inhabitants to the double process of "a densification of positive forces" and "the elimination of enemies of order." The eastern expanses were subdivided into dense zones of colonization (western Poland), marginal zones of colonization (all the way from Leningrad to the Crimea), and peripheral zones where the colonists would be concentrated in a few fortified localities. In this fashion the Spartan society would be recreated, with a German military elite, Baltic and Germanized Slav *perioikoi*, and Slav helots. An experimental prototype community was even established in a district near Lublin.[30]

The coherence of these projects depended upon ongoing

discussions between the thinkers and the activists concerning the concepts and problems involved. By 1940 certain historians among those most concerned decided their mission was "to supply the historical framework for the impending reorganization of Europe." They were already familiar with the principal elements in this intellectual construction: the resurrection of the Reich as a supernational entity, the permanent threat to civilization represented by Asia, and the establishment of "separate cultural levels" for Germans and Slavs respectively. Geographers perfected their theory of central areas, which began as descriptive and then became normative, and served to designate the positioning of networks of German colonies. Demographic economists worked on determining the rate of "overpopulation" in the towns and countryside of Poland, and proposed to bring it down to an acceptable level by getting rid of "dead ballast" in order to arrive at "an economic and social structure similar to that of the healthiest regions of Bavaria." Geneticist-anthropologists, who defined race "not as a group of men but as a group of genes," did away with physical categories and identified the social and moral characteristics of "Nordics" and "Orientals," concluding that "Race is an ideal to be achieved." It is worth noting that these contributions generally appealed to current ethical and cultural notions, and were thus opposed to the boorish materialism of ordinary racists. In this respect they were in tune with SS thinking, which likewise based its distinction between "people of value," the "educable," and the "ineducable" upon qualities of social adaptability and the performance of individuals. The boldest of them forthrightly recognized this similarity. One specialist in the organization of space wrote, "Our planning is not devoid of ethical values (*wertfrei*); the point of it is to serve the People. . . . Not only does it take account of the past but, by its constructive predictions, it collaborates in making things happen." However, they could not close their eyes to the concrete application of their theories. In the main they suggested that "dead ballast" should be evacuated or sent "to the East"; and when one of these professors traveling in the Ukraine discovered how SS intervention groups were carrying out that evacuation, he declared that it was terrible but very useful in reducing the number of superfluous consumers. Experts in the Ministry of Agriculture showed they were no less dehumanized by their so-called scientific rigor when they announced: "Tens of millions of people are going to become superfluous and will either die or emigrate to Siberia."[31]

Texts of this kind are so numerous that it has since been suggested that German science as a whole lost its way. In the preceding years of peace, careerist ambitions and a certain nationalistic tradition may have inclined some scientists to compromise their ethics by conniving with the authorities. But to go so far as to participate in genocide . . . ? The situation was summed up at the time by the geneticist Eugen Fischer, who had just resigned as director of the Emperor William Institute of Anthropology and Eugenics. His remarks have frequently been quoted for they are classic of their kind: "This is a rare chance for theoretical research, which finds itself in a period in which the official philosophy recognizes it and goes halfway to meet it, and in which its practical results are welcomed and treated as the bases of certain important laws and decisions."[32] The scientist flattered himself that it was he who inspired his Prince, not wishing to see that he was merely the latter's tool.

Postwar German public opinion for a long time clung to the reassuring illusion that the Black Order of the SS had merely been a monstrous excrescence on the Nazi system, with few members and altogether cut off from the rest of society. It could invoke the image the SS created for itself, that of an aristocracy full of scorn for ordinary Germans. Furthermore, every profession and every major civilian or military body through the mouthpiece of its re-created associations insisted it was important not to confuse it with the minority of its members who were criminals, fools, or mad. But what that illusion and those arguments ignore is that a minority or an aristocracy cannot retain or increase its power unless it is surrounded by a network of partners and auxiliaries.

On the periphery of the police offices a whole world of informers and spies was at work. The economic services of the *RSHA*
found industrialist clients to whom they could rent out the labor
of detainees, and among high-ranking, medium, and lowly cadres they found plenty of agents willing to enforce discipline. The
technocrats of euthanasia relied on members of the medical
profession to select their victims. The organizers of German
space—in effect the initiators of ethnic purges—could count on
the services of certain academics. Some sections of the army also
took part in the repression of occupied peoples. To be sure, the
decisive phase in the construction of this Eternal Empire, the
gassing of millions of human beings, was at first seen as the work
of a small number of initiates, distant bureaucrats, executioners
who worked with the assistance of helpers pulled out of the
crowd of victims. But thanks to the work of Raoul Hilberg, we
now know that their secret was shared by thousands of ordinary
policemen, secretaries, and transport technicians.[33]

Even so the SS was still not in total control of the German
people. Toward the end of the war, although they seemed to
have triumphed in their rivalry with the army, they were forced
to admit that among civilians there still remained many who
were "ineducable." Their blueprints had sketched out the
broad lines of a perfect society, but now it was too late to build it.

NOTES

1. Thamer H.-U., p. 684.
2. Gellately R., p. 44 (more precise figures than those of Höhne H., pp. 7–8); Mallmann K. M. and Paul G.; Gruchmann L., *Justiz*, p. 675.
3. Peukert D., *Volksgenossen*, pp. 162–67; id., *KPD*, p. 385; id., "Arbeiterwiderstand," p. 653; Huiskes M., "Einleitung," 73.
4. Gellately R., chap. 5; Mallmann K. M. and Paul G.; Frölich E., p. 626.
5. Wormser-Migot O., pp. 323–48 (with interpretations now superseded); above all
   Pingel F., pp. 64–73, 118–30.
6. Fabréguet M., p. 828 f.; Wormser-Migot O., p. 423; Arndt I., p. 105.
7. Kimmel G.
8. Bornemann M. and Broszat M.
9. Natzweiler (in French Nitzwiller) was the neighboring village; Struthof was a farm
   a few steps from the camp where various offices and the gas chamber were installed. A French thesis on the history of the camp is in preparation. On the *NN*,

see La Martinière J. de; on the *Kommandos, 28,* the introduction by Vorländer H. and the seven monographs; also Ziegler J.

10. Kimmel G. (Dachau); Siegert T. (Flossenbürg); Héran J. (Natzweiler); Lifton R. J. (Auschwitz and others), pp. 122 – 50, 305 – 29, 429 – 31.

11. Cited in *58,* p. 78.

12. According to the monographs in 7 and in *42.*

13. Pingel F., p. 73, 118, 130 – 58, 180 – 87.

14. Siegert T. (Flossenbürg); Fabréguet M., pp. 280 – 84 (Mauthausen); Bornemann M. and Broszat M. (Dora); Pingel F., p. 159 (Auschwitz).

15. Duhnke H., p. 512 f.; Fabréguet M., p. 296-303; Pingel F., p. 187 f., 218 f.

16. See the monographs in *28* and Ziegler J., for example p. 162 f., 253. *The Topography of Terrors* foundation, Berlin, is coordinating an inquiry into the reorganization of these sources of memories.

17. Durand Y., *La Vie quotidienne dans les Stalags, les Oflags et les Kommandos 1939 – 1945,* Paris: 1987.

18. Streit C., pp. 201 – 89.

19. Above all Herbert U., *Fremdarbeiter,* passim; see also Umbreit H., p. 262; Peukert D., *KPD,* p. 395; Grossmann A. J. (Bavaria); Roth K. H., pp. 239 – 48 (Daimler-Benz).

20. Kershaw I, *Nazisme,* chap. 5.

21. Mommsen H., "Réalisation de l'utopique"; Burrin P., chap. 3 and 5; Plum G., "Deutsche Juden," pp. 72 – 74; Dahm V., pp. 254 – 59; Kwiet K., pp. 566 – 659.

22. Benz W., "Überleben." Testimonies: Klemperer V., passim; Klepper J., *Unter dem Schatten,* Nov. 1939 – Jan. 1942; id., *Überwindung,* 21 Sept. 1941.

23. Stöver B., p. 269; Steinert M. G., *Hitlers Kreig,* pp. 236 – 62; Kershaw I., *L'Opinion,* p. 336 f. (Bavaria); Benz W., "Überleben"; Andreas-Friedrich R., passim; Klemperer V., passim.

24. Boyens A.; Hürten H., p. 347, 501 – 22; Hehl U. von, *Erzbistum Köln,* pp. 234 – 35.

25. Texts in 67, chap. II.

26. Schmuhl H. W.; Lifton R. J., pp. 74 – 94, 167 f., 467, 529; Müller-Hill B., pp. 37 – 99, and the communications in 24; Asseo H., *Les Tsiganes. Une destinée européenne,* Paris: 1994, chap. 5.

27. Lifton R. J., p. 103 f.; Hürten H., p. 492 f.; *63,* doc. of 15 Jan. 1942.

28. Krausnick H. and Wilhelm H.-H., in particular pp. 39 – 102, 142 – 287, 555; Burrin P., chap. 4.

29. Browning C., in particular chap. 18.

30. Klessmann C., "Osteuropaforschung"; Benz W., "Generalplan Ost"; Schpönwälder K., chap 5; Aly G., "Selektion"; id. and Heim S., *Vordenker,* in particular p. 60, 156, 394 – 432.

31. Schönwälder K., chap. 5 (historians); Rössler M. (geographers); Aly G. and Heim S., pp. 91 – 120, 156, 168 – 238, 372 – 92 (demographers); Massin B. (anthropologists); Pollak M., "Une politique scientifique" (anthropologists).

32. Cited at least by Müller-Hill B., p. 42; Pollak M., "Une politique scientifique," p. 88; Massin B. (with slightly different translations).

33. Hilberg R., "Bureaucratie."

9—The Front and the Rear

In communicating to their troops the leaders of all warring armies cultivate patriotism and hatred of the enemy. What was different about the army of the Third Reich was that it progressively adopted the Hitlerian philosophy of history. Since 1938, the High Command of the Armed Forces (*OKW*) and the Territorial Army (*OKH*) had passed into the hands of committed Nazis who, in a travesty of Clausewitz's formula, proclaimed that soldiers should share the fanaticism and objectives of the politicians. However, despite an influx of young cadets from the Hitler Youth and the Labor Service, some officers of fighting troops and most officers in the Staff Office still kept their distance from the Nazi leaders (drawing a distinction between them and the Supreme Leader to whom they had sworn loyalty), and continued to defend the singular combination of discipline and one's right to think for oneself which constituted the so-called "Prussian" model. The war against Poland was initially accepted as a further phase of revenge and was acclaimed as a success for the new military tactics. Only once soldierly operations were over and the methods of occupation and ethnic policy were revealed, did it prompt misgivings in some people. In the case of France, the most feared hereditary enemy, their objections were prompted not by an uneasy conscience but by anxiety about a project judged as too risky. Then, when all objections were swept aside by the successes, even the most skeptical were forced to recognize that the führer had proved his genius. It was when the USSR was attacked that a veritable intellectual and moral dereliction took place. Sharing the anti-Communism of their political leaders, the military commanders went along with the party's assimilation of Bolshevism and Judaism and issued its first criminal orders. And, with subordinate echelons similarly impregnated by the ideology, the crusading German army moved from the annihilation of enemy armies to the annihilation of its own people.

THE AVENGING ARMY, 1939-1940

It may seem somewhat facile to pick out in the German army of September 1939 certain weaknesses that would lead it into defeat five-and-a-half years later. Yet if we assume that it really was then that Hitler decided to go to war, it must be said that he did not prepare his army well. Of the one hundred or so divisions at the high command's disposal, only half were of "fighting quality": six armored divisions, four divisions of motorized infantry, three mountain divisions, and thirty-five infantry divisions, said to be "first wave infantry," made up of young, well-trained, and well-led troops. The sixteen divisions of second-wave infantry (reservists under age thirty-five) still included some former soldiers from the *Reichswehr* but also many civilians with virtually no training. As for the forty-five third- and fourth-wave divisions, they would have been incapable of standing up to a solid attacking enemy as they lacked modern weapons and suitable transport. With the elite units concentrated against Poland or in the West, it is reasonable to conclude that "had there been an [Allied] offensive on two fronts, the power of the National Socialists would rapidly have collapsed" (B. R. Kroener). The officer corps was also deficient. Staff offices were undermanned, and by men of poor quality, as their military training had been reduced from three years to two. The group of officers commanding fighting troops encompassed a wide range of backgrounds and ages and so no longer possessed the fine homogeneity of former times. Many reservists were quite elderly and may well have considered themselves victimized compared to the hundreds and thousands on special release (officials, business bosses, and so on) who remained at home. It is true that the "phony war" in the winter of 1939-40 made it possible to train reserve divisions and raise a number from their initial quality level to the level above. But the job of preparing troops for battle fell to old, noncommissioned officers who replaced combat training with drill and this certainly failed to inspire the men with ardor. The recall of men on special release despite the protests of economic circles nevertheless made it possible to reach the desired overall number of fighting men by the spring of 1940. But those reinforcements helped the elite units hardly at all, which explains the reluctance of the Staff Office to adopt Hitler's offensive plan. The strategy of a lightning war was thus no doubt determined partly by delays in the production of armaments and the mobilization of the civilian labor force, but also certainly by the structural weakness of the territorial army which had become a gigantic body with a weak head. Even Hitler himself considered the inflation of units of little value to be excessive. Soon after the armistice with France was signed and while preparing for the invasion of the British Isles, he ordered a massive demobilization of reservists and simultaneously reinforced the armored and motorized divisions. However he soon changed his mind and instead turned his eyes eastward, ordering that a giant army of two hundred divisions be created to invade and occupy all those great expanses![1]

Early victories were thus achieved principally thanks to the technical superiority of a relatively small number of forward units led by a majority of apolitical officers and a minority of young Nazis. One of the latter later recalled, "We National Socialists felt that the victory over France was a victory for the National Socialist ideal over Western democracy. But the bulk of our comrades never seized upon the meaning of the philosophical struggle." His opinion is confirmed by surveys of letters written by the military: praise of the führer was rare, even in June 1940. The fact is that many soldiers were in regular contact with not only their families but also their religious communities, which represented the war in the most traditional manner. The Evangelical Church sent them a whole series of edifying works such as *The Soldier's Catechism* by Ernst Moritz Arndt, which identified them as heirs to the patriots of 1813. The Catholic *Caritas* encouraged soldiers to stand firm in this test of endurance and patriotism, without bothering about its true significance, which was of course exactly what was expected of them. "A soldier knows of nothing but orders, . . . Christ, and Germany" wrote one former scout leader recently mobilized (even though he was just been released from prison). Those who were not practicing Christians received no less classic advice from their immediate officers: in Poland they were urged to behave with dignity, even toward Jews. The staff office of the airborne army, with great success, even among officers, distributed brochures that referred to Moltke the Elder and Hans von Seeckt as the patrons of the great military tradition of which Hitler was simply the heir. In fact the *OKW*, more Nazified than the staff offices of the armed forces, even began to worry about the spread of out-of-date values. They curtailed the services of mobilized priests (the professional military almoners were more reliable, but few in number) and ruled that parishes should no longer send their literature to soldiers. In December 1940 a circular from Brauchitsch ordered—possibly to forestall any intervention by the party—that meetings for ideological training should be resumed, but apparently this was not very effective: in the summer of 1941 during the advance into the heart of the USSR the protesting sermons of the bishop of Münster were still being passed from one Catholic to another.

Yet it would be wrong to regard these soldiers of 1939–41 as perfect models of discipline and moderation. In Poland when confronted with snipers, some without hesitation declared in their letters home that the orders for repression were far too generous, and explained (or confessed?) that this little war was "abominable because it often strikes at women and children." In occupied France there was sharp friction between the fighting officers and soldiers passing through, and the reservists and territorials stationed there permanently. The scorn of the fighting men for those staying behind the front line was matched by the territorials' criticisms of their disorderly requisition operations and private purchases. When the sabotage and first attacks of the French Resistance began, front line units complained about delays in the territorial High Command (*OBHF*) decisions to take reprisals. Material compromises if not actual corruption crept in, with more or less unrestrained violence against the guerillas: the seeds of the excesses of the war in the USSR were already planted.[2]

THE CRUSADING ARMY, 1941-1943

In June 1941 the German army certainly did have at its disposal the two hundred divisions planned by Hitler, but many were dispersed in the occupation of Europe and only 120 were available for the invasion of the vast USSR, that is to say only thirty more than were used to attack France the previous year. Furthermore, a quarter of the armored divisions and half of the rest were underequipped. So behind the spearhead units it proved necessary to fling into the battle reserve units of undertrained men led by inexperienced officers. The operations of that summer were a far cry from the triumphal advances shown in the newsreels: by the end of August the "combat power" of armored divisions had been halved as a result of human loss and wear and tear on materials, and that of infantry divisions had diminished by 60 percent. From now on the Staff Office was forced to ask constantly for reinforcements to be sent up from the rear, increasingly using young soldiers whose training had been hasty and workers whose departure from the factories slowed down weapons production. The airborne army also had to speed up the training of its crews, and this affected their quality: more planes were lost in accidents than in battle. So other Axis troops, Italians and Rumanians— soldiers of poor quality—and volunteers of all nationalities were called up to the front. Meanwhile, for services, workshops, and policing, autochthonous volunteers and prisoners of war were used. When winter arrived, the deficit grew yet greater with two hundred thousand men suffering from frostbite; the Staff Office calculated that 650,000 men were needed, to be provided by the civilian sectors. The two contrasting objectives of the political authorities, to conquer the vital spaces and keep up morale behind the lines, became irreconcilable. On top of all this, the tactics of spearheading and encirclement by the armored divisions had proved difficult in those vast empty steppes: the trailing convoys of food supplies had to travel hundreds of kilometers through no man's land, and the infantry with very few motorized vehicles followed far behind, making interminable marches that exhausted both men and horses. It is true that in the spring of 1942, on the eve of new offensives, the army had managed to restore total numbers to the initial level and even increase the number of its divisions on the eastern front, but the Staff Office experts knew this was only a facade and that many fighting units had been reduced to one third or even half of their theoretical strength. One example cited tells of an armored division which had lost six thousand men out of seventeen thousand and two hundred of its 212 tanks by the end of July 1941, then in August had been reequipped, only to once again lose all its material by November and during the winter be reduced to five thousand men obliged to move about on foot or on peasants' carts. It was built up again for the second year of the offensive, but only to 40 percent of its original strength. On the other hand the morale of the soldiers remained good. Hitler had deflected their rancor against the generals by dismissing the commander-in-chief of the territorial army and replacing half the division commanders. Losses among officers, particularly heavy in the assault regiments, were made good thanks to the speeded-up promotion of young second lieutenants and noncommissioned officers, whose relations with their men were more familiar than those of their predecessors. Pride at having survived Russian winter temperatures of minus forty degrees was combined with joy at the return of the fine weather that was supposed to herald the end of their trials.[3]

The years 1942 and 1943 saw more spectacular spearheading operations which, however, were costly in terms of both men and equipment. They also saw the first serious military reversals, many of them half-acknowledged in communiqués ("condensing of the front," "determined resistance by our troops"), but others mythified into salutary catastrophes—for example the destruction of the Sixth Army at Stalingrad. The losses in men killed, vanished, seriously wounded, ill, or taken prisoners by the enemy were higher than ever. Thus the Twelfth Infantry Division (an ordinary combat division singled out here purely because its archives were preserved), which had set out in June 1941 with 16,100 men, of whom 527 were officers, had by October 1943 lost 14,400 men of whom 336 were officers. The "Greater Germany" Grossdeutschland division, an elite unit created in May 1942 with eighteen thousand men, had lost almost all of them by one year later—which gave the lie to the theory of certain Staff Office specialists who attributed the heavy losses to the inferior quality of the troops and their officers. By the end of 1943 the armies of the East had in this fashion been reduced to two million men, fewer than in June 1941, and that level was to continue to decline.[4]

How can the endurance of these ordinary troopers be explained in these increasingly taxing advances and retreats? Years later in old soldiers' associations, the survivors invoked a number of factors which they insisted on distinguishing clearly from Nazi fanaticism: the instinct for self-preservation, fear of Bolshevism, pure patriotism, and the solidarity of small combat units. The first is too general to be either confirmed or denied. The fear of Bolshevism—assuming it was not a direct effect of party propaganda within the army—might have been fostered by messages coming from the churches; but from 1942 on those in command, suddenly surprisingly concerned to cut off communication with those in the rear, banned the circulation of all religious literature, even that sent by soldiers' individual families. Meanwhile, though, soldiers on the spot could see perfectly well the real living conditions of the Soviet people. Many were probably struck by the poverty of Russian and Ukrainian peasants and their haste to liberate themselves from the *Kolkhoz* (collective form) and "concluded that everything was even worse than what the National Socialist propaganda had led them to expect." However, that conclusion is drawn from a collection of letters published by Goebbels, and was no doubt constructed out of a systematic selection of letters. Others certainly discovered with surprise the existence of large factories, many schools, intelligent prisoners, and healthy, united families. So who was the enemy, Russia or the Bolsheviks? And what could explain the determined resistance of the Red Army soldiers, even when separated from their political commissars? Clearly ordinary soldiers sometimes asked themselves the same questions as their leaders when wondering how to define their enemy.

The third factor of perseverance, patriotism pure and simple, is supported chiefly by the correspondence of a cultivated minority of students and apolitical officers, and is expressed using a humanist vocabulary ("for the eternal cause of the spirit"), or a romantic one ("for the secret and eternal Germany"), or else sometimes Jüngian terms ("testing the most noble and best against materialism"). In the military memoirs and novels of the postwar period, "camaraderie" is the word that recurs most often. As early as 1948, American sociologists were explaining the long endurance of the men of the *Wehrmacht* by what they called "the cohesion of primary, informal groups": the infantry squadron, the tank crew, etc., small units of men bound together by the values of a virile community and solidarity in resistance to the enemy, the cold, the heat, and also possibly abusive superiors. However, one ambiguity is carefully blotted out by the filter of the collective memory: this camaraderie could quite easily evolve into complicity in acts of indiscipline. The fact that military tribunals had to pass sentence on over six hundred thousand cases in the course of the war says a great deal about this aspect of real daily life. And the fact that the number of death sentences increased regularly between autumn 1942 and the end of 1943 also shows that those in command did not shrink from using the deterrent—classic in every army—of the fear of immediate punishment. The conformism of a group could also lead to inhumanity: we have already seen above how ordinary men can turn into executioners.[5]

Should we conclude simply that these fighting men lived in a singularly closed mental world dominated by specifically military values and sheltered from all political contamination? That postwar slogan "The army was not Nazi" needs to be set alongside two phenomena we now know more about: the generalization of a new type of officer, and the growing role of ideology in determining the behavior of the troops.

The expression "officer corps" was already somewhat outdated even in 1938. By 1943 it would have been more accurate to speak of the "officer masses." They numbered about 250,000 men, 70 percent of whom were reservists, and by adding in the dead, the missing, and casualties invalided out that figure would be doubled. So what difference could the traditions of career officers make? At the beginning of the war Hitler had openly declared: "There will be no unity in the army until the spirit of the *Reichswehr* has been banished and that of the *Hitlerjugend* has penetrated the officer corps." The *Reichswehr* spirit had been created by recruiting young candidates through aptitude tests and diplomas, followed by incorporation into a regiment, promotion with seniority, and a code of honor. The realities of war undermined this fine edifice, and Hitler finished it off. To make good the losses in the ranks of aspiring officers and second lieutenants, new men were recruited from noncommissioned officers and *HJ* cadres, taking account solely of their "fighting qualities." Promotion to higher grades was purely selective and based on the same criteria, in which political conformism came to count for more and more. Eventually colonels and even division generals could be found who lacked any kind of intellectual ability. Once the regimentary framework had been dislocated into inter-army combat units, the institutions that had sustained the regimental *esprit de corps*, the honorary tribunals, and the colonel's control over his men's private lives all disappeared. Even staff officers had to prove their physical courage by fighting in the front line, and they furthermore lost their special insignia. The officer in the front line had become the *Volksoffizier* (Hitler even preferred the simple word *führer*, a copy of his own model), and was less and less likely to come from the upper classes of society and more and more likely to be politicized. In 1942–43, 44 percent of the officer cadets were former party members from whom there was no question of expecting political neutrality. Only the generals, who were older and had therefore passed through the filter of the imperial army and the *Reichswehr*, still preserved the manners of their caste and included a fair proportion of nobles' and officers' sons. As for reserve officers, almost all serving behind the front line and in units of lower "quality," they ended up constituting half the leadership, even in the fighting divisions. Although not as deeply political as young officer cadets in the front line, the fact that they were politicized at all was a new phenomenon, and they were in any case expected to prove themselves impeccable on the racial level. Those who had married Jewish women were ignominiously sent home.[6]

If the troops were not totally indoctrinated, that was due to clashes between competing psychological services. Keitel's circulars invited all officers of the *OKW* to develop closer relations with their men in order to foster the spirit of National Socialism. The new sheet edited under his auspices offered "the *Sturmer* a mixture of ideology, the cult of the Führer, and certain strategic considerations, with a vaguely religious veneer, to justify the crusading aspect" (M. Messerschmidt). At the grass roots level the party claimed a monopoly over communications between the front and the rear at the expense of religious and charitable associations. Meanwhile however, the *OKH* continued to refer to the old values, not without recourse to double-talk: for example, the "particular conditions of this war" (meaning the order to shoot all Red Army commissars) should not give rise to excesses; German soldiers should behave correctly toward occupied populations, etc. In military libraries, books by Hermann Hesse, E. Jünger, and even the Catholic Reinhold Schneider could still be found, while the *Weekly Military News Sheet* for officers kept strictly to studies of strategic science. An even more surprising sign of this incoherence is the fact that *Writings for the Knapsack*, a million copies of which were distributed, took as its model the free and human spirit (*sic*) of the army of Frederick II, yet it was published under the aegis of the *OKW*—which just goes to show that non-Nazi authors who knew how to practice the art of citations-with-a-wink could still infiltrate the rarefied spheres inhabited by the Nazi faithful.[7]

It is clearly difficult to gauge how these divergent if not contradictory publications affected the officers with educative responsibilities and, by repercussion, the beliefs of their men. One would need to take into account the antecedents of each man involved and whether he was a receiver or a diffuser of the message. The evidence certainly indicates that true Nazis, of whom there were many in civilian life, remained Nazis when serving the flag, as is testified by the reactions of German Communists who had taken refuge in the USSR and in the autumn of 1941 visited compatriots who had become Red Army prisoners of war. They were stupefied to find that 90 percent of these young soldiers—many of them workers—were convinced that the Third Reich had created true Socialism and that the conquest of extra vital space was legitimate.[8] The tone of letters home is more representative of general opinion, so far as can be told from the syntheses produced by the postal censorship. The most interesting example was based on eleven thousand letters sent or received by the men surrounded in Stalingrad, letters from which Hitler was keen to compile an anthology for the wider reading public. The report of the postal censorship was crushing, however. In the first days of the Sixth Army's encirclement in November 1942 both officers and men, certain their führer would manage to rescue them, were determined to face up heroically to the cold, the hunger, and the fighting. By early January 1943 their primary concerns were weakness due to hunger and their heavy losses, and by the second week of that month they were writing nothing but despairing letters of farewell. The postal censorship went so far as to convert this spectrum of attitudes into hard figures: 57 percent were blaming those in command, 33 percent passed no judgment, and the remainder fell into three small minorities—the faithful, the doubtful, and the politically hostile. The essential point was the collapse of the Hitler myth, and it was particularly dramatic in the case of disillusioned Nazis. One wrote, "It is horrifying to see how the people here are filled with doubt, and it is shaming to hear their words, in reply to which there is nothing to say, as the facts speak for themselves." And one officer exclaimed: "You're 26 years old, . . . you've shouted 'Heil Hitler' along with everybody else, and now you're off to rot in Siberia. And that is not the worst thing; it's knowing that it's all happening for a totally mad cause: it makes your blood boil." When Goebbels read the letters he recoiled in indignation, noting in his diary: "The letters are disastrous, indescribable: human weakness against which one is powerless." The idea of an anthology was obviously dropped.[9] Hitler for his part considered his prejudices against the officer caste to be vindicated and accused them of having failed in their educative task. At this point he elaborated an idea which, however, he did not realize until one year later, when the situation had become even graver: it was to set up a body of "National Socialist Officers for Psychological Action" (*NSFO*) consisting of several hundred party leaders who would be sent to carry the good news to every garrison and to the front. Their model was not to be so much the commissars of the Red Army (for German officers were to remain subordinate to their military commanders), but the führer himself, who had begun as a "teaching officer" in the *Reichswehr* in 1919. Meanwhile, but of course without saying so, he was also returning to Röhm's 1933 plans.[10]

However, some units still existed whose fanaticism should have been total, namely the *Waffen-SS*. Under pressure from Himmler who, not content to infiltrate the regular army, wanted to outweigh it, their numbers had increased from thirty thousand to five hundred thousand men and from three to forty or so divisions, divided into thirteen army corps. Their participation in the fighting was supposed to prove to the career officers that fanaticized troops did better than the rest, and to show the politicians that, in the words of one high dignitary, "it [was] neither the state nor the party as a whole that could resolve the Germanic problem, but only the SS." That expression "the Germanic problem," borrowed from an encoded vocabulary, meant that out of the various concepts of race the SS had chosen "Nordism," which attributed the domination of the future world not to the German people as such but to Germans and other Germanic elites. From now on the recruitment of its officers and men was to obey the same "ethnic" canon, that is to say selection would be based on character regardless of any intellectual or social hierarchy. But the speeded-up recruitment and need to replace huge losses (150,000 *Waffen-SS* killed or seriously wounded in four years) made it necessary to sacrifice those principles. As early as 1940 the units in barracks in Poland were recruiting *Volksdeutsche* classified as "Germanizable," some of whom did not even speak German. The next to arrive were Scandinavians, Dutch, and even Slavs and Turks (who were persistently described as "Aryans"). To get around the language problems they had to be kept in separate units, and these were disastrously short of officers. Indiscipline and discontent were so rife in them that by June 1943 20 percent of the Scandinavians and Dutch had returned home. The army of the "New Europe," three hundred thousand foreigners out of five hundred thousand men, presented a flattering enough image of itself but its operational efficiency was very disappointing. Even the flow of young German volunteers began to dry up, and by 1942 a contingent of young men just completing their Labor Service was automatically enrolled in the *Waffen-SS*. Perhaps it would have been possible to turn them into "fanatics filled with hatred" as Himmler kept repeating, but their weekly hour of doctrinal thinking amounted to little more than a mouthing of slogans. Nor did its officer corps ever measure up to the initial ideal. Young cadets trained in the corps' special schools were certainly trustworthy on both the political and military scores, and they were soon made commanders of companies, then battalions. The much trumpeted principle of "revolutionary" social mobility should then have assured them of equally rapid advancement to higher officer ranks, but here they were competing against either older officers or reservists who were both politically reliable and better educated. An analysis of the careers of SS colonels and generals shows that many were indeed ex-officers of the imperial army who had subsequently joined vigilante groups and then passed into either the police force or one of a variety of civilian professions that had allowed them to choose whether or not to be party militants. Eventually they had joined the SS. "Despite the low value set on culture in the SS system of values, a considerable proportion of their leaders are indeniably rooted in the middle class" (B. Wehner). At this level then, the new elite was hardly distinguishable except in nuanced ways from the regular army elite which was itself in a state of mutation. The authentic SS spirit—rabidly racist, antibourgeois, antireligious and anti-Communist—appears to have reigned only in a few units: the Death's Head division composed of former concentration camp guards; the "Adolf Hitler" division, formerly a bodyguard unit, and the "Hitler Youth" division in which ten thousand volunteers age seventeen or eighteen were under the command of officers who formerly belonged to the above-mentioned bodyguard unit.[11] Nor should it be forgotten that specially selected members of the *Waffen-SS* made up as much as one-third of the ranks of the "intervention groups." Thus despite the efforts of enthusiasts who assert there was a radical difference between the army and the *Waffen-SS* and between the latter and other subdivisions of the Black Corps, transitions between the three military bodies seem to have been as numerous as the cracks that threatened the cohesion of each of them—as is proved by their common participation in war crimes.

THE *WEHRMACHT* AND WAR CRIMES

Jurists draw a distinction between on the one hand war crimes, which violate international conventions on the treatment of civilian populations, military prisoners, and snipers, and on the other crimes against humanity committed against certain categories of human beings not because of their real or suspected activities but because of their nature. Whatever the justification for this casuistry which, most notably, has made it possible to declare the second category of crimes as indefensible, it helps the historical process not at all, for this is concerned not so much with defining actions as with uncovering the series of compromises that led a number of generals and their troops to commit them.

The German army had always been haunted by a fear of snipers and responded to their attacks with collective reprisals, hostage-taking, and shooting squads, imagining that these measures would solve the problem. Yet Clausewitz in his chapter on "small wars" had shown that guerillas are more or less invincible so long as they do not make the mistake of coming together in large groups. As early as 1871 during the campaign in France, Moltke had clashed with Bismarck who, for reasons more diplomatic than humanitarian, had wished to stop the reprisals. In 1914 the invasion of Belgium and northern France had produced similar excesses.[12] Perhaps such things always happen when regular armies are confronted with an enemy that does not play "fair," as is suggested by the history of many colonial wars. The *Wehrmacht* certainly pursued that policy during the campaign in Poland and the occupation that followed it. When German troops discovered the corpses of their compatriots killed by the Polish population in Bromberg (Bydgoszcz), their leaders did not hesitate to apply the "rights of war," a code of conduct that the high command had long since elaborated alongside the international conventions. As part of German reprisal policy, elements of the regular army teamed up with the SS and executed civilians by firing squad. After that the troops believed themselves authorized to commit every kind of excess, and in order to contain such "footsoldiers' behavior" the Staff Office set up "court martials" with the power of immediate execution.

It remained convinced that these apparently regular and controlled court martials were the only way to stop the actions of "bandits." The same kind of realistic considerations can be found even in the protests certain generals made against the massacres perpetrated by SS intervention groups. The famous memorandum by General Johannes Blaskowitz which is so often cited declared that the Polish population accepted the executions of saboteurs ordered by military tribunals, but the massive elimination of Jews and members of the Polish elite would simply strengthen the Resistance. He added that the spectacle of such killings demoralized the soldiers, who emerged from them either indignant or disposed to commit similar excesses themselves. His report was widely circulated, and Hitler was obliged to compose a reply. He wrote as follows: "The army must be glad to be rid of the responsibility for such diabolical work." The door was now open for a division of tasks that would satisfy the conscience of anyone at all accommodating: the army would maintain order; the SS would be responsible for "ethnic policy."[13]

In France the repression of sabotage and assassinations was at first the responsibility solely of the army services, in particular the "Campaign's Secret Police" which itself was under the control of the Second Bureau (*Abwehr*). Successive commanders-in-chief apparently applied the same classic methods: resistants were condemned to death by military tribunals and hostages were shot. Occasionally they tried to limit the use of such methods on the grounds that too many executions would simply make the population more hostile. But when picking out hostages they mostly selected Communists and Jews, implicitly manifesting of the official conception of the war as a crusade against Judeo-Bolshevism. Their entourage, composed of both officers on active service and conservative reservists extremely hostile to the party and SS, was eventually accused of being soft, so in June 1942 Himmler sent a "high-ranking head of the SS and the police" to Paris accompanied by members of the Gestapo and *SD* to stiffen the struggle against resistants. But the discussions between the two rival powers showed to what degree the military had become affected by anti-Semitism: in exchange for slowing down the executions of civilian hostages they quickly agreed to systematic arrests of first foreign then French Jews, reckoning that this would be a "more moderate" response to attacks, and to their subsequent deportation to the East "due to lack of space in France." The first steps in the collaboration of previously right-thinking people in genocide had been taken.[14] Meanwhile Hitler, Himmler, and Keitel had devised a new way to intimidate the occupied peoples: to avoid having resistants turn into martyrs, these would either be executed secretly or transferred to prisons in Germany and placed in the total isolation of "night and fog," after which they would be sentenced by civil courts. But the prisons were soon crammed, so the Gestapo took to sending an increasing number of these *NN* prisoners to concentration camps. Were the military magistrates ignorant of the final fate of these men who passed through their hands? In any case, in the role to which they were now reduced, simply that of a link in a chain, they could dispense with scruples.[15]

In Poland the military had been "complicit spectators"; in the USSR they were "co-actors" (C. Streit). Here the orders were clear: the SS would have freedom of action in the zone behind the lines and also the right to intervene in the battle zone, provided the army commanders gave their agreement; troops could shoot partisans and suspected civilians without trial (the Barbarossa circular); Red Army political commissars would be executed either by the soldiers who captured them or the SS, once they were transferred to the latter; "directives for the behavior of the troops" set them on their guard particularly against Bolsheviks, snipers, saboteurs, Jews, and Asiatics; and finally, military tribunals were to show leniency for any excesses committed by soldiers against civilians. These orders were passed from the *OKW* and the *OKH*, for once in agreement on all points, to the army and divisional commanders to be circulated among the smaller units. Only a few German generals, fearing to weaken the discipline of their men and to strengthen the resistance of the population, kept the circulars to themselves or asked for further explanations. But others, not all of them declared Nazis, even added their own comments to make it even clearer to their subordinates that this was no ordinary war. Only the treatment of nonsuspect civilians provoked serious disagreements, which produced a mini-war of memoranda between divisional staff offices, with some favoring letting them starve to death, others recommending better treatment to lure them away from the Bolsheviks or, if they belonged to ethnic minorities, from the Russians.[16] The practical application of terror thus varied from one division to another and from one time period to another. It is nevertheless possible to be more specific on three points: the military's relations with SS "intervention groups," the fate of prisoners of war, and the struggle against partisans.

The military could not possibly remain unaware of the massacres carried out by the SS intervention groups. Behind the lines the occupation troops and fighting units on rest leave rubbed shoulders with them daily. Further forward, plenty of corps leaders, whose agreement was theoretically necessary, simply let the SS units get on with it, preferring to spare their own men such dirty work. But they still needed to appease their consciences and try to reconcile the horror of these spectacles with the traditions that they remembered. Within the restricted circle of their staff office, some generals sadly confessed their impotence. One marshal, expressing his indignation in his diary, regretted the fact that the choice was made to eliminate the Jews by putting them brutally to death instead of sterilizing them all, which would have been more humane. . . . Others in the name of decency simply forbade their men to attend executions and, above all, to photograph them. But we also know that some proclaimed that the Jews, without distinguishing between age or sex, were "the initiators of sabotages and *Banden*"; in this way genocide was legitimized as part of the struggle against the partisans, an operation that apparently did not arouse so many objections. Reichenau, always distinguishing himself with particular zeal, outdid himself when he declared: "Soldiers must fully understand the necessity to punish the subhuman Jews harshly"; and his orders, considered a model, were distributed widely among the armies positioned close to the troops under his command. Such alignment with racial extremism was sometimes followed up with concrete action. In the Baltic States for example detachments of the army and navy (despite the latter's reputation of being less politicized) themselves carried out the first massive executions and organized militias of autochthonous killers before passing them on to the SS. Among these millions of soldiers some must have been indignant, but they were clearly obliged to be discreet in expressing their feelings both vocally and in their correspondence. Not until their first leave could they express themselves more freely in their homes, and this was when rumors of extermination began to spread throughout Germany. The members of the top staff offices, whose functions obliged them to travel everywhere, were better positioned to see how extensive the massacres were, and their attachment to traditional, religious, or "Prussian" values made them rebel: this is where the military Resistance germinated. Finally, a certain number of reservists who managed supply depots and repair shops tried to save their Jewish employees and workers from immediate death by emphasizing their high level of performance.[17]

The high command, confident in advance of its triumphs in Russia, had reckoned its troops would quickly take one or two million prisoners. However, it had prepared nowhere for them to live and only a minimum of rations to feed them. In seven months however the German forces had captured a total of 3.3 million! Under the very noses of the impotent, complicit, or (in rare cases) protesting prisoner of war camp commandants, the SS immediately executed not only Russians believed to be political commissars (the only category expressly indicated in the murderous orders mentioned above), but also party cadres, Communists, officials, and intellectuals among others. Their objective was to decapitate Soviet society and, in case some of these prisoners were transferred to the Reich, avoid contaminating the German population with the contagion of Bolshevist ideas (clearly little confidence was placed in Germany's civilian compatriots). Several hundreds of thousands of men, six hundred thousand during the entire war, disappeared in this manner. Soon army units received similar orders to act without flinching against prisoners of war and shoot all escapees and loners who tried to join up with the partisans. Circulars distributed among German troops reminded them that soldiers of the Red Army were "not comrades." On top of these deliberate executions, famine played its part, accounting for a further two million POW deaths by the end of 1942. In postwar attempts to defend the army, its lawyers attributed responsibility for this squarely to circumstances—the unexpected and unforseeably large number of mouths to feed. But in truth, priorities had clearly been defined from the outset: in order not to take rations from the Reich's population, the army had to feed itself on the spot. Once food supplies for Soviet civilians, already reduced to a minimum, were distributed to them, anything left would go to the prisoners of war, an amount of rations considered far lower than the vital minimum, sometimes no more than half. These enormous losses of life were thus not produced by chaos or impotence but resulted from a deliberate plan. In answer to protests he received from certain officers, Keitel retorted: "Those scruples correspond to the military concept of a war of chivalry; here, it is a matter of annihilating a concept of the world." Only after officials decided to employ a certain number of prisoners in agriculture and industry in the "old Reich" did rations increase slightly, an operation that was dubbed with cruel humor "bottle-feeding" (*Aufpäppelung*). The needs of the labor market were now to take precedence over those of the war of attrition. But the agricultural and industrial workers shunted to Germany as well as auxiliaries used by the fighting units continued to be treated in the hierarchy of slaves hardly better than Jews. Here again mass deaths can only be conveyed by horribly dry statis-

tics: of the 5.5 million Soviet prisoners of war officially recorded, by the end of 1942 just slightly over two million still
survived, three-quarters as auxiliaries for the army and "volunteers" in various militias in the occupied territories of the East,
the rest as workers in Germany. Taking into account a certain
number of escapees, the total number of Russian POW deaths
for the duration of the war has been calculated at 3.3 million.
"The army had sacrificed the honor of its uniform." (C. Streit)[18]

Propelled by official directives, encouraged by promises of
indulgence, if it so happened that too strict an officer had them
court martialed, and harrassed by partisans as they were, how
many officers and soldiers took to plunder, indiscriminately killing all captured "bandits" and hostages taken from a supposedly
complicit population? The first historical studies concentrated
on the small number of units whose archives had been preserved, and it is still difficult to draw any conclusions with regard to the *Wehrmacht* as a whole. In the two fighting divisions
selected for study, one infantry, the other armored, the hierarchy simultaneously manifested its concern to limit excesses
harmful to discipline and its determination to apply the extermination orders received from on high. The same generals who
in one breath alluded to the traditional rules of warfare in order
to deplore the execution of ordinary POW's, in the next proclaimed that no pity should be shown to Jews, political commissars, partisans, and their "agents," women and children
included. But the endless repetition of warnings against abuses
"contrary to the dignity of the German soldier" show that this
casuistry was unrealistic. We also know about the behavior of
the personnel responsible for guarding zones behind the army
lines (*Korück*), an amalgam or rather a juxtaposition of battalions of police, Hungarian, Rumanian, or even indigenous
troops, and German "security divisions" composed of old reservists and young men physically unsuited to combat. Most
were dispersed in sections in the forests, marshes, and villages of
the vast regions, their mission to protect crucial points and railway lines. Meanwhile a small number of units called "hunting

commandos" raked the countryside, encircling groups of partisans and destroying them. The reports of commanding officers present a singularly mixed image of these small, ill-controlled units: here a handful of soldiers "in carpet slippers" lived in symbiosis with peasant families; there hunting commandos assisted by the SS composed reports of victories in which the proportion of their losses and those of the bandits was one to seven, or even one to twenty. The population, initially passive, showed increasing solidarity with the partisans, despite or perhaps because of collective reprisals. At the end of 1942 a number of more humane or more realistic leaders ordered the shootings and hangings of hostages to be scaled down.

Should we assume that such behavior was general in *Wehrmacht* units as a whole? The testimony of former combatants does not provide much reliable information since the cloak of silence they were stifled under for so long has been followed by the effects of distancing, which tend to wipe out the most embarrassing memories even of those willing to talk. So we can only rely on written archives, and their preservation rate is, inevitably, patchy, so that even an exhaustive study of them can never produce a representative sample. Those defending the regular army at first tried to lay responsibility for most of the war crimes on SS units, "intervention groups" or *Waffen-SS* divisions. Then, giving ground in a strategic fashion, they tried to draw a distinction between the real military, the fighters who — they claimed — had behaved correctly, and those behind the lines whom they represented as having indulged in all kinds of excesses due to a lack of discipline and leadership. By so doing they were already abandoning the cause of the majority, since in those vast territories control of inhabitants, exploitation of resources, and the struggle against partisans had always immobilized at least 80 percent of the available manpower, leaving the attacking armies depleted. But even that line of qualified defense has had to be abandoned as more documents are discovered and shed unwelcome light on the behavior of some of the reputedly most glorious units. In the face of the pressure to obey orders from the high command, ideological contamination, in-bred reactions against "bandits," and group solidarity, any re-sistance was most likely limited to a relatively small number of individuals in isolated or relatively sheltered positions, such as for instance staff officers.[19]

THE MILITARY PLOTS AND THE DEFEAT

The abandonment of Russian territory, which began in the win-ter of 1943, initially alternating with counteroffensives and then proceeding in a continuous fashion, conjured up in many Ger-mans' minds the image of another retreat from Russia, that of Napoleon from Moscow in 1812. There was no shortage of such critical minds, particularly among staff officers professionally accustomed to analyzing the disposition of forces in a strictly objective manner. Even as they applied the führer's orders, some had long harbored doubts as to his strategic abilities, and their concerns were compounded by scruples of conscience due to the terror in which the military, or what was left of it, acted as accomplices. Realism alone showed that Germany must get rid of its Leader and his most fanatical collaborators, the SS. As a result, constant consultations took place in which majors and colonels begged their generals to place themselves at the head of a coup d'etat.

The first conspiracy was organized during the winter of 1939–40 to oppose the plan for a western offensive that spring, which many reckoned would fail. But already some officers were complementing those anxieties with considerations of a moral nature, with some pointing to the fate of the Poles and others condemning—despite the precedent of 1914—the violation of the neutrality of Belgium and the Netherlands. After contacts between the military and like-minded clandestine societies of diplomats and high-ranking civil servants were established, a change of regime was even considered. The plotters however ran into a vicious circle. Staff officers, who lacked the power to command the movements of troops, needed the cooperation of their generals. But the generals replied that they were uncertain whether they could carry the troops with them since their younger officers in particular were so besotted with Hitlerism that only defeat would open their eyes—the implication being that the planned conspiracy should be allowed to proceed. . . . Civilians against the regime made no bones about calling the generals "softies," but the subsequent triumph over France gave Hitler an aura of invincibility that dazzled even some conspirators.[20]

As early as late 1941 among the more lucid, and from 1942 on among a small but growing number of their comrades, strategic doubts and humanitarian scruples were again manifested during the war against the USSR. Some confessed to their impotence. U. von Kardorff recounts a visit one day by three officers on leave, two of whom would say only that they were defending their country (as opposed to the regime), while the third said: "But are we not defending ideals that our country has long since betrayed?" This was followed by a violent argument with an SS journalist present on the subjects of closing churches in Poznania and lies spread by propaganda. Others settled down to plot again, but not without internal disagreements over the legitimacy of tyrannicide. At least five successive plans for an assassination attempt existed, not counting the one put into effect on 20 July 1944.

The social structure of these resistant circles has often been described in a simplistic fashion, first by the SS and Ministry of Propaganda which, following the assassination attempt, dismissed it as the work of a clique of aristocrats completely cut off from the people. In truth—to concentrate solely on the military—even if this circle was sociologically homogeneous, it definitely included two generations. A statistical analysis of the 185 officers traced to the conspiracy shows that 49 percent of the generals came from the nobility as did 44 percent of the lower ranking officers. These proportions are much higher than those that obtained in the army as a whole, even the army on active service, and they reflect not only a consensus regarding old army values but also the persistence of certain family and social connections (what Goebbels called a "camarilla"). But on either side of the line dividing the generals from their subordinates, not only ages but also careers, political experiences, and everything that determines the attitudes of particular generations were different, indeed almost opposite. The generals, who were older, had grown up under the Empire, fought in 1914–18, and lived through the *Reichswehr*'s reservations during the Republic. They had welcomed the advent of the Third Reich only because it promised them both arms and their continuing autonomy, and repeal of the hated Versailles Treaty. Then their superiors had imposed upon these generals a number of moral capitulations before being themselves retired in 1938 and replaced by Hitler's "lackeys." The regime they hoped to establish was to be authoritarian if not monarchical: on that score they were in agreement with most civilian conspirators. Their officers, ranging from lieutenants to colonels who pressed them to take action, had for their part passed through an initial phase of enthusiasm and regarded the Third Reich as a prelude to a modern and harmonious society: an illusion, in their case, of "conservative revolutionaries" (readers of Spengler) rather than of retrograde conservatives. Of the two generations, the first to be won over was the more rapidly disappointed and the first to express indignation over the methods of terror that compromised the honor of their uniform. Logically enough, circles of these younger men initially made contact with the resistants in the non-Communist Left and set their sights on a regenerated Germany that was to be very different from the authoritarian regime their elders dreaming of. But that very hope shows that they represented only an avant-garde amid the greater mass of obedient officers. The coup's failure was, it is true, a result first of pure chance with the unfortunate displacement of the bomb that was to kill Hitler, and second of an accumulation of mistakes and lack of nerve on the part of the conspirators' Berlin staff office. But without indulging in facile lucidity after the event, it is fair to say that this failure was also predetermined by changes that had taken place in the military body as a whole. Some conspirators had already realized that, but in response to the objections of skeptics they insisted it was necessary to take action, even with no hope of success, simply for the sake of honor.[21]

Goebbels's diatribe against the "*Junker* caste" apparently boosted the morale of the army. According to information collected by the *SD*, soldiers and young officers alike displayed their indignation at the news of the assassination attempt, and approved of the trials that followed it and even the hanging of those judged guilty. It appears that only a few intellectuals and jurists thought the procedure of the "People's Court" was too reminiscent of the recent show trials in Moscow. Obviously our source here is suspect, above all on this particular point, which allowed the SS to give free rein to their hatred of the old elites. But the correspondence of soldiers shows that most were heartily relieved to learn that their Leader was still alive, and polls conducted by Americans among their German prisoners of war confirm their persistent attachment to the führer. Whereas 57 percent had expressed a continuing confidence in him at the beginning of July, that proportion rose to 68 percent by the end of the month, then fell considerably, after which it bounced back to 64 percent following one of his increasingly rare speeches in the autumn. Thereafter it steadily diminished but never fell below 30 percent. This confidence stemmed more and more from willful blindness, for the soldiers on the eastern front who peppered their letters home with exalted sentiments about the führer at the same time complained about the poor food and lack of reinforcements, and hinted at early signs of the army's decomposition, drunkenness, resentment against officers, and incipient panic. The most optimistic were counting on miracle weapons and in the meantime consoled themselves by reflecting, at Goebbels's suggestion, upon the hard trials that had beset Frederick II in the course of the Seven Years' War before he finally triumphed. Recently created "National Socialist officers for psychological action" preached relentlessly about fighting on to the bitter end, repeatedly asserting that Allied insistence on unconditional surrender would deliver Germany up to either Bolshevism or the Morgenthau Plan of deindustrialization.[22]

By the end of 1944 the armies of the eastern front, having lost their elite units in preparation for the December counteroffensive in the Ardennes, were composed mostly of units hastily reconstituted by collecting together soldiers who had survived earlier battles, the last men still on special release, now snatched away from their factories and offices, and youths from the class of '28. Their V-1 and V-2 rockets having failed to produce the desired effects in the West, there now remained only two weapons for army commanders to use, mass conscription and generalized terror. On 18 October 1944, the anniversary of the 1813 Battle of Leipzig, with the Americans already in German territory at Aachen and the Soviets in East Prussia, Hitler's order appeared mobilizing a militia (*Volkssturm*) of all men aged between 16 and 60 and even appealing for women volunteers. The response was poor: not only did this innovation acknowledge the gravity of the situation, propaganda made one clumsy mistake after another, urging the new militiamen to fight as snipers — something always deplored in the enemy — and giving them as leaders, party officials who were probably the most detested figures at this time. On paper this last reservoir of men seemed immense, and tens or even hundreds of new battalions sprang up in every *Gau*. Old men and youngsters, some not even in their teens, were herded into barracks and issued armbands instead of uniforms, old rifles, and anti-tank *panzerfausts*, portable "miracle weapons" based on the American bozooka and known as "the terror of armored vehicles." But as genuine military training was virtually nonexistent, they were initially used to dig earthworks or escort convoys of refugees. Hitler, possibly remembering the armies of the Convention, then proposed amalgamating the most solid of these *Volkssturm* in mixed brigades along with regular regiments. Some of these units fighting the Soviets put up desperate resistance at garrisons like Königsberg, Breslau, and finally Berlin, and despite enormous losses in killed, wounded, and deserted they seemed to preserve a core of irreducible fighters right to the very end. In contrast, on what remained of the southwestern front in Alsace and Baden, the militiamen's appalling morale speeded up the rout. Admittedly the so-called "elite troops" they fought alongside were not of the best quality: one unit, although known theoretically and grandiosely as "the 13th SS army corps," was by now essentially composed of customs officers, grounded airmen, and Ukrainians.[23]

The occasional tenacity of these skeletal regiments of adolescents and elderly men is all the more surprising because by this time Hitler's prestige was finally collapsing in the eyes of civilians. This fighting spirit can be explained in the East at least by their enduring hatred of Communism, reinforced by rumors concerning the barbaric behavior of Red Army soldiers. On top of all this, faced with growing signs of defeatism Hitler decided to radicalize the terror. "Martial courts" of SS hunted down deserters, wounded men who no longer wanted to fight, and civilians not zealous enough about digging trenches or blowing up bridges, and when they caught them proceeded to hang them publicly. Methods that in the past were reserved exclusively for "bandits" in all the countries of Europe were thus now turned against the German people and its army, now very confused by the enveloping scorn on the part of those who believed themselves still in charge. A few career officers tried to limit these excesses: in besieged Berlin the general of an armored division banned these "martial courts" from operating in his sector. Then in late April in Munich, a group of insurgent officers and noncommissioned officers seized control of the town hall and the radio, openly declared that "the pheasants would be hunted down," and even sketched a political program quite similar to the one the conspirators had presented the previous year. But the SS with the assistance of the last declared party members put an end to this revolt. The population had not budged: by now long inured to patience, it was waiting for the Americans.[24]

MORALE AT THE REAR

Propaganda experts analyzed the attitude of the average German now according to his "mood" (*Stimmung*) as shown by spontaneous but unstable and superficial gestures and words, now according to his "behavior" (*Haltung*) which was more constant and subject to fewer reversals because it was dictated by heredity, social position, and beliefs. A historian is clearly more interested in the second type of observations, even if he rejects the commentaries that accompany them, since for him the principal problem is how to explain the extraordinary endurance of the German people during the war. As already noted, there were a number of reasons for this stoicism: food supplies that were on the whole adequate, the unexpected reactions to the bombing and Allied insistence on capitulation, fear of the Red Asiatics on the one hand and the police on the other, etc. Then there is the notion of the belief in certain victory or, in the last analysis, confidence in the führer's "genius"—the principal reason behind peacetime cohesion—which still remained unlimited for about two years. After that the population alternated between periods of doubt and renewed confidence, but it is not always easy to establish their chronology. Professional observers, officials or members of information agencies, only dared to tackle the problem at moments when they risked nothing by doing so; and the few critical reports that can be contrasted to theirs, in particular those of the clandestine Socialists, became increasingly rare as the years passed. However it is possible to chronicle the developments, obviously prompted by major military events, which were reflected little by little in the telling signs leading up to the final despair.

* * *

During the Munich crisis the Germans had manifested more anxiety than enthusiasm, and they reacted similarly to the outbreak of war. The German-Soviet pact, hailed by the eulogists as further proof of the führer's skill, had unsettled many people. Claims on Danzig and the Polish Corridor were better received because they stemmed from the as yet unhealed wounds inflicted by the Treaty of Versailles and because the Poles were generally despised. But the response of France and Britain, in strong contrast to their capitulation of the preceding year, came as a shock (even, it was said, to Hitler). Nothing reveals the collective desires of the people better than the rumor that spread in October which suggested reassuringly that the king of England and the prime minister had both resigned and their successors were going to propose an armistice. There were demonstrations of joy even at the stock exchange and the University of Berlin. However there were no signs of open opposition or desertions among the mobilized men. Even those who had kept their distance from the regime and dismissed its propaganda were reassured by being integrated into the military world or, if they remained civilians, by living in symbiosis with it, because in their eyes it remained the last refuge of honesty and patriotism. These themes were developed by the churches in paraticular. Protestants felt a keen sympathy for their brothers in the German minority in Poland, and the official church had no difficulty in presenting the war as a crusade, declaring: "God is with us and our führer." Only a few individuals such as the bishop of Bavaria and a handful of pastors of the Confessional Church dared to remind people that war was always evil. Texts from the Catholic hierarchy resorted to the kind of vocabulary customary in such circumstances, calling for solidarity and prayers. But the police were alarmed by the "defeatist" tone in the sermons of some parish priests, which suggests that the latter were representing the war as a divine punishment: after all, the dissolution of certain ecclesiastical associations had still been in progress in

November before the führer had eventually decided to halt all antireligious measures.[25]

The crusading spirit was at first encouraged after the discovery in Poland of the corpses of "German civilians" allegedly massacred by the Poles: 58,000 of them according to German propaganda, 6,000 in reality. The Protestant Church on that account exalted the victory in Poland as prompt retribution for the persecutors. But soon letters from soldiers in Poland and accounts they gave when on home leave were drawing attention to an even more terrible reality, namely the treatment being inflicted on the Polish population, the systematic arrests of its elites, the hostages being shot, and the sufferings of the Jews. The rumors spread all the more easily thanks to the fact that Goebbels's propaganda services saw fit to respond with two contradictory declarations: 1. German soldiers do not commit atrocities and, 2. the German atrocities were only reprisals for Polish ones. The great ethnic roundups that began in late October in the newly annexed provinces, with their convoys of wretched people being expelled, came to the notice of even more witnesses, including German civilians sent to welcome home the "ethnic Germans." Even circles within the Protestant Church began to be concerned about this first application of racial purging.[26]

The victories in Norway and then Holland, Belgium, and France rekindled enthusiasm. The führer's genius had excelled itself against these redoubtable enemies. Everyone was convinced that Holland and Belgium were false neutrals, that blacks in the French army behaved like savages (to such a degree that some even considered the armistice to be too soft), and that Britain was about to be crushed by "new weapons"—the first appearance of a consoling myth that was to continue to resurface more and more frequently as the defeats multiplied. In the factories of Bavaria, pride at having produced the aircraft and tanks that had just proved their worth in the lightning war united all the workers, including—to the disappointment of the few remaining clandestine militants—many former Socialists and

Communists. Finally, the occupation of Alsace-Lorraine, hopefully for the last time, healed the last remaining scars left from 1919, and a number of university teachers hostile to Nazism but who had taught in Strasbourg under the Empire were delighted to see the western regions reintegrated into the mother country. Eventually this universal optimism alarmed the high command, particularly when it became clear to those in the know that their airmen would not prevail immediately over the British, so Goebbels was asked to prepare public opinion for a second winter of war. At this, enthusiasm rapidly cooled and gave way to more mundane preoccupations such as food and the evacuation of German children to the countryside: it seemed that the Royal Air Force might still present a threat.[27]

The invasion of the USSR had been prepared for by renewed polemics attacking Bolshevism and by information leaked to the concentrations of troops in the east; so only its timing came as a surprise, and it received general approval. Even Monsignor von Galen rejoiced at the news in the very same sermons in which he deplored the murder of the mentally ill. The enemy, which had revealed glaring weaknesses during its war with Finland in the winter of 1939–40, was underestimated (here, ordinary civilians shared the illusions of the staff office) and when the newsreels showed close-ups of women soldiers and Asiatic prisoners that were all the more horrifying because they were dying of starvation, the spectators were relieved to have escaped these barbaric hordes; and, according to police reports, they were positively glad to see Jews submitted to forced labor. Late August brought the first misgivings: while the nightly air raids certainly affected the nerves of city dwellers, the enormity of the Red Army's losses announced by the official communiqués counter-intuitively provoked a new anguish — the inexhaustible resources of the enemy. Soldiers' letters home from the East had already reflected a certain lassitude when the catastrophic December news broke: not only was the *Wehrmacht* halted at the gates of Moscow, the German population was now urged to sacrifice its own warm clothing for the soldiers. So Hitler had been wrong after all about the certainty of conquering the USSR before the winter. . . . No matter how hard he tried to shrug off personal responsibility by demoting certain generals, and despite efforts to assuage public opinion by rejecting both "euthanasia" and the battle against the churches, his popularity suffered a nasty knock. This can be seen in the announcements of soldiers' deaths in the newspapers. In these, families customarily invoked "the fatherland and the führer"; now, in the National Socialist daily paper in Augsburg, the proportion of these conformist announcements fell from 62 to 29 percent, and in the rest of the Bavarian press from 41-44 percent to 15-25 percent.[28]

In the following year such announcements became even more rare. Hitler, ignoring the pleas of his advisers, spoke less and less often on the radio, indeed so infrequently that the bewildered faithful began to worry about the state of his health. Good news from the Crimea and the submarine war raised morale for no more than a few days at a time; meanwhile the bombing raids increased relentlessly. The requisitioning and melting down of church bells in order to beat them into munitions, a seemingly patriotic measure, was instead regarded as a provocation by practicing Christians, who in southern Germany went so far as to organize farewell ceremonies for them. Well-informed British propaganda had organized an airdrop of false letters from Major Werner Mölders, an ace fighter pilot recently killed in an accident, in which this deeply religious Catholic was represented as violently critical of the regime's paganism. And the SD for the first time acknowledged that public opinion was "extraordinarily heterogeneous," which could be interpreted either as a confession of impotence or a dig at Goebbels. During these same months its reports began to admit to signs of ill-health among workers, both male and female, without interpreting these as in the past as merely "cunning tricks on the part of lazy workers." Meanwhile, doctors for their part were also concerned at the rising rate of infant mortality, cases of tuberculosis, and accidents at work.[29]

The Stalingrad catastrophe in early 1943 was thus not so

much a key point in sinking morale, but simply deepened skepticism in the official information being purveyed. Letters sent by families to their sons and husbands trapped there were, according to the postal censorship service, "sometimes confident, full of hope, and conscious of their duty even as they recognized the gravity of the situation, sometimes depressed or altogether despairing, but without turning to rancor." Official announcement of the Sixth Army's capitulation accompanied by ceremonies to honor the heroes sparked off a series of guesses as to what would happen in the event of total defeat. Thereupon the Soviet propaganda service in an extremely able move broadcast a list of prisoners' names over the radio and allowed them to write to their families using the intermediary of neutral countries. The police inadvertently allowed these letters to be distributed; then Hitler in a fury ordered that they be intercepted, whereupon the families had all the more reason to listen to Soviet radio. The latter then placed its transmitters at the disposal of the "Committee for Free Germany," which the Communists discreetly influenced from behind the more showy figures among a number of officer prisoners. In all its proclamations the USSR was naturally represented as the country of social justice par excellence. And to crown all these doubts about the inhuman nature of the enemy, the young Soviets that Germans worked alongside daily in the factories and fields turned out to be far more intelligent, honest, and even pious than anyone had imagined! In popular circles a new idea was soon circulating: that a Bolshevik Germany might in truth not be worse than the existing situation, for one would at least be rid of "the ten thousand at the top" and their "fine ladies." To counter this danger of alienation if not defection, Goebbels imbued his Sports Palace speech on 18 February with a demagogic tone, announcing that a new policy of "total war" would put an end to all privileges. But the immediate reception from his rapturous audience crammed with militants was quite different from the reservations that greeted it elsewhere. In the months that followed the *SD* even detected a change in not just people's "mood" but even in their "behavior": more and more were listening to radios, reading enemy tracts, and abandoning the Hitlerian salute. Soldiers' wives were losing interest in the war, quarreling with their husbands when they returned home on leave, and even entering into scandalous relationships. The only welcome news for authorities was that the hatred felt for the British was increasing along with the violence of their air raids. "The bourgeois is dead and the real Community is being created in the ruins," one procurator general announced. Meanwhile resistants were coming to realize that despite the general lassitude they constituted no more than a sprinkling of isolated groups. In a letter sent from Stockholm to an English friend, ex-diplomat U. von Hassel explained why there was no chance of a revolution, that is to say a change of regime: it could count on neither the middle classes, who were "infected by totalitarianism," nor the profiteers, nor the patriots, nor all those who believed Germany would be totally destroyed by the Allies; there were no young men left in Germany apart from the police and eight million foreigners; repression was secretly making sure that resistants were denied even the glory of martyrdom and, finally, "at least nine-tenths of the population are ignorant of the fact that we have murdered hundreds of thousands of Jews."[30]

In the East the regime was revealing its true nature while in Germany itself the agents of terror kept a low profile, and those who were naive could still draw a distinction between bad Nazis and good ones, placing Hitler at the head of the latter. Was there any chance of undermining this passivity by spreading news of these massacres, first of all in religious and cultivated circles that might be the most sensitive to maintaining the honor of the nation? Students grouped under the sign of the White Rose were hoping to do this when they addressed their friends at the University of Munich. Contrasting the high-flown promises that had won them over as adolescents with the appalling reality now occurring in the conquered countries, they called openly for them to help to topple the regime. But authorities caused the White Rose membership to disappear without creating much unrest. Priests and militants of the former Catholic Workers' Association were much less radical and simply defended what was left of their religious liberty against the attacks of Nazi fanatics without questioning the system as such. However, the police and judges drew no such fine distinctions. So the faithful saw their parish priests, vicars, and almoners now silenced, now ejected, now even serving preventive prison sentences and then being sent to concentration camps: the special section in Dachau eventually contained about one hundred priests and other concentration camps received pastors of the Confessional Church. These tribulations might perhaps have opened the eyes of their flocks had not the diocesan authorities, in Cologne for example, reacted by counseling greater prudence to those who remained. In short, in 1943, to resist, in the strongest sense of the word, was not so much to prepare for the future as to make an almost despairing gesture of protest, virtually without hope that it would be effective.[31]

A selection of *SD* reports describe the fluctuations of public opinion in the course of the following year. November 1943: the majority, influenced by letters from soldiers, no longer believed in victory and would have liked a compromise peace; Goebbels and Goering were detested more and more because of all their broken promises. But then, each time the führer decided to speak morale improved. However, by March 1944 the only remaining hope lay in miracle weapons. In April were heard growing fears of an invasion from the eastern provinces, where many Berliners had earlier been evacuated. By 4 May: "Many of our fellow-citizens will only preserve their stoical endurance if something truly decisive happens." June: news of the Allied landings in Normandy was greeted with relief, particularly because General Rommel—field marshal in charge of repulsing the attack—was still one of the few generals people trusted. The subsequent launch of the V-1s and V-2s rockets was hailed as the beginning of Germany's revenge on the British (V stood for *Vergeltung*, meaning reprisals). But people soon noticed that official news reports were again using expressions such as "determined resistance by our troops," unpleasantly reminiscent of phrases used on the eve of the Stalingrad disaster. The assassination attempt of 20 July provided propaganda with a perfect opportunity to rally the people more closely to their Leader by representing the conspirators as a clique of misguided aristocrats and trade unionists. But the propaganda campaign met with uneven reactions. In Freiburg a great rally of the faithful was attended by fifty thousand people. But in Berlin one Norwegian journalist noted: "The crowds are apathetic. . . . They are not weeping, not cheering, not angry." Elsewhere some Germans blamed the officer corps for the defeats and bewailed the fact that the poor führer was surrounded by such rotten advisers; others were surprised that he could allow himself to be so duped. Bavarian peasants, a more prudent group, remained totally silent[32]

The last months were characterized by a series of counterintuitive or "boomerang" reactions to the main themes purveyed by propaganda. When the party sought to rehabilitate itself by taking the *Volkssturm* militia under its wing, the chaos and vanity of the whole enterprise were laid at its door. When it gave the order for the last inhabitants of Aachen to evacuate the town as the Americans approached, they all hastened to burn their Nazi uniforms and refused to leave. When the radio announced that the Soviets were behaving in barbaric fashion in East Prussia, there were murmurs to the effect that "We did the same to the Jews and the concentration camp detainees." As early as the summer of 1944 in Bavaria and January 1945 in Königsburg, militant Nazis were announcing that in the event of defeat the führer in his great goodness would arrange for his people to die by gas. By mid-January the *SD* was finally admitting that the Führer's person was no longer spared criticism, and that public opinion was now split into three tendencies: defeatism in the West, endurance between Kiel and Frankfurt, and in the eastern regions the arrival of refugees provoked both indignation at the cowardice of the party and at the same time a surge of resistance against the Soviets. When they found themselves being shelled, Berliners cursed the army, the party, and all its leaders but still spared Hitler, except in the working quarters where the long-stifled Communist tradition was once again finding expression. Macabre humorists compared the last propaganda efforts there to "an orchestra continuing to play as the ship goes down."[33] Was it indeed lost with all hands and cargo?

NOTES

1. Kroener B. R., "Ressourcen," pp. 705–57, 816–50.
2. Messerschmidt M., *Wehrmacht*, pp. 251–79, 450; *60*, p. 215 f. (Protestants); Hürten H., p. 461 f., 473 (Catholics); soldiers' letters in *50*, in particular pp. 39–40; Umbreit H., pp. 101–18 (occupation).
3. Kroener B. R., "Ressourcen," pp. 871–984; Müller R. D., "Ausbeutungskrieg," pp. 183–85; id., "Scheitern," pp. 959–1029; Bartov O., *Army*, pp. 12–50; id., *Eastern Front*, pp. 12–39; Steinert M. G., *Hitlers Krieg*, pp. 272–74.
4. Bartov O., *Eastern Front*, pp. 12–39.
5. Bartov O., *Army*, pp. 12–39 and 116 f., 149 f.; Messerschmidt M., *Wehrmacht*, p. 279, 292; *50*, p. 28, 87, and 63, 17 August 1942, 26 July 1943 (visions of the USSR); Kühne T. (camaraderie); Messerschmidt M., "Zersetzer" (military tribunals). N.B. Bartov attributes the crimes not to solidarity, but on the contrary to the destruction of "primary groups"—but without many proofs.
6. Kroener B. R., "Auf dem Weg," pp. 653–78; Bald D., pp. 58–97; Bartov O., *Eastern Front*, pp. 40–67; Messerschmidt M., *Wehrmacht*, p. 422.
7. Messerschmidt M., *Wehrmacht*, pp. 258–72, 307–56, 441; Bartov O., *Eastern Front*, pp. 68–105.
8. Zimmermann M., "Ausbruchhoffnungen." Junge Bergleute in den 30er Jahren," in Niethammer L. (Hg.), *"Die Jahre weiss man nicht, wo man die heute hinsetzen soll." Faschismuserfahrungen im Ruhrgebiet. Lebensgeschichte und Sozialstruktur im Ruhrgebiet 1930 bis 1960*, Berlin and Bonn: 1983.
9. Steinert M. G., *Hitlers Krieg*, p. 328; doc. in *50*, pp. 16–20, and 72, XVIII, 3219, 2.
10. Messerschmidt M., *Wehrmacht*, p. 442.
11. Wegner B., pp. 150–92, 207–42, 263–98; Koch H. W., p. 364 f. (*HJ* division).
12. Aron R., *Penser la guerre. Clausewitz*, Paris: 1976, vol. 1, *L'Age européen*, p. 52, 162 f.; Ritter G., *Staatskunst und Kriegshandwerk*, Bd. I, *Die altpreussische Tradition*, Munich: 1954, pp. 279–88, 321–29.
13. Krausnick H. and Wilhelm H.-H., p. 39, 58–102; Müller K. J., *Heer*, pp. 429–59; 72, XIV, doc. 2882 (Blaskowitz).
14. Krausnick H. and Wilhelm H.-H., p. 108; Umbreit H., "Auf dem Weg." p. 194 f.; Herbert U., *Best*, pp. 252–64, 306 f.
15. La Martinière J. de. The *NN* procedure was applied only to occupied countries of northern and western Europe.
16. Krausnick H. and Wilhelm H.-H., pp. 116–36; Streit C., pp. 28–57; Förster J., "Barbarossa," p. 435; id., "Sicherung," pp. 1034–78; Müller R. D., "Scheitern," pp. 990–1014.

17. Krausnick H. and Wilhelm H.-H., pp. 205–59; Vestermanis M. (Baltic States).

18. 18. Streit C., pp. 73–256.

19. Bartov O., *Eastern Front*, passim; id., *Army*, pp. 77–141; Schulte T. J., pp. 42–85, 117–257. The exhibition entitled *Vernichtungskrieg. Die Verbrechen der Wehrmacht*, which was recently circulating in Germany provoked heated polemics. See the discussion between veteran soldiers, journalists, and historians, in *Die Zeit*, 3 March 1995.

20. Müller K. J., *Heer*, pp. 490–542; id., "Eliten," p. 30.

21. Kardorff U. von, 31 October 1942; Schieder W. A detailed account of these meetings is to be found in Hoffmann P. (contrary to its title, almost solely devoted to the conspiracy of 20 July).

22. *50*, pp. 142–48; Bartov O., *Army*, p. 176; Vogel D.; Steinert M. G., *Hitlers Kreig*, pp. 478–510; 72, XXI, doc. 3527, f.

23. Steinert M. G. *Hitlers Kreig*, pp. 540–60; Mammach K., pp. 43–130; Ueberschär G. R. (Baden).

24. *58*, p. 272 (martial courts in Berlin); Troll H., p. 660 f. (Munich).

25. Steinert M. G., *Hitlers Kreig*, p. 91 f. (this work has served as the basis for the whole of this part of the present work); Stöver B., p. 207; *63*, 11 Oct. 1939. 1 Dec. 1939; Schäfer H. D., "Das gespaltene Bewusstsein," p. 148, 160; *60*, doc. 53–66; Hürten H., p. 461 f.; Hehl U. von, *Erzbistum Köln*, p. 197 f.

26. Steinert M. G., pp. 98–104; 60, p. 171; *63*, 29 April 1940.

27. Steinert M. G., pp. 122–45; Kershaw I., *Hitler-Mythos*, pp. 135–94; Stöver B., pp. 213–15.

28. Steinert M. G., pp. 203–30; Stöver B., p. 218; *63*, 24 July 1941, 5 Jan. 1942; Kershaw I., *Hitler-Mythos*, p. 166.

29. Steinert M. G., p. 304-316, 343 f.; Kershaw I., *Hitler-Mythos*, pp. 157–66; *63*, 12 March 1942, 9 July 1942; Kater M., Doctors, p. 13 f., 42, 135–37.

30. *50*, pp. 16–20, 32, 196; Streit C., p. 236; *63*, 15 Feb. 1943, 8 July 1943; Steinert M. G., pp. 329–407, 425–449; Blessing W. K., p. 60 (Bavaria); Beck E. R., p. 102 (women); 72, XXI, doc. 3491 a (von Hassel).

31. Hürten H., pp. 535–38, and Hehl U. von, *Erzbistum Köln*, p. 222 (priests and militant Catholics).

32. Boberach H., "Chancen"; *63*, 20 April 1944, 4 May 1944; Klessmann C., "Volksbewegung"; Steinert M. G., pp. 456-489; Kershaw I., *Hitler-Mythos*, p. 187.

33. Steinert M. G., pp. 495–579; rumours of the gassings cited by Arendt H., *Eichmann*, pp. 183–84; Boberach H., "Chancen."

Conclusion

An official in the little town of Berchtesgaden, who conscientiously continued to listen to his fellow citizens, on 23 April 1945 wrote that they now had but one thought in mind: to get back to their prewar lives. According to him, they took no pleasure in becoming a part of history.[1] That laconic remark suggested the version of history heard during the previous three years that was to satisfy many Germans (in the West at least) for several decades: they would recognize, even proclaim, the achievements of nazism in the years of peace and conceal its wartime actions. The present work was not designed to study that posthumous and largely imaginary history of the Third Reich, which constitutes a component of the real history of the two states that succeeded it. Instead, let us return to Germany in the spring of 1945: total wretchedness and an abolished past. So was the slogan "zero year" in fact accurate?

The demographic dynamism which even in the thirties had been unable to repair all the consequences of the First World War now seemed smashed following losses so huge that experts came up with widely differing estimates. In outright deaths, deaths from wounds and sickness, and disappearances the armed forces had lost between 3.3 and 4.3 million men. Obviously casualties were heaviest in the twenty to thirty-five age group, in which some years of classes had been depleted by 20, 30, or even 40 percent. It was impossible to foresee how many of the two million prisoners of war would return, particularly from the USSR.[2] Among civilians, 400,000 to 500,000 had died in the bombing, 1.3 million in the exodus from the East, 300,000 in the gas chambers, and 130,000 to 140,000 in the concentration camps; 400,000 to 500,000 had emigrated, most of whom had no desire to return; and between 1.7 million and 2.3 million had been overtaken in their flight by the Soviet armies and were trapped beyond the 1937 frontiers.[3] It is tempting to add all those losses together in order to determine the total deficit accumulated between 1939 and 1945, but that would be a false calculation: during that time the description "German" was applied to hundreds and thousands of *Volksdeutsche* whose losses are consequently included in the above figures. Ethnic policy, as muddling as it was inhumane, made it impossible to produce any accurate evaluation of its consequences.

The human space once known as Germany and organized into its hierarchy of communities, districts, small rural villages, towns, and regions—a *Heimat* (home) for every individual—had long before the final defeat been dislocated by all the evacuations and transfers of factories, after which internal migrations relatively well-organized by the authorities had crossed paths with the exodus of fugitives from the East. Subsequent Allied occupation, which brought liberation for some and humiliation for others, then redivided this space into four parts with more or less artificial frontiers that were virtually sealed, within which a veritable disturbed anthill of agitation prevailed. Many liberated slaves now known as "displaced persons" became nomads to make their way back to their own countries and escape from the camps in which the all-too-well-meaning authorities tried to gather them together. What with the closed camps for prisoners of war and militant Nazis and semi-open camps for the refugees and homeless, the SS dream of a destructured society had paradoxically become a reality.

Even German families spared dispersion had lost their "natural head" and were to remain thus deprived for a long time. In 1950, even after the return of some prisoners of war, the proportion of women to men was still 114 percent in the new West Germany and as high as 125 percent in the new East Germany,[4] with the imbalance obviously greater in nubile age groups. Women therefore played a major role in the first tasks to wipe out the past, beginning with the clearing of ruins. Bourgeoises and proletarian women, social categories that had continued to exist despite all the constraints of the war economy and all the theoretical pronouncements of the Nazi leaders, now seemed to merge into a magma in which only individuals and micro-cells of one-parent families were distinguishable one from another.

Meanwhile, even at the heart of this chaos, new solidarities were being created and older ones resurfaced after being stifled for twelve years. After the war some groups of soldiers and officers managed to remain together after being captured, and in their camps they maintained a sense of having done their patriotic duty, in some cases even continuing to nurture a nostalgic loyalty to the führer. Natives of the eastern provinces began to form a category of their own, the "refugees," soon to be joined by the "expellees" of Poland and Czechoslovakia. This group was to become a powerful lobby. Once home, adolescents who had lived through a succession of exalting and traumatizing experiences retained a collective set of attitudes so distinctive that a number of aid and reeducation organizations were created expressly to help them. People evacuated from large towns wanted at all costs to return to their own neighborhoods, even if their ruined houses were in danger of collapsing. The universal desire to be home again sometimes took on a political tinge, but in that case it was accompanied by plans for the future. Even in the immediate aftermath of capitulation, individuals and groups reemerged from hiding, prisons, and camps, keen to close this parenthesis and begin rebuilding society. Some, former militants in the Social Democrat Party, hastened to open their offices and were soon accepting subscriptions. But new competition also materialized in the form of "anti-Fascist committees" where other resistants called vigorously for total denazification including in the ranks of the business bosses, thereby swiftly rendering themselves suspect to the western occupiers.[5]

The post-defeat period had been prepared for even better by some business circles. As early as 1943 the *RGI*, industry's official organ, had launched a program of studies on postwar economic policy under the leadership of Professor Ludwig Erhard. His team foresaw a return to liberalism as well as a struggle against inflation; but the final outcome of the war was not yet mentioned. In April 1944 a director of United Steelworks had intervened more forthrightly with Speer, warning him against the scorched earth strategy said to be contemplated by Hitler and urging him to consider ways to preserve "the necessary substance for industry after a lost war." During the next few months several study circles in which L. Erhard again figured looked forward to the transition to a peacetime economy "in a sovereign state with frontiers similar to those of 1919," a fond illusion that reflected to a certain lack of realism. Speer shared their desire to protect industrial installations against systematic destruction, but not their skepticism as to the chances of victory. He complained constantly about the lack of zeal displayed by certain large firms that reserved part of their manufacturing capability for products that would be relaunched into foreign markets as soon as hostilities ceased, or accumulated stocks of raw materials, or that perfected their machinery rather than produce vast quantities of weapons. The dispersion of factories to underground tunnels furthermore made it possible, at the cost of thousands of foreign deaths, to save a great deal of equipment and a considerable percentage of the skilled German labor force, as the Americans were startled to discover when they analyzed the small impact their bombing had on German production. In this way the principle of industry's "auto-responsibility" was respected from the years of destruction into the years of reconstruction, with no break in continuity apart from a phase of partial purging and decartelization sufficient to satisfy the victors.[6]

The new Germany, or rather the new Germanys taking shape in the four zones also needed political elites. Quite soon the Allies authorized the first local elections, and the prospect of later elections for even higher posts made the foundation of viable parties a matter of urgency. Should they simply re-create the parties inherited from the Weimar Republic? The Communists argued that they for their part had been constantly active in exile and in the concentration camps in order to reassociate themselves with revolutionary tradition and to present their party as a protagonist in a gathering of popular forces. The Social Democrats could also invoke their refusal to compromise, if not the active resistance of most of their leaders. But the same could not be said of other parties from the Weimar period, those of the Center and Right. If they were to be reborn, a fair amount of self-criticism would first have to take place. In the vast operation of collective conscience-searching that was to occupy the intellectual world between 1945 and 1949, the question of the responsibilities of conservatives, liberals, and Christians would necessarily occupy a central position. Across the board from the non-Stalinian Far Left to the non-Nazi Far Right, taking in the complete range of positions in between, denunciations and apologias relating to the Prussian tradition (with memories of the conspiracy of "20 July" lurking in the background) alternated with diagnoses of the weaknesses of the Weimar Republic, suggestions for the rejuvenation of conservatism and liberalism, and attempts to answer the piercing question, "Are we Germans different from other peoples?"[7] As nothing was sacrosanct in this debate, the position of the churches was also inevitably brought into question. Both Protestant and Catholic sides could evoke the heroism of certain martyrs, but the fact that there were so few of them combined with the prudence shown by both hierarchies precluded the churches from representing themselves as heirs to the Resistance. The line eventually adopted, not without arguments, by the Protestant Church expressed collective repentance for not having "confessed with greater courage, not having loved with more passion." The Catholic bishops for their part limited their regrets to the behavior of certain individuals: "Many Germans, including some from our ranks, allowed themselves to be fascinated by the false doctrines of National Socialism and remained indifferent before the crimes . . . , many themselves became criminals," and to justify the attitude of the most prudent of his colleagues, Cardinal Frings, the archbishop of Cologne, even added, "The Church is not responsible for controlling the state."[8] The faithful who were more or less accommodating to the Nazi regime and had simply lived in the "gray zone" were thus left to cope with their own individual consciences. Soon the CDU was to offer them, in default of an analysis of the past, a prospect for the future by proclaiming more forcefully than its predecessor, the *Zentrum*, that Christianity, democracy, and social justice were not simply reconcilable but positively indissociable. In this way the framework for a future western state emerged, founded upon the three pillars represented by big business, the churches, and socialism, which remained standing more or less intact amid the ruins of German society.

Of the trilogy consisting of the people, the empire, and the Leader, all that was left was the people. The word itself (*Volk*), disconnected from its racist meaning, remained in current use to symbolize an identity not highly perceptible in daily life. In the East, where the dominant classes of the past were abolished, all inhabitants were urged to merge into the workers' people. In the West, the political parties, one by one—with the Social Democrat Party lagging slightly behind the rest—were all to place the word *Volk* at the head of their political programs. But it would be almost half a century before German crowds would be heard shouting, "We are the people," then within a few days, "We are one people."

NOTES

1. Cited by Kershaw I., *Hitler-Mythos*, p. 193.
2. Kroener B. R., "Ressourcen," pp. 985–86 (4,300,000); *50*, p. 148 (same figure, but including the Austrians); *55*, Bd. I, p. 56 f. (3,800,000); Köllmann W., pp. 38–45 (same figure); Castell A. zu (3,300,000). The differences are probably due to the number of prisoners presumed dead at the date of each publication.
3. Ibid.; Marschalck P., pp. 83–85, 149. The differences are probably accounted for by the Sudetan Germans, who are included in some calculations but not in others.
4. Ibid.

5. This theme of continuities and new solidarities links together all the articles contained in collection *44*, tellingly entitled *De Stalingrad à la réforme monétaire*.
6. Herbst L., p. 322, 383–423; Hetzer G., p. 561 (MAN); Hayes P., p. 376 (*IG Farben*); Roth K. H., p. 317 f., and Fröbe R., "Arbeitseinsatz" (on Daimler-Benz, with a few rather forced interpretations).
7. A complete picture is to be found in Solchany J., *Comprendre le nazisme dans les années zéro, (1945–1949)*, Paris: 1997.
8. Cited by Hürten H., p. 548.

Chronology

1933

30 January	Hitler made chancellor.
27 February	The Reichstag fire.
28	Edict "for the protection of the people and the state."
5 March	Elections to the Reichstag.
21	The day of Potsdam.
23	The law granting full powers.
1 April	Boycott of Jewish businesses.
7	Abolition of the autonomy of the *Länder*. Statute for officials.
2 May	Dissolution of trade unions.
10	Burning of the books.
14 July	Banning of the parties. Law for "the prevention of descendants with hereditary flaws."
20	Concordat with the Vatican.
22 September	Chamber of Culture of the Reich.
29	Law on hereditary farms.
14 October	Departure from the League of Nations.
12 November	Plebiscite.

1934

20 April	Himmler head of the Gestapo in Prussia.
30 June	"Night of the Long Knives." (Röhm putsch).
25 July	Assassination of Dollfuss in Vienna.
2 August	Death of Hindenburg. Hitler head of state.

1935

13 January	Plebiscite in the Saar.

16 March	Universal military service.
26 June	Compulsory labor service.
15 September	Nuremberg laws on the Jews.

1936

7 March	Remilitarization of the Rhineland.
1 August	Olympic Games in Berlin.
9 September	Four-Year Plan.
25 October	Berlin-Rome Axis.
25 November	Anti-Komintern Pact with Japan.
1 December	Hitler Youth Organization becomes State Youth Organization.

1937

14 March	*Mit brennender Sorge* encyclical.
5 November	Hitler's address to the generals (the Hossbach deposition).
26	Schacht dismissed.

1938

4 February	Generals von Blomberg and von Fritsch dismissed.
	Hitler commander-in-chief of the armed forces.
	Ribbentrop minister of foreign affairs.
12–13 March	*Anschluss* of Austria.
29 September	Munich Conference.
9 November	"Night of Glass" pogrom.

1939

| 15 March | Invasion of Czechoslovakia. |
| 22 May | Pact of Steel with Italy. |

23 August	German-Soviet pact.
1 September	Invasion of Poland.
3	Britain and France declare war.
27	Capitulation of Warsaw. Creation of the *RSHA*.
October	"Euthanasia" program.

1940

9 April	Invasion of Denmark and Norway.
10 May	Western offensive.
22 June	Armistice with France.
13 August	Beginning of Battle of Britain.

1941

6 April	Invasion of Yugoslavia and Greece.
6 June	*OKW* order on the treatment of political commissars of the Red Army.
22	Invasion of the USSR.
15 July	"General plan for the East."
31	Heydrich ordered to prepare the "final solution for the Jewish problem."
19 September	Yellow stars compulsory for Jews in the Reich.
1 December	Offensive halted outside Moscow.
7	"Night and Fog" decree.
11	At war with the United States.
19	Hitler commander-in-chief of the territorial army.

1942

20 January	Wannsee Conference.
8 February	Speer minister of armament.

21 March	Sauckel plenipotentiary for labor.
30–31 May	First massive air raid by the RAF, on Cologne.
3 November	Battle of El Alamein.
11	Occupation of the free zone in France.

1943

31 January	Capitulation of the Sixth Army at Stalingrad.
18 February	Goebbels's speech on "total war."
	Arrest of members of the "White Rose."
19 April–19 May	Revolt of the Warsaw ghetto.
10 July	Allied landing in Sicily.
12	Soviet offensive.
24 July–3 Aug.	Hamburg bombed.
25 July	Fall of Mussolini.
2 September	Creation of Grand Ministry of War Production.
22 December	Creation of "NS officers for psychological leadership."

1944

19 March	Occupation of Hungary.
6 June	Allied landing in Normandy.
3 July	Collapse of the group of central armies on the eastern front.
20	Assassination attempt against Hitler and attempt at a *coup d'etat*.
1 Aug.–2 Oct.	Warsaw uprising.
11 September	Western allies reach the German frontier.
25	Creation of the *Volkssturm*.
16 December	Ardennes counteroffensive.

1945

14 January	Red Army in West Prussia.
23	Red Army reaches the Oder in Silesia.
13–14 Feb.	Dresden bombed.
19 March	Hitler's "scorched earth" order.
25 April	Americans and Russians meet at the Elbe.
30	Hitler's suicide.
8–9 May	German capitulation.

Bibliography*

The first part of this bibliography lists the collective works (colloquia, collections of articles, etc.) that are used repeatedly. They are listed in the alphabetical order of their titles, with the names of their editors (French abbreviation: "dir."; German: "Hg."; English/American: "ed."). The entries are numbered in alphabetical order.

The second part lists collections of documents, following the same method.

The third part lists books and individual articles in the alphabetical order of the names of their authors. Where an article is taken from a collective work cited in the first part, the title is not repeated, only its number.

N.B. Some works marginal to the subject, the complete references of which appear in the notes, are not in this bibliography.

1. Alltagsgeschichte. Zur Rekonstruktion historischer Erfahrungen und Lebensweisen. (Lüdtke A., Hg.), Francfort/M. and New York, 1989.

2. Anatomie des SS-Staates. (Broszat M. *et al.*), Bd. I-II, Olten, 1965.

3. *Angst, Belohnung, Zucht und Ordnung. Herrschaftsmechanismen in Nationalsozialismus.* (Sachse C. et al.), Opladen, 1982.

4. *Bayern in der NS-Zeit.* Munich: 1977–1983, 5 vol.

   Bd. I *Soziale Lage und politisches Verhalten der Bevölkerung im Spiegel vertraulicher Berichte.* (Broszat M., Fröhlich E., Wiesenmann F., Hg.).

   Bd. II *Herrschaft und Gesellschaft im Konflikt.* Teil A (Broszat M. and Fröhlich E., Hg.).

   Bd. III Teil B (Id. and Grossman A., Hg.).

   Bd. IV Teil C (Id., Hg.).

   Bd. V *Die Parteien KPD, SPD, BVP in Verfolgung und Wilderstand.* (Broszat M. et Mehringer H., Hg.).

5. *Berlin und die Provinz Brandenburg im 19. und 20. Jahrhundert.* (Herzfeld H. et Heinrich G., Hg.). Berlin: 1968.

---

*The list of abbreviations appears after the Bibliograpy.

6. *Das Daimler-Benz-Buch. Ein Rüstungskonzern im "Tausendjährigen" Reich.* (Hamburger Stiftung zur Geschichte des 20. Jahrhunderts). Nördlingen: 1987.

7. *La Déportation. Le système concentrationnaire nazi.* (Bédarida F. et Gervereau L., Dir.). Nanterre: 1995.

8. *Das deutsche Reich und der zweite Weltkrieg.* (Militärgeschichtliches kForschungsamt, Hg.), Stuttgart: 1979 – 1990, 6 vol.

Bd. I *Ursachen und Voraussetzungen der deutschen Kriegs politik. 2 (Deist W., Messerschmidt M., Volkmann H.-E. Wette W.).*

Bd. II *Die Errichtung der Hegemonie auf dem europäuschen Kontinent.* (Maier K. A., Rohde H., Stegemann B., Umbreit H.).

Bd. III *Der Mittlmeerraum und Südost-Europa. Von de "non-belligeranza" Italiens bis zum Kriegseintritt der Verenigten Staaten. 2 (Schreiber G., Stegemann B., Vogel D.).*

Bd. IV *Der Angriff auf die Sowjetunioin.* (Boog H., Förster J., Hoffmann J., Klink E., Müller R.-D., Ueberschär G.R.).

Bd. V *Organisation und Mobilisierung des deutschen Machtbereichs. 1.* Halbbd. *Kriegsverwaltung, Wirtschaft und personelle Ressourcen, 1939 – 1941.* (Kroener B. R., Müller R.-D., Umbreit H.).

Bd. VI *Der globale Krieg. Die Ausweitung zum Weltkrieg und der Wechsel der Initiative, 1941 – 1943.* (Boog H., Rahn W., Stumpf R., Wegner B.).

9. *Die deutsche Universität im 3. Reich.* (Eine Vortragsreihe der Unbiversität München). Munich: 1966.

10. *Die deutschen Eliten und der Weg in den zweiten Weltkrieg.* (Broszat M. et Schwabe K., Hg.). Munich: 1989.

11. *Erziehung und Schulung im 3. Reich.* (Heinemann M. Hg.), Stuttgaart: 1980, 2 vol. Teil 1. *Kindergarten, Schule, Jugend, Berufserziehung.* Teil 2. *Hochschule, Erwachsenenbildung.* Stuttgart: 1980.

12. *Faschismus als soziale Bewegung.* (Schieder W., Hg.), Hamburg: 1976.

13. *Femmes et Fascismes.* (Thalmann R., dir), Paris, 1986.

14. *Der Führerstaat. Mythos und Realität.* (Hirschfeld G., et Kettenacker L., Hg.). Stuttgart: 1981.

15. *Geschichte Berlins.* (Ribbe W., Hg.), Bd. II, *Von der Märzrefvolution bis zur Gegenwart.* Munich: 1987.

16. *Handbuch zur deutschen Militärgeschichte, 1648 – 1939.* (Militärgeschichtliches Forschungsamt, Hg.). Bd. VII *Wehrmacht und Nationalsozialismus, 1933 – 1939.* Munich: 1978.

17. *Intellektuelle im Banne des National-Sozialismus.* (Corino K., Hg.). Hamburg: 1980.

18. *Die Juden in Deutschland, 1933 – 1945.* (Benz W., Hg.). Munich: 1988.

19. *Katholische Kirche im 3. Reich.* (Albrecht D., Hg.). Mainz: 1976.

20. *Der Krieg des kleinen Mannes. Eine Militärgeschichte von unten.* (Wette W., Hg.). Munich: 1992.

21. *Kunst und Kultur im deutschen Faschismus.* (Schnell R., Hg.) Stuttgart: 1978).

22. *Life in the Third Reich.* (Bessel R., ed.). Oxford and New York: 1987.

23. *Machtbewuβtsein in Deutschland am Vorabend des zweiten Weltkrieges.* (Knipping F. et Müller K.-J., Hg.). Paderborn: 1984.

24. *Medizin im Nationalsozialismus.* (Kolloquein des Instituts für Zeitgeschichte). Munich: 1988.

25. *Nach Hitler. Der schwierige Umgang mit unserer Geschichte.* Beiträge von Martin Broszat. (Graml H. et Henke K. D., Hg.). Munich: 1987.

26. *Natinalsozialismus und die deutsche Universität.* (Universitätstage, 1966). Berlin: 1966.

27. *Nationalsozialistische Diktatur. Eine Bilanz.* (Bracher K. D., Funke M., Jacobsen H.-A., Hg.). Bonn: 1986.

28. *Nationalsozialistische Konzentrationslager im Dienste der totalen Kriegsführung. Sieben württembergische Auβenkommandos des KZ Natzweiler/Elsaβ.* (Vorländer H., Hg.). Stuttgart: 1978.

29. *Der nationalsozialistische Krieg.* (Frei N. et Kling H., Hg.). Frankfurt/M. and New York: 1990.

30. *Nazisme et Antinazisme dans la littérature et l'art allemands.* (Combes A., Vanousthuyse M., Vodoz I., Dir.). Lyons: 1986.

31. *1933. Fünfzig Jahre danach. Die nationalsozialistische Machtergreifung in historischer Perspektive.* (Becker J., Hg.). Munich: 1983.

32. *Oberbügermeister.* (Schwabe K., Hg.). Boppard.Rh.: 1981.

33. *La Politique nazie d'extermination.* (Bédarida F., Dir.). Paris: 1989.

34. *Regionale Eliten zwischen Diktatur und Demokratie. Baden und Württemberg, 1930-1952.* (Rauth-Kühe C. et Ruck M., Hg.). Munich: 1993.

35. *Regionen im historischen Vergleich. Studien zu Deutschland im 19. und 20. Jahrhundert.* (Bergmann J. et al. Hg.), Opla-den: 1989.

36. *Die Reihen fast geschlossen. Beiträge zur Geschichte des Alltags unter dem Nationalsozialismus.* (Peukert D. et Reulecke J., Hg.). Wuppertal: 1981.

37. *Die Schatten der Vergangenheit. Impulse zur Historisierung des Nationalsozialismus.* (Backes U., Jesse E., Zitelmann R., Hg.). Frankfurt/M: 1990.

38. *Schule und Unterricht im 3. Reich.* (Dithmar R., Hg.). Neuwied: 1989.

39. *La Science sous le Troisième Reich.* (Olff-Nathan J., Dir.). Paris: 1993.

40. *The Shaping of the Nazi State.* (Stachura P., Ed.). London: 1978.

41. *Sprache im Faschismus.* (Ehlich K., Hg.), Frankfurt/M.: 1989.

42. *Studien zur Geschichte der Konzentrationslager.* Stuttgart: 1970.

43. *Die Vertreibung der Deutschen aus dem Osten. Ursachen, Ereignisse, Folgen.* (Benz W., Hg.). Frankfurt/M.: 1985.

44. *Von Stalingrad zur Währungsreform. Zur Socialgeschichte des Umbruchs in Deutschland.* (Broszat M., Henke K.-D., Woller H., Hg.). Munich: 1988.

45. *Wer zurückweicht wird erschossen! Kriegsalltag und Kriegsende in Südwestdeutschland, 1944/45.* (Müller R.-D., Ueberschär G. R, Wette W.). Fribourg en B.: 1985.

46. *Der Widerstand gegen den Natigonalsozialismus. Die deutsche Gesellschaft und der Widerstand gegen Hitler.* (Schmädeke J. et Stein bach P., Hg.). Munich and Zurich: 1985.

47. *Wissenschaft in 3. Riech.* (Lundgreen P., Hg.). Francfort/M.: 1985.

48. *Wohnen im Wnadel.* (Niethammer L., Hg.). Wuppertal: 1979.

49. *Zweiter Weltkrieg und sozialer Wandel.* (Dlubogorski W., Hg.). Göttingen: 1981.

COLLECTIONS OF DOCUMENTS

50. *Das andere Gesicht des Krieges. Deutsche Feldpostbriefe, 1939 - 1945.* (Buchbender O. et Sterz R., Hg.). Munich: 1983.

51. *Die bildenden Künste im 3. Reich. Eine Dokumentation.* (Wulf J., Hg.). new ed. Francfort/M.-Berlin-Vienna: 1983.

52. *Die Daimler-Benz AG, 1916 - 1948. Schlüsseldokumente zur Konzerngeschichte.* (Roth K. H. et Schmid M., Hg.). Nördlingen: 1987.

53. *Documents on Nazism, 1919 - 1945.* (Noakes J. et Pridham, Ed. New York: 1975.

54. *Dokumentation zur Vertreibung der Deutschen aus Ost-Mittel-europa.* (Schieder T. et al., Hg.), Bonn: n.d.

Bd. I, 1 *Die Vertreibung der deutschen Bevölkerung aus den Gebieten östlich der Oder-Neisse.*

55. *Dokumente deutscher Kriegsschäden.* (Bundesministerium für Vertriebene, Flüchtige und Kriegsgeschädigte, Hg.).

Bd. I. Bonn: 1958.

Bd. II. 1, *Soziale und rechtliche Hilfsmaßnahmen . . . , Bonn: 1960.*

Bd. IV. 2, *Berlin. Kriegs- und Nachkriegsschicksal der Reichshauptstadt.* Bonn: 1967.

1. Beiheft, *Aus den Tagen des Luftkrieges und des Wiederaufbaus. Erlebnis- und Erfahrungsberichte.* Bonn: 1960.

2. Beiheft, *Der Luftkrieg im Spiegel der neutralen Presse.* Bonn: 1962.

56. *Es spricht der Führer. Sieben exemplarische Hitler-Reden.* (Krausnick H. et von Kotze H. von, Hg.). Gütersloh: 1966.

57. *Hitlers Machtergreifung. Dokumente vom Machtantritt Hitlers (30.1.1933) bis zur Besiegelung des Einparteistaates (14.7.1934).* (Becker J. et R., Hg.). 2d ed., Munich: 1992.

58. *Der Kampf um Berlin 1945 in Augenzeugenberichten.* (Gosztony P., hg.). Munich: 1975.

59. *Katholische Kirche und Nationalsozialismus. Dokumente, 1930–1935* (Müller H., Hg.). Introduction by K. Sontheimer. Munich: 1963.

60. *Kirche im Krieg. Der deutsche Protestantismus am Beginn des zweiten Weltkrieges.* (Braklmann G., Hg.). Munich: 1979.

61. *Lieber Stürmer! Leserbriefe an das nationalsozialistische Kampfblatt, 1924 bis 1945.* (Hahn F., Hg.). Stuttgart: 1978.

62. *Literatur und Dichtung im 3. Reich. Eine Dokumentation*. (Wulf J., Hg.). cf. **51.**

63. *Meldungen aus dem Reich. Auswahl aus den geheimen Lageberichten des Sicherheitsdienstes der SS, 1939–44.* (Boberach H., Hg.), 2d ed., Munich: 1968.

64. *Musik im 3. Reich. Eine Dokumentation.* (Wulf J., Hg.). cf. **51.**

65. *Nationalsozialismus im Alltag. Quellen zur Geschichte des Nationalsozialismus vornehmlich im Raum Mainz-Koblenz-Trier.* (Heyen F. J., Hg.). Boppard/Rh.: 1967.

66. *Der nationalsozialistische Alltag. So lebte man unter Hitler.* (Mosse G., Hg.). Königstein/Taunus: 1978.

67. *Les Chambres à gaz, secret d'État.* (Kogon E., Langbein H., Rückerl A. et al., Hg.). French trans. Paris: 1984 (1st ed. 1983).

68. *Presse und Funk im 3. Reich. Eine Dokumentation.* (Wulf J., Hg.). cf. **51.**

69. *Richterbriefe. Dokumente zur Beeinflussung der deutschen Rechtsprechung, 1942–1944.* (Boberach H., Hg.). Boppard/Rh.: 1975.

70. *Sozialgeschichtliches Arbeitsbuch.* (Petzina D., Abelschauser W., Faust A., Hg.). Bd. III. *Materialien zur Statistik des deutschen Reiches, 1914–1945.* Munich: 1978.

71. *Theater und Film im 3. Reich. Eine Dokumentation.* (Wulf J., Hg). cf. **51.**

72. *Ursachen und Folgen. Vom deutschen Zusammenbruch 1918 und 1945 bis zur staatlichen Neuordnung Deutschlands in der Gegenwart.* (Michaelis H. and Schraepler E., Hg.). Berlin: 1958–1978, Bd. 9–23.

73. *Die Wandinschriften des Kölner Gestapo-Gefängnisses im EL-DE Haus, 1943–1945.* (Huiskes M., Hg.). Cologne: 1983.

BOOKS AND ARTICLES

Abel T. *Why Hitler Came into Power. An Answer Based on the Original Life Stories of Six Hundred of his Followers.* New York: 1938.

Allen W. S. *Une petite ville nazie, 1930-1935.* French trans. Paris: 1969 (1st ed. 1965).

———. "Die deutsche Öffentlichkeit und die 'Reichskristallnacht' Konflikte zwischen Werthierarchie und Propaganda im 3. Reich." **36**. p. 397-411.

———. "Die sozialdemokratische Untergrundbewegung: zur Kontinuität der subkulturellen Werte." **46**. p. 849-66.

Aly G. "Bevölkerungspolitische Selektion als Mittel der sozialen 'Neuordnung.' **29**. p. 137-45.

———. et Heim S. *Vordenker der Vernichtung. Auschwitz und die deutschen Pläne für eine neue europäische Ordnung.* Hamburg: 1991.

Andreas-Friedrich R. *Schauplatz Berlin. Ein Tagebuch aufgezeichnet, 1938-1945.* Reinbek: 1964.

Arbogast C. et Gall B. "Aufgaben und Funktionen des Gauinspekteurs, der Kreisleitung und der Kreisgerichtsbarkeit der NSDAP in Württemberg." **34**. p. 151-169.

Arendt H. *Le Système totalitaire,* French trans. Paris: 1972 (1st ed. 1951).

———. *Eichmann à Jérusalem. Rapport sur la banalité du mal.* French trans. Paris: 1966; new ed. 1991; (1st ed. 1963).

Aretin K. O. von, "Der bayerische Adel. Von der Monarchie zum 3. Reich." **4**. Bd. III, p. 513-67.

Argeles J.-M. et Badia G. *république de Weimar-Tropisième Reich (Histoire de l'Allemagne contemporaine, t. 1).* Paris: 1987.

Arndt I. "Das Frauenkonzentrationslager Ravensbrück." **42**, p. 93-129.

Arndt K. "Die Münchener Architekturszene 1933-34 al ästhetisch-pllitisches Konfliktsfeld." **4**. Bd. III, p. 443-611.

Auerbach H. "Voksstimmung und veröffentlichte Meinung in Deutschland zwischen März und November 1938." **23**, p. 273-93.

Ayçoberry P. *La Question nazie. Essai sur les interprétations du national-socialisme, (1922-1975).* Paris: 1979.

Bachelier C. "La population des camps de concenetration nazis." **7**, p. 78-89.

Backes U., Jesse E., Zitelmann R. "Was heisst 'Historisierung' des Nationalsozialismus?" **37**. p. 25-57.

Baird J. W. *The Mythical World of Nazi War Propaganda, 1939-1945.* Minneapolis: 1974.

Bald D. *Der deutsche Offizier. Sozial- und Bildungsgeschichte des deutschen Offizierskorps im 20. Jahrhundert.* Munich: 1982.

Baldwin P. "Social Interpretations of Nazism: Renewing a Tradition." *JCH* (January 1990): p. 5-38.

Barkai A. *Das Wirtschaftssystem des Nationalsozialismus, new ed. Francfort/M.: 1988.*

Bartov O. *The Eastern Front, 1941-45. German Troops and the Barbarisation of Warfare.* Houndmills and London: 1985.

———. *Hitler's Army. Soldiers, Nazis and War in the Third Reich.* New York and Oxford: 1991.

Beck E. R. *Under the Bombs. The German Home Front, 1942-1945.* Lexington: 1986.

Bédarida F., " 'Kérygme' nazi et religion séculière." *Esprit* (January 1996): p. 89-100.

Beier G. "Gewerkschaften zwischen Illusion und Aktion." **46**. p. 99-111.

Benz W. "Der Generalplan Ost. Zur Germanisierungspolitik des NS-Regimes in den besetzten Ostgebieten, 1939–1945." **43.** p. 39–48.

——. "Prolog. Der 30. Januar 1933. Die deutschen Juden und der Beginn der nationalsozialistischen Herrschaft." **18.** p. 15–33.

——. "Der Novemberpogrom, 1938." **18.** p. 499–544.

——. "Überleben im Untergrund, 1943–1945." **18.** p. 600–700.

Béradt C. "Le cauchemar de l'histoire: rêver sous Hitler." *Le Débat* (May 1983): p. 178–84.

Bergmann J. et Mengerle K. "Protest und Aufruhr der Landwirtschaft in der Weimarer Republik, (1924–1933). Formen und Typen der politischen Agrarbewegung im regionalen Vergleich." **35.** p. 200–87.

Bernecker W. L. "Kapitalismus und Nationalisozialismus. Zum Problem der Unterstützung Hitlers durch die Wirtschaft." **31.** p. 49–88.

Berning C. *Vom "Abstammungsnachweis" zum "Zuchtwart." Vokabular des Nationalsozialismus.* Berlin: 1964.

Besier G. "Ansätze zum politischen Widerstande in der Bekennenden Kirche. Zur gegenwärtigen Forschungslage." **46.** p. 265–80.

Bessel R. *Political Violence and the Rise of Nazism. The Storm Troopers in Eastern Germany, 1925–1934.* New Haven and London: 1984.

Beyerchen A. D. *Scientists under Hitler. Politics and the Physics Community in the Third Reich.* New Haven and London: 1977.

Billig J. *L'Hitlérisme et le Système concentrationnaire.* Paris: 1967.

Blaich F. "Die bayerische Industrie, 1933–1939. Elemente von Gleichschaltung, Konformisus und Selbstbehauptung." **4.** Bd. II, p. 237–81.

——. "Wirtschaft und Rüstung in Deutschland, 1933–1939." **27.** p. 285–316.

Blasius D. "Psychiatrischer Alltag im Nationalsozialismus." **36.** p. 367–80.

Blessing W. K. " 'Deutsche in Not, wir im Glauben . . .' Kircheund Kirchenvolk in einer Katholischen Region, 1933–1939." **44.** p. 3–111.

Boberach H. "Einleitung." **63.**

——. "Chancen eines Umsturzes im Spiegel der Berichte des SD." **46.** p. 815–21.

Bock G. "Racisme, stérilisation obligatoire et maternité sous le natinal-socialisme." **13.** p. 99–113.

——. "Gleichheit und Differenz in der nationalsozialistischen Rassenpolitik." *GG* 3 1993): p. 277–310.

Boehnert G. C. "An Analysis of the Age and Education of the SS Führerkorps, 1925–1939." *HSR/HSF (October 1979).*

——. "The Jurists in the SS-Führerkorps, 1925–1939." **14.** p. 361–72.

Bornemann M. et Broszat M. "Das Konzentrationslager Dora-Mittelbau." **42.** p. 154–98.

Boyens A. "Wilderstand der evangelischen Kirche im 3. Reich." **27.** p. 669–86.

Bracher K. D.*Die Auflösung der Weimarer Republik. Eine Studie zum Problem des Machtverfalls in der Demokratie.* 2d ed., Stuttgart and Düsseldorf: 1957.

——. Sauer W. et Schulz G. *Die nationalsozialistische Mchtergreifung.* Cologne et Opladen: 1960.

——. "Die Gleichschaltung der deutschen Universität." **26.** p. 126–42.

——. *La Dictature allemande. Naissance, structure et consequences du nationalsocialisme,* French trans. Toulouse: 1986 (1st ed. 1969).

Bramke W. "Der unbekannte Widerstand in Westsachsen, 1933–1945." *JbRG* (1986): p. 220–53.

——. "Proletarischer Widerstand im Spektrum des Gesamtwiderstandes gegen de Faschismus.: *JbRG* (1987): p. 301–13.

Bramsted E. K. *Goebbels and National Socialist Propaganda, 1925–1945*. Michigan State U. P.: 1965.

Brenner, H. La Politique artistique du national-socialisme, French trans. Paris: 1980 (1st ed. 1963).

Breyvogel. W. et Lohmann T. "Schulalltag im nationalsozialismus." **36**. p. 199–221.

Broszat M. *L'État hitlérin. L'origine et l'évolution des structures du Troisième Reich*. French trans. Paris: 1985 (1st ed. 1970).

——. "Soziale Motivation und Führerbindung des Nationalsozialismus." *VfZG* 4 (1970).

——. "Eine Armutsregion im Spiegel vertraulicher Berichte: der Bezirk Ebermannstadt 1929 bis 1945." **4**. Bd. I. 1.

——. "Plaidoyer für Alltagsgeschichte. Eine Replik auf J. Kocka." **25**. p. 239–44 (1st ed. 1982).

——. "Alltagsgeschichte der NS-Zeit." **25**. p. 131–39 (1st ed. 1983).

——. "Resistenz und Widerstand." **25**. p. 68–91.

——. "Zur Struktur der nationalsozialistischen massenbewegung." *VfZG* 1 (1983).

——. "Plaidoyer pour une historisation du national-socialisme." French trans. *Bull. Ausch.* 24 (April-Sept. 1990): p. 276–42 (1st ed. 1985).

——. "Zur Sozialgeschichte des deutschen Widerstandes." *VfZG* (1986): p. 293–309.

——. et Friedländer S. "De l'historisation du national-socialisme. Échange de lettres." French trans. *Bull. Ausch.* 24 (April-Sept. 1990): p. 43–90 (1st ed. *VfZG*, 1988).

Browning C. *Des hommes ordinaires. Le 101ᵉ bataillon de réserve de la police allemande et la Solution finale en Pologne*, French trans. Paris: 1994 (1st ed. 1992) — *ordinary men: reserve police battalion 101 and the final solution in Poland*.

Buchheim H. *Die SS. Das Herrschaftsinstrument. Befehl und Gehorsam*. **2**, Bd. I.

Burden H. T. *The Nuremberg Party Rallies, 1923–1939*. New York: 1967.

Burrin P. *Hitler et les Juifs. Genèse d'un génocide*. Paris: 1989.

Caplan J. "Civil Service Support for National-Socialism: An Evaluation." **14**. p. 167–90.

Carroll B. A. *Design for Total War, Arms and Economics in the Third Reich*. The Itaghe and Paris:

Castell A. zu. "Die demographischen Konsequenzen des ersten und zweiten Weltkriegs für das deutsche Reich, die DDR und die BRD." **49**. p. 117–37.

Chaim H.-G. "Zur Verfolgung Berliner jüdischer Rechtsanwälte 1933 bis 1945." *ZfG* 11 (1988).

Childers T. *The Nazi Voter. The Social Foundations of Fascism in Germany, 1919–1933*. Chapel Hill and London: 1983.

Cluet M. "Idéologie national-socialiste et architecture du Troisième Reich." *RH2GM* (April 1981).

Conte E. "Völkerkunde und Faschismus? Fragen an ein vernachlassigtes kapitel deutsch-österreichicher Wissenschaftsgeschichte." In Stadler F., Hg., *Konti-*

nuität und Bruch, 1938–1945–1955. Beiträge zur österrichichen Kultur- und Wissenschaftsgeschichte. Vienna and Munich: p. 228-64.

——. et Essner C. *La Quête de la race. Une anthropologie du nazisme.* Paris: 1995.

Corino K. "Nachwort." **17**.

Courtade F. et Cadars P. *Histoire du cinéma nazi.* Paris: 1972.

Dahm V. "Kulturelles und geistiges Leben. **18**. p. 75–267.

Delage C. *La Vision nazie de l'histoire à travers le cinéma documentaire du Troisième Reich.* Lausanne: 1989.

Dipper C. "Der deutsche Widerstand und die Juden." *GG* (1983).

Dithmar R. "Richtlinien und Realität. Deutschunterricht im Gymnasium." **38**. p. 21-37.

Drobisch K. "Les camps allemands de 1933 à 1939.:" **7**. p. 42-48.

Dorz J., *Histoire de l'antifascisme en Europe, 1923–1939.* Paris: 1985.

Dülffer J. "Der Beginn des Krieges, 1939: Hitler, die innere Krise und das Mächtesystem." *GG* 4 (1976).

Duhnke H. *Die KPD von 1933 bis 1945.* Cologne: 1972.

Ebermayer E. ". . . und morgen die ganze Welt." Erinnerungen an Deutschlands dunkle Zeit. Bayreuth: 1966.

Eihholtz D. *Geschichte der deutschen Kriegswirtschaft, 1939–1945.*

Bd. I *1939–1941,* Berlin (Est), 1971.

Bd. II *1941–1943,* Berlin (Est), 1984.

Elias N. "Der Zusammenbruch der Zivilisation." *Studien über die Deutschen.* Francfort/M.: 1989 (published in 1961), p. 391-516.

Engeli C. and Ribbe W. "Berlin in der NS-Zeit." **15**. p. 927-1024.

Erger J. "Lehrer und Nationalsozialismus. Von den traditionellen Lehrerverbänden zum nationalsozialistischen Lehrerbund (NSLB)." **11**. Teil 2, p. 206-31.

Euler F. "Theater zwischen Anpassung und Widerstand. Die Münchner kammerspiele im 3. Reich." **4**. Bd. II, p. 91-174.

Fabréguet M. *Mauthausen. Camp de concentration national-socialiste en Autriche rattachée, (1938–1945),* thèse d'État, Paris-IV, 1995, 4 vol. typed.

Falter J. W. "Wer verhalf der NSDAP zum Sieg?" *PZG* (14 July 1979): p. 3-21.

——. et Hänisch D. "Die Anfälligkeit von Arbeitern gegenüber der NSDAOP bei den Reichstagswahlen, 1928–1933." *AfS* (1986): p. 179-216.

——. Lindenberger T. et Schumann S. *Wahlen und Abstimmungen in der Weimarer Republik.* Munich: 1986.

——. "Warum die Arbeiter während des 3. Reiches zu Hitler standen." *GG* 2 (1987): p. 217-32.

——. *Hitlers Wähler.* Munich: 1991.

——. et Kater M. H. "Wähler und Mitglieder der NSDAP. Neue Forschungsergebnisse zur Soziographie des Nationalsozialismus 1925 bis 1933." *GG* 2 (1993): p. 154-77.

Faust j A. "Professoren für den NSDAP. Zum politischen Verhalten der Hochschullehrer, 1932/33." **11**. Teil 2, p. 31-49.

Feit B. "Die Kreisleiter er NSDAP—nach 1945." **25**. p. 219-99.

Feldenkirchen W. *Siemens, 1918–1945.* Munich-Zurich: 1995.

Fest J. *Hitler. T. I. Jeunesse et Conquête du pouvoir.* T. ID *Le Führer,* French trans. 2 vol. Paris: 1973 (1st ed. 1973).

Fischer C. J. *Stormtroopers. A Social, Economical and Ideological Anaysis, 1929-1935.* London: 1983. *VfZG* 4 (1991): p. 534-49.

Fischer K. "Die Emigration von Wissenschaftlern nach 1933." VfZG 4(1991): p. 534-49.

Fischer W. *Die Wirtschaftspolitik des Nationalsozialismus.* Lunebourg: 1961.

Flessau I. *Schule der Diktatur. Lehrpläne und Schulbücher de Nationalsozialismus.* Frankfurt/M.: 1979.

Förster J. "Das Unternehmen 'Barbarossa' als Eroberung und Vernichtungskrieg." 8. Bd. IV, p. 413-47.

———. "Die Sicherung des 'Lebensraumes.'", ibid. p. 1030-78.

———. "La campagne de Russie et la radicalisation de la guerre: stratégie et assassinats de masse." *33.* p. 177-95.

Frei N. "Nationalsozialistische Eroberung der Provinzzeitungen. Eine Studie zur Pressesituation in der bayerischen Ostmark." 4. Bd. II, p. 1-90.

———. "Wie modern war der Nationalsozialismus?" *GG 3* (1993): p. 367-87.

———. *L'État hitlérien et la Société allemande, 1933-1945.* French trans. Paris: 1994 (1st d. 1987). Preface by Rousso H.

———. et Schmitz J. *Journalismus im 3. Reich.* Munich: 1989.

Friedländer S. "Réflexions sur l'historisation du national-socialisme." *Vingtième Siècle* 16 (1987): p. 43-54.

———. cf. Broszat M.

Fröbe R. "'Wie bei den alten Ägyptern.' Die Verlegung des Daimler-Benz-Flugmotorenwerks Genshagen nach Obrigheim am neckar, 1944/45." 6. p. 392-470.

———. Der Arbeitseinsatz von KZ-Häftlingen und die Perspktive der Industrie, 1943-1945." In Hamberger Stiftung zur Förderung von Wissenschaft und Kultur (Hg.). *"Deutsche Wirtschaft." Zwangsarbeit von KZ-Häftlingen für Industrie und Behörden.* Hamburg: 1991. p. 33-78.

Fröhlich E. "Die Herausforderung des Einzelnen. Geschichten über Widerstand und Verfolgung." 4. Bd. VI. p. 327-695.

Gay P. *Le Suicide d'une république. Weimar, 1918-1933.* French trans. Paris: 1993 (1st ed. 1968).

Geiger T. *Die soziale Schichtung des deutschen Volkes.* Stuttgart: 1932.

Gellately R. *The Gestapo and German Society. Enforcing Racial Policy, 1933-1945.* Oxford: 1990.

Gerstenberger H. "Alltagsforschung und Faschismustheorie." In Id. et Schmidt D., Hg. *Normalität oder Normalisierung? Geschichtswerkstätten und Faschismusanalyse.* Münster: 1987. p. 35-49.

Geyer M. H. "Soziale Sicherheit und wirtschaftlicher Fortschritt. Überlegungen zum Verhältnis von Arbeitsideologie und Sozialpolitik im 3. Reich." *GG 3* (1989): p. 382-406.

Girardet R. *Mythes et Mythologies politiques.* Paris: 1986.

Glass D V. "German Policy and the Birth-Rate." In *Population Policies and Movements in Europe.* New York: 1940. p. 269-314.

Golczewski F. "Die 'Gleichschaltung' der Universität Köln im Frühjahr 1933." In *Aspekte der nationalsozialistischen Herrschaft in Köln und im Rheinlande.* (Haupts L. et Möhlich G., Hg.). Colone: 1983. p. 48-72.

Goldhagen D. *Les Bourreaux volontaires de Hitler.* French trans. Paris: 1997 (1st ed. 1996).

Grimm D. "Die 'neue 'Rechtswissenschaft.' Über Funktion und Formation national-sozialistischer Jurisprudenz." **47**, p. 31–54.

Grossmann A. J. "Fremd- und Zwangsarbeiter in Bayern, 1939–1945". *VfZG* (1986): p. 481–521.

Gruchmann L. "Die bayerische ustiz im politischen Machtkampf, 1933/34. Ihr Scheitern bei der Strafverfolgung von Mordfällen in Dachau." **4**. Bd. II. p. 415–28.

———. *Justiz im 3. Reich. Anpassung und Unterwerfung in der Ara Gürtner.* Munich: 1987.]

Guyot A. et Restellini P. *L'Art nazi. Un art de propagande* Brussels: 1983.

Hachtmann R. "Industriearbeiterinnen in der deutschen Krieg wirtschaft, 1936–1944/45." *GG 3* (1993): p. 332–66.

Hamilton R. F. *Who Voted for Hitler?* Princeton: 1982.

Hanko H. M. "Kommunalpolitik in der "Hauptstadt der Bew gung," 1933–35. Zwischen "revolutionäer" Umgestaltum und Verwaltungskontinuität." **4** Bd. III. p. 327–441.

Hassell U. von. *D'une autre Allemagne. Journal posthume, 1938–44.* French trans. Paris: 1948 (1st ed. 1946).

Hayes P. *Industry and Ideology. IG Farben iln the nazi E.* Cambridge: 1987.

Hehl U. von. "Kirche, Katholizismus und das nationalsozial itische Deutschland. Ein Forschungsüberblick", **19**: p. 219–63.

———. *Katholische Kirche und Nationalsozialismus im Erzbist Köln, 1933–1945.* Mayence: 1977.

Héran J. "Les silnistres expériences médicales du Strutho Saisons d'Alsace *(Autumn 1993): p. 65–73.*

Herbert U. *Fremdarbeiter. Politik und Praxis des "Ausländer-Einsatzes" in der Kriegswirtschaft des 3. Reiches.* Berlin and Bonn: 1985.

———. "Arbeiterschaft im 3. Reich. Zwischenbilanz und offene Fragen." *GG 3* (1989): p. 320–60.

———. *Best. Biographische Studien über Radikalismus, Weltanschauung und Vernunft, 1903–1989.* Bonn: 1996.

Herbst L. *Der totale Krieg und die Ordnung der Wirtschaft. Die Kriegswirtschaft im Spannungsfeld von Politik, Ideologie und Propaganda, 1939–1945.* Stuttgart: 1982.

Herzfeld H. "Allgemeine Entwicklung und politische Geschichte." **5**, p. 119–39.

Hetzer G. "Die Industriestadt Augsburg. Eine Sozialgeschichte der Arbeiteropposition." **4**. Bd. III, p. 1–234.

Hilberg R. *La Destructioin des juifs d'Europe.* French trans. Paris: 1988 (1st ed. 1961).

———. "La bureaucratie de la solution finale." In *L'Allemagne nazie et le Génocide juif.* Paris: 1985. p. 219–35.

Hildebrand K. *Das Dritte Reich.* 3rd ed., Munich: 1987.

Hinkel H. *Zur Funktion des Bildes im deutschen Faschismus. Bildbeispiele - Analysen - Didaktische Vorschläge,* Steinbach/Giessen: 1974.

Hitler A. *Mon combat (Mein kampf).* French trans. Paris: 1934. new ed. 1979.

Hoffmann P. *La Résistance allemande contre Hitler.* French trans. Paris: 1984 (1st ed. 1979).

Höhne H. *L'Ordre noir. Histoire de la SS.* French trans. Paris: 1968 (1st ed. 1967).

Hopster N. "Ausbildung und politische Funktion der Deutschlehrer im Nationalsozialismus." **47**. p. 113-39.

Hürten H. *Deutsche Katholiken 1918 bis 1945*. Paderborn: 1992.

Husson E. *Une culpabilité ordinaire? Hitler, les Allemands et la Shoah*. Paris: 1997.

Hüttenberger P. "Heimtückefälle vor dem sondergericht München, 1933-1939." **4**. Bd. IV. p. 435-526.

———. "Interessenvertretung und Lobbyismus in 3. Reich." **14**. p. 429-55.

Jamin M. "Zur Rolle der SA im nationalsozialistischen Herrschaftssystem." **14**. p. 329-57.

Jarausch K. H. *The Unfree Professions. German Lawyers, Teachers and Engineers, 1900-1950*. New York and Oxford: 1990.

Johe W. "Das Konzentrationslager Neuengamme." **42** p. 29-49.

John J. "Rüstungsindustrie und NSDAP-Organisation in Thüringen 1933 bis 1939." *ZfG* 4 (1974).

Kardorff U. von. *Berliner Aufzeichnungen. Aus den Jahren 1942-1945*. Francfort/M.: 1964.

Kater M. *Studentenschaft und Rechtsradikalismus in Deutschland, 1918-1933*. Hamburg: 1975.

———. "Zum gegenseitigen Verhältnis von SA und SS in der Sozialgeschichte des Nationalsozialismus von 1925 bis 1934." *VSWG* 3 (1975).

———. "Sozialer Wandel in der NDAP im Zuge der nationalsozialistischen Machtergreifung." **12**. p. 25-68.

———. "Bürgerliche Jugendbewegung und Hitler-Jugend in Deutschland von 1926 bis 1939.:" *AfS* (1977). p. 128-74.

———. *The Nazi Party. A Social Profile of Members and Leaders, 1919-1945*. Oxford: 1983.

———. "Frauen in der NS-Bewegung." *VfZG* 2 (1983): p. 202-41.

———. *Doctors under Hitler*. Chapel Hill and London. 189.

———. "Forbidden Fruit? Jazz in the Third Reich." *AHR* (Feb. 1989): p. 1-43.

Kershaw I., *Der Hitler-Mythos. Volksmeinung und Propaganda im 3. Reich*. Stuttgart: 1980: *"The Hitler Myth" Image and Reality in the Third Reich*, Oxford. 1987.

———. *L'Opinion allemande sous le nazisme. Bavière, 1933-1945*. French trans. Paris: 1995 (1st ed. 1983).

———. "Alltägliches und Außeralltägliches: ihre Bedeutung für die Volksmeinung, 1933-1939." **36**. p. 273-92.

———. "Antisemitismus und Volksmeinung. Reaktionen auf die Judenverfolgung." **4**, Bd. II. p. 281-348.

———. " 'Widerstand ohne Volk'? Dissens und Widerstand im 3. Reich." **46**. p. 779-98.

———. *Qu'est-ce que le nazisme? Problèmes et perspective d'interprétation*. French trans. Paris: 1992 (2d ed. 1989).

———. *Hitler. Essai sur le charisme en politique*. French trans. Paris: 1995 (1st ed. 1991).

Kettenacker L. "Sozialpsychologische Aspekte der Führer-Herrschaft." **14**. p. 98-130.

Kimmel G. "Das Konzentrationslager Dachau. Eine Studie zu den nationalsozialistischen Verbrechen." **4**. p. 349-414.

Klaus M. *Mädchen in der Hitlerjugend. Die Erziehung zur "guten Frau."* Cologne: 1980.

Klee E., Dreesen W., Riess V. *Pour eux "c'était le bon temps."* *La vie ordinaire des bourreaux nazis.* French trans. Paris: 1990 (1st ed. 1988).

Klein U. "SA-Terror und Bevölkerung in Wupertal, 1933–34" **36**. p. 45–61.

Kleinberger A. F. "Gab es eine natinalsozialistische Hochschulpoliltik?" **11**. Teil 2. p. 9–30.

Klein G. H. "Adelsgenossenschaft und National-Sozialismus." *VfZG* 1 (1978).

Kleinert A. "La correspondance entre Ph. Lenard et J. Stark." **39** p. 149–66.

Kleinöder E. "Verfolgung und Widerstand der Katholischen Jugendverbände in Eichstätt." **4** II. p. 175–236.

Klemperer V. *LTI, la langue du IIIe Reich. Carnets d'un philologue.* French trans. by Guillot É. Paris: 1996 (1st ed. 1946).

Klepper J. *Unter dem Schatten deiner Flügel. Aus dem Tagebuch der Jahre 1932–1942.* Stuttgart: 1956.

———. *Überwindung. Tagebücher und Aufzeichnungen aus dem Krieg.* Stuttgart: 1958.

Klessmann C. "Das Problem der 'Volksbewegung' im deutschen Widerstand." **46**. p. 828–37.

———. "Osteuropaforschung und Lebensraumpolitik im 3. Reich." **47**. p. 350–83.

Klinksiek D. *Die Frau im NS-Staat.* Stuttgart: 1982.

Klöne A. *Jugend im 3. Reich. Die Hitlerjugend und ihre Gegner. Dokumente und Analysen.* Düsseldorf and Cologne: 1982.

———. "Jugendprotest und Jugendopposition. Von der Hitlerjugenderziehung zum Clilcquenwesen der Kriegszeit." **4**. Bd. IV. p. 527–620.

Klose W. *Histoire de la Jeunesse hitlérienne. Une génération au pas de l'oie.* French trans. Paris: 1996 (1st ed. 1964).

Klotzbach K. *Gegen den Nationalsozialismus. Widerstand und Verfolgung in Dortmund, 1930–1945. Eine historisch-politische Studie.* Hanover: 1969.

Koch H. W. *Geschichte der Hitlerugnd. Ihre Ursprünge und ihre Entwicklung, 1922–1945.* German trans., Percha/Starbergersee: 1979.

Kocka, J. *Les Employés en Allemane. Histoire d'un groupe social.* French trans. Paris: 1989 (1st ed. 1981).

Kogon E. *L'Enfer organisé. Le système des camps de concentration.* French trans. Paris: n.d.(1st ed. 1947).

Kolb E. "Bergen-Belsen." **42**. p. 130–54.

Köllmann W. "Bevölkerungsgeschichte, 1800–1970" In Zorn W., Hg. *Handbuch der deutschen Wirtschafts- und Sozialgeschichte.* Bd. 2. p. 9–51.

Könke G. "Modernisierungsschub" oder relatie Stagnation? Einige Anmerkungen zum Verhältnis von Nationalsozialismus und Moderne." *GG* 4 (1994): p. 584–608.

Konvitz J. "Représentations urbaines et bombardements stratégiques." *AESC* 4 (1989): p. 823–47.

Korinmann M. *Quand l'Allemagne pensait le monde. Grandeur et décadence d'une géopolitique.* Paris: 1990.

Koselleck R. "Terreur et rêve." *Le Débat* (May 1983). p. 185–92.

Krausnick H. et Wilhelm H.-H. *Die Truppe des Weltanschauungskrieges. Di Ein-*

satzgruppen der Sicherheitspolizei und des Sicherheitsdienstes, 1938–1942. Stuttgart: 1981.

Kroener B. R. "Auf dem Weg zu einer 'nationalsozialistischen Volksarmee.' Die sogenannte Öfnung des Heeresoffiziers-korps im 2. Weltkrieg." **44**. p. 651–82.

———. "Die personellen Ressourcen des 3. Reiches im Spannungs-feld zwischen Wehrmacht, Bürokratie und Kriegswirtschaft, 1939–1942." **8**. Bd. V, 1. p. 693–1001.

Krüger P. " 'Man lässt sein Land nicht im Stich, weil es eine schlechte Regierung hat.' Die Diplomatn und die Eskalation der Gewalt." **10**. p. 180–225.

Kühne T. "Kameradschaft—'das Beste im Leben des Mannes' Die deutschen Soldaten des 2. Weltkriegs in erfahrungs- und geschlehtergeschichtlicher Perspektive." *GG* 4 (1996): p. 504–29.

Kulka O. D. "Die Nürnberger Rassengesetze und die deutsche Bevölkerung im Lichte geheimer nationalsozialistischer Lage- und Stimmungsberichte." *VfZG* 4 (1984): p. 582–624.

Kunkel W. "Der Professor im 3. Reich." **9**. p. 103–34.

Küppers H. "Zum Gleichschaltungsprozess der öffentlich organisierten Erziehung in den Jahren 1933/34. Konkurrierende Kräfte und politisches Schicksal der Lehrerverbände." **11**. Teil 2. p. 232–45.

Kwiet K. "Nach dem Pogrom. Stufen der Ausgrenzung." **18**. p. 545–659.

La Martinière J. de. *Les N. N. Le décret et la procédure* Nacht und Nebel (*Nuit et Brouillard*). 2d ed., Paris: 1989.

Lämmert E. "Germanistik—eine deutsche Wissenschaft." **26**. p. 76–91.

Lehberer R. "Neusprachlicher Unterricht in der nationalsozialistischen Zeit . . ." **38**. p. 117–34.

Lehmann A. "In sowjetischer Kriegsgefangenschaft." **20**. p. 295–310.

Lewey G. *L'Église catholique et l'Allemagne nazie.* French trans. Paris: 1965 (1st ed. 1964).

Lifton R. J. *Les Médecins nazis, Le meurtre médical et la psychologie du génocide*, French trans. Paris: 1989 (1st ed. 1986) The Nazi doctors: medical killing and the psychology of genocide, London, 1987.

Löscher P. et Scholilng M. "In den Nischen des Systems. Der sozialdemokratische Pressespiegel 'Blick in die Zeit.'" **16**. p. 207–26.

Löwenthal R. "Widerstand im totalen Staat." **27**. p. 618–32.

———. "Wo blieb die 'rote Glut'? Areitererfahrungen und deutscher Faschismus." **1**. p. 224–82.

Lüdtke A. " 'Formierung der Massen' oder: Mitmachen und Hinnehmen? Alltagsgeschichte und Faschismusanalyse." In Gerstenberger H. et Schmidt D., hg. *Normalität oder Normalisierung? Geschichtswerkstätten und Faschismus-analyse.* Münster: 1987. p. 15–34.

———. "Wo blieb die 'rote Glut'? Arbeitererfahrungen und deutscher Faschismus." **1** p. 224–82.

Ludwig O. "Texte als Eplikationen von Haltungen. Zur Text-theorie der nationalsozialisten in Deutschland." **41**. p. 120–36.]

Mai G. "Die national-sozialistische Betriebszellen-Organisation. Zum Verhältnis von Arbeiterschaft und Nationalsozialismus." *VfZG* 4 (1983): p. 573–613.

———. " 'Warum steht der deutsche Arbeiter zu Hitler?' Zur Rolle der Deutschen Arbeitsfront im Herrschaftssystem des 3. Reiches." *GG* 2 (1986): p. 212–34.

Maier H. "Natinalsozialistische Hochschulpolitik." **9**. p. 71–102.

Maier J "Zu den Auseinandersetungen zwischen Staat and katholischer Kirche in Baden 1933–1945 in Fragen der Schule und des Religionsunterrichts." **11** Teil 1. p. 216–29.

Mallmann K. M. et Paul G. "Allwissend, allmächtig, allgegemwärtig: Gestapo. Gesellschaft und Widerstand." *ZfG* 11 (1993): p. 984–99.

Mamach K. *Der Volkssturm, Bestandteil des Kriegseinsatzes der deutschen Bevölkerung, 1944–1945.* Berlin (East): 1981.

Mann T. "Bruder Hitler." (1939). *Schriften zur Politik.* Francfort/M.: 1973.

Manstein P. *Mitgleder und Wähler der NSDAP 1919–1933. Untersuchungen zu ihrer schichtsmässigen Zusammenset-zung. 3d ed. Francfort/M.: 1990.*

Marschalck P. *Bevölkerungsgeschichte Deutschlands in 19 und 20. Jahrhundert.* Francfort/M.: 1984.

Mason T. *Arbeiterklasse und Volksgemeninschaft. Dokument und Materialien zur deutschen Arbeiterpolitik 1936–1939. Opladen: 1975.*

———. *Sozialpolitik im 3. Reich. Arbeiterklasse und Volksgemeinschaft.* Opladen: 1977.

———. "Die Bändigung der Arbeiterklasse im nationalsozialist schen Deutschland. Eine Einleitung." **3**. p. 11–53.

Massin B. "Anthropologie raciale et national-socialisme heurs et malheurs du paradigme de la 'race'" **39**. p. 197–261.

Matthias E. "Die SPD." In Id. et Morsey R., Hg., *Das Ende der Parteien, 1933.* 2d ed., Königstein and Düsseldorf. **19**. p. 101–278.

Matzerath H. *Nationalsozialismus und kommunale Selbstverwaltung.* Stuttgart: 1970.

———. "Oberbürgermeister im 3. Reich. Auswertung einer quantitativen Analyse." **32**. p. 157–99.

Mehringer H. "Die KPD in Bayern, 1919–1945. Vorgeschichte, Verfolgung und Widerstand." **4**. Bd. V. p. 1–285.

———. "Die bayerische SPD bis zum Ende des nationalsozialistischen Regimes. Voreschichte, Verfolgung und Widerstand." **4**. p. 287–431.

Mehrtens H. "Angewandte mathematik und Anwendungen der Mathematik im NS Deutschland." *GG* 3 (1986): p. 317–47.

———. "Mathermatik als Wissenschaft und Schulfach im nationalsozialistischen Staat. Nationalsozialistisch eingekleidetes Rechnen." **38**. p. 205–16.

———. "Mathématiques, sciences de la nature et national-socialisme; quelles questions poser?" **39**. p. 33–49.

Messerschmidt M. *Die Wehrmacht im NS-Staat Zeit der Indoktrination.* Hamburg: 1969.

———. "Der "Zersetzer" und sein Denunziant. Urteile des Zentralgerichts des Heeres — Aussentlle Wien — 1944." **20**. p. 255–78.

Michaud E. *Un art de l'éternité. L'image et le temps du national-socialisme.* Paris: 1996.

Miller G. "Erziehung des deutschen Reichsarbeitsdienstes für die weibliche Jugend." **11**. 2. p. 170–93.

Milward A. S. *Die deutsche Kriegswirtschaft, 1939–1945.* German trarns. Stuttgart: 1996 (1st ed. 1965).

Milza P. *Les Fascismes.* Paris: 1985

Mollin G. *Montankonzerne und "3. Reich." Der Gegenstaz zwischen Monopolindustrie und Befehlswirtschaft in der deutschen Rüstung und Expansion, 1936–1944.* Göttingen: 1988.

Mommsen H. "Der Reichstagsbrand und seine politischen Folgen." *VfZG* (1964): p. 351–413.

———. *Beamtentum im 3. Reich.* Stuttgart: 1966.

———. "Zur Verschränkung traditioneller und faschistischer Führungsgruppen in Deutschland beim Übergang von der Bewegungs- bis zur Systemphase." **12.** p. 158–81.

———. "La réalilsation de l'utopique:" la 'solutin finale de la question juive' dans le Troisième Reich." French trans. *Bull. Ausch.* 29 (July-Sept. 1991). (1st ed. 1983).

———. "Der Widerstand gegen Hitler und die deutsche Gesellschaft." *HZ* (1985).

———. "Noch einmal: Nationalsozialismus und Modernisierung." *GG 3* (1995): p. 391–402.

Morsch G. "Streik im 3. Reich." *VfZG* 4 (1988).

Mosse G. L. *The Nationalization of the Masses. Political Symbolism and Mass Movements in Germany from the Napoleonic Wars through the Third Reich.* New York: 1975.

Müller K. J. *Das Heer and Hitler. Arme und nationalsozialistisches Regime, 1933 – 1940.* Stuttgart: 1969.

———. "Armee und Drittes Reich. Versuch einer historischen Interpretation." In Id., Hg. *Armee, Politik und Gesellschaft in Deutschland, 1933 – 1945.* Paderborn: 1979. p. 11–50.

———. "National-Konservative Eliten zwischen Kooperation und Widerstand." **46.** p. 24-49.

Müller R. D. "Von der Wirtschaftsallianz zum kolnialen Ausbeutungskrieg." **8.** Bd. IV. p. 98–189.

———. "Das Scheitern der wirtschaftlichen 'Blitzkriegstrategie.'" **8.** Bd. IV. p. 936–1029.

———. "Die Mobilisierung der deutschen Wirtschaft für Hitlers Kriegsführung." **8.** Bd. V. 1. p. 349–689.

Müller-Hill B. *Science nazie, science de mort. L'extermination des Juifs, des Tziganes et des malades mentaux de 1933 à 1945.* French trans. Paris: 1990 (1st ed. 1984).

Muller J. Z. "Enttäuschung und Zweideutigeit. Zur Geschichte rechter Sozialwissenschaftler im 3. Reich." *GG 3* (1986): p. 289–316.

———. *The Other God that Failed. Hans Freyer and the Deradicalization of German Conservatism.* Princeton: 1987.

Muth H. "Jugendopposition im 3. Reich." *VfZG* (1982). p. 368–417.

Narthorff H. *Das Tagbuch der Hertha Nathorff. Berlin-New York. Aufzeichnungen 1933 bis 1945.* (Benz W. Hg.), republished Francfort: 1988.

Neebe R. *Grossindustrie, Staat und NSDAP. Paul Silverberg und der RDI in er Krise der Weimarer Republik.* Göttingen: 1981.

———. "Die Industrie und der 30. January 1933" **27** p. 155–176.

Neumann F. *Béhémoth. Sturcture et pratique du national-socialisme.* French trans. Paris: 1987. (1st ed. 1942).

Nicholaisen H.-D *Die Flak-Helfer. Luftwaffen- und Marinehelfer im 2. Weltkrieg.* Frankfurt/M.: 1981.

Olff-Nathan J. "Introduction." **39.** p. 7–29.

Orlow D. *The History of the Nazi Party, 1933–1945.* Pittsburg: 1973.

Ottweiler O. "Die nationalsozialistische Schulpolitik im Bereich des Volksschulwesens im Reich." **11.** Teil 1. p. 193–215.

Overy R. J. " 'Blitzkriegswirtschaft'? Finanzpolitik, Lebens-standard und Arbeitsein-satz in Deutschland, 1939 – 1942." *VfZG* 3 (1988): p. 379 – 436.

Palmier J.-M. *Weimar en exil.* Paris: 1988. 2 vols.

Pélassy D. *Le Signe nazi. L'univers symbolique d'une dictature.* Paris: 1983.

Peter R. "NS-Wirtschaft in einer Grenzregion. Die badische Rüstungsindustrie im 2. Weltkrieg." **34.** p. 171–93.

Petrick F. "Eine Untersuchung zur Beseitgung des Arbeitslosigkeit unter der deut-schen Jugend in den Jahren von 1933 bis 1935." *JbWG* (1967).

Petsch J. "Architektur und Städtebau im 3. Reich. Anspruch und Wirklichkeit." **36.** p. 175–95.

Petzina D. *Autarkiepolitik im 3. Reich. Der nationalsozialistische Vierjahresplan.* Stut-tgart: 1968.

———. "Die Mobilisierung der Arbeitskräfte vor und während des 2. Weltkrieges." *VfZG* (1970).

———. "Soziale Lage der deutschen Arbeiter und Probleme des Arbeitseinsatzes währ-end des 2. Weltkrieges." 49. p. 63–86.

Peukert D. *Die KPD im Widerstand. Verfolgung und Untergrundarbedit am Rhein und Ruhr 1933 bis 1945.* Wuppertal: 1980.

———. *Volksgenossenk und Gemeinschfaftsfremde. Anpassung, Ausmerze und Aufbegeh-ren unter dem nationalsozialismus.* Cologne: 1982.

———. "Der Arbeiterwiderstand, 1933–1945." **27.** p. 633–54.

———. "Das 3. Reich" aus der "Altaggs"-Perspektive." *AfS* (1986): p. 533–56.

——— *La République de Weimar.* Frence trans. Paris: 1995 (1st ed. 1987).

———. et Reulecke J. "Einleitung". **36.** p. 11–18.

Philipp W. "Nationalsozialismus und Ostwissenchaften." **26** p. 43–62.

Philippon J. *La Nuit des longs couteaux. histoire d'une intox.* Paris: 1992.

Pingel F. *Häftrlinge unter SS-Herrschaft. Winderstand, Selbstbehauptung und Ver-nichtung im Konzentrationslager.* Hamburg: 1978.

Plum G. "Deutsche Juden oder Juden in Deutschland?" **18.** p. 35–74.

———. "Wirtschaft und Erwerbsleben." **18.** p. 268–313.

Pohl H., Habeth S, et Brüninghaus B. *Die Daimler-Benz AG in den Jahren 1033 bis 1945. Eine Dokumentation.* Stuttgart: 1986.

Pois, R. A. *La Religion de la nature et le National-Socialisme.* French trans. Paris: 1993 (1st ed. 1986).

Pollak M. "Des mots qui tuent." *ARSS* 41 (1982): p. 25–45.

———. "Une politique scientifique: le concours de l'anthropologie, de la biologie et dudroit." **33.** p. 75–99.

Prinz M. *Vom neuen Mittelstand zum Volksgenossen. Die Entwicklung des sozialen Sta-tus des Angestellen von der Weimarer Republik bis zum NS-Zeit.* Munich: 1986.

———. "Der unerwünschte Stand. Lage und Status der Angestellt er im '3. Reich.' " *HZ* (1986): p. 327–59.

Prinz W. "Ganzheits und Gestalphyschologie und Nationalsozialismus." **47.** p. 55–81.

Rainbach A. "Die Ästhetik der Produktion im 3. Reich. " **21.** p. 57–85.

Rabitsch G. "Das Konzentratioinslager Mauthausen." **42.** p. 50–92.

Rebentisch D. "Die politische Stellung der Oberbürgermeister im 3. Reich." **32.** p. 125–55.

———. "Die 'politische Beurteilung' als Herrschaftsinstrumkent der NSDAP." **36.** p. 107–25.

Recker M. L. *Nationalsozialistische Sozialpolitik im 2 Weltkrieg.* Munich: 1985.
———. "Wohnen und Bombardierung im 2. Weltkrieg." **48.** p. 408–28.
Reichel P. *La Fascination du nazisme.* French trans. Paris: 1993 (1st ed. 1991).
Renneberg M. "La physique à l'université de Hambourg de 1933 à 1945." **39.** p. 133–47.
Repgen K. "Hitlers Machtergreifung und der deutsche Katholizismus. Versuch einer Bilanz." (1963) **19.** p. 1-34.
Reulecke J. "Die Fahne mit dem goldenen Zahnrad; der 'Leistungskampf der deutschen Betriebe,' 1937–1939." **36.** p. 245–69.
Reus G. " 'Brune comme la terre est la tunique des combatants': nature et société dans le lyrisme du Troisième Reich." **30.** p. 103–15.
Richard L. *Le Nazisme et la Culture.* new ed. Brussels: 1988.
Riemenschneider R. "L'enseignement de l'histoire en Allemagne sous le '3ᵉ Reich'" *Francia* (1979): p. 401–28.
Ringer F. K. *The Decline of the German Mandarins. The German Academic Community, 1890–1933.* Harvard: 1969.
Roegele O. B. "Student im 3. Reich." **9.** p. 135–74.
Rosenhaft E. *Beating the Fascists? The German Communists and Political Violence, 1929–1933.* Cambridge: 1083.
Rössler M. "Science et espace: l'histoire de la géographie, (1933–1945)." **39.** p. 303–17.
Roth K. H. "Der Weg zum guten Stern des 'Dritten Reiches': Schlaglichter auf die Geschichte der Daimler-Benz AG und ihrer Vorläufer, (1890–1945)." **6.** p. 28–373.
Ruhl K.-J. "Die nationalsozialistische Familienpolitik (1933–1945). Ideologie-Massnhmen-Bilanz." *GWU* (August 1991): p. 479–488.
Rüther M. "Lage und Abstimmungsverhalten der Arbeiterschaft: die Vertrauensrats sahlen in Köln 1934 und 1935." *VfZG* 2 (1991). p. 221–64.
Sachse C. "Hausarbeit im Betrieb. Betriebliche Sozialarbeit unter dem Nationalsozialismus." **3.** p. 209–74.
Saldern A. von. *Mittelstand im '3. Reich' Handwerker-Einzelhändler-Bauern.* Francfort/M.: and New York: 1979.
———. 'Alter Mittelstand im '3. Reich' *GG* 2 (1986). p. 235–43.
Salewski M. "Die bewaffnete Macht im 3. Reich, 1933–1939."
Sandkühler T. et Schmuhl H.-W. "Noch einmal: Die IG Farben und Auschwitz.", *GG* 2 (1993): p. 258–67.
Sauer W. W. "Sprachlosigkeit. Zum Problem der Sprachkritik und des Faschismus." **21.** p. 329–44.
Schäfer H. D. "Die nicht-nationalsozialistische Literatur der jungen Generation im 3. Reich." In Id., *Das gespaltene Bewusstsein. Deutsche Kultur und Lebenswirklichkeit.* Munich et Vienna: 1981. p. 7–54.
———. "Das gespaltene Bewusstsein. Über die Lebenswirklichkeit in Deutschland, 1933–1945." In Id., *Das gespaltene Bewusstsein. Deutsche Kultur und Lebenswirklichkeit,* Munich et Vienna: 1981. p. 114–162.
Schellenberger B. "Katholischer Jugendwiderstand." **46.** p. 314–26.
Schieder W. "Zwei Generationen im militärischen Widerstand." **46.** p. 436–59.
Schmidt C. "Zu den Motiven 'alter Kämpfer' in der NSDAP." **36.** p. 21–43.

Schmuhl H., W. "Die Selbstverständlichkeit des Tötens. Psychiater im Nationalsozialismus." *GG* 4 (1990): p. 411–39.

Schoenbaum D. *La Révolutin brune. Une histoire sociale due Troisième Reich.* French trans. Paris: 1979 (1st ed. 1966).

Scholder K. *Die Kirchen und das 3. Reich.*

Bd. I. *Vorgeschichte jund Zeit der Illusionen, 1933–34.* Frankfurt/M., etc. 1977.

Bd. II. *Das Jahr der Ernüchterung 1934. Barmen und Rom.* Berlin: 1985.

———. "Poilitischer Widerstand oder Selbstbehauptung als Problem der kirchlichen Leitungen." **46**. p. 244–54.

Scholdt G. *Autoren über Hitler. Deutschsprachige Schriftsteller 1919–1945 und ihr Bild vom "Führer."* Bonn: 1993.

Scholz H. *Erziehung und Unterricht unterm Hakenkreuz.* Göttingen: 1985.

———. et Strand E. "Nationalsozialistische Einflußnahmen auf die Lehrerbildung." 11. p. 110–24.

Schönhoven K. "Der politische Katholizismus in Bayern unter der nationalsozialistischen Herrschaft, 1933–1945." **4**. Bd. V. p. 541–646.

Schönwälder K. *Historikere und Politik. Geschichtswissenschaft im Nationalsozialismus.* Frankfurt/M. and New York: 1992.

Schreiner K. "Führertum, Rasse, Reich. Wissenschaft von der Geschichte nach der nationalsozialistischen Machtergreifung." **47**. p. 163–252.

Schulte T. J. *The German Army and Nazi Policies in Occupied Russia.* Oxford, etc.: 1989.

Schwabe K. "Deutsche Hochschullehrer und Hitlers Krieg." **10**. p. 291–333.

Schweitzer A. *Big Business in the Third Reich.* Bloomington: 1964.

Seidler F. W. "Lebensborn e. V. der SS. Vom Gerücht zur Legende." **37**. p. 291–318.

Siegel T. "Lohnpolitik im nationalsozialilstischen Deutschland." **3**. p. 54–139.

Siegert T. "Das Konzentrationslager Flossenbürg, gegründet für sogenannte Asoziale und Kriminelle." **4**. Bd. II. p. 429–92.

Silverman D. P. "Nazification of the German Bureaucracy Reconsidered: A Case Study." JMH (September 1988).

———. "Fantasy and Reality in Nazi Work-Creation Programs, 1933–1936." *JMH* 1 (1993): p., 112–51.

Sonnenberger F. "Der neue 'Kulturkampf' Die Gemeinschaftsschule und ihre historischen Voraussetzungen." **4**. Bd. III. p. 235–328.

Sontheimer K. "Die Haltung der deutschen Universitäten zur Weimarer Republik." **26**. 24–42.

Sösemann B. "Publizistische Opposition in den Anfängen des nationalsozialistischen Regimes." **46**. p. 190–206.

Spode H. "'Der deutsche Arbeiter resist.' Massentourismus im 3. Reich." *Sozialgeschichte der Freizeit* (Huck G., Hg.). Wuppertal: 1980. p. 281–306.

Stachura P. D. *Nazi Youth in the Weimar Republic.* Santa Barbara and Oxford: 1974.

———. "Das 3. Reich und die Jugenderziehung. Die Rolle der Hitlerjugend, 1933–1939." **27**. 224–44.

Stehkämper H. "Protest, Opposition und Widestand im Umkreis der untergegangenen Zentrumspartei." **46**. p. 113–150, 888–916.

Steiner J. M. "Über das Glaubensbekenntnis der SS." **27**. p. 206–223.

Steinert M. G. *Hitlers Krieg und die Deutschen. Stimmung und Haltung der deutschen Bevölkerung im 2. Weltkrieg.* Düsseldorf: 1970.

———. *Hitler et l'Allemagne nazie. L'Allemagne national-socialiste, 1933 – 1945.* Paris: 1972.

Stephenson J. *Women in Nazi Society.* London: 1975.

———. "'Verantwortungsbewusstsein': politische Schulung der deutchen Frauenorganisationen im 3. Reich." **11**. Teil 2. p. 194 – 205

———. "'Emancipation' and its Problems, War and Society in Wüttemberg, 1939 – 45." *EHQ 3* (1987). p. 345 – 65.

Stern J. P. *Le Führer et le peuple.* French trans. Paris: 1985. (1st ed. 1975)- *Hitler, The Führer and the People,* London, 1984.

Stollmann R. "Die krummen Wege zu Hitler. Das Nazi-Selbstbildnis im SA-Roman." **21**. p. 191 – 215.

Stommer R. "'Da oben versinkt der Alltag.' Thingstätten im. 3. Reich als Demonstration der Volksgemeinschaftsideologie." **36**. 149 – 73.

Stöver B. *Volksgemeinschaft im 3. Reich. Die Konsensbereitschaft der Deutschen aus der Sicht sozialistischer Exibelrichte.* Düsseldorf: 1993.

Streit C. *Keine Kameraden. Die Wehrmacht und die sowietischen Kriegsgefangenen, 1941 – 1945.* Stuttgart: 1978.

Struve W. *Elites against Democracy. Leadership Ideals in Bourgeois Political Thought In Germany 1890 – 1933.* Princeton: 1973.

Tenfelde K. "Proletarische Provinz. Radikalisierung in Penzberg/Oberbayern 1900 bis 1945." **4**. Bd. IV. p. 1 – 382.

Thalmann R. *Être femme sous le Troisième Reich.* Paris: 1982.

Thamer H.-U. *Verführung und Gewalt. Deutschland 193 – 1945.* Berlin: 1986.

Thierfelder J. "Die Auseinandersetzungen um Schulform und Religionsunterricht im 3. Reich zwischken Staat und evanglischer Kirshce in Wüttemberg." **11**. Teil 1. p. 230 – 50.

Troll H. "Aktionen zur Kriegsbeendignung im Frühjahr 1945. **4**, Bd. IV, p. 646 – 689.

Trumpp T. "Zur Finanzierung der NSDAP durch die Großindusstrie. Versuch einer Bilanz." **27**. p., 132 – 54.

Turner H. A. "Das Verhältnis des Großunternehmertums zur NSDAP. *Industrielles System und politische Entwicklung in der Weimarer Republik* (Mommsen H. et al., Hg.), Düsseldorf: 1974. p. 919 – 31.

Ueberschär G. R. "'Volkssturm' und 'Wehrwolf.' Das letzte Aufgebot in Baden." **45**. p. 23 – 37.

Umbreit H. "Auf dem Weg zur Kontinentalherrschaft." **8**. Bd. V. I. p. 3 – 345.

———. et Maier K. A. "Direkte Strategie gegen England." **8**. Bd. 2. p. 365 – 409.

Van Norden G. "Der Kirchenkampf im Rheinlande, 1933 – 1939." *GWU* (1960): p. 725 – 41.

———. "Zwischen Kooperation und Teilwiderstand. Die Rolle der Kirchen und Konfessionen. Ein Überblick über Forschungspositionen." **46**. p. 227 – 39.

Varga L. "La genèse du national-socialisme. Notes d'analyse sociale." *AHES* 48 (1937): p. 529 – 46.

Vestermanis M. "Der lettische Anteil an der 'Endlösung.'" **37** p. 426 – 49.

Vodoz I. "Viktor Klemperer: LTI (Lingua Tertii Imperii). Réflexions d'un linguiste juif: une forme de résistance." **30**. p. 189 – 99.

Vogel D. "Der Kriegstalltag im Spiegel von Feldpostbriefen, (1939 – 1945)." **20**. p. 199 – 212.

Voges M. "Klassenkampf als 'Betriebsgemeinschaft' Die len zum Widerstand der Industriearbeiter im 3. Reich." *AfS* (1981): p. 329-84.

Volk L. "Die Fuldaer Bischofskonferenz . . ." **19.** p. 35-102.

Volkmann H.-E. "Die NS-Wirtschaft in Vorvereitung des Krieges." **8.** Bd. I. p. 177-368.

———. Zum Verhältnis von Grosswirtschkaft und nationalsozialistischem Regime im 2. Weltkrieg." **27.** p. 480-508.

———. Deutsche Agrareliten und Revisions- und Expansions- kurs." **10.** p. 334-88.

Vollnhals C. "Jüdische Selbsthilfe bis 1938. **18.** p. 314-411.

———. "Die evangelische Kirche zwischen Traditionswahrung und Neuorientierung." **44.** p. 113-51.

Volmert J. "Politische Rhetorik des Nationalsozialismus." **41.** p. 137-61.

Vondung K. *Magie und Manipulation. Ideologischer kKult und politilsche Religion des Nationalsozialismus.* Göttingen: 1971.

———. "Der literarische Nationalsozialismus." **27.** p. 245-69.

Vorländer H. "Einleitung. Das Konzentrationslager Natzweiler-Struthof im Elsaβ und seine Auβenkommandos in Wüttemberg und Baden." **28.** *p. 1-18.*

———. "Nationalsozialistische Volswohlfahrt und Winterhilfswerk des deutschen Volkes." *VfG* (1986): p. 341-80.

Voszkamp W. "Kontinuität und Diskontinuität. Zur deutschen Literaturwissenschaft im 3. Reich." **47.** p. 140-62.

Walker M. "Une physique nazie?" **39.** p. 103-31.

Walther S. "Die Versorgungslage in Berlin im Januar 1940 und das politische Verhalten der Bevölkerung." *ZfG* 5 (1986)" p. 427-32.

Wegner B. *Hitlers politische Soldaten. Die Waffen-SS, 1933-1945.* Paderborn: 1982.

Weiss S. F. "Biologie scolaire et enseignement de l'eugénisme sous le Troisième Reich." **39.** p. 263-85.

Werner K. F. *Das NS-Geschichtsbild und die deutsche Geschichtswissenschafat.* Stuttgart: 1967.

———. "Machtstaat und nationale Dynamik in den Konzeptionen der deutschen Historiographie, 1933-1940." **23.** p. 327-63.

Wette W. "Ideologien, Propaganda und Innen politik als Voraussetzungen der Kriegspolitik des 3. Reiches." **8.** Bd. I. p. 25-173.

Wetzel J. "Auswanderung aus Deutschland." **18.** p. 412-98.

Wiesenmann F. "Juden auf dem Lande: die wirtschaftliche Ausgrenzung der jüdischen Viehhändler in Bayern." **36.** p. 381-96.

Wildt M. "Avant la 'solution finale' La politique juive du service de sésurité de la SS, 1935-1938." *Genèses* (21 December 1995): p. 29-52.

Wilke G. "Village Life in Nazi Germanuy." **22.** p. 17-24.

Winkler D. *Frauenarbeit im "3. Reich."* Hamburg: 1977.

Winkler H. A. *Mittelstand, Demokratie und Nationalsozialismus. Die politische Entwicklung von Hundwerk und Kleinhandel in der Weimarer Republik.* Cologne: 1972.

———. "Mittelstandsbewegung oder Volkspartei? Zur sozialen Basis der NSDAP." **12.** p. 98-118.

———. "Der entbehrliche Stand., Zur Miottelstandspolitik im 3. Reich." *AfS* (1977): p. 1-40.

Wisotzky K. "Der Ruhrbergbau am Vorabend des 2. Weltkrieges. Vorgeschichte, Entstehung und Auswirkung der 'Verordnung zur Erhöhung der Förderleistung und des Leistungslohnes im Bergbau' vom 2. März 1939." *VfZG* (1982): p. 418-61.

Wormser-Migot O. *Le Systèm3 concentrationnaire nazi, (1933–1945)*. Paris: 1968.

Zeman Z. A. B. *Nazi Propaganda*. London: 1964.

Ziegler H. F. "Fight against the Empty Cradle: Nazi Pronatal Policies and the SS-Führerkorps." *HSR/HSF 38 (April 1986)*.

——. *Nazi Germany's New Aristocracy. The SS Leadership, 1925–1939*. Princeton: 1989.

Ziegler J. *Mitten unter uns. Natzweiler-Struthof. Spuren eines Lagers*. Hamburg: 1986.

Zollitsch W. "Die Vertrauensratswahlen von 1934 und 1935. Zum Stellenwert von Abstimmungen im '3. Reich' am Beispiel Krupp." *GG 3* (1980): p. 361–81.

——. *Arbeiter zwischen Weltwirtschaftskrise und Nationalsozialismus*. Göttingen: 1990.

Abbreviations

(Only the titles of institutions are translated.)

AESC	*Annales. Economies. Sociétés. Civilisations*
AfS	*Archiv für Sozialgeschichte*
AHES	*Annales d'histoire économique et sociale*
AHR	*American Historical Review*
AO	*Auslandsorganisation* - Organization (of the Party) Abroad
APA	*Aussenpolitisches Amt der NSDAP* - Party Foreign Policy Office
ARSS	*Actes de la recherche en science sociales*
BdM	*Bund deutscher Mädel* - League of German Girls
Bull. Ausch.	Bulletin trimestriel de la Fondation Auschwitz
BVP	*Bayerische Volkspartei* - Bavarian Popular Party
DAF	*Deutsche Arbeitsfront* - German Labor Front
DDP	*Deutsche Demokratische Partei* - German Democratic Party
DFW	*Deutsches Frauenwerk* - German Women's Service
DNVP	*Deutschnationale Volkspartei* - German-National Popular Party
DVP	*Deutsche Volkspartei* - German Popular Party
EHQ	*European History Quarterly*
Gestapo	*Geheime Staatspolizei* - State Secret Police
GG	*Geschichte und Gesellschaft*
GWU	*Geschichte in Wissenschaft und Unterricht*
HJ	*Hitlerjugend* - Hitler Youth Organization
HZ	*Historische Zeitschrift*
HSR/HSF	*Historical Social Research - Historisch- Sozialwissenschaftliche Forschung*
JbRG	*Jahrbuch für Regionalgeschichte*
JCH	*Journal of Contemporary History*
JMH	*Journal of Modern History*

KdF	*Kraft durch Freude* - Strength through Joy
KL, KZ	*Konzentratzionslager* - Concentration camp
KPD	*Kommunistische Partei Deutschlands* - Communist Party of Germany
Napola	*Nationalpolitische Erziehungsanstalt* - Establishment of Political and National Education
NS	*Nationalsozialismus* - National Socialism
ns	*nationalsozialistisch* - National Socialist
NSBO	*Nationalsozialistische Betriebszellenorganisation* - National Socialist Organization of Business Cells
NSDAP	*Nationalsozialistische Deutsche Arbeiterpartei* - German National Socialist Workers' Party
NSFO	*Nationalsozialistische Führungsoffiziere* - *National Socialist Officers for Psychological Action*
NS Hago	*Nationalsozialistische Handwerks-, Handels- und Gewerbeorganisation* - National Socialist Organization of Artisans, Trade, and Light Industry
NSKK	*Nationalsozialistisches Kraftfahrerkorps* - National Socialist Motorized Corps
NSLB	*Nationalsocialistischer Lehrerbund* - National Socialist League of Teachers
NSV	*Nationalsozialistische Volkswohlfahrt* - National Socialist Popular Assistance
OBHF	*Oberbefehlshaber in Frankreich* - Commander-in-Chief in France
OKH	*Oberkommando des Heeres* - High Command of the Territorial Army
OKW	*Oberkommando der Wehrmacht* - High Command of the Armed Forces
PZG	*Aus Politik und Zeitgeschichte*
RAD	*Reichsarbeitsdienst* - Reich Labor Service
RdA	*Revue d'Allemagne*
RDI	*Reichsverband der deutschen Industrie* - Reich Federation of German Industry

RH2GM	*Revue d'histoire de la Deuxième Guerre mondiale*
RKF	*Reichskommissar für die Festigung deutschen Volkstums* - Reich Commissariat for the Consolidation of the German Race
RSHA	*Reichssicherheitshauptamt* - Principal Reich Security Office
RUSHA	*Rasse- und Siedlungshauptamt* - Principal Bureau for Race and Colonization
SA	*Sturmabteilungen* - Assault Sections
SD	*Sicherheitsdienst* - Security Service (of the SS)
Sopade	*Sozialdemokratische Partei Deutschlands (im Exil)* - Social Democrat Party of Germany in Exile
SS	*Schutzstaffein* - Protection squads
Stamokap	Staatsmonopolkapitalismus - State Monopolistic Capitalism
uk	*unabkümmlich* - Special auxiliary
VfZG	*Vierteljahrshefte für Zeitgeschichte*
VSWG	*Vierteljahrschrift für Sozial- und Wirtschaftsgeschichte*
WHW	*Winterhilfswerk* - Winter Assistance Service
ZfG	*Zeitschrift für Geschichtswissenschaft*